DEVON AND CORNWALL RECORD SOCIETY

New Series, Volume 47

DEVON AND CORNWALL RECORD SOCIETY

New Series, Volume 47

DEATH AND MEMORY IN MEDIEVAL EXETER

Edited by

David Lepine & Nicholas Orme

Exeter
2003

ISBN 0 901853 46 1

Designed and typeset by Mike Dobson, Quince Typesetting
Sabon 10/12.5

Printed and bound in Great Britain
by Short Run Press Ltd, Exeter

Contents

List of Illustrations and Text Figures

Illustrations

(Between pp. 54 and 55)

Text Figures

Preface and Acknowledgements

Death, burial, and the commemoration of the dead have been much studied by historians in recent years, but far less has been done to make available the sources on which these studies are based. Our book sets out to fill the gap with an anthology of the rich and varied evidence that survives from the medieval city of Exeter. It begins with a history of burial practices: where people were buried and why. This is followed by an edition of the only remaining local burial list, relating to the hospital of St John, and by a register of all the people known to have had a funeral or burial in Exeter between 1050 and 1540. The second part of the book deals with wills and executors. It prints the eighteen earliest Exeter wills that are relatively complete, and two rare documents drawn up by executors: an inventory of a will-maker's goods and a set of early executors' accounts. An index of all known Exeter wills up to 1540 is also provided. The third part is concerned with how the dead were remembered. This section contains over a dozen obituary records naming deceased men and women and the dates of their deaths, ranging from the tenth to the sixteenth centuries. The records include some early lists of members of guilds in the neighbourhood of Exeter, dating from about the year 1100; the obituary list of the Exeter guild of Kalendars in the twelfth and thirteenth centuries; the oldest specimens of the cathedral's 'obit accounts' from 1305-7; a document establishing a chantry in 1305; and various cathedral calendars recording the days on which dead people were commemorated. The result, it is hoped, will reveal something of the impact of death in a medieval English city, as well as providing evidence about some 1,500 individuals who lived there or elsewhere in the South West of England.

David Lepine is responsible for Documents 22 and 30 and for the introductory matter relating to them, while Nicholas Orme has undertaken the rest of the volume. We have shared ideas throughout, and co-operated in the editing process. Our grateful thanks are due to the dean and chapter of Exeter Cathedral and Devon County Council for permission to publish records in their ownership or care, to the Pierpont Morgan Library (New York) to reproduce the picture on the cover of the book, to Exeter Archaeology for Illustration 2, and to Professor R.J.P. Kain and the University of Exeter Press to reprint cartographic material. A grant by the British Academy enabled attendance at a conference of the Medieval

Academy of America in New York in 2002, devoted to urban history, which also advanced the project. Professor Maryanne Kowaleski contributed welcome advice on documentary sources, Professor Joelle Rollo-Koster on confraternities, Mr Nicholas Rogers on grave markers, Messrs John Allan, Stuart Blaylock, and Peter Weddell on Exeter archaeology, Professor Michael Swanton on Old English, and Mr Hugh Peskett on Sir William Pole's manuscript at Antony House. We are indebted to Mr Sean Goddard of the Department of Archaeology, University of Exeter, for drawing the maps and to Dr Mike Dobson, of Quince Typesetting, for designing and typesetting the book. The photography was chiefly carried out by Mr Richard Prince. Finally we would like to express our appreciation of the generous help forthcoming over many years from the librarians and archivists of Exeter Cathedral library and archives, the Devon Record Office, the Devon and Exeter Institution, Exeter University Library, and the West Country Studies Library in Exeter. Our special thanks are due in this respect to Mrs Audrey M. Erskine, Mrs Angela Doughty, and Mr Peter Thomas, and we dedicate our book to them with gratitude.

David Lepine
Nicholas Orme

Editorial Practice and Abbreviations

The documents in this volume have all been translated into modern English, mostly from medieval Latin, to bring them to the widest possible readership. There are, however, exceptions to this practice with regard to names. Names appear in their original documentary forms if they are Old English fore-names, later forenames that are unusual or unusually spelt, or surnames. Common forenames, on the other hand, such as John and William, Elizabeth and Mary, have been modernised, as have place-names unless they are unidentifiable or equivocal, in which case they appear in italics. When indexing names, the letter 'y' is treated as 'i' and grouped with it, except when it begins a word: as in 'Yonge'. Similar name forms are also brought together, irrespective of the strict alphabetical order.

Obsolete words have been rendered in the spellings followed by the *Oxford English Dictionary*, and are explained in the Glossary. Editorial additions to the texts are enclosed in square brackets [ ]: these consist of explanatory material and unusual or uncertain words in the original texts. Gaps in texts, due to manuscripts that are incomplete or illegible, are indicated by angle brackets < >. These gaps are supplied with conjectural readings when that is possible; otherwise they are left blank. All other editorial practices are explained in prefaces to the individual documents. The following abbreviations are used:

DRO   Exeter, Devon Record Office

D&C   Exeter Cathedral Archives, Dean and Chapter documents

ECA   Exeter City Archives (in Exeter, Devon Record Office)

MCR   Devon Record Office, Exeter City Archives, Mayor's Court Rolls

Reg.   Published editions of bishops' registers, listed in the bibliography

VC   Exeter Cathedral Archives, Vicars Choral documents

*   Indicates restored or conjectural names, e.g. Cook from Latin *cocus*.

Part I

Death and Burial

Introduction to Part I

Burial Places

The history of burial in Exeter is as old as the history of Christianity. Excavations in the 1970s on the site of the church of St Mary Major, near the west front of the cathedral, revealed a series of early cemeteries. This area was part of the Roman forum and basilica, and the oldest cemetery consisted of burials aligned with the Roman buildings, dating from about the fifth century but possibly later.[1] Although the religious context of these burials is not entirely clear, the fact that they were sited in the centre of the city, rather than outside the city according to pagan Roman practice, suggests that they were Christian and indicate the presence of a nearby church. Christianity became the official religion of the Roman Empire during the fourth century, making it likely that part of the complex of public buildings in Exeter was designated as a church. In turn that church would have attracted burials.

It is not certain how far urban life persisted in Exeter after the end of Roman Britain in the early fifth century, and the continued use of any late Roman church and burial ground is still unclear. A second cemetery, however, was identified in the same area as the first, containing graves from the late seventh to about the tenth century: graves apparently aligned with a different church (which has not been located). This evidence accords well with an assertion in Willibald's life of St Boniface, written between 754 and 768, that Boniface spent his boyhood at a monastery in Exeter, presided over by an abbot with the Anglo-Saxon name of Wulfhard.[2] Boniface was a boy in about the 690s, and the graves in the second cemetery may well relate to the church that he attended. In due course this cemetery was succeeded by a third, datable to the tenth century onwards, in which

---

[1] On the early cemeteries, see P.T. Bidwell, *The Legionary Bath-House and Basilica and Forum at Exeter* (Exeter, 1979), pp. 112–13, and C. Henderson and P. Bidwell, 'The Saxon Minster at Exeter', in *The Early Church in Western Britain and Ireland*, ed. S.M. Pearce (Oxford, British Archaeological Reports, British Series, 102 (1982)), pp. 145–75.

[2] *Vitae Sancti Bonifacii*, ed. W. Levison, Monumenta Germaniae Historica, Scriptores Rerum Germanicarum, 57 (Hannover and Leipzig, 1905), p. 6; translated by C.H. Talbot, *The Anglo-Saxon Missionaries in Germany* (London and New York, 1954), p. 28.

the graves were aligned with yet another church: that which later on became the parish church of St Mary Major. This church is thought to have originated as a minster church, staffed by a group of clergy and founded by King Æthelstan (925–39). In 1050 it acquired cathedral status when Leofric, bishop of Crediton and of Cornwall, united the two dioceses and moved his seat to Exeter.[3] Its cemetery then became the cathedral cemetery, and remained in use for the next six hundred years.

The first cathedral building at Exeter was that of Æthelstan's minster. It was replaced by a larger new structure in the Romanesque style, begun in about 1114, consecrated in 1133, and finished in about the 1180s. The old minster then became the church of St Mary Major. The Romanesque cathedral lasted until it was enlarged and converted into the third and present cathedral, built in the Decorated style, between about 1270 and about 1340. The clergy who staffed the minster and the cathedrals that followed it were 'secular clergy', apart from a short period between about 968 and 1000 when they were replaced by monks.[4] Secular clergy differed from monks in being active in the everyday world. At Exeter Cathedral they lived in private houses and rooms around the cathedral close, not in a single set of premises like a monastery, and they were allowed to travel and own property to a greater extent than monks. By the twelfth century they consisted of 24 canons, presided over by a precentor and a treasurer, together with a number of inferior clergy: 24 vicars-choral, who deputised for the canons in daily worship; 12 adolescent and young adult secondary clerks or 'secondaries'; and 14 boy choristers. A further group of chantry priests, called 'annuellars', came into existence in the thirteenth century. All these people, as we shall see, had functions in relation to funerals and the commemoration of the dead. In 1225 Bishop Brewer instituted the office of dean and, at about the same time, that of chancellor. This brought the constitution of Exeter Cathedral into line with other cathedrals of secular clergy such as Salisbury and York, in which the institution was led by four dignitaries: dean, precentor, chancellor, and treasurer. The dignitaries each had special responsibilities, but in other respects they were equal with the rest of the canons as members of the cathedral chapter, the cathedral's governing body. From 1225 onwards it is permissible to talk of the cathedral being ruled by a dean and chapter.

---

[3] On the history of the Anglo-Saxon minster and cathedral, see Henderson and Bidwell, 'The Saxon Minster at Exeter', pp. 145–75; J. Allan, C. Henderson, and R.A. Higham, 'Saxon Exeter', in *Anglo-Saxon Towns in Southern England*, ed. Jeremy Haslam (Chichester, 1984), pp. 385–414; and Patrick W. Conner, *Anglo-Saxon Exeter: a tenth-century cultural history* (Woodbridge, 1993), pp. 21–32. On the Norman and later cathedral, see V. Hope, L.J. Lloyd, and A.M. Erskine, *Exeter Cathedral*, 2nd ed. (Exeter, 1988), pp. 10–51.

[4] Conner, *Anglo-Saxon Exeter*, pp. 29–31.

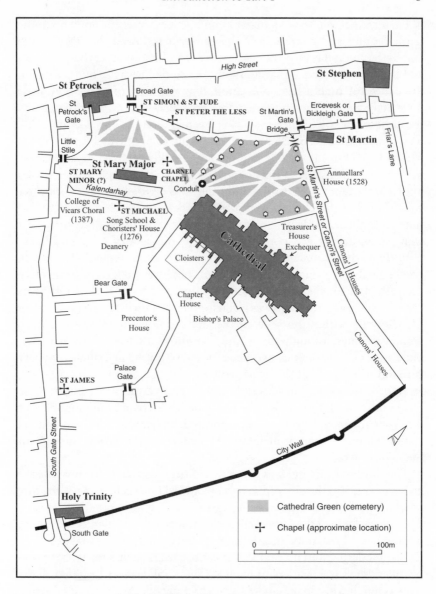

Fig. 1: Exeter Cathedral Close in the Middle Ages

Exeter, then, possessed a major church at least intermittently up to the tenth century and continuously thereafter. It followed that this church and its cemetery became the place where local people had their funerals and burials – a practice that no doubt developed casually but became in the course of time a legal obligation. The question of obligation arose once there were other churches in Exeter, which was certainly the case by the eleventh century. There may have been as many as 28 or 29 by 1100, including St George, St Olave, and St Martin, each of which can be dated before 1066, but these other churches are usually referred to as 'chapels' in early documents.[5] They did not possess full parochial rights or territories until 1222 when we are told that the city was divided into parishes, after which most of the chapels were designated as parish churches.[6] By that time the cathedral's claim to sole jurisdiction over funerals and burials was well established. It was not changed by the measure of 1222 and lasted until the early seventeenth century. Until then every person who died in Exeter (with a few exceptions to be identified) was obliged to be taken to the cathedral for his or her funeral service, and to be laid to rest in its cemetery unless permission was given for burial elsewhere. In consequence the churches within the walls of the city did not acquire graveyards in medieval times, though some came to allow interments within their buildings. The custom that everyone should be buried in a single cemetery is found in other English towns with a major ancient church – Chester, Hereford, Worcester, and possibly Bristol and Gloucester – but in these places other burial grounds were gradually created and the monopoly of the original cemetery eventually disappeared. Exeter Cathedral was unusual in the extent to which it maintained its control over burials throughout the middle ages.[7]

The diocese of Exeter was divided into rural deaneries for purposes of government, and the city of Exeter constituted one such deanery, the title of which in medieval times was the 'deanery of Exeter' or (to distinguish it from the deanery of the cathedral) as the 'deanery of Christianity of Exeter'. 'Deanery of Christianity' means 'rural deanery', and it is a mistake to think (as the modern Church does) that it is the specific name for what should be called 'the rural deanery of Exeter'. The rural deanery included all the parish churches inside the city walls and four outside: St David, St Edmund, St Leonard, and St Sidwell, but the application of the cathedral's funeral and burial rules to these four churches is less clear. St Edmund stood at one end of Exe Bridge and is not known to have had a burial ground. St

---

[5] On these chapels, see below, p. 235 and note 7.

[6] Ibid.

[7] Julia Barrow, 'Urban Cemetery Location in the High Middle Ages', in *Death in Towns*, ed. Steven Bassett (Leicester, 1992), pp. 78–100.

Leonard, on the other hand, lay well beyond the city limits and is mentioned as possessing one in 1397.[8] The status of St David and St Sidwell was complicated. Both functioned like parish churches and had parochial territories but they were technically chapels of ease within the parish of Heavitree. Heavitree church and much of its parish formed a 'peculiar jurisdiction' belonging to Exeter Cathedral, yet St David and St Sidwell were part of the rural deanery of Exeter. Both chapels of ease had room for open-air graveyards and eventually acquired them, although it is not certain when. In 1541 the bishop of Exeter licensed his suffragan bishop to consecrate the chapel and cemetery of St David, but this can only have been a regularisation of the status of the chapel (which had existed since at least the twelfth century) and is therefore not a sure guide to the history of the cemetery.[9] It is an open question at present whether the parishioners of St David, St Sidwell, and St Leonard were allowed funerals and burial at their local churches, or were obliged to go to the cathedral for the purpose.

Apart from this possible anomaly, the imposition of the cathedral's funeral and burial monopoly on the parish churches and chapels of Exeter was relatively easy to achieve. About half of them belonged to the cathedral and all were subject to the authority of the bishop, who was the ultimate ruler of the cathedral and could usually be relied on to defend its rights. More serious problems arose when other religious houses were founded in and around the city, because these had different patrons and affiliations and were less amenable to control. The issue first raised its head when the priory of St Nicholas was founded in Exeter in 1087 as a cell of Battle Abbey (Sussex), and grew more acute in the middle of the twelfth century when several more priories and hospitals made their appearance. It was already a sensitive matter in 1124 when Guy of Merton, prior of Bodmin (Cornwall), died on a visit to Exeter, upon which the cathedral clergy insisted on holding his funeral, although his body later appears to have been released to Bodmin.[10] In due course the cathedral elicited a privilege from a Pope Innocent, 'that no one should be allowed to establish a cemetery within the boundaries of the parish of the church of Exeter, without the consent of the [cathedral] chapter and the bishop'.[11] If this pope was Innocent II (1130–43), the privilege may represent an attempt to cope with the new foundations. The cathedral did not try (or failed) to stop them having

---

[8] *Reg. Stafford*, p. 99.

[9] DRO, Chanter XV, f. 108v.

[10] M.L. Colker, 'The Life of Guy of Merton by Rainald of Merton', *Mediaeval Studies*, 31 (1969), pp. 260–1; *The Heads of Religious Houses, England and Wales, I: 940–1216*, ed. D. Knowles, C.N.L. Brooke, and Vera M. London, 2nd ed. (Cambridge, 2001), p. 276.

[11] *Reg. Bronescombe*, ed. Hingeston-Randolph, p. 290.

cemeteries to bury their own clergy, but it was determined to prevent them from burying outsiders. There may have been an agreement to this effect with St Nicholas in or soon after 1087, and one was certainly made between 1139 and 1171, in which the cathedral conceded a cemetery in return for an undertaking by Battle Abbey that only monks of the priory should be buried in it.[12] A similar concession was made for the priory of St James, founded in about 1143 on the site of an earlier church off the Topsham Road. In that year its mother house, the priory of St Martin-des-Champs near Paris, consented to hold St James in dependency from the cathedral canons and promised not to receive any of their parishioners for burial without their permission.[13]

At about the same time as St James, another religious house appeared across the River Exe in Cowick. This was the priory of St Andrew, founded by 1144, which was a daughter house of the abbey of Bec-Hellouin in Normandy. Cowick Priory was also the parish church of Cowick (it may indeed have been a conversion of an earlier parish church to a monastery), and possessed a chapel of St Michael with a cemetery attached, which stood close to the priory site in Cowick Lane. Cowick parish was later regarded as part of the rural deanery of Kenn, not of Exeter, and, probably for that reason, no record survives of a cathedral grant for a cemetery belonging to Cowick Priory. The parish would have been regarded as lying outside the cathedral's jurisdiction. Later the chapel of St Thomas, which stood at the west end of Exe Bridge, became the parish church of Cowick for purposes of worship, but burials continued at the priory cemetery until 1412 when a new parish church of St Thomas was built on the present site in Cowick Street. The new church was provided with a new cemetery, which eventually (but not immediately) superseded the older one, and the dean and chapter were consulted before the bishop approved the new arrangements.[14] A fourth foundation of this period was Polsloe Priory, a house of nuns founded just over a mile to the east of the cathedral, in about 1160. This lay in the parish of Heavitree which belonged to the cathedral, and the canons were careful to ensure that the burial rights accorded to Polsloe were strictly limited. They granted a charter to the

---

[12] British Library, Cotton MS Vitellius D.ix, f. 181r. On f. 65v of the same manuscript is a grant by a Pope Honorius, either of 1129 or 1220, granting the prior and monks of St Nicholas right of free burial in their church, saving the rights of churches to whom the bodies of the dead belong.

[13] Exeter Cathedral Archives, D&C 2074; G. Oliver, *Monasticon Dioecesis Exoniensis* (Exeter and London, 1846), pp. 193–4.

[14] On the history of the priory and churches in Cowick, see G. Yeo, 'Where was Cowick Priory?', *Devon and Cornwall Notes and Queries*, 35/9 (1986), pp. 321–6; idem, *The Monks of Cowick* (Exeter, 1987); *Reg. Stafford*, p. 73.

priory allowing it to open a cemetery for its sisters and priests, but forbade anyone who was a parishioner of the church of Exeter to be buried there.[15] Three hospitals came into existence in or near the city during the twelfth century. The leper hospital of St Mary Magdalene in Magdalene Street is first documented in the reign of Bishop Bartholomew (1161–84), but may have originated earlier in the century.[16] Like other such houses it was a self-contained community with a chapel and cemetery, probably from the beginning, for the funerals and burials of its inmates.[17] The hospital of St Alexius, situated behind the priory of St Nicholas, is said to have been founded in 1164. It seems to have catered for infirm people who were not lepers, but it lasted for only about seventy years before it was united with the hospital of St John.[18] In view of its dedication it probably had a chapel, but no burial ground is recorded and the existence of such a place is unlikely, given what we know about St John. The latter house is first mentioned in a charter of 1184–5 confirming its property, but may be older. It stood in the High Street, just within the East Gate, and was staffed by brothers (and apparently also sisters) who seem to have ministered to travellers and to the poor: both the temporarily sick and the long-term infirm.[19] In 1351 Bishop Grandisson dedicated the hospital church, consisting of a choir and a nave, and gave permission for burials to take place there, subject to the rights of the cathedral.[20] This was evidently a new privilege, because in a document dated three years later he stated that those who died in the hospital had previously been buried in the cathedral cemetery, making heavy work for the hospital staff.[21]

The burial arrangements at all these houses required vigilance by the cathedral canons, but the problems they presented were much increased by the arrival of the friars in the thirteenth century. The Dominican Friars are first recorded in Exeter in 1232, where they established their church and friary in Bedford Street, while the Franciscans who followed them by 1240 took a site behind the priory of St Nicholas.[22] Each house duly acquired a cemetery for its members, and there was eventually a third because

---

[15] D&C 1374. There were subsequently burials both in the priory church and in a cemetery to the east of it: Leslie E. Webster and John Cherry, 'Medieval Britain in 1978', *Medieval Archaeology*, 23 (1979), pp. 250–1.

[16] Nicholas Orme and Margaret Webster, *The English Hospital, 1070–1570* (New Haven and London, 1995), pp. 226–31.

[17] The cemetery is mentioned in about 1233 (DRO, ED/M/39).

[18] Orme and Webster, *The English Hospital*, pp. 231–3.

[19] Ibid., pp. 233–9.

[20] *Reg. Grandisson*, ii, 1106–7.

[21] Ibid., ii, 1125.

[22] On the friaries, see A.G. Little and Ruth C. Easterling, *The Franciscans and Dominicans of Exeter* (Exeter, 1927).

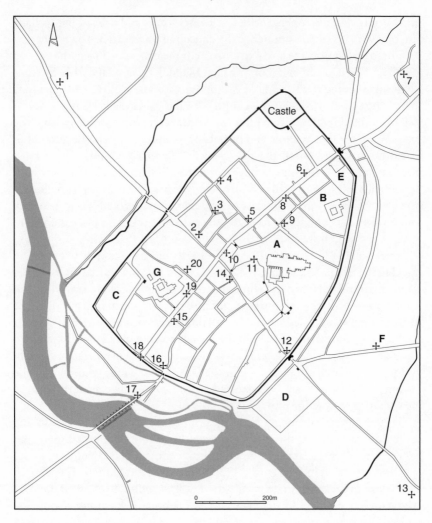

Fig. 2: Churches and Burial Places in Medieval Exeter

Religious houses

A	Cathedral and principal cemetery
B	Dominican Friary
C	Franciscan Friary, first site
D	Franciscan Friary, second site
E	St John Hospital
F	St Mary Magdalene Hospital
G	St Nicholas Priory

Parish churches

1	St David
2	St Kerrian
3	St Pancras
4	St Paul
5	All Hallows, Goldsmith Street
6	St Laurence
7	St Sidwell
8	St Stephen
9	St Martin
10	St Petroc
11	St Mary Major
12	Trinity
13	St Leonard
14	St George
15	St John Bow
16	St Mary Steps
17	St Edmund
18	All Hallows on the Wall
19	St Olave
20	St Mary Arches

Outside the map

H	Cowick Priory
I	Polsloe Priory
J	St James Priory
21	St Thomas parish church

the Franciscans moved in about 1300 to a new location outside the South Gate, near Holloway Street.[23] The old friary church, or part of it, remained as a chapel of St Mary and the graveyard there appears to have been preserved.[24] The friars threatened the cathedral's burial rights for two reasons. First their houses belonged to powerful international organisations with substantial privileges, including exemption from the authority of bishops. It is not clear that they even sought permission for their cemeteries. Secondly they were competitors (far more than monks had been) with cathedrals and parish clergy. Friars set out to make links with the laity through preaching, hearing confessions, and gathering alms. It naturally followed that the people they bonded with, especially wealthier people, should ask or be invited to have their funerals and burials in friary churches and cemeteries. This was the case all over western Europe, to the annoyance of the existing clergy who were deprived of rights and funeral revenues as a result. By the middle of the thirteenth century the popes were forced to arbitrate in the matter. There were several papal pronouncements, the most important and enduring of which was the bull *Super Cathedram*, issued by Boniface VIII in 1300. This laid down that anyone might choose burial at a friary but that, when this happened, a quarter of all the dues that were owed and the legacies that were made should go to the clergy of the dead person's parish.[25]

Disputes about burials in Exeter came to a head towards the end of the thirteenth century, and centred on the Dominicans. In 1281 there was a row over the body of a knight, Sir Henry de Pomeray, who seems to have requested burial in their church. The cathedral's rights were respected in so far that the body was taken there for its funeral, but the canons alleged that the friars carried it away for burial and removed the wax, cloths, and offerings associated with it, which rightfully belonged to the cathedral.[26] In 1301 there was a bitter clash over another knight, Sir Henry de Ralegh, who died in the friary where he had been living as a boarder with the status of a 'confrater' or associate member. The friars seem to have taken the view that Sir Henry was one of their own community, and prepared to organise not only his burial but also his funeral. The canons sent two of their number to request the body for the funeral, and it was eventually taken to the cathedral for this purpose, despite the friars' protests. After

---

[23]   Six burials have been identified on the later Franciscan site, probably within the east end of the church (Leslie E. Webster and John Cherry, 'Medieval Britain in 1978', *Medieval Archaeology*, 18 (1974), p. 188).

[24]   This is possibly the 'chapel called Our Lady chapel' with a cemetery in the parish of St John Bow, mentioned in 1578 (DRO, ECA, Misc. Roll 22, m. 38).

[25]   On the controversy, see David Knowles, *The Religious Orders in England*, 3 vols (Cambridge, 1948–59), i, 184–8.

[26]   Little and Easterling, *Franciscans and Dominicans*, pp. 40, 51, 72 .

the funeral the body was returned, but the friars refused to receive it and it lay for some time in the street before being taken back to the cathedral and buried there. The details of what happened are hard to perceive through the conflicting versions of the two sides, but the dispute was undoubtedly sharp and acrimonious. The friars complained to the court of the mayor of Exeter and then to the king's court. They declared the two canons to be subject to excommunication, and appealed to the pope. None of these authorities gave effective help to the friars, and in the end the controversy died down, though not until about 1305. The cathedral was left with its right to funerals; the friars with theirs to bury outsiders.[27]

There was a further proliferation of burial places in the later middle ages. One reason for this was a desire by wealthy people to be buried inside their parish churches, necessarily inside since most of the churches had no cemeteries. The earliest reference to such a burial is that of Agnes de Wodelegh in the church of St Mary Major in 1348 (Document 19), and there is a scattering of recorded instances later on – probably only a minority of those that occurred.[28] Such burials would have required the permission of the dean and chapter, and would always have followed a funeral in the cathedral. During the middle of the sixteenth century a burial ground was opened at Ringswell in Heavitree for criminals hanged on the gallows. The mayor of Exeter, John Peter, gave land for this purpose, and the place was blessed by the last Catholic bishop of Exeter, James Turberville, on 5 March 1558.[29] Ringswell post-dated the Reformation, but if we go back a few years to the 1530s, before the suppression of the religious houses, we can count up to about 27 burial sites in or near the city. They included the area in and around the cathedral (itself a complex of sites), six active or former religious houses, and about 20 parish churches.[30] A further unique site may have been a Jewish burial ground, since there was a Jewish community in Exeter from the twelfth century until the expulsion of Jews from England in 1290. It is likely that the community took advantage of a royal law of 1177 permitting Jews to acquire cemeteries outside city walls, but no record of such a place in Exeter has yet been found.[31]

---

[27] Ibid., pp. 40–6; see below, p. 196.

[28] See below, pp. 33–4.

[29] R. Pearse Chope, *Early Tours in Devon and Cornwall*, 2nd ed. (Newton Abbot, 1967), pp. 83–4.

[30] St Edmund, which stood on Exe Bridge, apparently had no room for internal burials (Beatrix F. Cresswell, *Exeter Churches* (Exeter, 1908), p. 29).

[31] On this subject, see Michael Adler, 'The Medieval Jews of Exeter', *Devonshire Association Transactions*, 63 (1931), pp. 221–40; Cecil Roth, *A History of the Jews in England*, 3rd ed. (Oxford, 1964), p. 13; and Bernard Susser, *The Jews of South-West England* (Exeter, 1993), pp. 4–25.

Mortality

If burial as an institution in medieval Exeter is comparatively well documented, the reverse is true of the individuals who died and were buried. Although the present volume lists some hundreds of known interments in the city up to 1540, these are only a tiny proportion of the whole, chiefly made up of wealthy people whose burials have been recorded. How many people lived and died in Exeter during the period of our study is impossible to say, since numbers are uncertain. The city has been conjectured as containing about three thousand inhabitants in 1377, based on two records of that year: the national poll-tax assessment and the local murage tax rolls.[32] Taxation sources, however, are not wholly reliable guides to population, because so many people are likely to have avoided the taxes or to have failed to pay them through poverty. The religious and economic infrastructure of Exeter (including the four suburbs beyond the main gates) suggests a larger figure: perhaps at least five thousand during the later middle ages.

A glimpse of the extent of mortality in the city during the early fourteenth century is afforded by the earliest cathedral obit accounts, which begin to survive in 1305 (Document 29).[33] These, until about 1327, include some records of funerals, because the offerings made on such occasions had to be divided among the canons in residence. A wealthy person's funeral generated enough money to be worth recording by itself, or rather some funerals did, because it is a puzzling fact that most of the citizens of Exeter who died bequeathing property in this period are not named in the accounts as having had funerals. Other funeral offerings, especially those of the poor, were lumped together as from 'certain corpses'. We do not therefore know the true number of funerals in these years, but we can identify a minimum by counting one for each named person and two for 'certain corpses'. Counting in this way gives us at least 40 funerals in 1306, the first year for which records are complete. From 1307 to 1314 the figures vary from 19 to 46, rising to 53 in 1315 and 84 in 1316 before falling again in the 1320s. After this the entries tail off (evidently for administrative reasons), and the accounts lose their value in this respect. The high figures of 1315–16 coincide with the well-known national crisis of these years, in which bad harvests in 1315 and 1316 led to high grain prices, malnutrition, and the outbreak of diseases termed by contemporaries 'pestilence' and 'dysentery'. Clearly Exeter did not escape this crisis.

---

[32] Maryanne Kowaleski, *Local Markets and Regional Trade in Medieval Exeter* (Cambridge, 1995), pp. 371–5.

[33] On what follows, see Nicholas Orme, 'Mortality in Early Fourteenth-Century Exeter', *Medical History*, 32 (1988), pp. 195–203.

These funeral statistics are chiefly of value for comparing different years. They undoubtedly fall short of the true numbers of people dying and being buried in the city. One sign of this is the absence, mentioned above, of the names of some wealthy citizens who died during the period. Another is provided by an interesting reference in connection with the establishment of the chantry of Dean Andrew Kilkenny in the cathedral in 1305 (Document 30). The foundation document stated that the endowments of the chantry were to supply six candles, apparently on a permanent basis, to burn in the cathedral before corpses that were brought to the cathedral 'without lights'. These were the bodies of adults or children whose families were too poor to afford such things. The candles were to burn in pairs before each corpse at the funeral mass, showing that it was envisaged that three poor deceased folk might be lying in the cathedral for this purpose at any one time. Indeed the ordinance foresaw that the total might even rise above three, but stated that on such occasions the number of candles was not to be raised.[34] This evidence confirms that we should mentally allow for more than two when encountering 'certain corpses' in the obit accounts. There were evidently occasions on which a group of bodies lay in the cathedral on the same day, since we must assume the presence of others besides the poor. Funerals, as we shall see, did not take place each day,[35] but there are likely to have been several every week. The Kilkenny evidence comes from the period before the great famine of 1315–16, and is likely to reflect normal conditions rather than outbreaks of high mortality.

Modern demographers emphasise the variety of diseases that caused mortality in the population of medieval England, rather than singling out the Black Death of 1348–9 as the only potent force in this respect. Still, the Black Death – the first major onset of the plague – was a notable event, and the reader will wish to be told of its history in Exeter. This too is still not clear in all respects. The plague appears to have had some severe effects in Devon, since it is said to have slain 20 of the 23 monks of Newenham Abbey near Honiton, and probably killed 9 of the 11 infirm priests in the hospital of Clyst Gabriel, four miles east of Exeter, between January and March 1349.[36] The seriousness of its impact on the city is suggested by the registration of a larger than usual number of wills in the mayor's court. Between 1301 and 1347 the number of wills so registered ranged from

[34] D&C 1927; below, p. 314.

[35] See below, pp. 19–20.

[36] On Newenham, see Oliver, *Monasticon*, p. 364, and on Clyst Gabriel, Nicholas Orme, 'A Medieval Almshouse for the Clergy: Clyst Gabriel', *The Journal of Ecclesiastical History*, 39 (1988), pp. 1–15, and idem, 'The Clergy of Clyst Gabriel, 1312–1509', *Devonshire Association Transactions*, 126 (1994), pp. 107–21.

one to 10 per annum, with a mean of about 4.3 per annum. In 1348 (the year that the plague arrived) there were 6 registrations, no more than usual, but in 1349 the number rose sharply to 55, particularly in February (10), March (13), and April (9).[37] Allowing for a lapse of time between death and registration, this points (as at Clyst Gabriel) to a large mortality in the first three months of the year. There were 12 registrations in 1350 and 8 in 1351, after which the totals fell to small figures before rising again to 11 in 1361 and 6 in 1362. These last two years saw another serious outbreak of the plague throughout England, and it seems that this was also the case in Exeter.[38]

The records of the cathedral show that about ten canons died between the autumn of 1348 and that of 1349, though not all may have died in Exeter and only four deaths are clearly attributable to the spring of 1349.[39] There were also at least five fatalities during the two years, and possibly fifteen or more, among the minor clergy of the cathedral: the vicars choral and annuellars.[40] Neither here nor in the city can we gain much sense of how the plague affected individual people, but clues may be found in the two wills that survive in complete form from the spring of 1349, both included in the present volume (Documents 19–20). One, that of Agnes de Wodelegh, is notable for its careful arrangements for the inheritance of her property, providing for its transmission in turn to her husband, daughter, step-daughter, and a city church, which appear to reflect concerns about mortality. The other, John Mounteyn's, appears to be that of a young man, possibly a widower, whose circumstances may also point to a period when death was more common than usual. In London the number of people needing to be buried caused new graveyards to be designated to receive them, but there is no evidence of this in Exeter.[41] Since any new burial ground would probably have been consecrated (as was the case in London), one would expect it to have stayed in being after the emergency and to have left some trace in local records, but none exists. It seems therefore that the cathedral set a priority on maintaining its rights, and either forbade interments outside its cemetery or (at most) allowed them to spread to the cemeteries that already existed in and outside the city.

---

[37] DRO, MCR 21–22 Edw III (1347–8), 22–23 Edw III (1348–9), 23–24 Edw III (1349–50).

[38] DRO, MCR 34–35 Edw III (1360–1), 35–36 Edw III (1361–2).

[39] J. Le Neve, *Fasti Ecclesiae Anglicanae 1300–1541*: vol. 9, *Exeter Diocese*, ed. Joyce M. Horn (London, 1964), passim.

[40] Nicholas Orme, *The Minor Clergy of Exeter Cathedral, 1300–1548* (Exeter, 1980), pp. 15–17, 53–4.

[41] Duncan Hawkins, 'The Black Death and the New London Cemeteries of 1348', *Antiquity*, 64 (1990), pp. 637–42.

The Cathedral Cemetery

The new burial sites established after the Norman Conquest catered primarily for small groups of clergy or élite laity, and were slow to affect the way in which most Exeter people were laid to rest. Until the early seventeenth century this involved a funeral in the cathedral followed by interment in a grave in the cathedral cemetery. The cemetery was a piece of consecrated ground, which had been formally made holy with prayers and rituals by a bishop.[42] Its supervision belonged to the cathedral treasurer, a responsibility first mentioned in the time of Bishop Bartholomew (1162–84), when we are told that the treasurer 'has the cemetery in his regulation and the right of burying'.[43] By 1337 he received 24s. a year from the cathedral exchequer to support the costs of this duty.[44] How well the duty was done became an issue during the treasurership of Robert Brok (1377–88), who prompted complaints from the rest of the chapter that he appropriated revenues that did not belong to him and neglected the tasks that did. Under his stewardship of the cemetery, his colleagues asserted, 'workmen make things there and timber belonging to outsiders is kept there, and pigs often enter there, and horses browse on the grass, and outsiders exhibit their goods there to sell them'. The treasurer rebutted these charges robustly. 'That some people work there is against his prohibition, and there is nothing that he can do further because they are not under his jurisdiction and he cannot expel them by force unless he is to set his hand to war.' The presence of horses, he claimed, was due to the canons themselves: 'this is to be imputed to you, since you have horses and vehicles brought to you, and they ought to receive fodder'. He closed light-heartedly with two lines of verse, in translation, 'If you love your guest, feed his mare with the best. You throw all to the air if you do not feed the mare!'[45]

Brok's remarks were justified in so far that the cemetery, a large open space at the heart of the city, attracted all kinds of activities that jarred with its function as a resting place for the dead. We are used to the convention that a cemetery should be landscaped, well kept, and quiet, but this was only a development of the late eighteenth and nineteenth centuries. Until that time burial grounds often lay close to the centres of settlements and were jostled by everyday life. Exeter's graveyard was crossed by paths and contained a well near the west front of the cathedral, where many in

[42] For the liturgy of consecration at Exeter, see *Liber Pontificalis of Edmund Lacy, Bishop of Exeter*, ed. Ralph Barnes (Exeter, 1847), pp. 42–6.

[43] D&C 3625, ff. 116v–117r; *Ordinale Exon*, ed. J.N. Dalton and G.H. Doble, 4 vols, Henry Bradshaw Society, 37–8, 63, 79 (1909, 1926, 1941), ii, 544–5.

[44] *Ordinale Exon*, ed. Dalton and Doble, i, 4.

[45] D&C 2920.

the city came to draw water. A drainage ditch ran down the north-east boundary of the cemetery, opposite the canons' houses. In the 1440s the city authorities complained that this was ill-maintained, causing flooding in the parts of the city it served.[46] Games took place alongside the trading and construction activities. In 1386 an adult cathedral vicar, John Forn, was censured for playing with a piece of wood among lay people in the cemetery – perhaps in some kind of caber-tossing contest.[47] But even the dean and chapter allowed the lighting of a bonfire on the vigil of the cathedral's feast-day, St Peter and St Paul (28 June), accompanied by ceremonial 'ridings' and the presentation of 'interludes' or dramas.[48]

The Church authorities seem to have tolerated a certain amount of pressure on the cemetery from the outside world. They strongly objected, on the other hand, to the spilling of blood, which sometimes resulted from fighting. This was held to pollute the ground and to compromise the area's sacred status. When an incident of blood-shedding took place, it was reported to the bishop who was usually living at a rural manor in Devon or out of the county altogether. He ordered an enquiry, suspended the use of the cemetery for burials, and (if appropriate) ordered the offenders to be summoned to a Church court or excommunicated. Suspensions lasted for anything from a week to a couple of months until the bishop consented to 'reconcile' the cemetery in a ceremony involving the sprinkling of holy water, blessed by himself.[49] Pollutions of this kind were a regular problem. Four allegations that they had happened occur in the 1380s alone and another four between 1426 and 1450.[50] The frequency with which reconciliations were needed in the diocese led bishops to get licences from the pope to appoint a deputy to do them – a device that also avoided the impression that ill-behaved people could put the bishop to trouble. In July 1381, for example, Bishop Brantingham, although not far away at Bishop's Clyst, empowered the cathedral precentor or treasurer to carry out the reconciliation, and sent the water required.[51] Where were bodies interred in the meantime? By about 1400 one option was to use the 'praiel', the open plot of land that lay in the middle of the newly completed

---

[46] *Letters and Papers of John Shillingford, Mayor of Exeter*, ed. S.A. Moore, Camden Society, new series 2 (1871), p. 89.

[47] D&C 3550, f. 21r.

[48] Nicholas Orme, *Exeter Cathedral as it Was, 1050–1550* (Exeter, 1986), pp. 80–1.

[49] For the rite of reconciliation, see *Liber Pontificalis*, ed. Barnes, pp. 46–52.

[50] *Reg. Brantyngham*, i, 157, 159; 169; ii, 582–3; *Reg. Lacy*, ed. Dunstan, I, 157–9; II, 62–4, 360; III, 56.

[51] *Reg. Brantyngham*, i, 157, 159.

cloister, south of the cathedral nave.[52] The praiel functioned as a burial ground (as it did at other cathedrals, such as Hereford and St Paul's) and, being an insulated area, it was not affected by pollution in the main cemetery. In the 1440s, at a time when the city authorities were making complaints against the cathedral clergy, one of their charges was that the latter were wont to shut the outer door of the cloisters, preventing people from going in to pray for the dead who lay in the cloisters and the praiel.[53] But the privilege of burial there may well have required permission and payment of fees.

Burial in the middle ages was part of an elaborate culture of death involving people, religion, money, art, and folklore.[54] It could be a simple process or a grand one, depending on one's wishes and resources. The religious ceremonies began as death drew near, with the arrival of the rector of the parish to administer the last rites. If a cleric was dying, other clergy would do this task. Departing persons were asked to declare their faith and to make their confession. They were then absolved, anointed, and commended in prayer. After death the body was washed and wound in a clean linen cloth or garment. It was placed on a bier and taken to the cathedral. The journey might be an elaborate one, with family, friends, and clergy accompanying the corpse bearing candles or torches, or it might be a poor affair without any lights. On reaching the cathedral the body of a canon or a member of the nobility was likely to be placed in the choir and that of an ordinary person outside the choir, probably in the nave. If death took place in the night or early morning the funeral may have taken place on the same day, but if it happened later in the day the body would have needed to lie in the cathedral overnight and be buried next morning. There appear to have been no funerals in the cathedral on Sundays, however, and it is not clear where the dead of the weekend rested until Monday.[55]

From about the thirteenth century it was probably usual for a funeral mass to be celebrated in the cathedral before a burial. This was certainly

---

[52] For the word, see Hans Kurath and Sherman M. Kuhn, *Middle English Dictionary* (Ann Arbor and London, 1956–2000).

[53] *Letters and Papers of John Shillingford,* pp. 85–6.

[54] There is a good body of recent literature on death and burial in medieval England (see the bibliography, below, pp. 349–55), of which Christopher Daniell, *Death and Burial in Medieval England, 1066–1550* (London and New York, 1997), is particularly to be recommended as a wide-ranging and well-written study.

[55] This and the following paragraph are based partly on the provisions in *Ordinale Exon*, ed. Dalton and Doble, i, 300, and partly on the 'Sarum' prayers and rites in use in southern England at the end of the middle ages, set out in *Manuale ad Vsum Percelebris Ecclesie Sarisburiensis*, ed. A. Jefferies Collins, Henry Bradshaw Society, 91 (1960), pp. 114–62.

the case by 1337, when Bishop Grandisson drew up his detailed guide to worship in the cathedral, known as the *Ordinale Exon*. The *Ordinale* assumes that funeral masses will be weekday events. On a normal weekday morning there was a series of services in the cathedral choir, beginning with prime which started between about 7.00 and 8.00am, followed (after an interval) by terce, sext, and high mass, the last of which was said at the high altar at about 9.00. If a body was present in church for funeral rites, the high mass was brought forward to follow prime and the funeral mass was celebrated after the service of sext, probably also at 9.00 or thereabouts. Like the high mass it took place at the high altar, and it included prayers for all the deceased persons present, of whom, as we have seen, there might be several. When this mass was over and more prayers had been said, each body would be brought to its grave by clergy and mourners. The grave was then dug, if this had not already been done, and was sanctified by the priest with holy water and incense. Then the body was placed in the grave, the priest threw earth upon it in the form of a cross, and the grave was filled, after which further prayers concluded the service.

Towards the end of the fourteenth century John Mirk, prior of Lilleshall (Shropshire), reflected on the burial service and what it symbolised in a model sermon for preaching at funerals. We are buried in holy ground because we come from earth and return there. Our bodies are covered by a white sheet to show that we have confessed and been cleanly absolved before we die. We lie with our head to the west and our feet to the east, so that we shall be ready to see the coming of Christ from the east at the Day of Judgment. A cross of wood stands by our head, as a reminder that we are saved by his passion on the cross, and another cross made of wax candles is placed on our breast, as a token that we die burning with charity to God and man. A measuring rod is laid beside us, like a staff, representing the fact that that we are going on a spiritual journey, but the staff is broken as a sign that there is no defence on this journey. We must take better or worse as we have deserved – a reference to the belief that one did not go to heaven merely through dying contrite and absolved. All sins must be paid for, and those who had not done enough good deeds in life to compensate must suffer pain in purgatory until their sins were expiated. When the earth is cast on our body, the door of the grave is shut, but so that fiends shall have no power over us, the priest sprinkles it with holy water and then goes on his way.[56]

Graves were often known in Exeter as 'pits' and may originally have been dug by anyone, but by the later middle ages there was a designated

---

[56] John Mirk, *Mirk's Festial*, ed. T. Erbe, Early English Text Society, extra series, 96 (1905), pp. 294–5.

person to make them, employed by the cathedral. He may well be the *fossor* (meaning 'digger') to whom a small annual fee of 1s. 8d. was paid from at least 1305 onwards.[57] In the early sixteenth century he was known both as the bellringer and the pitmaker, suggesting that he also advertised the funeral by ringing one of the cathedral bells or by walking the streets with a handbell.[58] At that time he charged 6d. for digging a grave, and he received a small share of the money distributed when obit masses were held in the cathedral in memory of the dead. The pitmaker in 1547, John Fynymore, was paid 3s. 2d. from this source. In about the 1520s or 30s the city authorities protested to the dean and chapter that the burial charge was levied even if the corpse was buried in another cemetery, but the dean and chapter replied that the pitmaker was bound to make the grave wherever it was needed. This was another of the ways in which the cathedral, while allowing some burials elsewhere, tried to maintain the principle that it was in charge of the operation throughout the city.

The earliest burials in the cathedral close, during the Roman and Anglo-Saxon periods, were centred at the south-western end, but they gradually spread northwards towards the street that runs from St Martin's church towards Southernhay. It was the normal practice in the close, as elsewhere, to dig graves on an east-west orientation, the orientation often varying from true east in order to align the graves with a nearby ecclesiastical building.[59] The dead were buried lying upwards and facing east in the manner that Mirk described. Some Anglo-Saxon corpses were simply laid in the grave, while others were placed on a layer of charcoal – a practice that seems to have died out in the twelfth century.[60] Occasionally stone slabs were placed beneath the buried person's head, as if for a pillow. Later medieval graves were sometimes lined with stone, and the cathedral fabric accounts mention stone being sold for this purpose, apparently for graves in the cemetery as well as in the church. Wooden coffins were in use from the Anglo-Saxon period onwards, but many bodies were deposited simply in shrouds. Goods were not normally placed in Christian graves other than personal jewellery: a gold ring was discovered in one of the early Exeter cemeteries. By the thirteenth century, however, some clergy were

---

[57] D&C 3673, f. 59r; below, p. 273.

[58] On this and what follows, see John Hooker, *The Description of the Citie of Excester*, ed. W.J. Harte and others, 3 parts, Devon and Cornwall Record Society (1919–47), pp. 213, 215–16; D&C 3686, ff. 44r, 46r.

[59] Daniell, *Death and Burial in Medieval England*, pp. 148–9; Philip Rahtz, 'Grave Orientation', *Archaeological Journal*, 135 (1978), pp. 1–14.

[60] On burial customs up to the twelfth century, see Henderson and Bidwell, 'The Saxon Minster', pp. 150–6.

coming to be buried in vestments while holding a chalice and paten, reflecting the importance attached to their power to say mass and to recreate the body of Christ under the form of bread and wine.[61] A chalice and paten were recovered from the grave of Bishop Bitton in 1763, although the site in that case was inside the cathedral.[62] And by the end of the middle ages, when literacy and writing were widespread, it was common for the priest at a burial to place a written document on the breast of the corpse.[63] Papal indulgences, granting full remission of penance to those who died contrite and confessed, were much in demand by this time, and the leaden bulls or seals attached to them have sometimes been found in graveyards elsewhere in England.[64]

Ground acquires significance when it is used for burial, and graves in history have often been marked and regarded as belonging to their occupants. There is no record of the dean and chapter granting anyone a space in the cemetery as was done inside the cathedral church, which implies that no right existed to possess a site in perpetuity. The use of the cemetery for animal grazing and human activities also indicates that there was a good deal of unimpeded space. It is not impossible, however, that some graves were marked, at least temporarily, with wooden crosses or stones. French manuscript illustrations of graveyards in the later middle ages show markers in the form of wooden crosses about a metre high, surmounted by a gable of two diagonal slats – perhaps as protection from rain.[65] In Kent there was a fashion for placing round-headed stones in churchyards, carved with a cross and supported on a short shaft.[66] Some Exeter burial sites were certainly remembered for years after they were made, because a few will-makers specified interment in or near an existing grave. This also indicates the possibility of being randomly buried, rather than in some serial order. Walter Gervas wished to be buried by his father; John Robyns by his wife Elizabeth.[67] If memorials were lacking, the numerous paths that criss-crossed the cemetery may have been helpful means by which graves could be visited and remembered.

It is also possible that burials were positioned according to rank, occupation, or parish, though evidence for this is elusive. Modern exca-

---

[61] On this subject, see Warwick Rodwell, *Wells Cathedral: Excavations and Structural Studies, 1978–93*, 2 vols (London, 2001), ii, 523–9.

[62] Hope, Lloyd, and Erskine, *Exeter Cathedral*, pp. 73–4.

[63] *Manuale*, ed. Collins, p. 157.

[64] Daniell, *Death and Burial in Medieval England*, pp. 168–9.

[65] See, for example, Roger S. Wieck, *Painted Prayers: the Book of Hours in Medieval and Renaissance Art* (New York, 1997), pp. 120, 129–31.

[66] Ben Stocker, 'Medieval Grave Markers in Kent', *Church Monuments*, 1 part 2 (1986), pp. 106–14.

[67] See below, pp. 72, 101.

vations have shown that a number of graves near the church of St Mary Major were aligned with the building, and these have been interpreted as forming a distinct burial ground for its parishioners.[68] The judgment may be insecure, however, because we know of two parishioners of St Kerrian who chose graves in the vicinity of St Mary Major.[69] Indeed that area may have been a popular burial place with wealthy Exonians, because it lay close to the route of religious and civic processions in and out of the cathedral. A request by a woman in the reign of Elizabeth I to be buried 'in the churchyard of St Peter, where St Petroc's parish use to be buried in' may or may not refer to a parochial sector, depending on how the sentence is interpreted.[70] The clearest reference to the reservation of a space for a group of people is the mention of the 'cemetery of the Kalendars' in 1308: an allusion to the guild of Kalendars, which included leading members of the clergy and laity of Exeter up to the middle of the fourteenth century.[71] The site concerned was in the cathedral close, possibly in Kalendarhay which takes its name from the same guild, and the fact that the site was so named suggests that it was appropriated to the burials of guild members. But it was perhaps a detached burial plot, rather than part of the main cemetery.

Graves, whether marked or not, cannot have endured indefinitely without disturbance, at least after the eleventh or twelfth century. As the city grew in population, its death rate rose higher still because towns harboured so much poverty and disease. More bodies came to be buried than the ground could easily absorb, causing bones to make their way to the surface or to be disturbed when new graves were dug. This problem was not confined to Exeter and seems to have been widespread in towns by the thirteenth century, causing the introduction of storehouses for cemetery bones, known as charnels. Exeter Cathedral cemetery acquired such a storehouse in 1286 in a form that was common elsewhere: a subterranean chamber with a small detached chapel above it.[72] The site lay close to the west front of the cathedral and the chapel was built at the expense of John of Exeter, formerly treasurer of the cathedral and a claimant to be its dean. This man was a principal suspect in relation to the murder of the cathedral precentor, Walter de Lechlade, which took place just outside the cathedral

[68] Henderson and Bidwell, 'The Saxon Minster', pp.148, 157.
[69] Below, pp. 75, 111 (John Hamond, John Tybot).
[70] Ethel Lega-Weekes, *Some Studies in the Topography of the Cathedral Close, Exeter* (Exeter, 1915), p.15.
[71] Exeter Cathedral Archives, D&C 2781–2. For the guild, see below, p. 235.
[72] On the Exeter charnel and chapel, see Nicholas Orme, 'The Charnel Chapel of Exeter Cathedral', in *Medieval Art and Architecture at Exeter Cathedral*, The British Archaeological Association Conference Transactions, 11 (1991), pp. 162–71

in 1283, and the building of the chapel seems to have been an act of reparation for his share in the crime. It was dedicated to St Edward the Confessor, probably in honour of King Edward I who was named after the Confessor and who visited Exeter in 1286 to oversee the trial of the precentor's murderers.[73] At the west end of the chapel a flight of steps gave access to the basement charnel in which loose bones were stored. When the charnel was excavated in 1971 it was found still to contain a mass of them, about one metre deep, many arranged into groups of arms, legs, and skulls. The chapel continued in use until about 1549 when it was destroyed as a consequence of the Reformation, and the use of the charnel may well have been discontinued at the same time.

The emphasis placed by the Church on holy burial had a contrary side: a refusal to admit certain kinds of the dead to consecrated ground. These included suicides, still-born children, thieves and adulterers slain in the act, those whom the Church had excommunicated, and unrepentant prostitutes.[74] The first two of these categories must have often caused problems in Exeter since they had to be buried somewhere, as we learn from an action for assault in the mayor's court in 1286. William Horman claimed that he had been told to bury a certain woman whom the bishop of Exeter had barred from consecrated ground, presumably because she was a suicide or a prostitute. He began to dig a grave in a part of the cemetery that the city authorities regarded as unconsecrated but the bishop as consecrated. While he was doing so John de Gorkelegh, a chaplain of the bishop, was alleged to have caused an affray by taking away his tools and striking him on the shoulder with a pick-axe.[75] The incident is interesting because it shows that part of the cemetery was apparently unhallowed (perhaps on or near the surrounding roads), and could be used for burying the excluded. It also indicates the clergy's fear of such burials invading the consecrated area, a fear that was not confined to Exeter. Evidence from elsewhere in England shows that stillborn children in particular were secretly interred in consecrated ground to give them validation as Christians.[76] The operation was best carried out after dark, but it would have been difficult to do so at Exeter after 1286 since that was also the year when the cathedral close was provided with gates and sealed off when night fell.

---

[73] *John Lydford's Book*, ed. Dorothy M. Owen, Devon and Cornwall Record Society, new series, 20 (1975), p. 106.
[74] Mirk, *Festial*, pp. 298–9; John Stow, *Survey of London*, ed. C.L. Kingsford, 2 vols (Oxford, 1908), ii, 55.
[75] DRO, MCR, 14 Edward I, m. 6.
[76] On this subject, see Nicholas Orme, *Medieval Children* (New Haven and London, 2001), p.126.

Burial inside the Cathedral

Even without violations the cemetery could not compete for sanctity with the cathedral church itself. The church was God's own house, the scene of the daily round of services. Not surprisingly there was a feeling that it was best to be buried inside the cathedral, where one's body would lie in more peaceful and holy surroundings close to the worship of God. Space for such burials, however, was limited and throughout the medieval period it was reserved for bishops, canons, and a few outsiders who were allowed in as a favour or for money. We know little about burial in the minster that became the cathedral. Bishop Leofric is said to have been laid to rest inside it at his death in 1072, and his successor Osbern (d. 1103) appears to have followed him there.[77] Whether their canons were allowed internal burials is not known. When the second cathedral was built it too was envisaged as a place for graves, at least of bishops. The bodies of Leofric and Osbern were transferred to it, probably at about the time that it was consecrated in 1133, and it is likely that most of their successors were laid to rest in the same way, except for Bishop William Warelwast who was buried at Plympton Priory.

Only the outlines of the second cathedral and its furnishings can be conjectured, but the building seems to have followed a simple plan. There was a choir surrounded by an ambulatory, a nave, and two towers, the latter linked to the nave by fairly restricted openings. There is no evidence that the building included any other units, such as small projecting chapels.[78] The plan suggests that the choir area – the holiest space – would have been used for burying bishops, though the only such burial that can be surmised is that of Bishop Brewer (d. 1244), whose tomb occupied a similar position in the third cathedral. However it is unlikely that every bishop of the second cathedral was interred in the choir, since the tomb of Bishop John the Chanter (d. 1191) stood in later times in the south tower, where there was an altar to St John Baptist – a cult that the bishop may have instituted or have chosen as his burial site. Canons were probably barred from the choir but permitted to lie in the nave and the ambulatories, as was the custom in the third cathedral. Thomas Boteler (d. 1264), Henry de Bracton (d. 1268), and Roger Torridge (d. 1274) were all buried (or asked to be) in front of altars in the nave, and the first dean, Serlo (d. 1231), may have been interred in the chapter house. Whether lay people were buried inside the second cathedral is not clear, but this is quite possible given that it happened in later times. Two thirteenth-century knights, Sir John de Montacute and Sir John Wyger, were involved in founding chantries in

---

[77] For references to this and all the individual burials that follow, see the register of burials, below, pp. 44–119.

[78] For the suggested plan, see Orme, *Exeter Cathedral As It Was*, p. 15.

the cathedral, with priests to pray for their souls, and they may have chosen graves near their chantry altars.[79] The basic funeral monument in the second cathedral was probably a flat ledger-stone, and even some bishops (like Brewer) may have been satisfied with this. Others in contrast sought to be remembered more grandly. Bishop John may have had an 'altar tomb' (like an altar but not necessarily used as one), and Bishops Henry Marshal (d. 1206) and Simon of Apulia (d. 1223) both had effigies that survive, each of which was probably elevated from the ground on a plinth or an altar-like structure.

Our knowledge of burial customs in the cathedral becomes clearer once we reach the era of the third and present building, erected after 1270. The chapter of Wells Cathedral enacted a statute about burial in 1243: canons were to lie in the cloisters unless they chose another site, vicars choral outside the eastern end of the church, and lay people beyond its western end.[80] No similar document survives from Exeter, but its clergy evidently observed conventions about grave sites and tombs that were broadly in line with those of other English cathedrals. The choir, or more specifically the presbytery and sanctuary that form its central and eastern parts, was reserved for bishops. Four of these were interred in altar tombs, with or without effigies, around the edge of this area. They included Bishop Marshal, translated from the second cathedral, and Bishops Stapledon (d. 1326), Berkeley (d. 1327), and Lacy (d. 1455). Another two had large ledger stones in the centre of the choir: Brewer and Bitton (d. 1307). As in the earlier building, however, certain bishops chose or were obliged to lie outside this area. Bishop Bronescombe (d. 1280) and his successor Quinil (d. 1291) preferred to be buried in the new Lady Chapel which they had instituted, perhaps because the choir of the second cathedral was full at that point and the choir of its successor had not yet been finished. The chapel, when built, included four large wall recesses, suitable for containing monuments, and at least two of these were subsequently used to house effigies from the tombs of earlier bishops, possibly Bartholomew (d. 1184) and Simon of Apulia (d. 1223). These effigies, and possibly the bodies of the bishops concerned, must have been moved from other sites in the second cathedral.

The choir of the third cathedral was larger than its predecessor, but it was still not large enough to hold many bishops unless they were prepared to lie, like Brewer and Bitton, beneath ledger stones. Room for raised monuments was limited, and Berkeley seems to have filled the last such space. His tomb was briefly the centre of a popular cult, following his

---

[79] See below, pp. 239–40.
[80] *Calendar of the Manuscripts of the Dean and Chapter of Wells*, 2 vols (London, Historical Manuscripts Commission, 1907), i, 73–4.

unexpected death on 24 June 1327, after a reign that had lasted for only three months. Candles and money were offered there, and the cult continued up to about the time of the Black Death, without attracting much official support and indeed arousing disapproval from Berkeley's successor, Grandisson.[81] Only two people are known to have been buried in the choir after 1327. One was Bishop Lacy in 1455, whose case will be examined presently. The other was not a bishop but a dean, Henry Webber, who died in 1477 after an exceptionally long and distinguished reign. He had chosen a burial place in the north choir aisle, and his colleagues had given permission for this, but the arrangement was superseded after his death and he was laid to rest in the choir, to the right of Bishop Bitton, beneath a ledger stone.[82] He was an exception, but an exception that proves the rule.

Since the choir had no room for raised tombs or effigies after 1327, later bishops requiring such monuments had to find space for them elsewhere in the cathedral. Grandisson (d. 1369), the next bishop after Berkeley, built a chapel for his tomb in the west wall of the cathedral nave and was buried there beside the great west door, as if to guard it. The tomb was destroyed in the late sixteenth century, and its precise form is unknown. His successor Brantingham (d. 1394) also planned his tomb while he was still alive, during the mid 1370s. It consisted of a large ledger stone, containing a monumental brass, in a new chantry chapel in the north arcade of the nave, balancing a similar chapel in the south arcade funded by Hugh Courtenay, earl of Devon (d. 1377), on the south side. The next bishop, Stafford (d. 1419), probably made his own arrangements in his lifetime, in his case a raised tomb with an effigy beneath an elaborate canopy. This was placed between the Lady Chapel and the chapel of St John Evangelist, and the tomb of Bishop Bronescombe was given a similar canopy on the opposite side of the Lady Chapel, in another matching scheme. Stafford's successor, Lacy (d. 1455), was buried in the cathedral choir, but this fact raises problems since there may not have been a vacant space. It is possible that Lacy planned to be buried elsewhere, and the tomb in the north choir aisle that contains a 'cadaver' or corpse may represent his intended monument.[83] The site of his present tomb seems unlikely to have been vacant up to that point, and its position acquires significance from the fact that it stands opposite (and resembles) that of Berkeley. Lacy died like Berkeley with a reputation for sanctity that may have led to his promotion to the

---

[81] On Berkeley and his cult, see Nicholas Orme, "Two Saint-Bishops of Exeter', *Analecta Bollandiana*, 104 (1986), pp. 403–11.

[82] See below, p. 115.

[83] For a discussion of this possibility, see Nicholas Orme, 'Whose Body?', *Friends of Exeter Cathedral Annual Report*, 66 (1996), pp. 12–17.

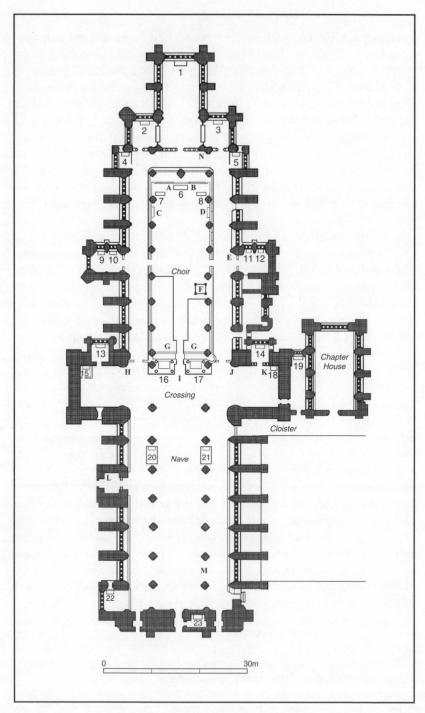

Fig 3: Exeter Cathedral 1300–1600

Altars and chapels

1   Lady chapel
2   St John the Evangelist
3   St Gabriel
4   St George
5   St Saviour
6   High altar (Our Lady, St Peter, and St Paul)
7   St Thomas Becket and St Alphege
8   St Stephen and St Laurence
9   St Andrew
10   St Katharine
11   St Mary Magdalene and St Thomas Becket
12   St James
13   St Paul
14   St John Baptist
15   Holy Cross
16   St Mary in the nave
17   St Nicholas
18   St Michael and the tomb of Bishop John
19   Holy Ghost
20   Trinity (Brantingham chantry)
21   Courtenay chantry, dedication unknown
22   St Edmund the King
23   Grandisson chantry (St Radegund?)

Images and other features

A   St Peter (image)
B   St Paul and Our Lady (image)
C   Tomb of Bishop Lacy
D   Tomb of Bishop Berkeley
E   St Mary Magdalene (image)
F   Bishop's throne
G   Choir stalls
H   Old Peter (image)
I   Choir screen (*pulpitum*) with cross above
J   St Mary (image)
K   St Michael (image)
L   St Mary (image)
M   Font (in this area)
N   St Mary and angels (painting)

Collecting boxes

These were sited by 10, 15, 18, 20, 21, 23, A, B, C, D, H, J, L, and perhaps in other places.

choir, room being found by removing an earlier tomb, possibly that of Blund (d. 1257) whose whereabouts is unknown.[84] The only other bishop to be buried in the cathedral before the Reformation was Oldham (d. 1519). He built a new chapel for the purpose off the south choir aisle, and he too had a partner for his project in Sir John Speke (d. 1518) who financed a similar chapel in a symmetrical position.

Bishops' tombs became more elaborate during the later middle ages and all those from Grandisson's onwards were housed in chapels, except for Lacy's which lay in the choir itself. This splendour was not matched in the case of the other cathedral clergy. Here simpler standards were observed and indeed enforced, since they were so rarely broken. The tombs of the deans, dignitaries, and canons were generally modest: a ledger stone on the floor with an incised inscription and sometimes minimal decoration such as a central cross. The stone of Dean Andrew Kilkenny once had inlaid brass lettering and an inlaid cross,[85] and that of Canon William Langton, a relative of Bishop Stafford, now in the chapel of St John Evangelist, still displays a brass portrait of the canon and inscriptions, but such embellishments may have been unusual. There is so much consistency in the non-episcopal tombs that they were clearly governed by an unwritten law or strong custom that there should be no raised monuments or effigies. The only sure exception is that of Precentor William Sylke (d. 1508). He was allowed an effigy, built into the screen of the chapel of the Holy Cross in the north transept, either because he paid for the screen or because his effigy was a cadaver and carried a message to passers by. Its Latin inscription states 'I am what you will be; I was what you are'.[86]

Deans, dignitaries, and canons had the privilege of burial in the cathedral interior, except for the choir, and nearly all seem to have taken advantage of it. Chancellor Robert Rygge (d. 1410) was unusual in his indifference as to whether he lay in the church or the cemetery. Canons often negotiated their burial sites with their colleagues during their lives, and (after the 1380s) had the requisite permission enrolled in the act-book of the dean and chapter. The most sought-after place may have been the eastern part of the nave in front of the great cross on the screen. Three deans had graves in this area by 1396, when the archbishop of Canterbury, William Courtenay (whose parents were buried nearby), proposed to turn them out for his own interment, but this plan did not materialise and he was eventually laid to rest in Canterbury Cathedral.[87] Altars and images were

---

[84] On Lacy and his cult, see Orme, "Two Saint-Bishops of Exeter', pp. 412–18.
[85] See below, p. 186.
[86] It is possible that the cadaver in the north choir aisle is a similar earlier monument to Canon William Browning (Orme, 'Whose Body?', pp. 12–17).
[87] See below, p. 63.

other favourite sites: John Cokworthy asked to be placed by St Mary Magdalene, Martin Lercedekne by St Gabriel, and William Pyl by St John Baptist. One would expect more such requests than have survived, but most of the evidence for them comes from after 1400 when the holiest locations may have been full. Doorways are occasionally mentioned: Robert Aiscough chose the one by the south choir-aisle vestry, William Brownyng its counterpart in the north choir-aisle that led to the exchequer, and Michael Lercedekne the door to the Lady Chapel. Here the motive may have been remembrance (the gravestone would be seen by passers by) or humility (it would be walked on). Other canons opted for burial in the choir aisles or the nave, sometimes moved by the wish to lie near a pre-decessor or (perhaps) a friend, so that small groups were established like that of the deans.

The minor clergy – the vicars choral and the chantry priests known as annuellars – outnumbered the canons in the later middle ages, but it was apparently rare for them to be allowed burial in the cathedral itself. Two such examples are known, Richard Brounste and John Hampton, but both were kept to modest places near doors. Originally most minor clergy may have reposed in the cemetery, but perhaps by 1342 (John Colbrok) and more certainly by 1387 (Stephen Drewe) they came to appropriate the cloisters as their special area. This gave them a status in accordance with their cathedral ranking: below that of the canons but above most of the laity.[88] A few of the latter were also allowed to lie in the third cathedral, but the number was not very large. There was a handful of knights, the earliest known being two early fourteenth-century figures in the south choir aisle (one probably a Ralegh), and a third opposite Bishop Stapledon's tomb in the north choir aisle (apparently his brother Richard, d. 1332). The earl of Devon, buried in the nave, was eventually accompanied by his widow and by his son Peter (d. 1408), and Sir John Speke and his wife occupied the chapel already mentioned. All the knights had stone effigies, except for Peter Courtenay who was commemorated by a brass effigy in a ledger stone, suggesting that the cathedral chapter regarded these leaders of local society as equal with bishops in terms of monumental privileges. A handful of citizens gained admission too: we hear for example of William Crugge, a former mayor, and his wife in about 1500. This involved gaining permission from the chapter, usually in return for a fee and might reflect links with the cathedral clergy. Thus William and Alice Oke, whose burial was sanctioned in 1391, were brother-in-law and sister of a canon, John

88 On the cloisters, see R.W. Parker, *Archaeo-Historical Assessment of Exeter Cathedral Cloisters*, Exeter Archaeology Report No. 97.42 (Exeter, privately printed, 1997).

Westcote. There is no evidence that citizens were accorded grand tombs, and the likelihood is that they were restricted to ledger stones.

Burial in other Places

Burial in the cathedral, as opposed to the cemetery, indicated special status. This was equally true of burial elsewhere in Exeter. The cathedral clergy, as we have seen, gave permission early on for the inmates of the religious houses of Exeter to be interred within their churches or precincts. Later there came to be a demand for outsiders to be buried in these houses or in the parish churches of the city. Such burials were marks of rank and wealth because there was limited room for them, because fees or benefactions might be expected in return, and because they breached the rule that bodies should lie in the cathedral cemetery. One had to apply to the cathedral authorities, meaning the dean and chapter, to be buried elsewhere, and although this does not seem to have cost money, the process required the consent of each member of the chapter.[89] This was most easily done in advance of one's death by making a request to a chapter meeting, but when permission was suddenly required following a death, the dead person's representatives had to consult each canon in residence individually – a fact that caused the city authorities to complain to the cathedral in the 1520s or 30s. In their reply the dean and chapter admitted that it was customary for the canons to be asked one by one, but they offered a concession, perhaps perceiving the strong feelings of anticlericalism in England at that time. In future, only two people would need to be consulted: the dean and the cathedral treasurer, or their deputies.[90]

Most of the churches in and around the city came to house the burials of rich or influential people during the later middle ages. Of the four small local monasteries two, St James Priory and the nunnery of Polsloe, have not left records of this practice, but the other two, St Nicholas and Cowick, both admitted at least a few outsiders and probably more than we know. St Nicholas was chosen by one gentlewoman of Devon, Lady Matilda Courtenay of Haccombe, and by two Exeter laymen, John and Nicholas Hamlyn – the latter of whom lived nearby in St Olave parish. Cowick Priory was the principal burying place of the Courtenay family of Okehampton and later of Tiverton, between 1292 and 1340. Hugh Court-enay (d. 1292), his widow Eleanor (d. 1328), his son Hugh, first earl of Devon (d. 1340), and the first earl's wife Agnes (d. 1340), were all interred there. Later the family changed its allegiance. The second earl, Hugh (d.

[89] See below, p. 75 (John Hamlyn)
[90] Hooker, *The Description of the Citie of Excester*, pp. 213, 215–16

1377), decided to be buried in Tiverton parish church, but altered his mind just before his death in favour of the cathedral, where he was duly followed by his wife. His descendants mostly reverted to his original choice and settled on Tiverton.

There are also records of lay burials in the Exeter friaries. We know by chance of about 13 in the Dominican house and 10 in that of the Franciscans, and the real totals are likely to have been much higher. The Dominicans were particularly successful in developing relationships with men and women of knightly rank. They secured the bodies of at least four members of the important Devon landholding family of the Dinhams between 1299 and 1497, as well as Lady Elizabeth Lercedekne, Sir William Martyn, Sir Henry de Pomeray, and (in intention if not in fact) Sir Henry de Ralegh. The discovery of a carved stone head of a warrior wearing a helmet, near the friary site in 1826, shows that there was at least one knightly effigy in its church.[91] Some Exeter laity also chose burial there, including John and Peter Colshill, Thomasia Davy, Richard Seler, and John Thomas. In the Franciscan friary, on the other hand, the only person of gentle rank known to have asked for a grave is Lady Katharine Huddesfeld. Here the evidence centres on Exeter people such as Aymer de Ponte, Thomas Parkes, John and William Wynard, and William Yorke. Excavations on the Franciscans' second site outside the South Gate have shown the presence of graves there, probably within the church, and have revealed one ledger stone with an inscription, belonging to a certain John Taylour.[92]

It was mentioned above that the parish churches of Exeter also came to be utilised as burial places by wealthy local people. Up to the middle of the fourteenth century, property owners like Walter Gervas (1258), three generations of the Collecote family (1269–1305), and Peter Soth (1327), as well as Nicholas de Durneford, a married clerk connected with the bishop's consistory court (1326), were content to be interred in the cathedral cemetery (Documents 5, 10, 13, 16–17). The change of fashion, as already noted, is first recorded in connection with Agnes de Wodelegh's request for burial in St Mary Major in 1349. The next such instance is that of Nicholas Taverner, mentioned as buried in one of the three churches of St Mary in 1373, and evidently a man of rank since the bishop granted an indulgence for those who prayed at his tomb. Other examples follow in the fifteenth century, and by the early sixteenth the practice was popular

---

[91] Now in the Royal Albert Memorial Museum, Exeter (Oliver, *Monasticon*, p. 336; T.W. Brushfield, 'Raleghana Part IV: Sir Henry de Ralegh, Knight, *Ob. 1301*', *Devonshire Association Transactions*, 34 (1902), pp. 455–81).

[92] The Greyfriars excavations have not been fully described in print; a drawing of the Taylour ledger stone is held by the Exeter Archaeology Unit.

among the leading citizen families, as their wills demonstrate. Besides St Mary Major there are examples of burials being planned or executed in St Mary Arches, St Martin, St Petroc, and St Sidwell, and it is unlikely that these were the only churches concerned.

The burials about which most is known, outside the cathedral, are those in the hospital of St John. When Bishop Grandisson allowed the hospital to bury people in 1351, he specified the privilege as being for the brothers (who ran the hospital), the infirm men (who were maintained there), and anyone else who wished.[93] This final clause was a large concession, equivalent to the rights claimed by the friars, and was ill received at the cathedral. On 26 February 1354 the bishop issued another document, in which he said that he had considered a paper schedule (presumably from the hospital) concerning damage that it had suffered at the hands of the dean and chapter. He restated his grant of burial, which was evidently the point at issue, and ruled that if the dean and chapter impeded burials in future, they would be charged 100 marks (£66 13s. 4d.) in alms to the bishop.[94] A month later, on 31 March, the bishop made a further order about the matter, this time with the consent of the cathedral. He recalled the difficulties caused to the hospital by lack of burial rights, and reaffirmed his grant of these, specifying that they were to apply in the hospital church, part of the cloister, and certain adjoining grounds. But he defined the right of burial more narrowly as applying to the prior, brethren, and poor of the hospital, and added 'always saving in all things the rights of us and of our said cathedral church with regard to others choosing burial there'.[95] These words probably satisfied the dean and chapter by confirming that the interment of outsiders must first have their permission.

A few records of burials in the hospital after 1351 survive by chance in extraneous records, as for other churches, but our knowledge of them improves considerably in the second half of the fifteenth century, thanks to a list drawn up on behalf of the hospital and recorded in its cartulary (Document 1). The list is in two parts. The first claims to be 'The names of outsiders buried in the hospital of St John, Exeter, within human memory'. It is not dated but, as the second part implies, it is likely to have been compiled at or before 1492. Sixty-five people are named in it, the earliest of whom died at the turn of the fourteenth and fifteenth centuries, but the list is not complete since it excludes one or two people whose burials in the hospital are known from other records. Its contents seem therefore to have been based, as it implies, on memory or perhaps in part on tombs, and after it was drawn up many of the names in the list were annotated to

---

[93] *Reg. Grandisson*, ii, 1106–7.

[94] DRO, Exeter City Archives, Book 53A, f. 74v.

[95] *Reg. Grandisson*, ii, 1125.

indicate their parish of residence. The first list is followed by a second entitled 'The names of strangers buried in the aforesaid hospital, namely in the church, from the year of the Lord 1492 to the year of the Lord 1520'. This list was later supplemented with records of burials up to the year 1535, and contains a total of 81 names, making 146 in both lists together. Most of the names in the second list are given their parish affiliations, and some are followed by their family relationships, occupations, and places of burial in the hospital.

The purpose of the lists is not fully clear. They may have been compiled for the benefit of the hospital authorities to remind themselves of those whom they had buried and, eventually, of the approximate places where those burials lay. But it is possible that the documents reflect continuing tensions between the hospital and the cathedral. In 1448 the hospital secured a confirmation of Grandisson's grant of 1354 from Pope Nicholas V, in which the pope conceded that all persons who chose burial in the hospital church and its precincts might be buried there freely and lawfully.[96] This may have led to the hospital receiving corpses for which the cathedral clergy had not given permission, leading to a demand from the bishop or cathedral that the hospital kept a record of those it buried. The naming of parishes may also be significant, and may represent an attempt to ensure that the hospital did not subvert the rights of the city clergy. Under the papal decree *Super Cathedram*, drawn up with the friars in mind, a quarter of the funeral legacies of anyone buried outside their parish church had to be paid to the rector of the church. That this was an issue in Exeter emerges from a suit brought in the bishop's consistory court between 1437 and 1446 by James Richard, rector of St Olave, who claimed that his parishioner Peter Yonge had been buried in the hospital, whose clergy had withheld the rector's share of Yonge's legacies, valued at £1 0s. 2d.[97] Accordingly the burial records may reflect the hospital's obligations to the outside world as well as its internal procedures.

The lists provide some tantalising evidence about the layout of the hospital church, which cannot easily be translated into a plan. The church contained a choir and a nave, the choir presumably including a high altar dedicated to St John Baptist, as well as stalls for the prior and hospital brethren. Three other altars stood in the church, dedicated to Jesus, St Katharine, and St Thomas. Mentions of the high cross presumably refer to a large 'rood' or crucifix on a screen separating the choir from the nave. There was also a chapter house, a chapel of the Trinity, and a cloister on the south side of the church. The clergy of the hospital numbered four: a prior and three brothers, living under the rule of St Augustine. Some of

---

[96] *Calendar of Papal Letters, 1447–55*, pp. 309–10.
[97] British Library, Harley MS 862, ff. 14r–15r.

them are included in the hospital burial lists, usually with tombs in the choir or the chapter house, although one lay by the altar of St Katharine. The other inmates of the hospital included servants, twelve infirm brothers who were permanent residents, nine scholars (boys or adolescents) studying at the city high school, and probably some casual visitors suffering from short-term illnesses. A few of these inmates are mentioned in the lists: two butlers, an inmate of the infirmary, and one person (Master John Hylle) described as 'our guest'. He may have been a 'corrodarian', someone who had purchased board and lodging for life. But as so few of the servants, brothers, scholars, or visitors are mentioned, it is likely that the rest were laid to rest in the 'adjoining grounds' mentioned by Grandisson, in other words in an open-air graveyard.

The outsiders who came for burial can be analysed on the basis of their social and geographical origins. The highest in status were a few Devon gentry, the most important being Sir John Hulle, justice of the king's bench (d. 1416), and his two wives. Others included three members of the Copplestone family, together with Lady Elizabeth Ralygh, Mistress Elizabeth Speke, and her heir Master Robert Speke, the last three of whom were buried in the choir. The secular (parish) clergy numbered about fourteen, including the rectors or vicars of Chagford, Peter Tavy, Plymtree, Rockbeare, and St Laurence and St Olave in Exeter. One wonders if two of these (Henry Grymstone and William Reygny) were men who had retired to live in the hospital. There was an untypical annuellar of the cathedral, Richard Smyth, who preferred the hospital church to his own place of employment, and some unidentifiable clergy who appear to have been relatively humble chaplains. These may have been victims of sickness while visiting Exeter. The great majority of the burials, however, were those of laymen and women from the city itself, doubtless of some economic status. They embraced two mayors, John Lympeny and John Talbot, and several men and women styled 'master' or 'mistress' who must have been members of the city élite. The people of lowest rank to be mentioned were a cathedral canon's cook and a shoemaker. One or two outsiders, apart from the gentry, were specially favoured in where they were buried. A certain John Maye was laid in the choir and Alice ap Ryse, mother of a sub-prior, was allowed a grave in the chapter house. In general, however, both clerical and lay outsiders seem to have been restricted to the nave and the Trinity chapel.

A geographical analysis of the burials can also be made when the parish affiliation of the dead person is given. This shows a marked bias towards the eastern half of the city, as against the western. If we divide the intramural part of the city into four quarters, following the four main streets, the parish churches of the north-east quarter predominate, with 51 burials. Most of the latter (40) were in the parish of St Laurence, in which the hospital lay. The south-east quarter provides 23 burials, to which we can add 11 from St Sidwell's which lay outside the walls on the east side. The other half of the city, west of North Street and South Street, provides far fewer examples: 7 in the north-west quarter, 5 in the south-west, and 2 outside the walls on the south and west sides. This probably reflects the fact that the hospital was sited near the East Gate and had most links with those who lived nearby, but economic factors may also have some relevance. The western half of the city tended to be poorer than the eastern, and had fewer people of wealth and status to be buried in the hospital. A few of those with graves came from outside Exeter, including some of the parish clergy mentioned above, a child from Cornwall, and a man from Iddesleigh. These cases may represent sick people who sought support from the hospital while in Exeter, or who retired to live in the hospital. It is likely that some people of means in poor health gravitated to the city because of its economic, cultural, and medical amenities, just as they are known to have done in the eighteenth and nineteenth centuries.

The history of burial in medieval Exeter reveals a number of changes between 1100 and 1540. We began with a community whose lay members were usually buried in the cathedral cemetery, which acted as the churchyard of the city and provided a unifying element. As time went on this unity fragmented and choice of one's burial place became possible, at least for the wealthy: a process that is paralleled in other towns.[98] Additional religious houses were founded (especially the friaries) in which the rich might be buried, and eventually the fashion for burial elsewhere spread to the parish churches. As diversity grew, we can see some evidence of neighbourhood links. Nicholas Hamlyn of St Olave parish in 1504 sought a resting place nearby in St Nicholas Priory. William Wynard, who founded his almshouse near the Franciscan Friary in 1436–9, chose his burial site in the friary church. Neighbourliness is most obvious in the case of St John's hospital where, although those buried came from a wide range of parishes in the city, the greatest number lived near the building. It looks as if some people made links with the churches close to them, even if these churches were not parish churches. Burial practices, then, reflected relationships within the local community. They also signified status. The right to bury gave status to the cathedral as mother church of the city, and eventually to some other churches. Burial also conferred, or acknowledged, status in respect of those who were buried. Medieval moralists liked to remind their listeners that the distinctions of this life would not survive the equality brought by death. The author of the great poem *Piers Plowman*, writing in the 1370s, warned knights that

[98] Barrow, 'Urban Cemetery Location', pp. 81–95; Vanessa Harding, 'Burial Chocie and Burial Location in Later Medieval London', in *Death in Towns*, ed. Steven Bassett (Leicester, 1992), pp. 119–35.

In charnel at church, churls are evil [i.e. hard] to know,
Or a knight from a knave there; know this in thine heart.[99]

But the study of burial shows that such sentiments fell short of the truth.
The churl's bones might lie in the charnel, but the knight's reposed in the
cathedral and the merchant's in the friary, hospital, or parish church. The
distinctions of worldly life outlasted life itself, and long endured in monuments and graves.

---

[99] William Langland, *Piers Plowman*, ed. W.W. Skeat, 2 vols (Oxford, 1969),
B.vi.50–1; C.ix.45–6.

1. Burial Lists of St John's Hospital, Exeter, *c*.1492–1535

(Source: Devon Record Office, Exeter City Archives, Book 53A (Cartulary of St John's Hospital). Latin text. Abbreviations have been expanded, the use of capital letters has been modernised, and 'u' rather than 'v' is used at the beginnings of words. Additions to the list made before about 1535 are in italics. The names of churches represent the parishes in which the deceased persons lived.)

[f. 94v]

The names of outsiders buried in the hospital of St John, Exeter, within human memory.

John Boys, *of St Laurence*
John Webbe, *of St Laurence*
Sir John Hille, *justice of the king's bench*
Denise and Lady Matilda, his wives
Master William Leche, *of St Paul*
Sir William Aller, rector of St Olave
Newant
Sir John Burley
Master Walter Robert, principal portionist of the church of Tiverton
Master William Wellis, *of St Martin*
The wife of Walter Gyst, *of St Laurence*
Richard Bere, *of St Laurence*
Richard Quylter, *of St Laurence*
Trewynard of Cornwall, *of All Hallows Goldsmith Street*
Stafford, *of St Mary Major*
John Tynle and Margaret his wife, *of St Laurence. His wife, namely this Margaret, died in the parish of Holy Trinity*
John Talbot, formerly mayor of the city of Exeter, *of St Kerrian*
Master Richard Talbot, *of St Laurence*
Sir Thomas Lusquyt, *of St Edmund on the bridge*

Johan Manscomb and his wife, *of St Stephen*

Thomas Law and Joan his wife, *of St Laurence. This Joan died in the parish of St Stephen, namely as the wife of Master Drew*

Richard Cokeworthi, *of All Hallows on the Walls*

Peter Sturt, his wife and their son, *of St Martin*

John Tremayn, *of St Martin*

The wife of John Smert, *of St Pancras*

The wife of Thomas Coke, *of St Petroc*

Alice Bewcham and William her son, *of St Laurence*

Alice Brokyn, *of St Martin*

Sir Richard Donscombe

Walter Coke

The mother of Adam Summayster

Richard Dygon, *of St Sidwell*

William Hodel, *of St Sidwell*

Sir Robert Dawe

The mother of John Huesch

John Cole

The wife of Thomas Hawkyn

The son of Nicholas Trelawny, *of St Petroc*

A child of Cornwall, *of St Petroc*

John Roos

The daughter of Thomas Dourissh, *of St Sidwell*

Sir John Bealle, vicar of Rockbeare

Sir John Frank, rector of Peter Tavy

Sir Nicholas Coldecote, rector of St Laurence

The sister of William Hethfeld, *of St Laurence*

Richard Mylle, *of St Stephen*

Yerde

John Sawle, *of St Laurence, in the bailey*

The cook of Canon Dodyngton, *of St Martin*

Peter Yeonge, *of St Olave*

Elizabeth Chuselden, *of St Laurence*

Margaret Hydon, *of St Sidwell*

Lady Joan Lerchedekne, *of St Laurence*

Joan Herlewynyne, of St George, in the year of the Lord one thousand four hundred and fifty seven, on the feast of the Assumption

John Pyttes, of St Martin

John Harlewyne, of St George

Master John Hylle, our guest

Thomas Mayer, of the parish of Iddesleigh

The names of strangers buried in the aforesaid hospital, namely in the church, from the year of the Lord 1492 to the year of the Lord 1520.

Master Henry Grymstone, in the chapel of the Holy Trinity
John Whytelock, *of St Stephen*
Sir Roger Wheler, *of St Laurence*
Richard Waggot, *of St Laurence*
John Broke, *of St Sidwell*
John Sayer, *of St Stephen*
John Coppleston, esquire ⎫
Richard Coppleston, son ⎪ in the parish of St Laurence
John Copplestone   ⎬
Mistress Joan, wife of the same ⎭
Mistress Christina Hyngstecote, *of St Stephen*
William Obeley, *of St Mary Arches*
Willmot, his wife ⎫ *of St George*
Elizabeth, daughter of the same ⎭
Margery Page, of St Sidwell
Alice Norrys, *of St Laurence*
John Boddely, *of St Stephen*
Peter Williams ⎫ *of St Petroc*
Agnes, his wife ⎭
Thomas Clerck, *within the hospital*
Joan Byshoppe ⎫ *of St Laurence, wives of one husband*
Elizabeth Byshoppe ⎭
John Colcharde, *of St George*
Thomas Cogworthy, *of St Kerrian*
Roger Schordyche ⎫ *of St Stephen*
Johanna, his wife ⎭
Thomas Gele, *within the hospital*
John Boteler, *within the hospital*
Philip Skyce, *of St Laurence* ⎫ *These two were our butlers*
Thomas Elycotte, of St Sidwell ⎭
John Harrys, within the hospital

[f. 95r]

Michael Payne, shoemaker, of St Laurence
Master John Hull, of St Paul
John Cliffton ⎫ All Hallows on the Walls
Joan, his wife ⎭
John Bolter ⎫ St Lawrence
Mistress Joan Duke, his daughter ⎭
Mistress Juliana Duke, of St Stephen

William Genyan
Lady Elizabeth Ralygh
Mistress Elizabeth Speke ⎫ these are buried in the choir; of St
Master Robert Speke, her heir ⎭ Laurence
Master John Lympeny, mayor of the city, is buried before the altar of St
   Katharine
John Newcomb, before the high cross
Edmund Bodon, beneath the altar of St Thomas
Master Oliver, prior, in the chapter house
Master Peter, prior, before the altar of John Baptist
Brother John Lug, in the chapter house
Brother Richard Willys, before the altar of St Katharine
Brother John Preste, confrater, buried at Bridgwater
Brother Robert Bernard, brother of Bridgwater, buried here in our chapter
   house, 1531 in the month of April, the eighth day
Alice Rede, of St Laurence, next to the wall by the altar of St Katharine
Sir William Reyny, in the hospital next to the cloister door inside the church
Master Henry Coppleston, of St Laurence, before the altar of St Thomas
Brother John Kokel, by [*per*] the altar of St John Baptist
Alice ap Ryce, of St Sidwell, in the chapter house
John Awells, of St Paul, in the nave of the church
Sir Richard Smyth, annuellar of St Peter, before the altar of Jesus.
Sir Henry Bery, in the hospital in the choir
Margaret Norbroke, her husband and herself within one grave
John Colman ⎫ of St Laurence, in the nave of the church
and Joan his wife ⎭
Thomas Elycot ⎫ of St Sidwell, before the door of the dormitory
and Elizabeth his wife ⎭
Brother Richard Hylle, prior, in the hospital before his stall
Richard Boodon ⎫ in the hospital, at the end of the church
and Joan his wife ⎭
Sir John Goodefello, of St Laurence, in the church at the end
Nicholas Byschopp, of St Laurence, in the north part
William Chubbe, of St Paul
John Norbroke, of St Sidwell
John May, one of the infirmary, in the north part of the church, at the end
   of the church
John Calwodly ⎫ of St Laurence, before the image of the high cross
Alicia, his wife ⎭
John Maye, was buried before the high altar

Joan Hull, of St Paul, in the middle of the church
William Hull, her son, of St Laurence, at the head of
   his mother
Beatte Warner, of St Laurence, in the chapel of the
   Blessed Trinity
John Trewarak, of St Laurence, near the door on
   the west
Brother Robert Lawrens, prior, in the chapter house
Brother Arnulph ap Pryss, subprior, in the chapter
   house

in the year of the
Lord 1535

2. A Register of all known Burials and Funerals in Exeter, 1050–1540

(Sources: original records, as stated. The full references will be found in the bibliography at the end of the volume.)

Unnamed People

Boy of Cornwall, parish of St Petroc
Buried in the hospital of St John before 1492 (DRO, ECA, Book 53A, f. 94v).

Cadaver in the north choir aisle of Exeter Cathedral.
For possible identifications of the person commemorated, see Orme, 1996, pp. 12–17.

The cook of Canon [John] Dodyngton, St Martin's parish.
Dodyngton died 1400 (see below). Buried in the hospital of St John (DRO, ECA, Book 53A, f. 94v).

The rector of St Martin, Exeter
The record of his funeral in Exeter Cathedral occurs in Christmas term 1322–3 (D&C 3764, f. 37r).

Named People

Aiscough, Robert
Archdeacon of Exeter. Died 23 October 1482 (Le Neve, p. 14). In his will, dated 10 October 1482, he asked to be buried in the ambulatory of Exeter Cathedral on the south side of the choir near the door of the vestibule, before the image of the Blessed Virgin Mary (PRO, PROB 11/7, f. 45r–v).

Aiscough, William
Canon of Exeter Cathedral. Died by 25 June 1486 (Le Neve, p. 55). The cathedral bells are recorded being rung for him between Michaelmas 1485 and Michaelmas 1486 (D&C 3779, f. 231r).

John Ayssh

Annuellar of the Montacute and Bollegh chantry. Died between Mid-summer term 1484 and Michaelmas term 1487 (Orme, *Minor Clergy*, p. 73). The cathedral bells were recorded being rung for him between Michaelmas 1485 and Michaelmas 1486 (D&C 3779, f. 231r).

Ayschele, Richard

Master; probably identical with Master Richard Aysshulle, clerk, created notary public by the bishop of Exeter, 3 February 1351 (*Reg. Grandisson*, ii, 1098). Buried in Exeter Cathedral by 1 November 1391 when William and Alice Oke were licensed to be buried at his feet (D&C 3550, f. 95v).

Aldryngton, Richard (Allerton)

Canon of Exeter Cathedral. Died by 17 December 1429 (Le Neve, p. 45). The record of his funeral in Exeter Cathedral occurs in Christmas term 1429–30 (D&C 3771).

Alyn, —

Wife of Henry Alyn. The bells of Exeter Cathedral are recorded being rung for her in Christmas term 1395–6 (D&C 3773, f. 70v).

Aleyn, John

The record of his funeral in Exeter Cathedral occurs in Michaelmas term 1305 (D&C 3673, f. 63v).

Aller, William

Rector of St Olave, Exeter. Died by 6 January 1404 (*Reg. Stafford*, p. 171). Buried in the hospital of St John (DRO, ECA, Book 53A, f. 94v).

Andrewe, Thomas

Parish of St Mary Arches, Exeter; sometime mayor. Father of Joan Blackaller (see below). Died 9 March 1519. In his will, dated 28 April 1517, he requested burial in the church of St Mary Arches (MCR 23–24 Hen VIII, m. 7; PRO, PROB 11/18, f. 238v). His monument survives in the church, with a recumbent effigy in civil dress, inscription, and date.

Annore

The record of his funeral in Exeter Cathedral occurs in Midsummer term 1307 (D&C 3673, f. 79v).

Apothecary – see Espicer

Arblaster, John le

The record of his funeral in Exeter Cathedral occurs in Easter term 1306 (D&C 3673, f. 67v).

Archedekne – see Lercedekne

Arundell, Lady Katherine

Daughter of Sir John Chidiock; married first William Stafford of Hook, Dorset, secondly Sir John Arundell of Lanherne (Cornwall) (Cokayne, iv, 327). Died *c.* 1479 (see below). In her will, dated 2 April 1479, she asked that her body 'be buried in the chancel of the church of the Grey Friars without [the] South Gate of the city of Exeter' (Cornwall Record Office, Arundell Deeds, ARB 217/4).

Audley, James

Lord Audley. In his will, dated 1385, he asked to be buried in the abbey of Hulton (Staffs.) if he died in the Marches and in the choir of the Friars Preachers if he died in Devon or Somerset (Lambeth Palace Library, Reg. William Courtenay, f. 121v). Died 1 April 1386, and buried at Hulton Abbey, Staffs. (Cokayne, i, 339–40).

Austell, Thomas

Treasurer of Exeter Cathedral. Died by 5 April 1515 (Le Neve, p. 12), probably on 18 March 1515, the apparent date on his ledger stone, now in the 5th bay of the north choir aisle (Hope, Monumentarium, p. 34). In his will, dated 24 August 1509, he asked to be buried in the cathedral by the tomb of Master Thomas Kirkeby (see below), a previous treasurer (PRO, PROB 11/18, f. 58r–v).

Baker, Andrew

The cathedral bells were recorded being rung for him in Michaelmas term 1396 (D&C 3773, f. 70r). Possibly identical with Andrew Polworthy, baker (see below).

Baker, Richard

Probably parish of All Hallows, Goldsmith Street. Citizen of Exeter. Died between 14 February 1484 and 10 January 1485. In his will, dated 14 February 1484, he asked to be buried in the church of the hospital of St John, and bequeathed the hospital an annual rent of 5s. to hold his obit (British Library, Add. Charter 27631; MCR 2 Ric III– 1 Hen VII, m. 18). He is not mentioned in the hospital burial list in DRO, ECA, Book 53A, ff. 84v–95r.

Baker, Roger

The cathedral bells are recorded being rung for him in Easter term 1393 (D&C 377s, f. 71r). Possibly identical with Roger Hethman, died by 12 May 1393 (MCR 16–17 Ric II, m. 32).

*Baker, Th[omas] (*Pistor)

Son of Thomas the Baker (*Pistor*). The record of his funeral in Exeter Cathedral occurs in Easter term 1309 (D&C 3673, f. 90v).

Bald, Richard

Apothecary. The record of his funeral in Exeter Cathedral occurs in Midsummer term 1306 (D&C 3673, f. 68v).

Bampton, Walter

Canon of Exeter Cathedral. Died by 24 March 1383 (Le Neve, p. 38). Probably buried in the cathedral or its cemetery; one of the officers at his funeral was attacked in the cemetery, shortly before 1 April 1383, by unknown persons, causing blood to be shed (*Reg. Brantyngham*, i, 159).

Bampton, William

Canon of Exeter Cathedral. Died by 1 November 1396 (Le Neve, p. 43). The cathedral bells are recorded being rung for him in Michaelmas term 1396 (D&C 3773, f. 70v). Stone was sold for his tomb in Exeter Cathedral between Michaelmas 1396 and Michaelmas 1397 (D&C 2656).

Barbour, John

Canon of Exeter Cathedral. Died by 6 November 1455 (Le Neve, p. 53). A sum of 2s. was received from his executors for stone, lime and sand for his tomb between Michaelmas 1455 and Michaelmas 1456 (D&C 2700). Buried in the nave by 1 September 1464, when Canon John Pyttys (see below) chose to be buried near him (DRO, Chanter XII (ii), Reg. Bothe, ff. 50v–51v).

Barforth, Robert

Archdeacon of Barnstaple. Died by Michaelmas term 1486 (Le Neve, p. 21). The bells of Exeter Cathedral are recorded being rung for him between Michaelmas 1485 and Michaelmas 1486 (D&C 3779, f. 231r).

Bartholomew

Bishop of Exeter. Died 1184, probably on 14 December, the date on which Exeter Cathedral subsequently kept his obit (D&C 3518, f. 58v; 3625, f. vi verso). Possibly buried in the cathedral (Erskine, Hope, and Lloyd, p. 99; Hope, Monumentarium, p. 109).

Barton, Thomas

Canon of Exeter Cathedral. Died by 24 March, probably 16 March, 1416 (Le Neve, p. 42). In his will, dated 27 June 1415, he asked to be buried 'near the tomb or oratory of my lord of good memory, Thomas [Brantingham], formerly bishop of Exeter, on the south side, marble stones for sufficiently covering the tomb having been ordained for me' (*Reg. Stafford*, p. 411). The record of his funeral in the cathedral occurs in Easter term 1416 (D&C 3770). A sum of 6s. 8d. was paid for stone for the pavement of his tomb and that of Hugh Hickelyng between Michaelmas 1415 and Michaelmas 1416 (D&C 2671).

Bastow, John

Master; perhaps a layman. A sum of 12d. was paid for lime and sand for his tomb in Exeter Cathedral or its cemetery between Michaelmas 1493 and Michaelmas 1494 (D&C 2704/4).

Batte, John alias Richard

In his will of 1457 he requested burial in front of the door of the church of St Mary the Virgin [probably St Mary Major: the document is partly illegible] (D&C 2538/2).

Batyn, —

Wife of. The cathedral bells are recorded being rung for her in Christmas term 1396–7 (D&C 3773, f. 70v).

Beauprey
>   A record of his funeral in Exeter Cathedral occurs in Michaelmas term
>   1307 (D&C 3673, f. 78r).

Bekwyth – see Grymstone

Belde, John
>   Vicar of Rockbeare (Devon). Died by 24 August 1439 (*Reg. Lacy*, i,
>   253). Buried in the hospital of St John (DRO, ECA, Book 53A, f. 94v).

Beleboche, Martin
>   A record of his funeral in Exeter Cathedral occurs in Midsummer term
>   1307 (D&C 3673, f. 77r).

Beare, Alexander
>   Vicar choral of Exeter Cathedral. Died between Michaelmas term 1455
>   and Easter term 1456 (Orme, *Minor Clergy*, p. 29). A sum of 16d. was
>   received by the cathedral between Michaelmas 1455 and Michaelmas
>   1456 for lime, sand and stone sold to the executors of 'Sir Alexander'
>   and for a marble stone on his tomb in the cloister of Exeter Cathedral
>   (D&C 2700).

Bere, J. de
>   Master. A record of his funeral in Exeter Cathedral occurs in
>   Midsummer term 1315 (D&C 3764, f. 13v).

Bere, Richard.
>   Parish of St Laurence, Exeter. Buried in the hospital of St John by
>   1492 (DRO, ECA, Book 53A, f. 94v).

Bere, —
>   Wife of. The cathedral bells are recorded being rung for her in Christmas
>   term 1396–7 (D&C 3773, f. 70v).

Berkeley, James
>   Bishop of Exeter. Died 24 June 1327 (Dalton and Doble, i, p. xxiii; Le
>   Neve, p. 1). His funeral was held in Exeter Cathedral on 27 June
>   (D&C 3764, f. 59r). His tomb chest lies on the south side of the pres-
>   bytery, formerly bearing an inscription (Leland, i, 226; Hope, Monu-
>   mentarium, p. 1).

Bernard, Robert
>   Brother of the hospital of St John, Bridgwater. Buried in the chapter
>   house of the hospital of St John, Exeter, 8 April 1531 (DRO, ECA,
>   Book 53A, f. 95r).

Bery, Henry
>   'Sir', i.e. priest. Resident in the hospital of St John; buried in the choir
>   of the church between 1520 and 1535 (DRO, ECA, Book 53A, f. 95r).

Betty, John
>   The cathedral bells are recorded being rung for him between Michael-
>   mas 1490 and Michaelmas 1491 (D&C 3779, f. 231v).

Bewchamp, Alice

Buried in the hospital of St John by 1492 (DRO, ECA, Book 53A, f. 94v).

Bewcham, William

Son of Alice. Buried in the hospital of St John by 1492 (DRO, ECA, Book 53A, f. 94v).

Byshoppe, Elizabeth

Parish of St Laurence, Exeter. Married to the same husband as the next. Buried in the hospital of St John between 1492 and 1520 (DRO, ECA, Book 53A, f. 94v).

Byshoppe, Joan

Parish of St Laurence, Exeter. Married to the same husband as the preceding. Buried in the hospital of St John between 1492 and 1520 (DRO, ECA, Book 53A, f. 94v).

Byschopp, Nicholas

Parish of St Laurence, Exeter. Buried in the north part of the hospital of St John between 1520 and 1535 (DRO, ECA, Book 53A, f. 95r).

Bismano, William de

Treasurer of Exeter Cathedral. Died possibly by 30 December 1309, certainly by 22 February 1310 (Le Neve, p. 10). A record of his funeral in Exeter Cathedral occurs in Christmas term 1309–10 (D&C 3673, f. 95v).

Bythewall, —

Mother of Robert Bythewall, rector of Lawhitton (Cornwall), 1312–16. The record of her funeral in Exeter Cathedral occurs in Christmas term 1314–15 (D&C 3764, f. 12r).

Bitton, Thomas

Bishop of Exeter. Died 21 September 1307 (Le Neve, p. 1). A record of his funeral in Exeter Cathedral occurs in Michaelmas term 1307 (D&C 3673, f. 77v). Buried in the middle of the presbytery of the cathedral before the high altar (Leland, i, 226; D&C 4037, 4708, P/2/1; Hope, Monumentarium, p. 44). For details and expenses of his funeral and burial, see Hale and Ellacombe, pp. 22–4, and for a reconstruction of his ledger stone and monumental brass, Swanton, pp. 126–9.

Blackall, Roger

Layman of Exeter. In his will, dated 5 July 1537, he requested burial 'within the churchyard of St Peter', i.e. of Exeter Cathedral (PRO, PROB 11/28, f. 217r).

Blackaller, Alice

Daughter of Thomas Andrewe (see above). Died 31 July 1535. Her ledger stone, now inside but once outside St Mary Arches church, carries the inscription 'Orate pro anima Alicie Blackaller, filie magistri

Thome Andrew, qui obiit ultimo die julii anno domini mo vxxxv...'
(Cresswell, pp. 94–5).

Blakeborn, Henry de

Canon of Exeter Cathedral. Died probably on either 29 June (D&C
3765, f. 29v) or 30 June 1399 (D&C 3625, f. iii verso). The cathedral
bells were rung for him in Easter term, allegedly 1398 but presumably
more accurately 1399 (D&C 3773, f. 70r).

Bloyou, Henry

Canon of Exeter Cathedral. Died on or shortly before 30 July 1334,
when his funeral was held in the cathedral (D&C 3764, f. 94v).

Blund, Richard (Blond, Blondy)

Bishop of Exeter. Died 1257, probably on 23 December, the date on
which Exeter Cathedral subsequently kept his obit (D&C 3625. f. vi
verso). Probably buried in the cathedral; 'said to have been buried on
the north side of the choir of his church' (Oliver, *Lives of the Bishops*,
p. 39). For a possible surviving part of his monument, see Hope, Monumentarium, p. 26.

Boddely, Joan

Parish of St Stephen, Exeter. Buried in the hospital of St John between
1492 and 1530 (DRO, ECA, Book 53A, f. 94v).

Bodeham, Thomas

Archdeacon of Totnes. Died by 1297, perhaps on 4 April when his
obit was subsequently held (*Reg. Bronescombe*, ed. Hingeston-Randolph, pp. 400–1). Possibly buried in the chapel of St Gabriel in Exeter
Cathedral, where a chantry was established in his memory on 15
October 1297 (D&C 1471; Oliver, *Lives of the Bishops*, pp. 429–31).

Bodon, Edmund

Buried beneath the altar of St Thomas in the hospital of St John between
1520 and 1535 (DRO, ECA, Book 53A, f. 94v).

Boodon, Richard

Married layman, resident in the hospital of St John. Buried 'at the end
of the church' of the hospital between 1520 and 1535 (DRO, ECA,
Book 53A, f. 95r).

Boodon, Joan

Wife of Richard Boodon. Resident in the hospital of St John. Buried
'at the end of the church' of the hospital between 1520 and 1535
(DRO, ECA, Book 53A, f. 95r).

Bodrygan, —

Son of Sir Henry de Bodrygan, knight. A record of his funeral in Exeter
Cathedral occurs in Midsummer term 1308 (D&C 3673, f. 84v).

Bohun, Humphrey de

Earl of Essex and Hereford. Died 16 March 1322 and buried in the
Dominican Friary, York (Cokayne, vi, 470). Since the late sixteenth

century, the right-hand of the two monuments of knights in the south choir aisle of Exeter Cathedral has been conjectured to represent him, because it formerly appeared to bear the coat of arms of the Bohun family (azure, a bend argent cotised or between six lioncels or) (Carew, p. 5; Legg, p. 74; Pole, p. 109; Symonds, pp. 38, 89; BL, Add. MS 29931, ff. 33, 127; BL, Add. MS 17459, f. 7r; Hope, Monumentarium, p. 79). No medieval evidence exists to support this theory, and it is possible that the coat of arms was that of Henry de Boxe (see below).

Bokebroke

Presumably a member of the Boggebroke family of Exeter, unless a mistake for Nicholas Braybroke, canon of Exeter Cathedral, who died by July 1401 (MCR 2 Henry IV, m. 40). The cathedral bells were rung for him in 1401 (D&C 3773, f. 54v).

Bollegh, Henry

Archdeacon of Cornwall. Died after 13 July 1289, when he laid plans to be buried in the chapel, later known as St John Evangelist, in Exeter Cathedral, where his chantry was established (D&C 343).

Bolter, John

Parish of St Laurence, Exeter. Father of Joan Duke (see below). Buried in the hospital of St John between 1520 and 1535 (DRO, ECA, Book 53A, f. 95r).

Bolter, Roger

Precentor of Exeter Cathedral. Died probably on 5, certainly by 6, December 1436 (Le Neve, p. 7). His funeral was held in the cathedral in Michaelmas term 1436 (D&C 3771). In his will, dated 8 June 1436, he asked to be buried in the cathedral 'at the feet of the tomb of Amma Fylham, if the canons and my co-brethren are willing to offer this concession', or otherwise in some other place in the cathedral or cemetery (*Reg. Lacy*, IV, 27). Between Michaelmas 1436 and Michaelmas 1437 the cathedral received 10d. from his executors for large stones for making his tomb (D&C 2687).

Bonde, —

Mother of William Bonde, vicar choral. Her funeral was held in Exeter Cathedral on 24 January 1311 (D&C 3673, f. 102r).

Boskom, —

The bells of Exeter Cathedral were rung for him in 1401 (D&C 3773, f. 54v).

Boscum, —

Wife of. The bells of Exeter Cathedral were rung for her in 1401 (D&C 3773, f. 54v).

Bosoun, Joan

Died by 18 November 1392 (MCR 16–17 Ric II, m. 8). Wife of Richard Bosoun; the bells of Exeter Cathedral were rung for her in about 1392 (D&C 3773, f. 71r).

Bosoun, Robert

> Chancellor of Exeter Cathedral. Died probably on 21 January, certainly by 30 January, 1400 (Le Neve, p. 9). On 16 December 1396 the cathedral chapter gave him licence to be buried 'in the nave . . . next to the burial place of Master John Wylyet, formerly chancellor, that is to say on the south side of the same Master John' (D&C 3550, f. 103r). A sum of 2s. was paid for 24 feet of Raddon stone for his tomb between Michaelmas 1399 and Michaelmas 1400 (D&C 3658).

Boteler, John

> Resident in the hospital of St John. Buried in the hospital church between 1492 and 1530 (DRO, ECA, Book 53A, f. 94v).

Boteler, Thomas le

> Archdeacon of Totnes. Died between 5 and 11 January 1264 (*Reg. Bronescombe*, ed. Hingeston-Randolph, p. 187; see below). In his will, dated 1 November 1263, he asked to be buried in Exeter Cathedral before the altar of St Edmund (D&C 3672, p. 339). On 5 January following he established a perpetual chantry of a chaplain celebrating at the same altar in the early morning (ibid., pp. 340–1).

Boxe, Henry de (de la Boxe)

> Probably a knight: a man or men of this name occur with lands and interests in Dorset, Somerset, and Wiltshire (*Feudal Aids*, ii, 19, 38; iv, 303; v, 208). The record of his funeral in Exeter Cathedral occurs in Christmas term 1316–17, including the gift of his horse (D&C 3764, f. 22r). A Surrey or Sussex knight of the same name, contemporary and possibly identical, had a coat of arms (or, a bend argent between six lioncels gules) remarkably similar (except in colour) to that of the Bohun family (*The Parliamentary Writs and Writs of Military Summons*, ed. F. Palgrave, 2 vols in 4 (London, Record Commission, 1827–34), i, 412). It is possible therefore that the tomb of the cross-legged knight on the right-hand side in the south choir aisle of the cathedral was that of Boxe, whose coat of arms was misread as that of Humphrey de Bohun (see above).

Boys, John

> Parish of St Laurence, Exeter. Buried in the hospital of St John by 1492 (DRO, ECA, Book 53A, f. 94v).

Boyton, W.

> The record of his funeral in Exeter Cathedral occurs in Midsummer term 1306 (D&C 3673, f. 68v).

Bracton, Henry (Bratton)

> Chancellor of Exeter Cathedral. Died by September 1268 (*Reg. Bronescombe*, ed. Hingeston-Randolph, p. 136). Buried before 'the altar of the Blessed Virgin in the nave of Exeter' Cathedral (D&C 1846, 1848). See also Hope, Monumentarium, p. 182.

Bradeworthi, John
> Citizen of Exeter. In his will of 1499 he asked to be buried in the church of St Martin before the altar of St Mary (D&C 2538/1).

Braylegh, Richard de
> Dean of Exeter Cathedral. Died 13 August 1352 (Le Neve, p. 4). He paid 2s. 8d. to the cathedral fabric fund between Michaelmas 1340 and Michaelmas 1341 for the cost of making his grave, presumably reserving a place for it in the cathedral (D&C 2631; Erskine, *Fabric Accounts*, ii, 259).

Brantingham, Thomas
> Bishop of Exeter. Died 23 December 1394 (Le Neve, p. 2). In his will, dated 13 December 1393, he asked to be buried 'in the nave of the said church of Exeter, on the north side, that is to say before the altar formerly constructed by us and dedicated by us in honour of the holy and undivided Trinity' (PRO, PROB 11/1, f. 24v; *Reg. Brantyngham*, ii, 742). This was between the pillars of the second bay of the nave from the east on the north side. The cathedral bells are recorded being rung for him in Christmas term 1394–5 (D&C 3773, f. 70v). See also Hope, Monumentarium, p. 250.

Brewer, William
> Bishop of Exeter. Died 1244, either on 24 October according to an Exeter Cathedral chronicle (Dalton and Doble, i, p. xxii) or on 24 November, the date on which Exeter Cathedral subsequently kept his obit (D&C 3625, f. vi recto). Buried in the cathedral, probably in or near the choir or presbytery. In 1319–20 the cathedral chapter spent 9d. on digging and making his grave, presumably in consequence of the rebuilding of the cathedral (Erskine, *Fabric Accounts*, i, 114). Thereafter buried in the middle of the presbytery in front of the high altar, west of the grave of Thomas Bitton (Leland, i, 226; D&C 4037, 4708, P/2/1). His ledger stone is now in the first bay of the north choir aisle, with an inscription (Hope, Monumentarium, p. 41).

Broke, John
> Parish of St Sidwell, Exeter. Buried in the hospital of St John between 1492 and 1520 (DRO, ECA, Book 53A, f. 94v).

Brokyn, Alice
> Parish of St Martin, Exeter. Buried in the hospital of St John by 1492 (DRO, ECA, Book 53A, f. 94v).

Bronescombe, Walter
> Bishop of Exeter. Died 22 July 1280 (Dalton and Doble, i, p. xxii). On 20 July 1280 he chose his burial place as the chapel in Exeter Cathedral now known as St Gabriel (*Reg. Bronescombe*, ed. Hingeston-Randolph, pp. 38–9). His tomb now stands between the Lady Chapel and the chapel of St Gabriel (Hope, Monumentarium, p. 121). For a rather later inscription on his tomb, see Leland, i. 226).

Brownyng, William

Canon of Exeter Cathedral. Died 13 November 1454 (see below). His funeral in the cathedral is recorded in Michaelmas term 1454 (D&C 3772). In his will, dated 15 August 1454, he asked to be buried in the cathedral 'near the image which I have ordained at my own costs in the ambulatory, in the ground next to the entrance to the exchequer' (*Reg. Lacy*, IV, 60). For a discussion whether that image is the cadaver in the wall of the north choir aisle, see Orme, 1996, pp. 12–17. His ledger stone survives in the floor of the 3rd bay of that aisle with an inscription and date (Hope, Monumentarium, p. 39).

Brounste, Richard (Brownste)

Vicar choral of Exeter Cathedral. Died in Christmas term 1453–4, probably on 26 March 1454 (Orme, *Minor Clergy*, pp. 29–30). Between Michaelmas 1441 and Michaelmas 1442 the chapter conceded to him 'his burial place in the same church right inside the small west door on the south side, etc., in the ambulatory' (D&C 2689).

Buffet, William

Died by 30 October 1312 (MCR 6–7 Edw II, m. 5). The record of his funeral in Exeter Cathedral occurs in Michaelmas term 1312 (D&C 3673, f. 115v).

Bulwyke, Philip

Layman. In his will, dated 24 September 1499, he asked to be buried in the church of the Friars Preachers (Dominican Friary) 'before the image of Pity' (PRO, PROB 11/12, f. 151v). The location of the church is not mentioned but may have been in Exeter; the will mentions Plymouth, which did not possess such a friary.

Bund, John

The record of his funeral in Exeter Cathedral occurs in Christmas term 1307–8 (D&C 3673, f. 80v).

Burgoun, John

Rector of St Stephen-in-Brannel (Cornwall), previously of St Olave, Exeter. Died by 6 December 1425 (*Reg. Lacy*, i, 29). His executors paid 40s. between Michaelmas 1425 and Michaelmas 1426 for his tomb in Exeter Cathedral (perhaps for permission for burial there) and 2s. for lime to make the tomb (D&C 2680).

Burlegh, John (Burley)

Rector of Farringdon (Devon). Probably died by 30 April 1397 (*Reg. Stafford*, p. 172). The bells of Exeter Cathedral were rung for him in Christmas term 1396–7 (D&C 3773, f. 70v). He is probably identical with the Sir John Burley mentioned as buried in the hospital of St John by 1492 (DRO, ECA, Book 53A, f. 94v).

Busse, —

Mother of John Busse. The record of her funeral in Exeter Cathedral occurs in Michaelmas term 1308 (D&C 3673, f. 86r).

1. A late sixteenth-century plan of Exeter Cathedral cemetery, showing numerous paths, some fencing, and the conduit by the north-west corner of the cathedral. The charnel chapel, formerly near the conduit, had disappeared by this date.

2. Above, burials from the cathedral cemetery, excavated in the 1970s, showing interment on the back with heads facing towards the east.

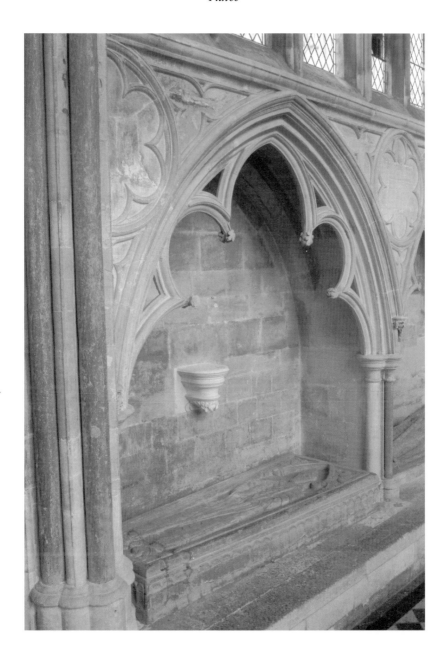

3. Tomb recess in the cathedral Lady Chapel, late thirteenth century, used for reburying an earlier bishop of Exeter with more grandeur. The effigy may be that of Bishop Bartholomew (d. 1184).

4. The cathedral chapel of St Andrew, built in the early fourteenth century and chosen by Dean Andrew Kilkenny (d. 1302) for his chantry. The ledger stone above his grave still lies before the altar; the stone pinnacles were not originally in this chapel.

5, 6. Early fourteenth-century effigies of knights in the south choir aisle. Above, one of the Ralegh family, possibly Sir John or Sir Thomas. Below, what is traditionally called the cenotaph of Humphrey de Bohun, earl of Hereford (d. 1322); more probably the tomb of a different knight.

7. The grand monument of Walter Stapledon (d. 1326). Bishop when the choir of the cathedral was being completed, and a generous benefactor of the building, he was able to secure the burial place of honour, north of the high altar.

8. Probably Sir Richard Stapledon (d. 1332), brother of the bishop. His tomb, like the bishop's, publicised the importance of a family that had recently risen from relatively humble status.

9. Hugh Courtenay, earl of Devon (d. 1377) and his wife Margaret (d. 1391).
The swans at her feet were the badge of her family, the Bohuns, one of several
noble houses that claimed descent from the Knight of the Swan.

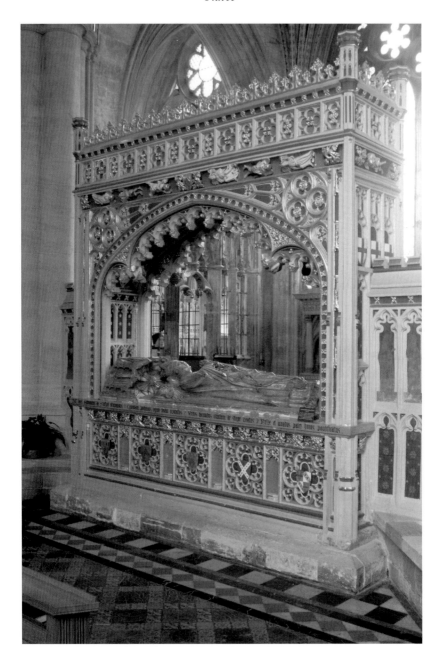

10. Another splendid bishop's tomb, that of Edmund Stafford (d. 1419), himself the son of an earl. He complemented it by giving an earlier bishop, Walter Bronescombe, a similar tomb on the opposite side of the Lady Chapel.

11, 12. Above, the plain tomb of Bishop Lacy (d. 1455), venerated as a shrine up to the 1530s. Below, a typical 'cadaver' or 'transi' monument of the fifteenth century: possibly intended by Lacy for his tomb, possibly a memento mori erected by Canon William Browning.

13, 14. Above, The brass of Canon William Langton (d. 1414), kinsman of Bishop Stafford, buried by Stafford's tomb. Below, the tomb of Archdeacon John Fulford (d. 1519), a typical cathedral ledger stone.

15, 16. Above, Sir John Speke (d. 1518); below, Bishop Hugh Oldham (d. 1519). Their tombs and chantries, planned as a pair, were the last great funeral monuments in the cathedral before the Reformation.

Calwodly, Alice
Parish of St Laurence, Exeter. Buried before the image of the high cross in the hospital of St John between 1520 and 1535 (DRO, ECA, Book 53A, f. 95r).

Calwoodlegh, Elizabeth
Mother of Thomas 'junior' (see below), and probably wife of Thomas 'senior' (see below). Buried in the Dominican Friary, Exeter, by 1480 (DRO, Chanter XII (ii), Reg. Fox, f. 126r).

Calwodly, John
Parish of St Laurence, Exeter. Buried before the image of the high cross in the hospital of St John between 1520 and 1535 (DRO, ECA, Book 53A, f. 95r).

Calwoodlegh, Thomas
'Junior'; esquire. Probably son of the next. In his will, dated 1 March 1480, he asked to be buried in the Dominican Friary, Exeter, near Elizabeth Calwoodlegh, his mother (DRO, Chanter XII (ii), Reg. Fox, f. 126r).

Calwodely, Thomas
Esquire; probably father of the preceding. Died between 24 February 1492 and 4 March 1493. In his will, dated 24 February 1492, he asked to be buried in the Dominican Friary, Exeter (MCR 8–9 Hen VII, m. 24).

Camelford, Thomas
Rector of St Mary Steps, Exeter. Died by 12 May 1393 (MCR 16–17 Ric II, m. 32). The bells of Exeter Cathedral were rung for him in Easter term 1393 (D&C 3773, f. 71r).

Camville – see Kamuyle

Caperon, William
The record of his funeral in Exeter Cathedral occurs in Midsummer term 1312 (D&C 3673, f. 114r).

Carewe, Isabel
Of Antony (Cornwall) Perhaps the widow of Alexander Carew of Antony, d. 1492. In her will, dated 1521, she requested burial in the church of St Thomas, Cowick Street, Exeter (Truro, Royal Institution of Cornwall, Henderson MS 66, p. 165).

Carpenter, Ralph
The record of his funeral in Exeter Cathedral occurs in Midsummer term 1306 (D&C 3673, f. 68v). Possibly the same as Ralph de Christchurch, carpenter, died by 5 June 1307 (MCR 34–35 Edw I, m. 33).

Carslegh, James
Archdeacon of Exeter. Died by 5 December 1438 (*Reg. Lacy*, i, 238). The record of his funeral in Exeter Cathedral occurs in Christmas term 1438–9 (D&C 3771).

Carslegh, Peter

> Canon of Exeter Cathedral. Died 24 December 1534 (Le Neve, p. 60). In his will, dated 5 August 1534, he asked to be buried in the Lady Chapel of the cathedral (PRO, PROB 11/25, f. 230v).

Carswyll, —

> Wife of William de Carswylle. The record of her funeral in Exeter Cathedral occurs in Midsummer term 1307 (D&C 3673, f. 77r).

Carter, Peter

> Secondary clerk and holder of various minor offices in Exeter Cathedral (Orme, *Minor Clergy*, p. 97). Probably died between Michaelmas 1464 and Michaelmas 1465, when his executors paid the cathedral 8d. for sand: evidently for his grave in the cathedral or cemetery (D&C 2704).

Chaldon, Thomas

> Annuellar of the Bratton chantry in Exeter Cathedral (Orme, *Minor Clergy*, p. 73). Probably died between Michaelmas 1484 and Michaelmas 1485, when the cathedral bells were rung for him (D&C 3779, f. 231r).

Chalmore, —

> Buried in the cathedral cemetery by 13 April 1514 when his son John requested burial next to him (PRO, PROB 11/18, f. 34v).

Chalmore, John

> Apparently of Exeter. In his will, dated 13 April 1514, he asked to be buried in the cathedral cemetery next to his father (PRO, PROB 11/18, f. 34v).

Champernon, Agnes

> Between Michaelmas 1430 and Michaelmas 1431 her executors paid Exeter Cathedral £3 6s. 8d. for permission for her burial in the cathedral, and 3s. 4d. and 2s. for stones, 1s. 6d. for lime, and 6d. for sand to make her tomb (D&C 2683).

Charlton, Roger de

> Archdeacon of Totnes. Died probably 10 June, certainly by 13 June, 1338 (Le Neve, p. 17). The record of his funeral in Exeter Cathedral occurs in Midsummer term 1338 (D&C 3765).

Charlton, Thomas de

> Canon of Exeter Cathedral. Died shortly before 8 March 1331 when his funeral is recorded in the cathedral (D&C 3674, f. 77v). His tomb is mentioned between Michaelmas 1330 and Michaelmas 1331 (D&C 2628, m. 1; Erskine, *Fabric Accounts*, ii, 234).

Cheyne, —

> Son of Cheyne. The record of his funeral in Exeter Cathedral occurs in Midsummer term 1316 (D&C 3764, f. 19r).

Chichester, —

> The effigy of the left-hand knight in the south choir aisle of Exeter Cathedral was attributed to a member of the Chichester family by

antiquaries of the late sixteenth and seventeenth centuries, because it appeared to bear this family's coat of arms (Leland, i, 227; Legg, p. 74; Symonds, p. 89; Hope, Monumentarium, p. 79). The arms, however, were previously those of the Ralegh family of Raleigh, Devon, whose heiress married Sir John Chichester in about 1385, and more probably relate to Henry or Thomas de Ralegh (see below) (Brushfield, pp. 455–8, 463–81).

Choun, John
   Parish of St Pancras, Exeter. Died between 24 April and 3 May 1474. In his will, dated 24 April 1474, he asked to be buried in the cathedral cemetery (MCR 13–14 Edw IV, m. 34).

Christchurch – see Carpenter

Chubb, —
   Wife of Robert Chubb. The bells of Exeter Cathedral were rung for her between Michaelmas 1488 and Michaelmas 1489 (D&C 3779, f. 231v).

Chubbe, William
   Parish of St Paul, Exeter. He was buried in the hospital of St John between 1520 and 1535 (DRO, ECA, Book 53A, f. 95r).

Chuselden, Elizabeth
   Parish of St Laurence, Exeter. She was buried in the hospital of St John by 1492 (DRO, ECA, Book 53A, f. 94v).

Clare, Richard de
   Canon of Exeter Cathedral. Died between 26 November 1337 and 4 April 1338, probably nearer the latter (Le Neve, p. 26; *Reg. Grandisson*, ii, 857, 870; D&C 2792). The record of his funeral in Exeter Cathedral occurs in Midsummer term 1338 (D&C 3765).

Clerck, Thomas
   Resident in the hospital of St John. Buried there between 1492 and 1520 (DRO, ECA, Book 53A, f. 94v).

Cleyhangre, R. de
   His funeral was held in Exeter Cathedral on 8 April 1311 (D&C 3673, f. 104r).

Clifford, Thomas
   Canon of Exeter Cathedral. Died by 1 February 1419 (Le Neve, p. 47). In his will, dated 18 December 1418, he asked to be buried in the cathedral (ibid., p. 422). The record of his funeral in the cathedral occurs in Christmas term 1418–19 (D&C 3770).

Cliffton, Joan
   Parish of All Hallows on the Wall, Exeter. Buried in the hospital of St John between 1520 and 1535 (DRO, ECA, Book 53A, f. 95r).

Cliffton, John
   Parish of All Hallows on the Wall, Exeter. Buried in the hospital of St John between 1520 and 1535 (DRO, ECA, Book 53A, f. 95r).

Cobethorn, John

Dean of Exeter Cathedral. Died in about Michaelmas term 1458 (Le Neve, p. 5). The record of his funeral in the cathedral occurs in Christmas term 1458–9 (D&C 3772).

Cofyn, William

Said to have been buried in the Dominican Friary, Exeter, before 1301 (DRO, Exeter City Archives, Misc. Roll 67). A William Coffin held land at Caffins Heanton in Lynton parish in 1285 (*Feudal Aids*, i, 336).

Cogworthy, Thomas

Parish of St Kerrian, Exeter. Buried in the hospital of St John between 1492 and 1520 (DRO, ECA, Book 53A, f. 94v).

Cokworthy, John

Canon of Exeter Cathedral. Died 4 June 1433, according to his ledger stone now in the 4th bay of the south choir aisle (Hope, Monumentarium, p. 96). He is presumably the John Cokworthy, 'clerk', who made his will on 27 October 1431 and asked to be buried in the cathedral 'outside the vestibule before the image of St Mary Magdalene', i.e. near the entrance to the double chapel off the south choir aisle (*Reg. Lacy*, IV, 23). The record of his funeral in the cathedral occurs in Easter term 1433 (D&C 3771).

Cokeworthi, Richard

Parish of All Hallows on the Wall, Exeter. Buried in the hospital of St John by 1492 (DRO, ECA, Book 53A, f. 94v).

Colcharde, John

Parish of St George, Exeter. Buried in the hospital of St John between 1492 and 1520 (DRO, ECA, Book 53A, f. 94v).

Cole, John

Buried in the hospital of St John by 1492 (DRO, ECA, Book 53A, f. 94v).

Colebrok, R.

A sum of 3s. 4d. for his grave in the cloister of Exeter Cathedral was paid to the fabric fund between Michaelmas 1341 and Michaelmas 1342 (Erskine, *Fabric Accounts* ii, 267). Possibly the same as John Colbrok who occurs as an annuellar of the cathedral between 1330 and 1337 and might have qualified for such a grave (Orme, *Minor Clergy*, p. 52).

Collecote, Adam de

Father of Henry de Collecote (see below) (D&C 277a). Died after making his will on 2 December 1269 (D&C VC/3053); later commemorated on 12 June (DRO, ECA, Book 53A, f. 8r). Buried in the cathedral cemetery by 11 December 1294 when Henry requested burial in his parents' grave (see below).

Collecote, Henry de

Parish of St Mary Steps, Exeter; married layman. In his will, dated 11

December 1294, he asked to be buried 'in the cemetery of St Peter of Exeter, in the place where my father and my mother rest' (D&C 2121; *Reg. Bronescombe*, ed. Hingeston-Randolph, pp. 435–6).

Collecote (Coldecote), Margaret de
Wife of John de Beare, tanner, of Exeter. In her will, dated 7 May 1305, she asked to be buried in the cathedral cemetery (D&C VC/ 3018).

Collecote, Nicholas
Rector of St Laurence, Exeter. Died by 2 June 1424 (*Reg. Lacy*, i, 79). In his will, dated 27 March 1424, he wished to be buried 'in the church of the hospital of St John' (*Reg. Lacy*, IV, 1); subsequently buried there (DRO, ECA, Book 53A, f. 94v).

Collecote, Rose de
Wife of Adam and mother of Henry de Collecote (see above). Died after December 1269 (D&C VC/3053). Buried in the cathedral cemetery by 11 December 1294 when Henry requested burial in his parents' grave (see below).

Colyns, Arnulph
Canon of Exeter Cathedral. Died between 8 March and 29 May 1490 (Le Neve, p. 58). By his will, dated 8 March 1490, he asked to be buried in the cathedral (PRO, PROB 11/8, f. 273r–v). A sum of 20d. was paid, between Michaelmas 1493 and Michaelmas 1494, for lime, sand and tilestone for his tomb: probably in the cathedral (D&C 2704/4).

Collys, Walter
Precentor of Exeter Cathedral. Died by 16 May 1453 (Le Neve, p. 7). Between then and Michaelmas 1453 his executors paid 9s. 11d. for stone, lime and sand sold to them for his tomb in the cathedral and for the work of masons and labourers (D&C 2697).

Colman, Joan
Wife of John Colman. Buried in the nave of the hospital of St John between 1520 and 1535 (DRO, ECA, Book 53A, f. 95r).

Colman, John
Husband of Joan Colman. Buried in the nave of the hospital of St John between 1520 and 1535 (DRO, ECA, Book 53A, f. 95r).

Colshill, John
Parish of St Petroc, Exeter. Citizen; first husband of Elizabeth Speke (see below), and possibly father of the next two entries. In his will, dated 12 June 1495, he asked to be buried in Exeter Cathedral (MCR 11–12 Hen VII, m. 40; PRO, PROB 11/10, f. 207r).

Colshill, John
In his will, dated 28 April 1518, he asked to be buried (if he died in Exeter) 'in the conventual church of the Friars Preachers [i.e. Dominican

Friars] . . . before the image of St George and next to the grave in which Peter Colshill my brother was buried (PRO, PROB 11/19, f. 81r).

Colshill, Peter

Buried in the Dominican Friary, Exeter, before the image of St George by 28 April 1518, when his brother John Colshill requested to be buried next to him (PRO, PROB 11/19, f. 81r).

Comb, —

A record of this person's funeral in Exeter Cathedral occurs in Easter term 1315 (D&C 3764, f. 12v).

Comb, J. de

His funeral was held in Exeter Cathedral on 14 August 1332 (D&C 3764, f. 85r).

Conant, Denise

The bells of Exeter Cathedral were rung for her in Easter term 1395 (D&C 3773, f. 70v).

Conant, Hugh

The bells of Exeter Cathedral were rung for him in about 1392 (D&C 3773, f. 71r).

*Cook, — (*Cocus*)

Wife of William *Cook (*Cocus*). A record of her funeral in Exeter Cathedral occurs in Midsummer term 1307 (D&C 3673, f. 75v).

*Cook, — (*Cocus*)

Wife of Simon *Cook (*Cocus*). A record of her funeral in Exeter Cathedral occurs in Easter term 1308 (D&C 3673, f. 83r).

*Cook, — (*Cocus*)

Wife of Richard *Cook (*Cocus*). A record of her funeral in Exeter Cathedral occurs in Michaelmas term 1316 (D&C 3764, f. 21r).

Coke, —

Parish of St Petroc, Exeter. Wife of Thomas Coke. Buried in the hospital of St John by 1492 (DRO, ECA, Book 53A, f. 94v).

*Cook, R. (*Cocus*)

Possibly Richard Cook (see the second entry above). A record of his funeral in Exeter Cathedral occurs in Easter term 1322 (D&C 3764, f. 33r).

Cook, Thomas

Vicar choral of Exeter Cathedral. Died by 16 May 1438 (*Reg. Lacy*, i, 234). Between Michaelmas 1437 and Michaelmas 1438 his executors paid 20s. for large stones, lime, and sand for making his tomb in the cathedral cloister, and 20s. as a legacy to the cathedral fabric and for an old marble stone for his tomb (D&C 2688).

Coke, Walter

Buried in the hospital of St John by 1492 (DRO, ECA, Book 53A, f. 94v).

Coppleston, Henry
Parish of St Laurence, Exeter. 'Master.' Buried before the altar of St Thomas in the hospital of St John between 1520 and 1535 (DRO, ECA, Book 53A, f. 95r).

Coppleston, Joan
Parish of St Laurence, Exeter. Wife of John (next entry); 'Mistress.' Buried in the hospital of St John between 1492 and 1520 (DRO, ECA, Book 53A, f. 94v).

Coppleston, John
Parish of St Laurence, Exeter. Husband of Joan (previous entry); esquire. Buried in the hospital of St John between 1492 and 1520 (DRO, ECA, Book 53A, f. 94v).

Coppleston, Richard
Parish of St Laurence, Exeter. Son of John (previous entry). Buried in the hospital of St John between 1492 and 1520 (DRO, ECA, Book 53A, f. 94v).

Cornew, Robert
Knight; patron of Brushford church, Somerset (*Reg. Stafford*, p. 190). The bells of Exeter Cathedral were rung for him in Easter term 1398 (D&C 3773, f. 70r).

Coryngdon, John
Canon of Exeter Cathedral. Died on about 20 July 1495 (Le Neve, p. 57). In his will, dated 20 February 1494, he asked to be buried in the cathedral nave 'near and next to the grave' of Archdeacon David Hopton (PRO, PROB 11/10, f. 184r).

Coscum, Margery (Coscumbe, Koskom)
See below.

Coscum, William (Coscumbe, Koskom)
The bells of Exeter Cathedral were rung for 'Koskom' and the wife of 'Coscum' in about 1401 (D&C 3773, f. 54v). He is very likely William Coscumbe and she Margery, who died as his widow by 4 December 1402 (MCR 4 Hen IV, m. 10)

Couertocke, R.
A record of his funeral in Exeter Cathedral occurs in Easter term 1317 (D&C 3764, f. 23r).

Courtenaye, —
The bells of Exeter cathedral were rung for this person between Michaelmas 1487 and Michaelmas 1488 (D&C 3779, f. 231v).

Courtenay, Agnes
Countess of Devon; wife of Hugh Courtenay, first earl of Devon (see below). Died at Tiverton (Devon), 11 June 1340 (Oliver, *Monasticon*, p. 346). Her funeral was held in Exeter Cathedral (D&C 3765), and she was buried at Cowick Priory on 27 June 1340 (Oliver, *Monasticon*, p. 346).

Courtenay, Eleanor de.

Daughter of Hugh Lord Despenser, widow of Sir Hugh Courtenay (d. 1292) (see below), and mother of Hugh, first earl of Devon (d. 1340) (see below). Died at London, 26 September 1328; buried in Cowick Priory (Oliver, *Monasticon*, p. 344).

Courtenay, Hugh de

Knight; baron of Okehampton. Husband of Eleanor (see above) and father of Hugh, first earl of Devon (see below). Died at Colcombe in Colyton parish (Devon), 28 February 1292; buried at Cowick Priory (Oliver, *Monasticon*, p. 344). For an indulgence of 1300 mentioning his burial place, see British Library, Additional Charter 13913.

Courtenay, Hugh de

Earl of Devon. Son of Hugh and Eleanor Courtenay (see above), wife of Agnes (see above), and father of Earl Hugh (d. 1377) (see below). Died at Tiverton (Devon), 23 December 1340 (Oliver, *Monasticon*, p. 346). His funeral mass was celebrated by Bishop Grandisson who also preached the sermon on 5 February 1341; it is not clear if this was in Exeter Cathedral or Cowick Priory (*Reg. Grandisson*, ii, 939). Buried at Cowick Priory (Oliver, *Monasticon*, p. 346).

Courtenay, Hugh

Earl of Devon; son of Earl Hugh (d. 1340) (see above); and husband of Margaret (see below). Died 2 May 1377 (Cokayne, iv, 324). In a codicil to his will, dated 28 April 1377, he asked to be buried in Exeter Cathedral (*Reg. Brantyngham*, i, 382). His tomb was subsequently placed in the second bay of the nave from the east, on the south side. See also Hope, Monumentarium, p. 165.

Courtenay, Margaret

Countess of Devon; wife of Earl Hugh d. 1377 (see above). Died 16 December 1391 (Cokayne, iv, 324). She intended to be buried in Exeter Cathedral by 24 June 1385 (*The Register of Nicholas Bubwith, Bishop of Bath and Wells*, ed. T.S. Holmes, vol. ii (Somerset Record Society, xx, 1914), pp. 361–73). Her monument subsequently lay with that of her husband (see previous entry).

Courtenay, Matilda

Lady; daughter of Sir William Beaumont, wife of Sir Hugh Courtenay of Haccombe (Devon). On 20 August 1464 she endowed prayers for her soul in St Nicholas Priory, Exeter, where she intended to be buried (DRO, ED/M/838), and in her will, dated 10 July 1466, she asked to have her funeral in Exeter Cathedral and her body taken for burial in the priory (PRO, PROB 11/5, f. 161r).

Courtenay, Peter

Knight; seventh son of Earl Hugh (d. 1377) and Countess Margaret (see above). Died not long before 18 November 1408 (*Cal. Fine Rolls*

1405–13, p. 134). He was buried under a ledger stone on the north side of the tomb of Earl Hugh and Countess Margaret (Pole, p. 109; Symonds, p. 88). In 1864 this was moved to the first bay of the south choir aisle. The stone contains a brass indent and inscription (Oliver, *Lives of the Bishops*, p. 238; Hope, Monumentarium, p. 101).

Courtenay, William

Archbishop of Canterbury; fourth son of Earl Hugh (d. 1377) and Countess Margaret (see above). In his will, not dated but prior to 28 July 1396, he asked to be buried 'in the nave of the cathedral church of Exeter in the place where now lie three deans in order before the high cross', i.e. in the very centre of the nave before the screen. On 28 July 1396 he changed his mind in favour of the collegiate church of Maidstone (Kent), but after his death on 31 July 1396 he was interred in Canterbury Cathedral (L.L. Duncan, 'The Will of William Courtenay, Archbishop of Canterbury, 1396', *Archaeologia Cantiana*, 23 (1898), pp. 58–9, 66–7; Joseph Dahmus, *William Courtenay, Archbishop of Canterbury, 1381–1396* (University Park, Pa., and London, 1966), pp. 228, 266–7).

Courtenay, William

Knight; of Powderham (Devon). Died by 19 December 1485 (MCR 1–2 Hen VII, m. 12). The bells of Exeter Cathedral were rung for him between Michaelmas 1484 and Michaelmas 1485 (D&C 3779, f. 231r).

Courtour, Philip

In his will, dated 26 May 1421, he asked to be buried in the church of St Sidwell before the image of St Katherine (DRO, ED/M/682).

Cremell, William

Probably parish of St Kerrian, Exeter. Died between 20 November 1483 and 12 April 1484. In his will, dated 20 November 1483, he asked to be buried in the cathedral cemetery (MCR 1–2 Ric III, m. 28).

Crese, Nicholas

Rector of St Mary Steps, Exeter. Died by 1 June 1398 (*Reg. Stafford*, p. 171). The bells of Exeter Cathedral were rung for him in Easter term 1398 (D&C 3773, f. 70r).

Cristischerche, Thomas de

Baker. The record of his funeral in Exeter Cathedral occurs in Christmas term 1310–11 (D&C 3673, f. 102v).

Crugg, [Katherine?]

Lady; wife of William Crugge (see below). Died 8 May 1500, according to her ledger stone, now in the 5th bay of the south side of the nave of Exeter Cathedral. The inscription appears to refer to 'Domine . . . rine nuper uxoris Willelmi Crugg, maior civitatis Exon' (Hope, Monument-arium, p. 243).

Crugge, William

Formerly mayor of Exeter; husband of Katherine [?] (see above). Died by about 1500, when a sum of 13s. 4d. was paid to Exeter Cathedral 'for his grave', probably in the cathedral in view of the presence of his wife's ledger stone there (see above) (D&C 3680).

Cullompton, Walter (Columpton)

Canon of Exeter Cathedral. Died by 20 March 1401 (Le Neve, p. 39). On 21 June 1393 the cathedral chapter gave him permission to have 'his tomb on the north side of the tomb of Master John More' (D&C 3550, f. 89r). More had been licensed to be buried in the nave (see below). The cathedral bells were rung for him in 1401 (D&C 3773, f. 54v).

*Cutler, Walter (*Cultellarius*)

The record of his funeral in Exeter Cathedral occurs in Midsummer term 1306 (D&C 3673, f. 68r). Joan, widow of Walter le Cotiller died in about 1315 (MCR 8–9 Edw II, m. 33)

Danby, John

Vicar choral of Exeter Cathedral. Died between Michaelmas 1485 and Michaelmas 1486 when the cathedral bells were rung for him (D&C 3779, f. 231r; Orme, *Minor Clergy*, p. 35.

David

Vicar of 'Nymet', i.e. Bishop's Nympton (Devon); died by 13 December 1319 (*Reg. Stapeldon*, p. 190). Buried in or near Exeter Cathedral between Michaelmas and December 1319, when a sum of 8d. was paid from his estate to the cathedral fabric (Erskine, *Fabric Accounts* i, 113).

David, William

The record of his funeral in Exeter Cathedral occurs in Easter term 1332 (D&C 3764, f. 83v).

Davy, Thomasia

Parish of St Petroc, Exeter. Widow of Simon Davy, citizen and tailor. Died between 20 May and 31 August 1517. In her will, dated 20 May 1517, she asked to be buried in the Dominican Friary, Exeter (MCR 8–9 Henry VIII, between mm. 48 and 49).

Dawe, Robert

'Sir'; probably priest. Buried in the hospital of St John by 1492 (DRO, ECA, Book 53A, f. 94v).

Denner, John

Annuellar of the Bodeham and Puntingdon chantry in Exeter Cathedral. Died in Easter term 1389 (D&C 2598/2; Orme, *Minor Clergy*, p. 74). The cathedral bells were rung for him, probably in that term (D&C 3779, f. 231v).

Dyer, Martin

Canon of Exeter Cathedral. Apparently died in Michaelmas term 1464;

the record of his funeral in Exeter Cathedral occurs in that term (D&C 3772/1). In his will, dated 6 September 1464, he asked to be buried in the cathedral 'or elsewhere if it does not happen that I die there' (DRO, Chanter XII (i), Reg. Nevill, f. 141v). His obit, however, was subsequently held on 12 March (D&C 3675, f. 27r).

Dygon, Richard
Parish of St Sidwell, Exeter. Buried in the hospital of St John by 1492 (DRO, ECA, Book 53A, f. 94v). Possibly the same as Richard Dygon, died by 5 August 1398 (MCR 21–22 Ric II, m. 45).

Dynham, Isabel
Daughter of Hugh de Vere, earl of Oxford; widow of Oliver Lord Dynham (see below). Died 11 August 1300 (DRO, ECA, Book 53A, f. 66r). Buried in the Dominican Friary, Exeter, on the south side of the presbytery, opposite her husband (Oliver, *Monasticon*, p. 344).

Dynham, Jane
Lady; widow of Sir John Dynham, knight (see below). In her will, dated 26 January 1497, she asked to be buried in the Dominican Friary, Exeter, 'by my lord my husband, as use is, where our tomb is made' (PRO, PROB 11/11, f. 87r).

Dynham, John
Of Hartland, Nutwell, and other places in Devon and Cornwall; knight. Died 25 January 1458 (Cokayne, iv, 378). Buried in the Dominican Friary, Exeter, by 1497 when his widow Jane requested burial by him (PRO, PROB 11/11, f. 87r).

Dynham, Oliver
Lord Dynham. Died 26 February 1299 (Cokayne, iv, 370–1). Buried in the presbytery of the Dominican Friary, Exeter, by 1300, when his wife Isabel was buried opposite him (Oliver, *Monasticon*, p. 344).

Dyrewyne, J.
The record of his funeral in Exeter Cathedral occurs in Easter term 1312 (D&C 3673, f. 112v).

Dyreweyne, John (de Exonia)
Canon of Exeter Cathedral. Died on about 5 September 1314; his funeral took place in the cathedral on that day (D&C 3764, f. 9r; cf. MCR 7–8 Edw II, m. 49; *Reg. Stapeldon*, p. 213).

Dobell, Laurence
Rector of St Mary Major, Exeter. Died by 23 January 1532 (DRO, Chanter XIV, f. 58v). On 14 April 1527 the chapter of Exeter Cathedral agreed at his request that the cathedral choristers should say the psalm *De Profundis*, three times a week, while standing in the west porch of the cathedral facing his intended tomb (D&C 3551, f. 39r–v). This suggests that he planned to be buried in the cemetery near the west doors. The agreement was confirmed on 27 January 1532 after his death (ibid., f. 79r).

Dodderygg, Alice de
> The record of her funeral in Exeter Cathedral occurs in Midsummer term 1305 (D&C 3673, f. 59r).

Doddisscombe, —
> Son of John de Doddisscombe. Apparently buried in Exeter between Michaelmas 1341 and Michaelmas 1342, when the mayor ordered 16d. worth of wine to be sent for his funeral (Rowe and Draisey, p. 17).

Dodyngton, John
> Treasurer of Exeter Cathedral. Died probably 14 April, certainly by 20 April 1400 (Le Neve, p. 11). In his will, dated 26 March 1400, he requested burial by the side of Dounebrygge, 'my master, while he lived' (*Reg. Stafford*, p. 379): this was beneath the south tower (see below: William Ekerdon). The cathedral bells were rung for him, apparently in 1401 (D&C 3773, f. 54v).

Donscombe, Richard
> Rector of North Hill (Cornwall) and prebendary of Cutton in the chapel of Exeter Castle. Died 7 June 1421 (*Reg. Lacy*, i, 9, 15). Buried in the hospital of St John by 1492 (DRO, ECA, Book 53A, f. 94v).

Doulys, John de
> Married layman. In his will, dated 25 October 1267, he asked to be buried in the cathedral cemetery (British Library, Add. Charter 27523; DRO, ECA, Book 53A, f. 6r).

Doune, Matthew
> Canon of Exeter Cathedral. Died by 19 June 1430 (Le Neve, p. 48). A record of his funeral in Exeter Cathedral occurs in Midsummer term 1430 (D&C 3771).

Dounebrygge, William
> Canon of Exeter Cathedral. Died 5 January 1393 (Le Neve, p. 40: D&C 3625, f. i recto; *Reg. Brantyngham*, i, 125). The cathedral bells are recorded being rung for him in Easter term 1393 (D&C 3773, f. 71r). Buried in the cathedral by 26 March 1400 beneath the south tower (see below: William Ekerdon), when Canon John Dodyngton, his former pupil or servant, chose to be buried next to him (*Reg. Stafford*, p. 378).

Dourissh, —
> Parish of St Sidwell, Exeter. Daughter of Thomas Dourissh. Buried in the hospital of St John by 1492 (DRO, ECA, Book 53A, f. 94v).

Dove, Roger
> The bells of Exeter Cathedral were rung for him in Michaelmas term 1397 (D&C 3773, f. 70r).

*Drawer, Walter (*Tractor*)
> The record of his funeral in Exeter Cathedral occurs in Easter term 1308 (D&C 3673, f. 82r)

Drewe, Stephen
Vicar choral of Exeter Cathedral. Died by 17 August 1387 (Orme, *Minor Clergy*, p. 21). Between then and 11 September 1387, his body, which had been buried in the cathedral cloister, was removed by 'certain sons of iniquity' and transferred to another place, against the sacred canons of the Church (*Reg. Brantyngham*, i, 175–6).

Drew – see also Steyner

Drewell, —
Wife of [Richard?] Drewell (see below). The bells of Exeter Cathedral were rung for her between Michaelmas 1484 and Michaelmas 1485 (D&C 3779, f. 231r).

Druell, John (Drewell)
Archdeacon of Exeter. Died between 29 March and 8 June 1453 (Le Neve, p. 14). In his will, dated 29 March 1453, he asked to be buried in the cathedral 'wherever the dean and my brethren shall assign' (Lambeth Palace Library, Reg. John Kempe, f. 290r). Between Michaelmas 1452 and Michaelmas 1453 the cathedral received 8s. 10d. from his executors for stone, lime and sand for his tomb and 11d. for a marble stone to lay on him (D&C 2697).

Druell, Richard
The bells of Exeter Cathedral were rung for him between Michaelmas 1490 and Michaelmas 1491 (D&C 3779, f. 231v).

Dreyton, John de
Precentor of Exeter Cathedral. Died by 12 June 1301 (*Reg. Stapeldon*, p. 153; D&C 3673, p. 17). Conjectured to be the precentor commemorated on a ledger stone now in the chapel of St Andrew in the cathedral (Hope, 1964, pp. 102–6). However, the surname on the stone (ibid.) is restricted to the last three poorly legible letters, which might relate to Precentor Ralph Germeyn, who died in 1316 (see below).

Duke, Joan
Parish of St Laurence, Exeter. Daughter of John Bolter; 'Mistress'. Buried in the hospital of St John between 1520 and 1535 (DRO, ECA, Book 53A, f. 95r).

Duke, Juliana
Parish of St Stephen, Exeter. Buried in the hospital of St John between 1520 and 1535 (DRO, ECA, Book 53A, f. 95r).

Durneford, Nicholas de
Parish of St Martin, Exeter. Married clerk. In his will, dated 17 August 1326, he asked to be buried in the cathedral cemetery (DRO, ECA, Book 53A, f. 53v).

Edmund
The record of his funeral in Exeter Cathedral occurs in Midsummer term 1316 (D&C 3764, f. 19r).

Edward, Thomas
> Dominican friar. Buried in the cemetery of Modbury church (Devon) by 10 January 1373 when Bishop Brantingham, at the request of the prior of the Dominican Friary, Exeter, sanctioned the reburial of his body in the friary (*Reg. Brantyngham*, i, 294).

Ekerdon, William
> Canon of Exeter Cathedral. Died by 4 December 1413, probably on 3 December (Le Neve, p. 45). In his will, dated 8 November 1413, he asked to be buried 'next to [John] Dodyngton in the south tower' of the cathedral, probably in or near the chapel of St John Baptist (*Reg. Stafford*, p. 402).

Elycot, Elizabeth
> Parish of St Sidwell, Exeter. Wife of Thomas (see below). Buried before the door to the dormitory in the hospital of St John between 1520 and 1535 (DRO, ECA, Book 53A, f. 95r).

Elycotte, Thomas
> Parish of St Sidwell, Exeter. Butler of the hospital of St John. Buried in the hospital church between 1492 and 1520 (DRO, ECA, Book 53A, f. 94v).

Elycot, Thomas
> Parish of St Sidwell, Exeter. Husband of Elizabeth (see above). Buried before the door to the dormitory in the hospital of St John between 1520 and 1535 (DRO, ECA, Book 53A, f. 95r).

Elyot, William
> Rector of Aveton Giffard and vicar of Blackawton (Devon). Died by October 1494 (Orme, 2001, pp. 12–17). Possibly uncle of the next. A sum of 3s. 4d. was paid to Exeter Cathedral between Michaelmas 1493 and Michaelmas 1494 for stone, lime and sand for making his tomb, probably in Exeter Cathedral (D&C 2704/4).

Elyot, William
> Archdeacon of Barnstaple; possibly nephew of the above. Died probably on 18 June 1506 (D&C 3675, f. 2r). A sum of 3s. 4d. was paid to Exeter Cathedral between Michaelmas 1505 and Michaelmas 1506 for lime and sand for his grave, probably in Exeter Cathedral (D&C 2704/5).

Eprestone, Simon de
> Rector of St Olave, Exeter. Died between 30 September and 6 December 1341 (*Reg. Grandisson*, iii, 1332). A sum of 3s. 4d. was paid to Exeter Cathedral between Michaelmas 1341 and Michaelmas 1342 for making his grave in the cloister of the cathedral (Erskine, *Fabric Accounts* ii, 266).

Espicer, Adam (*Ypotecar'*)
> Died by 12 September 1317 (MCR 10–11 Edw II, m. 48). The record

of his funeral in Exeter Cathedral occurs in Midsummer term 1317 (D&C 3764, f. 24v).

Estbroke, Thomas

Subdean of Exeter Cathedral. Died by 28 August 1441 (Le Neve, p. 6). A sum of 26s. 8d. was paid to the cathedral by his executors between Michaelmas 1441 and Michaelmas 1442 for his burial in the cathedral, as conceded by the chapter, plus 3s. 4d. for lime, sand and stones for making his tomb (D&C 2689).

Eston, Agnes

Wife of Thomas Eston. A sum of 26s. 8d. was paid by her husband for her grave in the cathedral, by concession of the chapter, between Michaelmas 1407 and Michaelmas 1408 (D&C 2664). She was buried in the nave of the cathedral by 18 January 1410 (D&C 3550, f. 129v).

Eston, Thomas

Parish of Holy Trinity, Exeter. Citizen of Exeter; husband of Agnes. Died after October 1423. On 18 January 1410 the chapter of Exeter Cathedral gave him permission to make his tomb next to that of his wife in the cathedral, if he died in or near Exeter (D&C 3550, f. 129v). On 16 October 1423 the permission was extended to allow his burial 'in the nave of the church . . . next to the grave or tomb of his wife, formerly deceased and buried in the same'. He paid 26s. 8d. to the cathedral fabric (ibid., f. 152v).

Evelyn, John

Canon of Exeter Cathedral. Died between Michaelmas 1484 and Michaelmas 1485, when the cathedral bells were rung for him (D&C 3779, f. 231r).

Exebrigge, Walter

The bells of Exeter Cathedral were rung for him in Easter term 1396 (D&C 3773, f. 71v).

Fairchild, —

Wife of Thomas Fairchild. The record of her funeral in Exeter Cathedral occurs in Michaelmas term 1311 (D&C 3673, f. 110r).

Fayreman, Thomas

Vicar choral of Exeter Cathedral. His funeral took place in the cathedral on 4 January 1314 (D&C 3764, f. 6r).

Fardeyn, —

Wife of Thomas Fardeyn. Her funeral took place in Exeter Cathedral on 17 May 1315 (D&C 3764, f. 13r).

Faryngdon, George

Rector of Chawleigh (Devon). Died by 15 April 1542 (DRO, Chanter XIV, f. 107v), probably on about 1 April 1542 when the chapter of Exeter Cathedral gave permission for his burial in the cathedral, in return for a payment of 10s. to the fabric (D&C 3552, f. 20v).

Faukun, Hugh

The record of his funeral in Exeter Cathedral occurs in Michaelmas term 1305 (D&C 3673, f. 62r).

Feere

The bells of Exeter Cathedral were rung for him between Michaelmas 1485 and Michaelmas 1486 (D&C 3779, f. 231v).

Feriby, William de

Canon of Exeter Cathedral. Died by 1 November 1392 (Le Neve, p. 38). The cathedral bells were rung for him (D&C 3773, f. 71r).

Ferrour, —

Wife of Thomas Ferrour. On 26 January 1391 the chapter of Exeter Cathedral gave permission to her husband 'to bury the body of his wife' in the cathedral (D&C 3550, f. 71r).

Ferrour, Thomas

A sum of 20d. was received from his executors between Michaelmas 1390 and Michaelmas 1391 for his burial in the cathedral (D&C 2650), and a further sum of £21 6s. 8d. between Michaelmas 1391 and Michaelmas 1392 (ibid., 2651).

Fylham, Amma

Mother of William Fylham (see below) (*Reg. Lacy*, IV, 32). Buried in Exeter Cathedral by 8 October 1435 (ibid.). On 8 June 1436 Roger Bolter, precentor of Exeter Cathedral chose to be buried, if possible, at the foot of her tomb (*Reg. Lacy*, IV, 27).

· Fylham, William

Chancellor of Exeter Cathedral. Died by 11 March 1439 (Le Neve, p. 9). The record of his funeral in the cathedral occurs in Easter term 1439 (D&C 3771). In his will, dated 8 October 1435, he asked to be buried in the cathedral 'next to the grave of my mother' (see above) (*Reg. Lacy*, IV, 32). The identification of his tomb and inscription made by George Oliver (*Lives of the Bishops*, p. 241) is a mistake for that of William Brownyng (see above).

Flower, John (Floure, Flowre)

Canon of Exeter Cathedral. Died by Easter term 1463 (Le Neve, p. 53), when a record occurs of his funeral in the cathedral (D&C 3772). In his will, dated 20 February 1463, he asked to be buried in the cathedral according to the will of his brother canons, and if they so agreed, 'in one side or ambulatory outside the choir (DRO, Chanter XII (i), Reg. Nevill, f. 138r–v).

Fox, John

The record of his funeral in Exeter Cathedral occurs in Easter term 1307 (D&C 3673, f. 75r).

Frank, John

Rector of Peter Tavy (Devon). Died by 19 April 1441 (*Reg. Lacy*, i,

264). Buried in the hospital of St John (DRO, ECA, Book 53A, f. 94v).

Fry, John

Rector of St Mary Arches, Exeter. Died by 19 August 1393 (*Reg. Brant-yngham*, i, 131). The bells of Exeter Cathedral were rung for him in Midsummer term 1393 (D&C 3773, f. 71r).

Fulford, John

Archdeacon of Exeter. Died 19 January 1519 (see below). Buried in Exeter Cathedral; his ledger stone now lies in the retrochoir, with inscription and date (Oliver, *Lives of the Bishops*, p. 242; Hope, Monu-mentarium, p. 53).

Fulford, William

Archdeacon of Barnstaple. Died by 27 October 1475, probably on 24 October, the date of his obit (Exeter Cathedral Library, MS 3508, f. 9v; Le Neve, p. 20). In his will, dated 31 January 1475, he asked to be buried in Exeter Cathedral (PRO, PROB 11/6, f. 196v). Buried in the nave by 18 February 1476, when Canon John Ward (see below) asked permission to be buried next to him (Reg. Booth, f. 51v).

Gabriel, Richard

Canon of Exeter Cathedral. Died by 2 August 1419 (Le Neve, p. 47). The record of his funeral in the cathedral occurs in Midsummer term 1419 (D&C 3770).

Gatepath, Beatrice de

Died and buried, probably in Exeter, by 13 May 1331 when Serlo att Hole promised to pay John Treydeners a debt of 17s. 6d. for wax purchased for her burial (MCR 4–5 Edw III, m. 32d).

Gatepath, William de

Died by 6 December 1316 (MCR 10–11 Edward II, m 10). The record of his funeral in Exeter Cathedral occurs in Michaelmas term 1316 (D&C 3764, f. 21r); his burial in the cathedral is recorded between Michaelmas 1316 and Michaelmas 1317 (Erskine, *Fabric Accounts* i, 73). Between Michaelmas 1324 and Michaelmas 1325 a sum of 6s. 8d. was paid to the cathedral for a stone for his tomb (ibid., p. 155).

Gaudechon, W.

The record of his funeral in Exeter Cathedral occurs in Michaelmas term 1316 (D&C 3764, f. 21r).

Gefferey, Richard

Parish of St George, Exeter. Died by 25 November 1476. In his will, dated 6 April 1472, he asked to be buried in the church of the hospital of St John (MCR 16–17 Edw IV, m. 9). He is not mentioned in the hospital burial list in DRO, ECA, Book 53A, ff. 84v–95r.

Gele, Thomas

Resident in the hospital of St John. Buried in the church there between 1492 and 1530 (DRO, ECA, Book 53A, f. 94v).

Genyan, William

Buried in the hospital of St John between 1520 and 1535 (DRO, ECA, Book 53A, f. 95r).

Germyn, —

Wife of W. Germyn. The record of her funeral in Exeter Cathedral occurs in Michaelmas term 1311 (D&C 3673, f. 108v).

Germeyn, Adam

Rector of St Paul, Exeter. Probably died 9 October 1310 (*Reg. Stapeldon*, p. 216; cf. MCR 4–5 Edw II, m. 2). His funeral in Exeter Cathedral is recorded in Michaelmas term 1310 (D&C 3673, f. 100r).

Germyn, John

Chancellor of Exeter Cathedral. Died between 21 February and 24 June 1460 (Le Neve, p. 9). The record of his funeral in Exeter Cathedral occurs in Easter term 1460 (D&C 3772). A sum of 3s. was paid to the cathedral by his executors between Easter and Michaelmas 1460 for lime, sand and stone, probably to make his tomb in the cathedral (D&C 2702).

Germeyn, Ralph

Precentor of Exeter Cathedral. Died 3 December 1316 (Le Neve, p. 7). His funeral took place in the cathedral on the same day (D&C 3764, f. 21r). A sum of 3s. 8d. for his burial, probably in the cathedral, was paid to the fabric fund between Michaelmas 1316 and Michaelmas 1317 (Erskine, *Fabric Accounts* i, 73). For his possible tomb, see John de Dreyton, above.

Gerveys, —

Wife of. The bells of Exeter Cathedral were rung for her in 1401 (D&C 3773, f. 54v).

Gervas, Nicholas

Married layman. Buried in the cathedral cemetery by 1258 when his son Walter (see below) chose to be buried beside him (D&C VC/3345). This fact casts doubt on the assertion of John Hooker, 1919–47, iii, 602, that he and his wife were buried in the chapel on Exe Bridge.

Gervas, Walter

In his will, dated in the spring of 1257, but possibly more correctly 1258, he asked to be buried in the cathedral cemetery near the body of his father (see above) (D&C VC/3345; see below, p. 140).

Gybbes, Walter

Canon of Exeter Cathedral. Died by 24 May 1413, probably on 14 May (Le Neve, p. 44). In his will, dated 1 February 1412, he asked to be buried in the cathedral 'next to Sir Walter Trote' (see below) (Lambeth Palace Library, Reg. Thomas Arundel, ii, f. 168r). A sum of 18d. was paid for stones for his tomb between Michaelmas 1412 and Michaelmas 1413 (D&C 2668).

Giffard, Aveline
>Lady. The record of her funeral in Exeter Cathedral occurs in Easter term 1327 (D&C 3764, f. 98v).

Gyffard, John
>Apparently of Withycombe Raleigh (Devon). Died not long before November 1492 (see below). The bells of Exeter Cathedral were rung for him between Michaelmas 1487 and Michaelmas 1488 (D&C 3779, f. 231v). In his will, dated 9 November 1487 and proved 3 November 1492, he asked to be buried in Exeter Cathedral (Lambeth Palace Library, Reg. John Morton, i, f. 130r; *Reg. Morton*, ii, 87–8).

Giffard, Walter
>Chancellor of Exeter Cathedral. Died by 14 April 1322 (Le Neve, p. 8). The record of his funeral in the cathedral occurs in Easter term 1322 (D&C 3764, f. 32v).

Gilbert, Richard
>Canon of Exeter Cathedral. Died 11 April 1524, according to his ledger stone in the chapel of St Paul in the cathedral (Hope, Monumentarium, p. 137). Mentioned as buried in the chapel of St Paul by 1543 (D&C 2924).

Gyst, —
>Parish of St Laurence. Wife of Walter Gyst. Buried in the hospital of St John by 1492 (DRO, ECA, Book 53A, f. 94v).

Glasney, John de (de Glason)
>Rector of Clyst St George (Devon), and a past, possibly present, vicar choral of Exeter Cathedral (Orme, *Minor Clergy*, p. 13). Died 22 March 1322 (*Reg. Stapeldon*, p. 202). His funeral was held in the cathedral on 26 March (D&C 3764, f. 32v). Buried in the cathedral by 1331, when John Jackes (see below) asked to be buried near him (Erskine, *Fabric Accounts* ii, 235).

Golde, Adam
>Died by 14 August 1396 (MCR 19–20 Ric II, m. 46); the bells of Exeter Cathedral were rung for him in Easter term 1396 (D&C 3773, f. 71v). A sum of 20s. was paid for his grave in the cathedral between Michaelmas 1395 and Michaelmas 1396 (D&C 2655), and stone was later purchased for his tomb (D&C 2656).

Goodefello, John
>Parish of St Laurence, Exeter. 'Sir', i.e. priest. Buried in the hospital of St John at the end of the church between 1520 and 1535 (DRO, ECA, Book 53A, f. 95).

Goos, Raymond
>Citizen of Exeter; died by 13 April 1394 (MCR 17–18 Ric II, m. 28). The bells of Exeter Cathedral were rung for him in about 1394 (D&C 3773, f. 71r).

Gorgys, Thomas

A sum of 40s. was paid for his tomb in Exeter Cathedral (probably as a licence for burial), and 2s. for stones for the tomb, between Michaelmas 1403 and Michaelmas 1404 (D&C 2662).

Gosse, Nicholas

Chancellor of Exeter Cathedral. Died between Michaelmas 1485 and Michaelmas 1486, when the cathedral bells were rung for him (D&C 3779, f. 231r).

Govys, John

Vicar choral of Exeter Cathedral. Died between 31 March and 15 April 1416 (see below). In his will, dated 31 March 1416, he asked to be buried in the cathedral cemetery (*Reg. Stafford*, p. 415).

Grandisson, John de

Bishop of Exeter. Died 16 July 1369 (Le Neve, p. 1). In his will, dated 8 September 1368, he asked to be buried 'outside the west door of the church of Exeter' (*Reg. Grandisson*, iii, 1549) and gave directions for an inscription on his tomb (ibid., p. 1557). Buried in the chapel immediately outside and on the south side of the main west door (Leland, i, 227; Hope, Monumentarium, p. 151). His monument was removed in the late 16th century.

Grandisson, William de

Archdeacon of Exeter. Died 5 June 1330 (Le Neve, p. 13). The record of his funeral in Exeter Cathedral occurs in Easter term 1330 (D&C 3764, f. 74r).

Grendon, Simon

Citizen of Exeter; his will suggests that he or his ancestors originated in Staffordshire. Died between 30 July and 2 September 1411 (see below). In his will, dated 30 July 1411, he asked to be buried in Exeter Cathedral under the north tower, before the image of the Blessed Mary (*Reg. Stafford*, p. 397).

Grymstone *alias* Bekwyth, Henry

Master of Exeter High School in 1479–80 (Orme, *Minor Clergy*, p. 9). Rector of St Stephen, Exeter, instituted 8 January 1480 (DRO, Chanter XII (ii), Reg. Courtenay, f. 89v). Rector of Chagford and Stoke Fleming (Devon), died by 30 March 1499 (ibid., Reg. Redman, f. 9r). Buried in the Trinity chapel of the hospital of St John (DRO, ECA, Book 53A, f. 94v).

Guscott, —

Husband of Joan Guscott (see below). Buried in the Franciscan Friary, Exeter, by 1508, when his wife asked to be buried beside him.

Guscott, Joan

Widow. In her will, dated 5 September 1508, she asked to be buried in the Franciscan Friary, Exeter, next to her husband (DRO, St Mary Arches Exeter, 332A/PF 248).

Haccombe, —

Son of O. de Haccombe. The record of his funeral in Exeter Cathedral occurs in Midsummer term 1317 (D&C 3764, f. 25r).

Hakeworth

The record of his funeral in Exeter Cathedral occurs in Easter term 1311 (D&C 3673, f. 105r).

Haliburton, Patrick

Canon of Exeter Cathedral. Died by 2 December 1493 (Le Neve, p. 58). A sum of 10d. was paid between Michaelmas 1493 and Michaelmas 1494 for lime and sand and one of 12d. for tile-stones and a marble stone for lying on his tomb (D&C 2704/4).

Hals, Richard

Treasurer of Exeter Cathedral. Died between 1 and 25 May 1417 (Le Neve, p. 11). The record of his funeral in the cathedral occurs in Easter term 1417 (D&C 3770). In his will, dated 1 May 1417, he asked (if he died in Devon or nearby) to be buried in the cathedral 'by the side of the grave of Master William Trevellys, formerly treasurer or Exeter, at the foot of his grave at the entrance to the choir on the north side' (*Reg. Stafford*, pp. 416–17).

Hamlyn, John

On 19 January 1497 the prior of St Nicholas, Exeter, acknowledged the permission granted by the dean and chapter to bury his body in the priory (D&C 2371).

Hamlyn, Nicholas

Parish of St Olave; merchant. In his will, dated 2 October 1504, he asked to be buried in the church of St Nicholas Priory (PRO, PROB 11/14, f. 164r).

Hamm, John

The record of his funeral in Exeter Cathedral occurs in Midsummer term 1316 (D&C 3764, f. 19r).

Hamond, John

Parish of St Kerrian, Exeter. Died by 5 May 1477. In his will, dated 21 April 1474, he asked to be buried in the cathedral cemetery 'on the east and the south side of the chapel called the charnelhouse' (MCR 16–17 Edw IV, m. 32).

Hampton, John

Annuellar of the Grandisson chantry in Exeter Cathedral. Died between 1522 and 1532 (Orme, *Minor Clergy*, p. 78). On 1 March 1522 the chapter of Exeter Cathedral conceded to him a burial place within the cathedral, 'next to the door of the aforesaid church, near the chapel of John de Grandisson'. He promised in return a sum of 13s. 4d. to the canons in residence who would be present at his funeral (D&C 3551, f. 5r).

Hanforth, Henry
>Parish of St Petroc; married layman. Died between 12 December 1492 and 12 January 1493. In his will, dated 12 December 1492 and proved 12 January 1493, he asked to be buried in the cathedral cemetery (Lambeth Palace Library, Reg. John Morton, i, f. 130v; *Reg. Morton*, ii, 89).

Herlewyne, Joan
>Parish of St George, Exeter. Buried in the hospital of St John, 15 August 1457 (DRO, ECA, Book 53A, f. 94v).

Harlewyne, John
>Parish of St George, Exeter. Buried in the hospital of St John by 1492 (DRO, ECA, Book 53, f. 94v).

Harpeton, Thomas de
>Chaplain. The record of his funeral in Exeter Cathedral occurs in Midsummer term 1312 (D&C 3673, f. 114v).

Harrys, John
>Resident in the hospital of St John. Buried there between 1520 and 1535 (DRO, ECA, Book 53A, f. 94v).

Harrys, Thomas
>Precentor of Exeter Cathedral. Died 31 December 1511, according to his ledger stone now in the retrochoir of the cathedral (BL, Add. MS 29931, f. 112; Hope, Monumentarium, p. 49). In his will, dated 1 November 1511, he asked to be buried in the cathedral 'before the image of the Blessed Mary in the south part of the said church' (DRO, Chanter XIII, Reg. Oldham, f. 172r–v). His ledger stone is now close to the wall painting of the Assumption of the Virgin Mary, and probably in or near its original position.

Hawkyn, —
>Wife of Thomas Hawkyn. Buried in the hospital of St John by 1492 (DRO, ECA, Book 53A, f. 94v).

Haydon, Roger de
>The record of his funeral in Exeter Cathedral occurs in Michaelmas term 1305 (D&C 3673, f. 62r).

Helyer, Richard
>Archdeacon of Cornwall. Died 19 December 1446 according to his ledger stone, now in the 4th bay of the north choir aisle (Hope, Monumentarium, p. 36). The record of his funeral in Exeter Cathedral occurs in Christmas term 1446–7 (D&C 3771).

Hendeman, Thomas
>Chancellor of Exeter Cathedral. Died by 23 February 1429 (Le Neve, p. 9). The record of his funeral in the cathedral occurs in Christmas term 1428–9 (D&C 3771).

Henshaw, Nicholas
>Canon of Exeter Cathedral. Died 10 (Le Neve, p. 63), or 14 (Polwhele,

ii, 39) December 1524. His ledger stone, with an inscription, lay in the retrochoir in the 18th century (Polwhele, ii, 39; BL, Add. MS 29931, f. 113; Hope, Monumentarium, p. v, with incorrect year).

Hereward, Robert

Canon of Exeter Cathedral. Died by 15 March 1363 (Le Neve, p. 25). Buried in the cathedral by 21 June 1393 when Archdeacon John Lydford (see below) received permission to be buried at his feet (D&C 3550, f. 89r). Lydford's tomb was stated on 12 March 1407 to be 'on the north side of the choir' (*Reg. Stafford*, p. 389).

Hereward, Thomas de

Archdeacon of Exeter. Died by 25 November 1329 (Le Neve, p. 12). The record of his funeral in Exeter Cathedral occurs in Michaelmas term (by 25 November) 1329 (D&C 3764, f. 71v; *Reg. Grandisson*, iii, 1275).

Hethffeld, —

Parish of St Laurence, Exeter; sister of William Hethffeld. Buried in the hospital of St John by 1492 (DRO, ECA, Book 53A, f. 94v).

Hethman, John

Citizen of Exeter. In his will, dated 20 July 1432, he envisaged his funeral taking place in Exeter Cathedral, but did not specify a place of burial (DRO, ECA, ED/M/733).

Hethman, Roger – see Baker

Hewet, Joan

Wife of Richard Hewet (see below). Buried in the chancel of St Laurence church by 2 March 1520, when her husband Richard requested burial beside her (PRO, PROB 11/19, f. 181r).

Hewet, Richard

Parish of St Laurence, Exeter; citizen and merchant of Exeter. In his will, dated 2 March 1520, he asked to be buried in St Laurence church and bequeathed 6s. 8d. for his 'pit' in the chancel beside Joan, his late wife (PRO, PROB 11/19, f. 81r).

Hewysch

The record of his funeral in Exeter Cathedral occurs in Midsummer term 1324 (D&C 3764, f. 45r).

Hewysch – see also Huesch

Hickelyng, Hugh

Precentor of Exeter Cathedral. Died by 30 January 1416, probably 28 January (Le Neve, p. 7). The record of his funeral in the Cathedral occurs in Easter term 1416 (D&C 3770). In his will, dated 8 August 1415, he asked to be buried in the cathedral 'near the altar of the chantry' of Bishop Brantingham, i.e. near the second bay of the nave on the north side (*Reg. Stafford*, p. 410). A sum of 6s. 8d. was paid for stones for the pavement of his tomb and that of Thomas Barton between Michaelmas 1415 and Michaelmas 1416 (D&C 2671).

Hylle, John
    'Master'. Guest or inmate of the hospital of St John. Buried in the
    hospital church by 1492 (DRO, ECA, Book 53A, f. 94v).

Hylle, Richard
    Prior of the hospital of St John. Died 1524 (Oliver, *Monasticon*, p.
    301). Buried before his stall in the choir of the hospital church (DRO,
    ECA, Book 53A, f. 95r).

Hyngstecote, Christina
    Parish of St Stephen, Exeter. 'Mistress'. Buried in the hospital of St
    John between 1492 and 1520 (DRO, ECA, Book 53A, f. 94v).

Hodell, William (Hodel)
    Parish of St Sidwell, Exeter; married layman. In his will, dated 17
    March 1400, he asked to be buried in the church of the hospital of St
    John (British Library, Add. Charter 27580). Buried in that church by
    1492 (DRO, ECA, Book 53A, f. 94v).

Hoige, Richarda
    Wife of Thomas Hoige; died 1531. Buried beneath a ledger stone in
    the church of St Olave, with an inscription and year date (Cresswell,
    p. 133).

Holebroke, Thomas (Holbrok)
    Died by 26 January 1400 (MCR 1 Hen IV, m. 16). The bells of Exeter
    Cathedral were rung for him in about 1399 (D&C 3773, f. 70r).

Holond, Roger
    Parish of St Thomas, Cowick. In his will, dated 4 September 1506, he
    asked to be buried 'in the guild of St Michael within the parish church
    of St Thomas' (PRO, PROB 11/15, f. 137v).

Homans, Thomas
    Vicar choral of Exeter Cathedral. Died Michaelmas term 1393 (Orme,
    Minor Clergy, p. 20). The bells of the cathedral were rung for him in
    Michaelmas term 1393 (D&C 3773, f. 71r).

Hopton, David
    Archdeacon of Exeter. Died between 17 January and 3 February 1492
    (Le Neve, p. 14). In his will, dated 17 January 1492, he asked to be
    buried in Exeter Cathedral 'next to the gravestone of Master John
    Warde, formerly canon' (PRO, PROB 11/9, f. 60r–v). Mentioned as
    buried in the nave in 1494, when Canon John Coryngdon (see above)
    chose to be buried by him (PRO, PROB 11/10, f. 184r). His ledger
    stone now lies in the 4th bay of the north side of the nave; the incom-
    plete date contains only the figures equivalent to '149' (Hope, Monu-
    mentarium, p. 246).

Horsey, William
    Canon of Exeter Cathedral. Died 10 April 1543 (Le Neve, p. 62). In
    his will, dated 6 June 1531, he asked to be buried in the cathedral

'near the earl's tomb', i.e. near the tomb of the earl and countess of Devon in the second bay of the nave on the south side (PRO, PROB 11/29, f. 198r).

Huddesfeld, Katherine

Lady; widow successively of Thomas Rogers, serjeant of the law, and Sir William Huddesfeld (d. 1499), lord of various manors in Devon. In her will, dated 21 November 1510, she asked to be buried in the Franciscan Friary, Exeter, 'before [the image of] St Francis beside the high altar in the same church' (PRO, PROB 11/18, f. 30v).

Huesch, —

Mother of John Huesch. Buried in the hospital of St John by 1492 (DRO, ECA, Book 53A, f. 94v).

Hull, —

The bells of Exeter Cathedral were rung for him in 1401 (D&C 3773, f. 54v). Possibly identical with Roger atte Hille, died by 29 May 1402 (MCR 3 Hen IV, m. 34).

Hull, —

Wife of Henry Hull. The bells of Exeter Cathedral were rung for her between Michaelmas 1486 and Michaelmas 1487 (D&C 3779, f. 231r).

Hull, Joan

Parish of St Paul, Exeter. Mother of William Hull (see below). Buried in the middle of the church of the hospital of St John, 1535 (DRO, ECA, Book 53A, f. 95r).

Hulle, Denise

First wife of Sir John Hulle (see below). Buried in the hospital of St John some time before his own burial there in about 1416 (DRO, ECA, Book 53A, f. 94v).

Hulle, Sir John (Hille)

Knight; justice of the king's bench. Died by 13 May 1416, when his son John did homage for the family property (DRO, Chanter IX, f. 311r). In his will, dated 2 June 1407, he asked to be buried in the church of the hospital of St John 'next to the gate called *Vestvente*' (PRO, PROB 11/2A, f. 128v). Buried there by 1416 when his second wife, Lady Matilda Latymer (see below), requested burial near him (see also DRO, ECA, Book 53A, f. 94v).

Hull, John

Parish of St Paul, Exeter; 'Master'. Buried in the hospital of St John between 1530 and 1535 (DRO, ECA, Book 53A, f. 95r).

Hull, William

Son of Joan Hull (see above). Buried by the head of his mother in the middle of the church of the hospital of St John, 1535 (DRO, ECA, Book 53A, f. 95r).

Hunden, William

> Canon of Exeter Cathedral. Died between 21 January and 21 February 1416 (Le Neve, p. 46). The record of his funeral in the cathedral occurs in Christmas term 1415–16 (D&C 3770).

Hunte, Thomas

> Alderman and mayor of Exeter; died 15 May 1548. In his will, dated 20 April 1548, he asked to be buried 'within the parish church of St Petroc' if he happened to die in Exeter, and 'that a tombstone now being at my house be laid upon my burial' (PRO, PROB 11/32, f. 80r). Buried in St Petroc, where his ledger stone bore an inscription and the date of his death (Cresswell, p. 153).

Ilminystr', Nicholas de

> The record of his funeral in Exeter Cathedral occurs in Midsummer term 1314 (D&C 3764, f. 8r).

Jakes, John

> Vicar choral of Exeter Cathedral. Died probably between 1331 and 1337 (Orme, *Minor Clergy*, p.14). Between Michaelmas 1330 and Michaelmas 1331 he paid 6s. 8d. to the cathedral for his grave in the cathedral, next to John de Glasney (see above), and 5s. for a marble stone (Erskine, *Fabric Accounts*, ii, 235).

John the Chanter

> Bishop of Exeter. Died 1191, probably on 1 June, the date on which Exeter Cathedral subsequently kept his obit (D&C 3518, f. 24v; 3625, f. iii verso). Buried in the south tower of the cathedral, which later became the south transept (Leland, i, 227). The altar tomb now by the south wall of the transept is more probably his, albeit later than his time, than that of Canon John Michel (see below), because canons were not normally commemorated with such tombs (arguing against Hope, Monumentarium, p. 172).

Jon, Margaret

> Parish of St Mary Major. Widow of John Serle; wife of William Jon, cook, of Exeter. In her will, dated 30 November 1384, she asked to be buried in the cathedral cemetery (D&C VC/3164).

Jugement, Walter

> The record of his funeral in Exeter Cathedral occurs in Easter term 1316 (D&C 3764, f. 17v).

Kamuyle, William de

> 'Sir'; i.e. priest or knight. No doubt a member of the Devon knightly family of Camville. The record of his funeral in Exeter Cathedral occurs in Easter term 1307 (D&C 3673, f. 75r).

Karswylle, Nicholas de

> The record of his funeral in Exeter Cathedral occurs in Midsummer term 1306 (D&C 3673, f. 68v).

Kelbryg, —

Wife of Kelbryg. The bells of Exeter Cathedral were rung for her in about 1399 (D&C 3773, f. 70r).

Kelly, John (Kylly)

Probably parish of St Petroc, Exeter. Died between 16 November 1486 and 3 December 1487. In his will, dated 16 November 1486, he asked to be buried 'in the south part of the guild [i.e. probably aisle] of the parish church of St Petroc (MCR 3–4 Hen VII, m. 10). The bells of Exeter Cathedral were rung for him between Michaelmas 1486 and Michaelmas 1487 (D&C 3779, f. 231r), and again for him (or for another John Kelly) between Michaelmas 1488 and Michaelmas 1489 (ibid., f. 231v).

Kerdewelle, —

Wife of Kerdewelle. The record of her funeral in Exeter Cathedral occurs in Midsummer term 1305 (D&C 3673, f. 59v).

Keys, Roger

Precentor of Exeter Cathedral. Died 5 November 1477 (Exeter Cathedral Library, MS 3508, f. 10r; Le Neve, p. 8). Possibly buried in the chapel of St Paul in the cathedral, where he established a chantry for his soul on 20 June 1472 (D&C 2367).

Kilkenny, Andrew de

Dean of Exeter Cathedral. Died 4 November 1302 (Le Neve, p. 3). Probably buried in the chapel of St Andrew in the cathedral, where a chantry was established for his soul on 30 August 1305 (D&C 1927) and where his probable ledger stone now lies (Hope, 1964, pp. 102–6; Hope, Monumentarium, p. 135).

Kilkenny, William de

Canon of Exeter Cathedral. Died by 6 May 1329 (Le Neve, p. 23). The record of his funeral in the cathedral occurs in Easter term 1329 (D&C 3764, f. 68r).

Kyrke, Giles

Citizen and merchant of Exeter. In his will, dated 12 March 1546, he asked to be buried 'under the foot of [the image of] Our Lady at the side aisle in St Mary Arches church, and there to have a tomb upon my grave, if it fortune me to die within the city [of Exeter]' (PRO, PROB 11/31, f. 41r–v).

Kirkeby, Thomas

Treasurer of Exeter Cathedral. Died between 8 and 10 December 1476 (Le Neve, p. 11). In his will, dated 7 October 1474, he asked to be buried in the cathedral (PRO, PROB 11/6, f. 218v). His tomb is mentioned in 1509 when Thomas Austell, also treasurer, chose to be buried next to him (PRO, PROB 11/18, f. 58r–v). Austell's ledger stone now lies in the 5th bay of the north choir aisle (see above).

Knollys, Robert

'Sir'; probably priest. Perhaps identical with the rector of St Mellion (Cornwall), instituted 13 October 1457, resigned 1462 (DRO, Chanter XII (i), ff. 6r, 17r). The bells of Exeter Cathedral were rung for him between Michaelmas 1486 and Michaelmas 1487 (D&C 3779, f. 231r).

Knovile, John de

Canon of Exeter Cathedral. Died in August 1322 (Le Neve, p. 23). The record of his funeral in the cathedral occurs in Midsummer term 1322 (D&C 3764, f. 34r).

Kokel, John

Brother of the hospital of St John. Buried by the altar of St John Baptist in the hospital church between 1520 and 1535 (DRO, ECA, Book 53A, f. 95r).

Laci, —

The record of his funeral in Exeter Cathedral occurs in Michaelmas term 1330 (D&C 3764, f. 75v).

Lacy, Edmund

Bishop of Exeter. Died 18 September 1455 (Le Neve, p. 2). Buried in the second bay on the north side of the choir of Exeter Cathedral in an altar tomb, formerly bearing a brass indent depicting an effigy of a bishop surrounded by a rectangular inscription plate (Hope, Monumentarium, p. 4). The brass was defaced in about 1538 by Dean Heynes (Leland, i, 227). For his claim to be the person commemorated in the cadaver monument in that aisle, see Orme, 1996, pp. 12–17.

Lacy, Philip

Brother of Bishop Lacy, and a married esquire of his household. Died not long before 11 February 1445 (D&C 764). His tomb in the cathedral is mentioned in association with that of Edmund Lacy on 2 May 1499 (D&C 2395), and is likely to have been situated in the north choir aisle. For his claim to be the person commemorated in the cadaver monument in that aisle, see Orme, 1996, pp. 12–17.

Lane, Jordan de la (Venell')

Died by 27 January 1314 (MCR 8–9 Edw II, m. 18) The record of his funeral in Exeter Cathedral occurs in Christmas term 1314–15 (D&C 3764, f. 11v).

Langeden, W. de

The record of his funeral in Exeter Cathedral occurs in Midsummer term 1312 (D&C 3673, f. 113v).

Langrigg, Walter (Langrygge)

Vicar choral of Exeter Cathedral (Orme, *Minor Clergy*, p. 20). Died Easter term 1394, when the bells of Exeter Cathedral were rung for him (D&C 3773, f. 71r).

Langton, William

Canon of Exeter Cathedral; relative of Bishop Stafford. Died 29 January 1414 (see below). In his will, dated 29 January 1414, he asked to be buried in the cathedral, either on the right or on the left of Stafford's tomb (*Reg. Stafford*, p. 404). Buried on the north side of the tomb, in the chapel of St John Evangelist, where his ledger stone and brass indent survive, with an inscription and date (Hope, Monumentarium, p. 117).

Latoun, Roger

The record of his funeral in Exeter Cathedral occurs in Easter term 1310 (D&C 3673, f. 97v).

Latymer, Matilda

Lady; widow first of Sir John Hulle (see above) and second of Sir Robert Latimer. In her will, dated 21 April 1416, she asked to be buried in the church of the hospital of St John near the grave of Hulle (*Reg. Stafford*, p. 415). Her burial in the church is recorded in 1492 (DRO, ECA, Book 53A, f. 94v).

Law, Joan

Parish of St Stephen, Exeter. Widow first of Thomas Law (see below) and later of 'Mr [Benedict?] Drew'. Buried in the hospital of St John by 1492 (DRO, ECA, Book 53A, f. 94v).

Law, Thomas

Parish of St Laurence, Exeter. Husband of Joan (see above), whom he predeceased. Buried in the hospital of St John by 1492 (DRO, ECA, Book 53A, f. 94v).

Laurauns, Richard

Rector of St Stephen, Exeter, collated 1392 (*Reg. Brantyngham*, i, 119). The bells of Exeter Cathedral were rung for him in Easter term 1394 (D&C 3773, f. 71r).

Lawrens, Robert

Prior of the hospital of St John from 1524 to before 1534 (Oliver, *Monasticon*, p. 301). Buried in the chapter house of the hospital in 1535 (DRO, ECA, Book 53A, f. 95r).

Leche, William

Parish of St Paul, Exeter; 'Master'. Buried in the hospital of St John by 1492 (DRO, ECA, Book 53A, f. 94v).

Lechlade, Thomas de

Dean of Exeter Cathedral. Died 15 April 1309 (Le Neve, p. 4). His funeral took place in the cathedral on 16 April (D&C 3673, f. 90r).

Lechlade, Walter de

Precentor of Exeter Cathedral. Died 9 November 1283 (the date of his cathedral obit: D&C 3625, f. vi recto; 3675, f. 31r), or the 10th (Rose-Troup, 1942, p. 45). Mentioned on 30 December 1292 as buried opposite the altar of St Edmund the Confessor in the cathedral (D&C 1930).

Leofric

> Bishop of Exeter. Died 10 February 1072; buried in the first, Saxon, building of Exeter Cathedral (Barlow, p. 13). His body was transferred from this to the Norman cathedral in the time of Bishop William Warelwast (1107–37), probably in 1133 (Chambers, 1933, p. 50 (f. 5v)). A sum of 20d. was paid by the cathedral between 8 May and 29 September 1418 for 'writing on the stone of Lord Leofric, first bishop of Exeter Cathedral' (D&C 2672). For possible identifications of his tomb, see Hope, Monumentarium, pp.109, 133.

Le Archedeakene, —

> A sum of 5s. for his or her tomb was paid to the fabric fund of Exeter Cathedral between Michaelmas 1316 and Michaelmas 1317 (Erskine, *Fabric Accounts*, i, 72). None of the archdeacons of Exeter diocese died at this time, so the reference is to a member of the Lercedekne family.

Lercedekne, Elizabeth

> Haccombe (Devon). Lady; widow of Sir Warin Lercedekne. In her will, dated 12 December 1406, she asked to be buried in the choir of the Dominican Friary nearest to the place of her death; this may well have been at Exeter (*Reg. Stafford*, p. 388).

Lerchedekne, Joan

> Parish of St Laurence, Exeter. Lady. Buried in the hospital of St John by 1492 (DRO, ECA, Book 53A, f. 94v).

Lercedekne, Martin

> Canon of Exeter Cathedral. Died 4 April 1433, according to his ledger stone now in the chapel of St Gabriel (Hope, Monumentarium, p. 128, correcting Le Neve, p. 42). On 25 March 1411 the cathedral chapter granted him permission to be buried before the altar of St Gabriel in the cathedral (D&C 3550, f. 120v). In his will, dated 5 June 1430, he asked to be buried 'in the chapel of St Gabriel ... as was otherwise conceded to me and registered in the [cathedral] exchequer, if it happens to me to die in the city [of Exeter] or nearby (*Reg. Chichele*, ii, 476). The record of his funeral in the cathedral occurs in Easter term 1433 (D&C 3771).

Lercedekne, Michael

> Treasurer of Exeter Cathedral. Died between 5 and 20 January 1442 (Le Neve, p. 11). In his will, dated 5 January 1442, he asked to be buried in the cathedral 'before the door of the chapel of the Blessed Virgin Mary ... or as near to the door of the same as may honestly be done' (*Reg. Lacy*, IV, 37–8). The record of his funeral in the cathedral occurs in Christmas term 1441–2 (D&C 3771). Between Michaelmas

1441 and Michaelmas 1442 the his executors paid the cathedral 4s. for stones and 1s. 8d. for lime and sand for making his tomb in the cathedral (D&C 2689).

Archedekene, Richard

Died by 21 March 1306 (MCR 33–34 Edw I, m. 25). The record of his funeral in Exeter Cathedral occurs in Christmas term 1305–6 (D&C 3673, f. 65v).

Lercedekne, —

Wife of Sir Thomas Lercedekne. The record of her funeral in Exeter Cathedral occurs in Midsummer term 1316 (D&C 3764, f. 20r).

Levenaunt, Walter

Canon of Exeter Cathedral. Died by 1 November 1404 (Le Neve, p. 39). On 23 June 1385 the cathedral chapter gave him licence to have his grave next to John More (see below), i.e. in the cathedral nave (D&C 3550, f. 14r). See also above: Walter Cullompton.

Lewer, Robert (Lywer)

Canon of Exeter Cathedral. Died 20 September 1444, according to his ledger stone formerly in the north transept of the cathedral but not now extant (Oliver, *Lives of the Bishops*, p. 241; Hope, Monument-arium, p. vi). The record of his funeral in the cathedral occurs in Midsummer term 1444 (D&C 3771).

Lydford, John

Archdeacon of Totnes. Died by 13 December 1407 (Le Neve, p. 18). On 21 June 1393 the chapter of Exeter Cathedral conceded him a tomb at the feet of Canon Robert Hereward (see above) (D&C 3550, f. 89r). In his will, dated 12 March 1407, he asked to be buried in the cathedral 'on the north side of the choir in the place chosen by me' and assigned to him by the chapter (*Reg. Stafford*, p. 389).

Lyf, Joan – see More

Lyf, Richard

Buried before the font in the bell-tower of the church of St Mary Major before 1406, when his widow Joan atte More (see below) asked to be buried in the same tomb (DRO, 51/1/3/8).

Lymmer, Andrew (Lymmere)

Died by 25 April 1401 (MCR 2 Hen IV, m. 30). The bells of Exeter Cathedral were rung for him in 1401 (D&C 3773, f. 54v).

Lympeny, John

'Master'; mayor of Exeter. Buried before the altar of St Katherine in the hospital of St John between 1520 and 1535 (DRO, ECA, Book 53A, f. 95v).

Lingham, Robert

Rector of St Mary Major, Exeter. Died between 6 March (see below) and 29 June 1428 (*Reg. Lacy*, i, 111). In his will, dated 6 March 1428, he asked to be buried 'before the altar of the Blessed Appollonia, virgin and martyr, in the bell-tower of the said church [of St Mary Major] in the tomb which has been made ready for me for a long while' (*Reg. Lacy*, IV, 12).

Loue, W. le

Master. His funeral took place in Exeter Cathedral on 22 February 1315 (D&C 3764, f. 12r). Compare Walter le Wolf (possibly alias le Lowe), rector of Kentisbury 1312–14 (*Reg. Stapeldon*, p. 225).

Lovecok, —

Wife of. The record of her funeral in Exeter Cathedral occurs in Michaelmas term 1311 (D&C 3673, f. 109v).

Lovecok, —

Wife of Philip Lovecok (see below). Her funeral took place in Exeter Cathedral on 19 May 1314 (D&C 3764, f. 7v).

Lovecok, Philip

His funeral took place in Exeter Cathedral on 4 November 1315 (D&C 3764, f. 16r).

Lovecock, Walter

The record of his funeral in Exeter Cathedral occurs in Midsummer term 1316 (D&C 3764, f. 18v).

Lug, John

Brother of the hospital of St John. Buried in the chapter house of the hospital between 1520 and 1535 (DRO, ECA, Book 53A, f. 95).

Lusquyt, John

Rector of St Kerrian, Exeter. Died by 14 December 1398 (*Reg. Stafford*, p. 171; cf. MCR 1 Hen IV, m. 5). On 28 October 1391 the chapter of Exeter Cathedral licensed him to have his grave in the cathedral when he died, on payment of 20s. (D&C 3550, f. 75v). The bells of the cathedral were rung for him in 1399 (D&C 3773, f. 70r), and the sum of 2s. was paid for stone for his tomb between Michaelmas 1397 and Michaelmas 1398 (D&C 2657).

Lusquyt, Thomas (Losquyt)

Parish of St Edmund, Exeter; priest. Chantry priest of the chapel of the Virgin Mary on Exe Bridge, appointed 1403 (DRO, ED/M/572); executor of the will of Walter Trote, canon of Exeter Cathedral, dated 1404 (DRO, Chanter VIII, f. 303r). Buried in the hospital of St John by 1492 (DRO, ECA, Book 53A, f. 94v).

Manchester, Richard

Canon of Exeter Cathedral and of Crantock College (Cornwall). Died on the 20th day of an unknown month in 1541, perhaps October, according to his ledger stone in the 6th bay of the nave (Hope, *Monumentarium*, p. 243). Dead by 12 November 1541 (DRO, Chanter XIV, f. 106r, 107r; cf. Le Neve, p. 65).

Manscombe, —

Parish of St Stephen, Exeter. Wife of John Manscombe (see below). Buried in the hospital of St John by 1492 (DRO, ECA, Book 53A, f. 94v).

Manscombe, John

Parish of St Stephen, Exeter. Buried in the hospital of St John by 1492 (DRO, ECA, Book 53A, f. 94v).

Marchont, Robert le

The record of his funeral in Exeter Cathedral occurs in Easter term 1310 (D&C 3673, f. 97r).

Marshal, Henry

Bishop of Exeter. Died 1206, probably on 26 October, the date on which Exeter Cathedral subsequently kept his obit (D&C 3625, f. v verso). Buried, by the sixteenth century, in an altar tomb with an effigy on the north side of the cathedral presbytery (Leland, i, 227; Hope, *Monumentarium*, pp. 4, 27).

Marescall, Roger le

The record of his funeral in Exeter Cathedral occurs in Midsummer term 1316 (D&C 3764, f. 19v).

Mareys, W.

The record of his funeral in Exeter Cathedral occurs in Midsummer term 1316 (D&C 3764, f. 18v).

Martyn, H.

Son of W. Martyn. His funeral took place in Exeter Cathedral on 26 June 1316 (D&C 3764, f. 18v).

Martyn, Richard

Canon of Exeter Cathedral. Died in Christmas term 1462–3, when the record of his funeral in the cathedral occurs in its records (Le Neve, p.52; D&C 3772). In his will, dated 31 July 1461, he asked to be buried in the cathedral 'before the images of the Blessed Mary and St Peter the Apostle in the north part of the nave of the said church' (DRO, Chanter XII (i), Reg. Nevill, f. 137v).

Martyn, Eleanor

Née Mohun; wife of Sir William Martyn (see below). Buried in the Dominican Friary, Exeter, by 20 May 1329, when an arrangement was made for candles to burn on 3 February, the anniversary of her death (*Reg. Grandisson*, i, 497).

Martyn, William

Knight; husband of Eleanor (see above). Buried in the Dominican Friary, Exeter, by 20 May 1329, when an arrangement was made for candles to burn on 26 November, the anniversary of his death (*Reg. Grandisson*, i, 497).

Matthew
> Rector of St Leonard, Exeter. The record of his funeral in Exeter Cathedral occurs in Easter term 1308 (D&C 3673, f. 82v).

Maye, Joan
> Buried before the high altar of the church of the hospital of St John between 1520 and 1535 (DRO, ECA, Book 53A, f. 95r).

May, John
> Resident in the infirmary of the hospital of St John. Buried at the end of the hospital church on the south side (DRO, ECA, Book 53A, f. 95r).

Mayer, Thomas
> Parish of Iddesleigh (Devon). Buried in the hospital of St John by 1492 (DRO, ECA, Book 53A, f. 94v).

Maynard, John
> Merchant of Exeter. In his will, dated 4 December 1546, he asked to be buried 'within the parish church of St Mary Arches... in the chapel of the Holy Trinity' (PRO, PROB 11/31, f. 244v).

Maynwaryng, Nicholas
> Canon of Exeter Cathedral. Died 15 January 1537 (Le Neve, p. 64). In his will, dated 7 December 1536, he asked to be buried 'between the two pillars nigh and beneath th'earl of Devonshire's tomb', i.e. in the vicinity of the second bay of the arcade on the south side of the nave, where the Courtenay tomb and chantry stood (PRO, PROB 11/27, ff. 45v–46r).

Meler, Luke le
> The record of his funeral in Exeter Cathedral occurs in Midsummer term 1305 (D&C 3673, f. 59v).

Membury, Simon de
> Annuellar of the Winkleigh chantry, Exeter Cathedral, till 1309 (*Reg. Stapeldon*, p. 270). His funeral took place in the cathedral on 29 August 1320 (D&C 3764, f. 25r).

Meriet, Walter
> Chancellor of Exeter Cathedral. Died on, or his funeral in the cathedral took place on, 18 May 1345 (D&C 3765).

Merle, Alexander
> The bells of Exeter Cathedral were rung for him in Easter term 1393 (D&C 3773, f. 71r).

Merton, Guy de
> Augustinian canon and prior of Bodmin, Cornwall. Died in Exeter 15 May 1124. His funeral was held in Exeter Cathedral on the following day, and his body was probably buried at Bodmin later (M.L. Colker, 'The Life of Guy of Merton by Rainald of Merton', *Mediaeval Studies*, 31 (1969), pp. 260–1; *The Heads of Religious Houses, England and*

Wales, I: 940–1216, ed. D. Knowles, C.N.L. Brooke, and Vera M. London, 2nd ed. (Cambridge, 2001), p. 276).

Michel, John

Canon of Exeter Cathedral. Died by 20 September 1397 (Le Neve, p. 43). A record of the bells of the cathedral being rung for him occurs in Michaelmas term 1397 (D&C 3773, f. 70r); stone was sold for his tomb between Michaelmas 1396 and Michaelmas 1397 (D&C 2656). At Michaelmas 1398 the cathedral fabric accounts record the building of 'a base for the image of [St] Michael, placed on the wall next to the tomb of Sir John Michel', probably in the south-east corner of the south tower (D&C 2657). The altar tomb now by the south wall of the transept is less probably his, than that of Bishop John the Chanter (see above), because canons were not normally commemorated with such tombs (arguing against Hope, Monumentarium, p. 172).

Mylle, Richard

Parish of St Stephen. Buried in the hospital of St John by 1492 (DRO, ECA, Book 53A, f. 94v).

Mogryche, John (Mogrigge)

Canon of Exeter Cathedral. Died 28 June 1524, according to his ledger stone now in the 1st bay of the nave on the south side (Hope, Monumentarium, p. 254a). In his will, dated 27 June 1524, he asked to be buried in the cathedral (PRO, PROB 11/21, f. 182v; D&C 2418). Said in about the1530s to have been buried near the tomb of Hugh Courtenay (see above), earl of Devon (D&C 2924), which was also on the south side of the nave.

Molton, Roger de

Canon of Exeter Cathedral. Died in January 1307, when a record occurs of his funeral in the cathedral (D&C 3673, f. 72v).

Molyneux, Henry

Canon of Exeter Cathedral. Died between 4 and 12 March 1490 (Le Neve, p. 57). In his will, dated 4 March 1490, he asked to be buried before the image of St Michael (in the south tower) if possible, or else before the image of St Christopher (location unknown) (PRO, PROB 11/8, f. 359r–v). The bells of Exeter Cathedral were rung for him between Michaelmas 1489 and Michaelmas 1490 (D&C 3779, f. 231v).

More, Joan atte

Widow of Richard Lyf (see above), later married to Richard atte More. In her will, dated 30 January 1406, she asked to be buried before the font in the bell-tower of the church of St Mary Major in the grave of Richard Lyf (DRO, 51/1/3/8).

More, John

Rector of St Petroc, Exeter. Died by 20 October 1386 (*Reg. Brant-*

yngham, ii, 628–9). On 23 June 1385 the chapter of Exeter Cathedral licensed him to be buried 'in the middle of the church . . . that is to say in the nave' (D&C 3550, f. 14r). A sum of 5s. was paid for stones for his grave between Michaelmas 1386 and July 1387 (D&C 2646). Buried in the cathedral by 1393, when the chapter licensed Walter Cullompton (see above) to be buried on the north side of his tomb (D&C 3550, f. 89r).

More, John
   A sum of 11d. was paid for stone, lime and sand for his tomb in Exeter Cathedral between Michaelmas 1513 and Michaelmas 1514 (D&C 2704/7).

More, Richard
   Treasurer of Exeter Cathedral. Died 20 February 1517, according to his ledger stone now in the retrochoir of the cathedral (Oliver, *Lives of the Bishops*, p. 242; Hope, Monumentarium, p. 48).

Morewell, Ralph
   Canon of Exeter Cathedral. Died by 20 March 1465 (Le Neve, p. 52). Money was paid by his executors for tile, lime and sand, probably for making his grave in the cathedral, between Michaelmas 1464 and Michaelmas 1465 (D&C 2704).

Morton, John (Bovy)
   Canon of Exeter Cathedral. Died by Michaelmas term 1459 (Le Neve, p. 49). In his will, dated 9 September 1457, he asked to be buried in the cathedral 'in the ambulatory on the north side of the choir before the image of the crucifix depicted there' (DRO, Chanter XII (i), Reg. Nevill, f. 139r–v).

Moset, —
   The record of his funeral in Exeter Cathedral occurs in Midsummer term 1316 (D&C 3764, f. 19r).

Mounteyn, —
   Father of William Mounteyn (see below). Buried probably in the cathedral cemetery by 1349, when his son requested burial in his grave.

Mounteyn, William
   In his will, dated 3 May 1349, he asked to be buried 'in the [probably cemetery] of St Peter of Exeter' in the grave where his father lay (D&C 2232).

Muelis, Matilda
   Lady; wife of Sir John de Muelis (Moelis), knight. The record of her funeral in Exeter cathedral occurs in Midsummer term 1309 (D&C 3673, f. 93v).

Mugge, William
   Canon of Exeter Cathedral. Died by 9 June 1381 (Le Neve, p. 34). In his will, dated 15 April 1380, he asked to be buried either in the Chapel

Royal at Windsor, Berks., or in Exeter Cathedral (Lambeth Palace Library, Reg. Courtenay, ff. 201v–202r).

Nans, John

Canon of Exeter Cathedral. Died by 17 September 1508 (Le Neve, p. 60). In his will, dated 31 July 1507, he asked to be buried in the cathedral (PRO, PROB 11/16, f. 63v). Buried there by 1517, when Thomas Tomyowe (see below) asked for burial next to him (PRO, PROB 11/19, f. 71r–v).

Nassington, William de

Canon of Exeter Cathedral. Died 19 June 1359 (Le Neve, p. 27). The record of his funeral in the cathedral occurs in Easter term 1359 (D&C 37

Nave, John

Master; perhaps a layman, as no such cleric is known. A sum of 7s. 5d. was paid for stone for his grave, probably in Exeter Cathedral or its cemetery, between Michaelmas 1507 and Michaelmas 1508 (D&C 2704/6).

Nelme, William

'Sir'; probably priest. Very likely identical with the rector of Clyst Hydon (Devon), previously rector of Roche (Cornwall), instituted on 8 May 1475 (DRO, Chanter XII (ii), Reg. Bothe, f. 34v). The bells of Exeter Cathedral were rung for him between Michaelmas 1486 and Michaelmas 1487 (D&C 3779, f. 231r). Within the same period the cathedral received a sum of 53s. 4d. as a bequest by him for licence for his burial, probably inside the cathedral (ibid., f. 5r), and 5s. 8d. was paid for lime, sand, stones, and tile for marking his tomb (D&C 2704/3).

Newant, —

Buried in the hospital of St John by 1492 (DRO, ECA, Book 53A, f. 94v).

Newcourt, John

Buried before the high cross in the church of the hospital of St John between 1520 and 1535 (DRO, ECA, Book 53A, f. 95r).

Neweton, —

Son of Robert de Neweton. The record of his funeral in Exeter Cathedral occurs in Easter term 1307 (D&C 3673, f. 74r).

Nymet, Alice

Of Exeter. Apparently buried in or near Exeter Cathedral between Michaelmas 1411 and Michaelmas 1412 (D&C 2667). Between Michaelmas 1412 and Michaelmas 1413 her executor Richard Bosoun owed the cathedral a sum of 20s. for her tomb, part or all of which was probably in return for permission for her burial (D&C 2668).

Nymeton, — (Nyweton?)

Two children of Robert de Nymeton (or Nyweton?) The record of their funerals in Exeter Cathedral occurs in Christmas term 1305–6 (D&C 3673, f. 65v). A Robert de Nywton died in 1311 (MCR 4–5 Edw II, m. 46).

Norbroke, John

Parish of St Sidwell, Exeter. Buried with his wife Margaret (see below) in one grave in the hospital of St John between 1520 and 1535 (DRO, ECA, Book 53A, f. 95r).

Norbroke, Margaret

Parish of St Sidwell, Exeter. Buried with her husband John (see above) in one grave in the hospital of St John between 1520 and 1535 (DRO, ECA, Book 53A, f. 95r).

Norrys, Alice

Parish of St Laurence, Exeter. Buried in the hospital of St John between 1492 and 1530 (DRO, ECA, Book 53A, f. 94v).

Norton, Richard

Precentor of Exeter Cathedral. Died by 24 February 1524 (Le Neve, p. 8). In his will, dated 5 August 1523, he asked to be buried 'where it pleases God, but if I die in Exeter I wish to be buried in the wall of the chapel of St Mary of the [cathedral] church of Exeter in a place where no image or other burial or enclosure is found. And that provision be made for a marble stone in which a memorial may be made of my name and my titles with all things belonging to my dignity in the same church, together with the coats of arms belonging to each of my parents' (DRO, Chanter XIV, ff. 31v–32r).

Obeley, Elizabeth

Parish of St George, Exeter. Daughter of William (and probably Willmot) Obeley (see below). Buried in the hospital of St John between 1492 and 1520 (DRO, ECA, Book 53A, f. 94v).

Obeley, William

Parish of St Mary Arches, Exeter; citizen and merchant. Father of Elizabeth (see above) and wife of Willmot (see below). In his will, dated 29 May 1505, he asked to be buried in the church of the hospital of St John 'before the image of St Michael the Archangel' (MCR 2–3 Hen VIII, m. 26). Buried in the hospital between then and 1520, probably by 1511 (DRO, ECA, Book 53A, f. 94v).

Obeley, Willmot

Wife of William and probably mother of Elizabeth Obeley (see above). Buried in the hospital of St John between 1492 and 1520 (DRO, ECA, Book 53A, f. 94v).

Obelyn, —

The record of his funeral in Exeter Cathedral occurs in Midsummer term 1314 (D&C 3764, f. 8v).

Oke, Alice

Née Westcote. Sister of John Westcote, canon of Exeter Cathedral, and wife of William Oke (see below). Died 1415 (D&C 3550, f. 95v). On 1 November 1391 the cathedral chapter licensed William and Alice Oke to be buried in the cathedral in return for a fee of 40s.; a further sum of 6s. 8d. for the privilege was paid on behalf of Alice in 1415 (ibid., ff. 75v, 95v).

Oke, William

Husband of Alice Oke (see above). Died by 22 June 1416 (MCR 3–4 Hen V, m. 38). On 1 November 1391 the cathedral chapter licensed William and Alice Oke to be buried in the cathedral in return for a fee of 40s. (D&C 3550, ff. 75v, 95v). The tomb is described as recently made on 20 July 1411 when Canon John Westcote, Oke's brother-in-law, asked to be buried next to it (*Reg. Stafford*, p. 418).

Oldham, Hugh

Bishop of Exeter. Died 25 June 1519 (Le Neve, p. 3). In his will, dated 16 December 1518, he asked to be buried in the south part of the cathedral 'in the chapel that I have caused to be made in the honour of my lord God and Saviour', i.e. the chapel of St Saviour in the retrochoir (PRO, PROB 11/19, ff. 147v–148r). Buried there by about 1540 (Leland, i, 227; Hope, Monumentarium, p. 131).

*Oldland, Robert de (*Veteri Terra*)

Canon of Exeter Cathedral. Died by 17 February 1308 (Le Neve, p. 22). The record of his funeral in Exeter Cathedral occurs in Christmas term 1307–8 (D&C 3673, f. 81v).

Olneye, Th. de

The record of his funeral in Exeter Cathedral occurs in Michaelmas term 1323 (D&C 3764, f. 41r).

Oliver, John

Master. Prior of the hospital of St John. Died 1497 (Oliver, *Monasticon*, p. 301). Buried in the chapter house of the hospital (DRO, ECA, Book 53A, f. 95r).

Ordgar

Ealdorman. Died in the early or mid 11th century. Said to have been buried in Exeter (H.P.R. Finberg, 'The House of Ordgar and the Foundation of Tavistock Abbey', *English Historical Review*, 58 (1943), p. 191).

Orum, John

Chancellor of Exeter Cathedral. Died between 16 August and 21 September 1436 (Le Neve, p. 9). In his will, dated 16 August 1436, he asked to be buried in the north porch of the cathedral (*Reg. Lacy*, IV, 24). The record of his funeral in Exeter Cathedral occurs in Michaelmas term 1436 (D&C 3771).

Osbern

> Bishop of Exeter. Died 1103. Buried in Exeter Cathedral; his body was transferred from the Saxon to the new Norman building in the time of Bishop William Warelwast (1107–37), probably in 1133 (Chambers, 1933, p. 50 (f. 5v)).

Otery, H. de

> The record of his funeral in Exeter Cathedral occurs in Michaelmas term 1321 (D&C 3764, f. 31v).

Otery, Roger de

> Chancellor of Exeter Cathedral. Died by 2 December 1314, when his funeral took place in the cathedral (D&C 3764, f. 10v).

Otery, Walter de

> The record of his funeral in Exeter Cathedral occurs in Midsummer term 1311 (D&C 3673, f. 107r).

Oxton

> The record of this person's funeral in Exeter Cathedral occurs in Easter term 1324 (D&C 3764, f. 44r).

Oxton, John de

> Vicar choral of Exeter Cathedral (Orme, *Minor Clergy*, p.14). Died by 13 November 1315, when his funeral took place in the cathedral (D&C 3764, f. 16r).

Page, Margery

> Parish of St Sidwell, Exeter. Buried in the hospital of St John between 1492 and 1530 (DRO, ECA, Book 53A, f. 94v).

Palmer, John

> Of Exeter, baker. Died between 26 October and 18 November 1487 (see below). In his will, dated 26 October 1487, he asked to be buried in the church of the Holy Trinity (DRO, Holy Trinity Exeter, 1718A add./PFW 1–2).

Parchemyner, Roger

> The record of his funeral in Exeter Cathedral occurs in Christmas term 1310–11 (D&C 3673, f. 103r).

Paris, Maior (Parys)

> Canon of Exeter Cathedral. Died 8 July 1438 according to his ledger stone now in the 3rd bay of the north choir aisle (Hope, Monumentarium, p. 40, where the month is given inaccurately as June). In his will, dated 8 July 1438, he asked to be buried in the cathedral (*Reg. Lacy*, IV, 33). The record of his funeral in the cathedral occurs in Midsummer term 1438 (D&C 3771).

Parke, John

> Canon of Exeter Cathedral. Died by 28 September 1422 (Le Neve, p. 45). The record of his funeral occurs in Christmas term 1422–3, possibly in the cathedral (D&C 3770).

Parker, Thomas
Parish of Holy Trinity, Exeter. In his will, dated 6 September 1506, he asked to be buried in the Franciscan Friary, Exeter, 'before the image of Our Lady in the body [i.e. nave] of the church there' (PRO, PROB 11/15, f. 188v).

Parkhouse, William
Canon of Exeter Cathedral. Died 1 March 1541 (see below). His ledger stone formerly lay in the chapel of St Andrew in the cathedral (Oliver, *Lives of the Bishops*, p. 242; Hope, Monumentarium, p. v).

Pascow, John
Canon of Exeter Cathedral. Died between 8 February and 11 March 1494 (Le Neve, p. 58). In his will, dated 8 February 1494, he asked to be buried in the cathedral 'before the image of St Michael the archangel in the south part of the same', i.e. in the south-east corner of the south tower (PRO, PROB 11/10, ff. 115v–116r).

Paston, Benedict de
Canon of Exeter Cathedral. Died by 25 October 1330 (Le Neve, p. 26). Possibly given a funeral and buried in the cathedral; the value of his palfrey was given to the canons of the cathedral in Christmas term 1330–1 (D&C 3764, f. 78r).

Payne, Michael
Parish of St Laurence, Exeter; shoemaker. Buried in the hospital of St John between 1520 and 1535 (DRO, ECA, Book 53A, f. 95r).

Pencryche, William
Canon of Exeter Cathedral. Died by 10 September 1446 (Le Neve, p. 49). The record of his funeral in the cathedral occurs in Midsummer term 1446 (D&C 3771).

Penels, Richard
Archdeacon of Cornwall. Died between 28 December 1418 and 11 January 1419 (Le Neve, p. 16). In his will, dated 28 December 1418, he asked to be buried in the cathedral (*Reg. Stafford*, p. 420).

Pentecoste
The record of his or her funeral in Exeter Cathedral occurs in Christmas term 1306–7 (D&C 3673, f. 73r).

Perour, —
Children of John de Perour. The record of their funerals in Exeter Cathedral occurs in Christmas term 1310–11 (D&C 3673, f. 102r).

Pers, John
The bells of Exeter Cathedral were rung for him in Christmas term 1393–4 (D&C 3773, f. 71r).

Peter
Master. Prior of the hospital of St John; death date not known. Buried before the altar of St John Baptist in the church of the hospital by 1535 (DRO, ECA, Book 53A, f. 94v).

Peuton, —

>   Wife of Peuton. The bells of Exeter Cathedral were rung for her in Midsummer term 1393 (D&C 3773, f. 71r).

Pyl, John

>   Master. A sum of 2s. 6d. was paid by his executors to Exeter Cathedral between Michaelmas 1465 and Michaelmas 1466 for small stones, lime and sand, probably for making his tomb in the cathedral or cemetery (D&C 2704/1).

Pyl, William

>   Canon of Exeter Cathedral. Died by 18 December 1392 (Le Neve, p. 38). On 27 April 1392 the cathedral chapter licensed him to make 'his tomb before the altar of St John Baptist' (D&C 3550, f. 78v). The bells of the cathedral were rung for him (D&C 3773, f. 71r), and 3s. was received between Michaelmas 1392 and Michaelmas 1393 for stone sold for his tomb (D&C 2652).

Pilton, William

>   Canon of Exeter Cathedral. Died by 24 June 1435 (Le Neve, p. 46). The record of his funeral in the cathedral occurs in Midsummer term 1435 (D&C 3771). Buried in the chapel of St Paul in the cathedral, where his monument no longer contains a legible date (Pole, p. 109; BL, Add. MS 29931, f. 98; Oliver, *Lives of the Bishops*, p. 241; Hope, Monumentarium, p. 137).

Pinchun, Bartholomew

>   In his will, dated 10 October 1244, he asked to be buried in the cathedral cemetery (DRO, ECA, Book 53A, f. 16r).

Pytte, Thomas

>   A sum of 20d. was received by the clerk of the works of Exeter Cathedral between Michaelmas 1390 and Michaelmas 1391 from Robert Bosoun, chancellor of the cathedral, for the tomb of Thomas Pytte, probably in the cathedral or cemetery (D&C 2650).

Pyttes, John

>   Canon of Exeter Cathedral. Died by 19 September 1467 (Le Neve, p. 53). In his will, dated 1 September 1464, he asked to be buried 'in the nave of the [cathedral] . . . near the burial place of John Barbour, formerly canon of the same church, with these verses following inscribed on the marble stone placed upon it, so that the faithful may be the more moved to offer prayers to God for me: Subiacet hoc lapide Johannes Pyttys musicus ille, Qui fuit ecclesie quondam canonici huius, Presulis Edmundi Lacy cantor que capella, Rector de Tavy Petri Parkham simul extans, Pro quo mente pie rogo dicite sancta Maria' (DRO, Chanter XII (ii), Reg. Bothe, ff. 50v–51r). The record of his funeral in the cathedral occurs in Midsummer term 1467 (D&C 3772).

Pyttes, John
    Parish of St Martin, Exeter. Buried in the hospital of St John by 1492
    (DRO, ECA, Book 53A, f. 94v).

Plente, John
    Canon of Exeter Cathedral. Died 10 May 1483 (Le Neve, p. 57). In
    his will, dated 9 May 1483, he asked to be buried in the cathedral next
    to Robert Aiscough (see above), i.e. on the south side of the choir near
    the door of the vestibule before the image of the Virgin Mary (PRO,
    PROB 11/7, ff. 55v–56r).

Poddesdon, John
    Subdean of Exeter Cathedral. Died by 9 October 1399 (Le Neve, p.
    6). The cathedral bells were rung for him (D&C 3773, f. 70r).

Poltimor, Agnes de
    The record of her funeral in Exeter Cathedral occurs in Easter term
    1322 (D&C 3764, f. 33r).

Polworthy, Andrew
    Baker. Died by 19 February 1397 (MCR 20–21 Ric II, m. 23). In his
    will, dated 3 October 1396, he asked to be buried in the cathedral
    cemetery (DRO, ECA, ED/M/551). Possibly identical with Andrew
    Baker (see above).

Pomeray, Henry de
    Knight. Died 1281. His funeral took place, at least in part, in Exeter
    Cathedral, but his body was allegedly taken from there for burial to
    the Dominican Friary (Little and Easterling, pp. 51, 70).

Ponte, Aymer (Emer) de
    In his will, dated 14 September 1290, he asked to be buried in the
    Franciscan Friary, Exeter (MCR 18–19 Edw I, m. 14).

Porte, W. de
    The record of his funeral in Exeter Cathedral occurs in Easter term
    1313 (D&C 3764, f. 2r).

Pottere, Gervase le
    The record of his funeral in Exeter Cathedral occurs in Midsummer
    term 1305 (D&C 3673, f. 59v).

Praywell, Adam
    Annuellar of Exeter Cathedral. Died after 1361 (Orme, *Minor Clergy*,
    pp. 53–4). Probably buried in the cathedral, the cloister, or just outside;
    a door near his grave is mentioned between Michaelmas 1377 and
    Michaelmas 1378 (D&C 2640; cf. 2659).

Prenn, Walter
    Apparently buried in Exeter Cathedral; between Michaelmas 1442
    and Michaelmas 1443 2d.was spent on wire 'for angels at the new
    tomb of Walter Prenn' (D&C 2690).

Proffett, Richard
    Parish chaplain of Clyst Honiton (Devon). Died in the 15th century;
    date not known. He bequeathed his body to be buried in the church of
    St Sidwell, Exeter; it was brought to St Sidwell on a 23 April and was
    taken next morning to Exeter Cathedral, presumably for the funeral
    (D&C 2862).
Prout, Alice
    The record of her funeral in Exeter Cathedral occurs in Easter term
    1323 (D&C 3764, f.38r).
Puntyngdon, William de
    Archdeacon of Totnes. Died probably 24 July 1307 (Le Neve, p. 17;
    D&C 3625, f. iv recto). The record of his funeral in Exeter Cathedral
    occurs in Midsummer term 1307 (D&C 3673, f. 76r). Possibly buried
    near the altar of SS Mary Magdalene and Thomas the Martyr in the
    chapel off the south choir aisle, where he established a chantry for his
    soul on 2 February 1302 (D&C 2129).
Quylter, Richard
    Parish of St Laurence, Exeter. Buried in the hospital of St John by
    1492 (DRO, ECA, Book 53A, f. 94v).
Quinil, Peter
    Bishop of Exeter. Died 1 October 1291 (*Reg. Bronescombe*, ed.
    Hingeston-Randolph, pp. xxi–ii), or the 6th (Dalton and Doble, i, p.
    xxii). His obit, however, was subsequently held at Exeter Cathedral
    on the 4th (D&C 3625, f. v verso). Buried in the Lady Chapel of the
    cathedral beneath a ledger stone (Leland, i, 226; Hope, Monument-
    arium, p. 108).
Ralegh, —
    The effigy of a knight on the north side of the third bay of the south
    choir aisle in Exeter Cathedral was said to bear the arms of the Ralegh
    family in the early seventeenth century (Pole, p. 109). If so, it may
    relate to one of the Raleghs mentioned below. See also Brushfield, pp.
    455–81, and Hope, Monumentarium, p. 79.
Ralygh, Elizabeth
    Parish of St Laurence Exeter. Lady. Buried in the choir of the church
    of the hospital of St John between 1520 and 1535 (DRO, ECA, Book
    53A, f. 94v).
Ralegh, Henry de
    Parish of St Pancras, Exeter; knight. Died 1301 as a *confrater* in the
    Dominican Friary, Exeter, having allegedly wished for burial in the
    friary. His body was taken by force to Exeter Cathedral for its funeral
    and was then returned to the friary, upon which the friars refused to
    receive it. It was later buried in the cathedral, and was still there on 13
    February 1306 when the dean and chapter agreed that it should be

removed if his widow or two other named people so desired, but the outcome is not known (Little and Easterling, pp. 40–4). In the seventeenth century, Sir William Pole identified the left-hand of the two knights' effigies in the south choir aisle of the cathedral as bearing the Ralegh coat of arms (Pole, p. 109), while other antiquaries believed the arms were those of the Chichester family (Legg, p. 74; Symonds, p. 89), to whom the Ralegh property descended. On this basis, some modern writers have suggested that the effigy is that of Henry de Ralegh. The theory is plausible but not certain because there was another Ralegh with Exeter Cathedral connections (see below).

Ralegh, Thomas de

Knight; sheriff of Devon. The record of his funeral in Exeter Cathedral occurs in Christmas term 1308–9, including the offering of his palfrey and arms (D&C 3673, f. 88v). He is as good a candidate as Henry de Ralegh (see above) for the attribution of the left-hand effigy of a knight in the south choir aisle of the cathedral.

Ralph

Rector of St Edmund, Exeter. The bells of Exeter Cathedral were rung for him in Easter term 1395 (D&C 3773, f. 70v).

Ralph

'Sir'; i.e. priest or knight. The bells of Exeter Cathedral were rung for him between Michaelmas 1485 and Michaelmas 1486 (D&C 3779, f. 231r).

Rawlens, Robert

Exeter, probably parish of St Sidwell; probably layman. In his will, dated 1503 and proved on 23 July 1503, he asked to be buried in the cathedral cemetery (PRO, PROB 11/13, f. 240v).

Rede, Alice

Parish of St Laurence, Exeter, 'next to the city wall'. Buried by the altar of St Katherine in the hospital of St John between 1530 and 1535 (DRO, ECA, Book 53A, f. 95r).

Redman, Thomas

Canon of Exeter Cathedral. Died by 6 February 1432 (Le Neve, p. 44). The record of his funeral in the cathedral occurs in Christmas term 1431–2 (D&C 3771).

Redully, John

Dominus; probably priest. A sum of 10s. was paid to Exeter Cathedral for stone, lime, and sand, possibly for his tomb in or near the cathedral, between 25 March 1393 and 25 March 1394 (D&C 2653).

Reygny, William

Canon of Chulmleigh church and Crediton College (Devon); rector of Plymtree (Devon). Died by 12 January 1521 (DRO, Chanter XIV, f. 8r). In his will, dated 15 April 1519, he asked to be buried (if he died in Exeter) 'within the choir of the hospital of St John . . . within and fast by the south door of the said choir, if it shall fortune none other person there to be buried before I shall decease'; if then, 'I will, desire, and pray that my body may rest as nigh to that place as it shall be convenient' (PRO, PROB 11/20, f. 83v). Died a resident in the hospital, and buried in the church next to the door of the cloister (DRO, ECA, Book 53A, f. 95r).

Renbaud, H.
The bells of Exeter Cathedral were rung for him in Easter term 1398 (D&C 3773, f. 70r).

Reve, Simon le
The record of his funeral in Exeter Cathedral occurs in Michaelmas term 1313 (D&C 3764, f. 4v).

Reven, James
A sum of 40s. for his burial, probably in Exeter Cathedral or cemetery, was paid to the cathedral between Michaelmas 1323 and Michaelmas 1324 (Erskine, *Fabric Accounts*, i, 146).

Ryce, Alice ap
Parish of St Sidwell, Exeter. Probably mother or sister of Arnulph ap Ryse (see below). Buried in the chapter house of the hospital of St John between 1520 and 1535 (DRO, ECA, Book 53A, f. 95r).

Ryce, Arnulph ap
Subprior of the hospital of St John; probably godson of Arnulph Colyns (see above). Buried in the chapter house of the hospital in 1535 (DRO, ECA, Book 53A, f. 95r).

Riche, Gil'
A sum of 6s. 8d. for making his or her grave in Exeter Cathedral was paid to the cathedral between Michaelmas 1341 and Michaelmas 1342 (Erskine, *Fabric Accounts*, ii, 266).

Ridmore, John de
The record of his funeral in Exeter Cathedral occurs in Midsummer term 1305 (D&C 3673, f. 61r).

Ruyggeway, —
Wife of Stephen Ruyggeway (see below). Buried in the church of St Nicholas Priory by 1496, when her husband asked to be buried by her.

Ruyggeway, Stephen
Parish of St Olave, Exeter. Citizen. In his will, dated 5 December 1496, he asked to be buried in the church of St Nicholas Priory 'as near to my wife as possible' (MCR 14–15 Hen VII, m. 47).

Rygge, Robert
Chancellor of Exeter Cathedral. Died 26 March 1410 (Le Neve, p. 9). In his will, dated 24 March 1410, he asked to be buried 'in the cemetery or [cathedral] church of Exeter according to the discretion of my executors' (PRO, PROB 11/2A, f. 160r).

Ryse, John
> Treasurer of Exeter Cathedral. Died 7 May 1531 (Le Neve, p. 12).
> Buried in the cathedral; his ledger stone had disappeared by the mid
> nineteenth century (Oliver, *Lives of the Bishops*, p. 240).

Robert II, 'of Chichester'
> Bishop of Exeter. Died 10 March 1160. Said to have been buried in
> the cathedral by Oliver, *Lives of the Bishops*, p. 18, but the information
> relates to his predecessor, Bishop Robert Warelwast.

Robert, Walter
> Master. Principal portionist of the rectory of Tiverton (Devon). Died
> by 27 September 1415 (*Reg. Stafford*, p. 214). Buried in the hospital
> of St John (DRO, ECA, Book 53A, f. 94v).

Robyns, Elizabeth
> Wife of John Robyns (see below). Buried in the cathedral cemetery by
> 1516 when her husband wished to be buried beside her (PRO, PROB
> 11/19, f. 27v).

Robyns, John
> Parish of St Petroc, Exeter; citizen and saddler. In his will, dated 10
> June 1516, he asked to be buried 'in the cemetery of the cathedral
> church of . . . Exeter next to the grave of Elizabeth, formerly my wife'
> (PRO, PROB 11/19, f. 27v).

Roger, —
> Daughter of Master Roger. The record of her funeral in Exeter
> Cathedral occurs in Christmas term 1310–11 (D&C 3673, f. 103r).

Rokes, —
> Wife of Rokes. The bells of Exeter Cathedral were rung for her in
> 1398–9 (D&C 3773, f. 70r).

Roos, John
> Buried in the hospital of St John by 1492 (DRO, ECA, Book 53A, f.
> 94v). Possibly identical with John Roos, died by 29 September 1410
> (MCR 11 Hen IV, m. 52).

Rotherham, Richard
> Chancellor of Exeter Cathedral. Died by 10 September 1455 (Le Neve,
> p. 9). In his will, dated 4 October 1454, he asked to be buried in the
> cathedral 'next to the tomb of Master John Snetysham, the last
> chancellor, . . . my predecessor' (*Reg. Lacy*, IV, 62); Snetysham (see
> below) asked to be buried 'as nearly beneath the *pulpitum* as possible'.
> The record of his funeral in the cathedral occurs in Midsummer term
> 1455 (D&C 3772). A sum of 1s. 8d. was paid between Michaelmas
> 1456 and Michaelmas 1457 for stone, lime and sand for making his
> tomb (D&C 2701).

Rowe, John   .
> Subdean of Exeter Cathedral. Died by 10 November 1463 (Le Neve,
> p. 6). In his will, dated 8 September 1462, he asked to be buried in the

cathedral 'if it happens that I die within the kingdom of England and if my body may be carried to the said church without grave danger' (DRO, Chanter XII (i), Reg. Nevill, ff. 139v–140r). His funeral is not mentioned in the cathedral obit accounts.

Rugge, John

Vicar of St Thomas, Cowick. Died by March 1537. In his will, dated 1 April 1536 he asked to be buried in the choir of the church of St Thomas before the image of St Thomas' (Beatrix F. Cresswell, 'John Rugge, Vicar of St Thomas by Exeter', *Devon and Cornwall Notes and Queries*, 17 (1932–3), p. 166).

Russheton, Nicholas (Ryssheton)

Canon of Exeter Cathedral. Died by Christmas term, 1462–3, when his funeral in the cathedral is recorded (D&C 2834; 3772).

Russell, John

Parish of St Mary Major. In his will, dated 4 October 1497, he asked to be buried in the church of St Mary Major (DRO, 51/1/5/5).

Sage, —

Child of John le Sage (see below). The record of his or her funeral in Exeter Cathedral occurs in Easter term 1309 (D&C 3673, f. 91v).

Sage, John le

The record of his funeral in Exeter Cathedral occurs in Easter term 1314 (D&C 3764, f. 7r).

St Helen, William of (*de Sancta Elena*)

Canon of Exeter Cathedral. Died shortly before 10 March 1316, when his funeral is recorded in the cathedral (D&C 3764, f. 17r).

St Laurence, Bartholomew of (*de Sancto Laurentio*)

Dean of Exeter. Died shortly before 26 November 1326, when his funeral is recorded in the cathedral (D&C 3764, f. 56v).

St Leonard, Matill' of (*de Sancto Leonardo*)

Wife of Walter of St Leonard. The record of her funeral in Exeter Cathedral occurs in Midsummer term 1312 (D&C 3673, f. 113r).

St Paul, Michael of

Chaplain. The record of his funeral in Exeter Cathedral occurs in Midsummer term 1307 (D&C 3673, f. 76v).

Sares, Alan

Master; layman. The bells of Exeter Cathedral were rung for him between Michaelmas 1486 and Michaelmas 1487 (D&C 3779, f. 231v). During the same period, money was paid for stone, tile-stone, lime and sand for his tomb, probably in or near the cathedral (D&C 2704/3).

Sares, Joan

Daughter of Alan Sares (see above). The bells of Exeter Cathedral were rung for her between Michaelmas 1485 and Michaelmas 1486 (D&C 3779, f. 231r).

Saundford, W. de

The record of his funeral in Exeter Cathedral occurs in Christmas term 1311–12 (D&C 3673, f. 110v).

Sawle, John

Parish of St Laurence, Exeter, 'in la baly', presumably living in the bailey of Exeter Castle. Buried in the hospital of St John by 1492 (DRO, ECA, Book 53A, f. 94v).

Sayer, John

Parish of St Stephen, Exeter. Buried in the hospital of St John between 1492 and 1520 (DRO, ECA, Book 53A, f. 94v).

*Seamstress, Joan (*Sutrix*)

The record of her funeral in Exeter Cathedral occurs in Christmas term 1305–6 (D&C 3673, f. 65v.

Seler, Richard

Citizen and mayor of Exeter, resident at Marsh near Exeter. In his will, dated 23 July 1344, he asked to be buried in the Dominican Friary, Exeter (MCR 1 Hen IV, m. 41d).

Seler, Matill'

Wife of Richard le Seler. Her funeral took place in Exeter Cathedral on 31 October 1320 (D&C 3764, f. 26r).

Serle, Sara

Parish of St Mary Major, Exeter. Wife of John Serle. In her will, dated 28 November 137[4?], she asked to be buried in the cathedral cemetery (D&C VC/3103).

Serlo

Dean of Exeter. Died 1231, probably on 21 July, the date of his obit (D&C 3518, f. 36v; 3625, f. iv recto). A ledger stone in the chapter house of the cathedral is traditionally said to mark his grave (Erskine, Hope, and Lloyd, pp. 20–1).

Schaplegh, —

Wife of Schaplegh (presumably first wife; see below). The bells of Exeter Cathedral were rung for her in Christmas term 1396–7 (D&C 3773, f. 70v).

Schaplegh, —

Wife of Schaplegh (presumably second wife; see above). The bells of Exeter Cathedral were rung for her in 1401 (D&C 3773, f. 54v).

Shillingford, Baldwin de

Canon of Exeter Cathedral. Died by 23 February 1418, probably 19 February (Le Neve, p. 39). The record of his funeral in the cathedral occurs in Easter term 1418 (D&C 3770). Stone for his tomb, probably in the cathedral, was sold to his executors between 8 May and Michaelmas 1418 (D&C 2672).

Schordyche, —

Wife of Roger Schordyche (probably the canons' baker, see below next but one). The bells of Exeter Cathedral were rung for her between Michaelmas 1487 and Michaelmas 1488 (D&C 3779, f. 232r).

Schordych, Joan
Parish of St Stephen, Exeter. Wife of Roger Schordych (see below, next but one). Buried in the hospital of St John, between 1492 and 1520 (DRO, ECA, Book 53A, f. 94v).

Shardych, Roger (Shordych)
Baker to the canons of Exeter Cathedral. A sum of 6s. 8d. was paid for Beer stone for his tomb, probably in or near the cathedral, between Michaelmas 1486 and Michaelmas 1487 (D&C 2704/3). This entry seems incompatible with the one next following, suggesting that there were two men with this name.

Schordych, Roger
Parish of St Stephen, Exeter. Husband of Joan Schordych (see above). Buried in the hospital of St John, between 1492 and 1520 (DRO, ECA, Book 53A, f. 94v).

Schute, John
Archdeacon of Exeter. Died by 27 September 1425 (Le Neve, p. 14). The record of his funeral in Exeter Cathedral occurs in Michaelmas term 1425 (D&C 3770).

Sylke, William
Precentor of Exeter Cathedral. Died on or before 25 April 1508, when his funeral was held in the cathedral (D&C 3771, loose sheet). In his will, dated 24 November 1506, he asked to be buried in the north part of the cathedral 'near the chapel of the Holy Cross' (PRO, PROB 11/15, f. 280r). His monument subsequently formed part of the south wall of the chapel, in the north transept of the cathedral, with an inscription but no date (Oliver, *Lives of the Bishops*, p. 241; Hope, Monumentarium, p. 194).

Simon of Apulia
Bishop of Exeter. Died 1223, probably on 9 September, the date on which Exeter Cathedral subsequently kept his obit (D&C 3518, f. 49v; 3625, f. v recto). An effigy of a bishop in the Lady Chapel of the cathedral is ascribed to him (Oliver, *Lives of the Bishops*, pp. 190–1; Hope, Monumentarium, p. 109).

Symon, Alsyn
Wife of John Symon (see below). Buried in the church of St Petroc by 1524, when her husband asked to be buried next to her (PRO, PROB 11/22, f. 8r).

Symon, John
Mayor of Exeter; husband of Alsyn (see above). In his will, dated 26 September 1524, he asked to be buried in the church of St Petroc 'as nigh to Alsyn Symon, late my wife, as it may be' (PRO, PROB 11/22, f. 8r).

Skeltone, Peter de
Rector of St Stephen-by-Saltash (Cornwall). Died, probably in Exeter, 6 September 1316 (*Reg. Stapeldon*, p. 258). The record of his funeral in Exeter Cathedral occurs in Midsummer term 1316 (D&C 3764, f. 20r).

*Skinner, Richard (*Pelliparius*)
The record of his funeral in Exeter Cathedral occurs in Midsummer term 1307 (D&C 3673, f. 77r).

Skynner, Richard
Annuellar of the Brantingham chantry, Exeter Cathedral. Died 4 May 1418 (Orme, *Minor Clergy*, p. 56). On 7 January 1391 the cathedral chapter conceded to him licence to glaze a small window in the cathedral cloister, the last and nearest to the door of the west part of the cloister, and to be buried on the floor of the cloister before the said window (D&C 3550, f. 70r).

Skot, —
Wife of Skot. The bells of Exeter Cathedral were rung for her in Christmas term 1396–7 (D&C 3773, f. 70v).

Skyce, Philip
Parish of St Laurence, Exeter. Butler of the hospital of St John. Buried in the church of the hospital between 1492 and 1520 (DRO, ECA, Book 53A, f. 94v).

Smale, Robert
Annuellar of the Brantingham chantry, Exeter Cathedral (Orme, *Minor Clergy*, p. 74). Died between Michaelmas 1485 and Michaelmas 1486, when the cathedral bells were rung for him (D&C 3779, f. 231r).

Smalecumb, William de
The record of his funeral in Exeter Cathedral occurs in Michaelmas term 1311 (D&C 3673, f. 109r).

Smert, —
Parish of St Pancras, Exeter. Wife of John Smert. Buried in the hospital of St John by 1492 (DRO, ECA, Book 53A, f. 94v).

Smith, Richard
Annuellar of the Stafford chantry, Exeter Cathedral. Died by 19 March 1524 (Orme, *Minor Clergy*, p. 80). Buried before the altar of Jesus in the church of the hospital of St John (DRO, ECA, Book 53A, f. 95r).

Smyth, Julyan
Parish of St Mary Arches, Exeter. Widow of Robert Smythe (see below). In her will, dated 1547, she asked to be buried in the cathedral cemetery next to her husband (Exeter, West Country Studies Library, and DRO, Moger Will Abstracts, xix, 6688).

Smythe, Robert
Husband of Julyan Smyth (see above). Died by 1547, and buried in

the cathedral cemetery (Exeter, West Country Studies Library, and DRO, Moger Will Abstracts, xix, 6688).

Snape, William

A sum of 3s. 4d. was paid to the clerk of the works of Exeter Cathedral between Michaelmas 1390 and Michaelmas 1391 for his tomb, probably in or near the cathedral (D&C 2650).

Snetysham, John

Chancellor of Exeter Cathedral. Died by 3 July 1448 (Le Neve, p. 9). In his will, dated 5 March 1448, he asked to be buried in the cathedral 'as near beneath the *pulpitum* as possible' (*Reg. Lacy*, IV, 44). The record of his funeral in the cathedral occurs in Midsummer term 1448 (D&C 3771). Buried in the cathedral by 1454 when his successor, Richard Rotherham (see above), asked to be buried next to him.

Somaister, Joan

Widow of Richard Somaister of Netherexe (Devon). In her will, dated 30 October 1407, she asked to be buried 'in the church of St John', Exeter, probably meaning the hospital church of St John (Antony House, Sir William Pole, 'Extracts from Deeds, Charters and Grants', no. 1978). She is presumably the 'mother of Adam Summayster' mentioned as buried in the hospital by 1492 (DRO, ECA, DRO, ECA, Book 53A, f. 94v).

Somersete, Henry de

Dean of Exeter. Died in late December 1306, probably on 22 December, the date on which his obit was later held (D&C 3625, f. vi verso). The record of his funeral in the cathedral is recorded in that season (D&C 3673, f. 72r).

Soth, Peter

Parish of St Kerrian, Exeter. In his will, dated 3 April 1327, he asked to be buried in the cathedral cemetery (DRO, ECA, ED/M/276). The record of his funeral in Exeter Cathedral occurs in Easter term 1327 (D&C 3764, f. 59r).

Souder, John

Dominus; probably priest. A sum of 40d. was paid to Exeter Cathedral for stones sold to his executors, probably for his tomb in or near the cathedral, between 7 July and 29 September 1387 (D&C 2647).

Speke, Elizabeth

Of White Lackington, Somerset. Lady. Third wife of Sir John Speke (see below), and previously of John Colshill (see above). Died between 18 December 1518 and 17 June 1519 (see below). In her will, dated 18 December 1518, she asked to be buried in Exeter Cathedral 'by the body of my said husband, Sir John Speke, within the new chapel of St George which he late made and founded' (PRO, PROB 11/19, f. 136r).

Speke, Elizabeth
Parish of St Laurence, Exeter. Mistress; mother of Robert Speke (see below). Buried in the choir of the church of the hospital of St John between 1520 and 1535 (DRO, ECA, Book 53A, f. 95r).

Speke, John
Of White Lackington, Somerset; knight. Husband of Elizabeth (see next but one above). Died 28 April 1518. In his will, dated 20 February 1517, he asked to be buried in Exeter Cathedral 'within my chapel of St George' (PRO, PROB 11/19, f. 70r), a chapel erected by him in about the 1510s (Orme, 1986, pp. 25–41). He was buried there by 1518 (see Elizabeth Speke, next but one above). See also Hope, Monumentarium, p. 129.

Speke, Robert
Parish of St Laurence, Exeter. Master. Heir of Elizabeth Speke (see next but one above). Buried in the choir of the church of the hospital of St John between 1520 and 1535 (DRO, ECA, Book 53A, f. 95r).

Spenser, Henry le
Parish of St Olave. In his will, dated 21 June 1311, he asked to be buried in the cathedral cemetery (MCR 4–5 Edw II, m. 46).

Spurway, Thomas
Of Exeter; gentleman. In his will, dated 29 March 1548, he asked to be buried 'in St Nicholas churchyard [presumably the graveyard of the former priory of St Nicholas]' or 'in holy earth' if he died out of Exeter (PRO, PROB 11/32, f. 41v).

Stafford, —
Parish of St Mary Major, Exeter. Buried in the hospital of St John by 1492 (DRO, ECA, Book 53A, f. 94v).

Stafford, Edmund
Bishop of Exeter. Died 3 September 1419 (Le Neve, p. 2). In his will, dated 24 July 1418, he asked to be buried 'in the cathedral church of Exeter in the monument which I have made to be newly erected there' (*Reg. Chichele*, ii, 154). His tomb stands in the cathedral on the north side of the Lady Chapel and the south side of the chapel of St John Evangelist (Leland, i, 226; Hope, Monumentarium, p. 114).

Stapledon, [Mabel?] (Stapeldon)
Wife of William de Stapledon (see below); very likely therefore Mabel, mother of Bishop Walter de Stapledon (see below) (Buck, p. 11). The record of her funeral in Exeter Cathedral occurs in Michaelmas term 1307 (D&C 3673, f. 77v).

Stapledon, Richard
Brother of Bishop Stapledon (Buck, p. 11); knight. Probably died 11 March 1332 (D&C 3625, f. ii; 3764, f. 88r). He is probably the knight buried in the north wall of the 1st bay of the north choir aisle, opposite

Bishop Stapledon's tomb (cf. Leland, i, 227; Hope, Monumentarium, p. 22).

Stapledon, Richard
Probably the illegitimate son of Sir Richard Stapledon (see above) (Buck, p. 11; cf. D&C 2881). The bells of Exeter Cathedral were rung for him in Midsummer term 1394 (D&C 3773, f. 70v).

Stapledon, Thomas de
Canon of Exeter Cathedral; brother of Bishop Walter de Stapledon (see below) (Buck, p. 11). Said to have died 3 October 1342 (Le Neve, p. 25), but his funeral in the cathedral is elsewhere dated as 2 October (D&C 3765).

Stapledon, Walter de
Bishop of Exeter. Died 15 October 1326 (Dalton and Doble, i, p. xxiii; Le Neve, p. 1; Buck, p. 220). First buried in the cemetery of Holy Innocents, London, 16 October (Buck, p. 221). Reburied in Exeter Cathedral in Easter term 1327 (D&C 3764, f. 58r); his tomb lies on the north side of the first bay of the presbytery (cf. Leland, i, 227; Hope, Monumentarium, p. 5).

Stapeldon, William de (Stapeldon)
Very likely the husband of Mabel and father of Bishop Walter de Stapledon (see above) (Buck, pp. 10–12). The record of his funeral in Exeter Cathedral occurs in Easter term 1309 (D&C 3673, f. 91r).

Steyner, Drew
Burnt, probably as a Lollard, at Livery Dole in Heavitree parish, 7 August 1431 (Exeter Cathedral Library, MS 3508, f. 8v). His existence has not yet been corroborated from other sources, and it is unclear whether Drew was his forename or surname, and Steyner his surname or occupation: 'stainer' meaning dyer (Orme, 1998, p. 22).

Sterre, John
'From outside the East Gate'. The bells of Exeter Cathedral were rung for him in Michaelmas term 1393 (D&C 3773, f. 71r). Probably identical with John Storre, died by 21 September 1394 (MCR 17–18 Ric II, m. 51).

Stephyns, Henry
Annuellar of the Torridge Chantry in Exeter Cathedral (Orme, *Minor Clergy*, p. 83). In his will, dated 8 August 1537, he asked to be buried in the garden of the cathedral cloister; dead by September 1537 (DRO, 1049M/FW 33).

Stevenys, John
Canon of Exeter Cathedral. Died by 27 February 1461 (Le Neve, p. 47). The record of his funeral in Exeter Cathedral occurs in Christmas term 1460–1 (D&C 3772).

Stoke, Roger de
Vicar choral of Exeter Cathedral (Orme, *Minor Clergy*, p. 13). Died in January 1307, when the record occurs of his funeral in the cathedral (D&C 3673, f. 72v).

Stokes, R.
Possibly Ralph, rector of Ashcombe (Devon) (*Reg. Stapeldon*, p. 185). His funeral took place in Exeter Cathedral on 5 October 1316 (D&C 3764, f. 20v).

Storre – see Sterre

Stowford, John
Prebendary of Chulmleigh church (Devon). Died by 18 July 1393 (*Reg. Brantyngham*, i, 130). The bells of Exeter Cathedral were rung for him in Midsummer term 1393 (D&C 3773, f. 71r).

Strange, John
Canon of Exeter Cathedral. His funeral took place in Exeter Cathedral between 29 September and 24 November 1320 (D&C 3764, f. 26v; MCR 14–15 Edw II, m. 8).

Strange, R.
'Sir'; i.e. priest or knight. His funeral took place in Exeter Cathedral on 12 September 1321 (D&C 3764, f. 30r). Possibly the annuellar of the cathedral who resigned in 1309, but equally the annuellar may be the next entry (*Reg. Stapeldon*, p. 270).

Strange, Roger
Vicar choral and succentor of Exeter Cathedral. His funeral took place in Exeter Cathedral on 1 August 1316 (D&C 3764, f. 19r).

Strete, William de
Prebendary of Hayes in the chapel of Exeter Castle. Died 14 February 1312 (*Reg. Stapeldon*, p. 214). Buried 'at Cowick', probably in the cemetery of the priory church, possibly on 1 March (D&C 3673, f. 110v).

Stubbys, John
Precentor of Exeter Cathedral. Died by Michaelmas term 1486 (Le Neve, p. 8). The bells of the cathedral were rung for him between Michaelmas 1485 and Michaelmas 1486 (D&C 3779, f. 231r).

Sturt, —
Parish of St Martin, Exeter. Wife of Peter Sturt (see below). Buried in the hospital of St John by 1492 (DRO, ECA, Book 53A, f. 94v).

Sturt, —
Parish of St Martin, Exeter. Son of Peter Sturt (see below). Buried in the hospital of St John by 1492 (DRO, ECA, Book 53A, f. 94v).

Sturt, Peter
Parish of St Martin, Exeter. Wife of Peter Sturt. Buried in the hospital of St John by 1492 (DRO, ECA, Book 53A, f. 94v).

*Summoner, Peter the (*Apparitor*)
  The record of his funeral in Exeter Cathedral occurs in Easter term
  1312 (D&C 3673, f. 112).

Susseter, John (Surcetere)
  Rector of Holy Trinity, Exeter. Died between 1374 and 1385 (*Reg.
  Brantyngham*, i, 333; ii, 595). Buried in the lower or chancel part of
  Holy Trinity church by 1442 (*Reg. Lacy*, II, 263).

Suttis, John
  The record of his funeral in Exeter Cathedral occurs in Christmas
  term 1305–6 (D&C 3673, f. 65v).

Swayn, —
  Wife of R. Swayn. The bells of Exeter Cathedral were rung for her in
  Easter term 1398 (D&C 3773, f. 70r).

Talbot, John
  Parish of St Kerrian, Exeter; citizen of Exeter. In his will, dated 21
  September 1420, he asked to be buried in the church of the hospital of
  St John (DRO, ECA, Book 53A, f. 84r). Buried there by 1492 (ibid., f.
  94v).

Talbot, Matilda
  Prioress of Polsoe Priory near Exeter. Died and buried in the priory by
  17 May 1439, when an indulgence was granted for prayers for her
  soul (*Reg. Lacy*, II, 146).

Talbot, Richard
  Parish of St Laurence, Exeter. Master. Buried in the hospital of St John
  by 1492 (DRO, ECA, Book 53A, f. 94v).

Tancret, John (Tankaret)
  Vicar choral of Exeter Cathedral. Died Christmas term 1488–9 (Orme,
  Minor Clergy, p. 34). The cathedral bells were rung for him between
  Michaelmas 1488 and Michaelmas 1489 (D&C 3779, f. 231v).

Tauntifer, —
  Child of Walter Tauntifer. The record of its funeral in Exeter Cathedral
  occurs in Midsummer term 1308 (D&C 3673, f. 85v).

Taverner, Nicholas
  Died by 12 March 1373. Buried 'in the church of the Blessed Mary' of
  Exeter (which church – St Mary Arches, St Mary Major, or St Mary
  Steps – is not specified), when an indulgence was granted for prayers
  for his soul (*Reg. Brantyngham*, i, 340).

*Taverner, Reginald (*Tabernarius*)
  The record of his funeral in Exeter Cathedral occurs in Midsummer
  term 1306 (D&C 3673, f. 68v).

Taverner, Robert
  Parish of St Mary Major. Son of William Taverner. In his will, dated 28
  August 1383, he asked to be buried in the cathedral cemetery (DRO,
  ECA, 51/1/3/4).

Taylour, John

Tin-merchant. A merchant of this name occurs in Exeter in 1471–7 (Rowe and Jackson, p. 56; *Calendar of Close Rolls 1476–85*, p. 73). Buried in the Franciscan Friary in the late fifteenth or early sixteenth century; his ledger stone was found during the digging of a sewer trench in Friars Walk (Exeter Archaeology, drawing).

Tayllur, Roger le

The record of his funeral in Exeter Cathedral occurs in Christmas term 1315–16 (D&C 3764, f. 16v).

Thomas, John

Parish of St Petroc, Exeter. In his will, dated 31 May 1469, he asked to be buried in the Dominican Friary, Exeter (PRO, PROB 11/5, f. 237r).

Thorneby, W.

The record of his funeral in Exeter Cathedral occurs in Midsummer term 1316 (D&C 3764, f. 20r).

Tybot, John

Parish of St Kerrian, Exeter; married layman. In his will, dated 4 June 1474, he asked to be buried 'in the cemetery of [the cathedral church of] St Peter, Exeter, before the door of the church of the Blessed Mary there', i.e. St Mary Major (MCR 3–4 Henry VIII, m. 1).

Tynle, John

Parish of St Laurence, Exeter. Husband of Margaret Tynle (see below). Buried in the hospital of St John by 1492 (DRO, ECA, Book 53A, f. 94v).

Tynle, Margaret

Parish of Holy Trinity, Exeter. Wife of John Tynle (see above). Buried in the hospital of St John by 1492 (DRO, ECA, Book 53A, f. 94v).

Tyrel, John

The bells of Exeter cathedral were rung for him in about 1399 (D&C 3773, f. 70r).

Toker, Robert

Of Exeter; gentleman. In his will, dated 27 December 1546, he asked to be buried in the parish church of St Mary Major (PRO, PROB 11/31, f. 242r).

Tollet, Richard

Archdeacon of Barnstaple. Died between 27 March and 26 April 1528 (Le Neve, p. 21). In his will, dated 27 March 1528, he asked to be buried in Exeter Cathedral 'afore Our Lady chapel, betwixt my Lord Oldam is chapel and Sir John Speke is', i.e. in the retrochoir (PRO, PROB 11/22, f. 270r).

Tomyow, Thomas

Canon of Exeter Cathedral. Died by 1 April 1518 (Le Neve, p. 58). In his will, dated 30 September 1517, he asked to be buried in the cathedral 'next to Master [John] Nans' (see above) (PRO, PROB 11/19, f. 71r–v).

Torre, William de

> Baker. The record of his funeral in Exeter Cathedral occurs in Christmas term 1305–6 (D&C 3673, f. 65r).

Torridge, Roger (de Toriz)

> Dean of Exeter. Died 1274, probably on 29 April, the date on which his obit was subsequently kept at the cathedral (D&C 3625, f. ii verso). Mentioned on 18 January 1284 as buried near or before the altar of St Richard and St Radegund in the cathedral (D&C 1936).

Toryton, Pauline de

> The record of her funeral in Exeter Cathedral occurs in Christmas term 1308–9 (D&C 3673, f. 89v).

*Totnes, Nicholas of (*de Tottonia*)

> Rector of Thorverton, Exeter. The record of his funeral in Exeter Cathedral occurs in Michaelmas term 1311 (D&C 3673, f. 109v).

Tracy, —

> Son of Sir Henry Tracy of Fremington (Devon), possibly the knight who occurs in Devon in the reign of Henry III. Buried by the entrance to the cloister of Exeter Cathedral at an unknown date (Dalton and Doble, ii, 545).

Tregonwell, Robert

> Canon of Exeter. Died 13 January 1543, adjusting the incomplete inscription on his ledger stone now in the chapel of St Andrew to what else is known of his career (Hope, *Monumentarium*, p. 134, with incorrect date; Emden, 1974, p. 576).

Tregrisiow, Ralph

> Dean of Exeter. Died 25 July 1415 (Le Neve, p. 4). On 21 June 1393 the cathedral chapter licensed him to make his tomb 'against the west door in the middle of the church, as near to the wall in the middle of the said door as he can conveniently make it' (D&C 3550, f. 89r). In his will, dated 16 June 1411, he asked to be buried in the cathedral if he died in Devon (*Reg. Stafford*, p. 405). Buried in the cathedral 19 August 1415 (DRO, Chanter IX, f. 169v), perhaps having died elsewhere.

Trelawny, —

> Parish of St Petroc, Exeter. Son of Nicholas Trelawny. Buried in the hospital of St John by 1492 (DRO, ECA, Book 53A, f. 94v).

Trelosk, Andrew de (Treluyk)

> Knight, of Cornwall, with property in Exeter. Died by 8 November 1305 (MCR 33–34 Edw I, m. 6). The record of his funeral in Exeter Cathedral occurs in Michaelmas term 1305 (D&C 3673, f. 62r).

Tremayn, John

> Parish of St Martin, Exeter. Buried in the hospital of St John by 1492 (DRO, ECA, Book 53A, f. 94v).

Tremayn, Thomas
>Canon of Exeter Cathedral. Died by 15 July 1420 (Le Neve, p. 48). The record of his funeral in the cathedral occurs in Midsummer term 1420 (D&C 3770).

Trendelbeare, William
>Priest; clerk of the works of Exeter Cathedral in 1371–5 (Orme, *Minor Clergy*, p. 3). Rector of Alphington (Devon), died by 7 May 1403 (*Reg. Stafford*, p. 141). Between Michaelmas 1402 and Michaelmas 1403 a sum of 3s. 4d. was paid to the cathedral for stones for his tomb (D&C 2661).

Trevellys, William
>Treasurer of Exeter Cathedral. Died by 26 September 1399 (Le Neve, p. 11). The cathedral bells were rung for him (D&C 3773, f. 70r); a sum of 2s. 6d. was paid between Michaelmas 1399 and Michaelmas 1400 for tilestone for paving his tomb (D&C 2658). Buried in the cathedral by 1417, when his successor Richard Hals (see above) asked to be buried next to him (*Reg. Stafford*, pp. 416–17).

Trewarak, John
>Parish of St Laurence, Exeter. Buried by the west door of the church of the hospital of St John by 1535 (DRO, ECA, Book 53A, f. 95r).

Trewynard, —
>Of Cornwall; parish of All Hallows Goldsmith Street, Exeter. Buried in the hospital of St John by 1492 (DRO, ECA, Book 53A, f. 94v).

Trote, Walter
>Canon of Exeter Cathedral. Died by 12 March 1404 (Le Neve, p. 44). In his will, dated 4 November 1399, he asked to be buried in the cathedral (*Reg. Stafford*, p. 381). Buried there by 1412 when Canon Walter Gybbes (see above) asked to be buried beside him (Lambeth Palace Library, Reg. Thomas Arundel, ii, ff. 167v–168r).

Udy, John
>Canon of Exeter Cathedral. Died between 18 February and 14 June 1463 (Le Neve, p. 54). In his will, dated 18 February 1463, he asked to be buried in the nave of the cathedral 'next to the *pulpitum*' (DRO, Chanter XII (i), Reg. Nevill, f. 140v).

Vaggescombe, Robert
>Canon of Exeter Cathedral. Died by 16 June 1382 (Le Neve, p. 39). In his will, dated 23 June 1381, he asked to be buried in the cathedral 'or wherever God disposes' (Lambeth Palace Library, Reg. Courtenay, f. 200r).

Venella – see Lane

Veteri Terra – see Oldland

Veysi, Robert
>A sum of £1 6s. 8d. was paid to Exeter Cathedral by his wife between

Michaelmas 1430 and Michaelmas 1431 for his tomb in the cathedral (D&C 2683).

Veysey, William (Veisei)

Relative of Bishop John Veysey; apparitor general of the bishop. In his will, dated 1 January 1535, he asked to be buried in the cathedral cemetery, at the end near the charnel house (DRO, Moger Wills, xxi, 7428).

Vyel, Cecilia

The record of her funeral in Exeter Cathedral occurs in Easter term 1313 (D&C 3764, f. 2r).

Vude, Richard (Unde?)

Parish of St Petroc, Exeter; citizen and merchant. In his will, dated 8 February 1506, he asked to be buried in the church of St Petroc before the image of the Virgin Mary (PRO, PROB 11/15, f. 184v).

Wadham, John

Knight, with property in Devon, Somerset, and elsewhere. Died by 12 August 1412 (*Cal. Fine Rolls, 1405–13*, p. 216). A sum of 3s. 2d. was paid between Michaelmas 1412 and Michaelmas 1413 for stones for his tomb in the cathedral (D&C 2668).

Wagot, —

Wife of Richard Wagot. The bells of Exeter Cathedral were rung for her between Michaelmas 1485 and Michaelmas 1486 (D&C 3779, f. 231r).

Waggot, Richard

Parish of St Laurence. Buried in the hospital of St John between 1492 and 1530 (DRO, ECA, Book 53A, f. 94v).

Wagott, William

Canon of Exeter Cathedral. Died between Michaelmas 1484 and Michaelmas 1485, when the bells of the cathedral were rung for him (D&C 3779, f. 231r).

Walys

The bells of Exeter Cathedral were rung for him in about 1399 (D&C 3773, f. 70r).

Ward, John

Canon of Exeter Cathedral. Died between 18 February and 27 March 1476 (Le Neve, p. 52). In his will, dated 18 February 1476, he asked to be buried 'in the nave of the cathedral church . . . next to the tomb of Master William Fulford' (see above) (DRO, Chanter XII (ii), Reg. Bothe, ff. 51v–52r). Buried there by 1492, when David Hopton (see above) asked for burial near him.

Warelwast, Robert

Bishop of Exeter. Died 1155, perhaps on 22 March, the date on which Exeter Cathedral subsequently kept his obit (D&C 3625, f. ii recto).

Buried in the choir of the cathedral (D&C 3625, f. 116v; Dalton and Doble, ii, 543). His tomb is mentioned in 1320–1 (Erskine, *Fabric Accounts*, i, 130).

Warelwast, William

Bishop of Exeter. Died 26 September 1137 (Oliver, *Monasticon*, p. 37). He was not buried in Exeter Cathedral but in Plympton Priory (Devon) (Leland, i, 215).

Waryn, John

Archdeacon of Barnstaple. Died by 31 July 1442 (Le Neve, p. 20). The record of his funeral in Exeter Cathedral occurs in Midsummer term 1442 (D&C 3771).

Webber, Henry

Dean of Exeter. Died 13 February 1477, according to his ledger stone, now in the 8th bay of the north choir aisle (Hope, Monumentarium, p. 28). In his will, dated 25 February 1472, he asked to be buried in the cathedral 'in the north ambulatory, which place was assigned to me by the [cathedral] chapter' (D&C 2365). In fact, he was given the rare honour, for someone not a bishop, of burial beneath a ledger stone in the presbytery, between the stone of Thomas Bitton and the south wall. This is shown by a plan and inventory of ledger stones in the cathedral choir, of about 1763, which describes the inscription on his stone in detail. It was moved at that date to the north choir aisle (D&C 4037–8, 4708).

Webber, John, senior

Parish of St Laurence, Exeter. On 29 April 1389 the dean and chapter of Exeter licensed the prior of the hospital of St John to bury his body in the hospital church (D&C 3559, f. 54v). Buried in the hospital by 1492 (DRO, ECA, Book 53A, f. 94v).

Wele, Letice

The record of her funeral in Exeter Cathedral occurs in Michaelmas term 1312 (D&C 3673, f. 116r).

Wells, John a

Parish of St Paul, Exeter. Buried in the nave of the church of the hospital of St John between 1520 and 1535 (DRO, ECA, Book 53A, f. 95r).

Wellis, William

Parish of St Martin, Exeter. Master. Buried in the hospital of St John by 1492 (DRO, ECA, Book 53A, f. 94v).

Westcote, John

Canon of Exeter Cathedral; related to Alice and William Oke (see above). Died by 23 June 1418 (Le Neve, p. 47). The record of his funeral in the cathedral occurs in Midsummer term 1418 (D&C 3770). In his will, dated 20 July 1411, he asked to be buried near the tomb of William Oke (*Reg. Stafford*, p. 418). A sum of 4s. was paid between

Michaelmas 1418 and Michaelmas 1419 for stone for paving his tomb (D&C 2673).

Wheler, Roger

Parish of St Laurence, Exeter. Rector of Yarcombe (Devon). Died by 17 February 1494 (DRO, Chanter XII (ii), Reg. King), f. 168r). Buried in the hospital of St John by 1530 (DRO, ECA, Book 53A, f. 94v).

Whetere, Thomas le

The record of his funeral in Exeter Cathedral occurs in Christmas term 1307–8 (D&C 3673, f. 81v).

Whytelock, John

Parish of St Stephen, Exeter. Buried in the hospital of St John between 1492 and 1520 (DRO, ECA, Book 53A, f. 94v).

Wych, John

'Sir'; i.e. priest or knight. A sum of 12d. was paid to Exeter Cathedral by his executors between Michaelmas 1493 and Michaelmas 1494 for stone, and 13d. for lime and sand, for his tomb, probably in the cathedral or its cemetery (D&C 2704/4).

Wyk, J. de

The record of his funeral in Exeter Cathedral occurs in Midsummer term 1326 (D&C 3764, f. 54v).

Wyke, Sar' de

Her funeral took place in Exeter Cathedral on 6 April 1315 (D&C 3764, f. 12v).

Wilford, —

Wife of Robert Wilford (see below). A sum of £2 was paid to Exeter Cathedral by her between Michaelmas 1397 and Michaelmas 1398 for her tomb: probably for permission to be buried in the cathedral with her husband. The cathedral bells were rung for her in about 1399 (D&C 3773, f. 70r).

Wilford, Elsote

Apparently the first wife of William Wilford (see below). A sum of 3s. 8d. was paid to Exeter Cathedral between Michaelmas 1405 and Michaelmas 1406 for her tomb, probably in the cathedral, and a further sum of 26s. 8d. was paid in the same period by William Wilford 'for the tomb of his dead wife in the [cathedral] church' (D&C 2663).

Wilford, Robert

Married layman; probably husband of the unnamed woman (see above). The bells of Exeter Cathedral were rung for him in Christmas term 1395–6 (D&C 3773, f. 70v). A sum of 20s. was paid to the cathedral between Michaelmas 1397 and Michaelmas 1398 for stone for his tomb (D&C 2657).

Wilford, William

Citizen of Exeter. Died between 30 June and 2 October 1413 (see below). In his will, dated 30 June 1413, he asked to be buried in Exeter Cathedral or its cemetery as his executors should determine (*Reg. Stafford*, p. 401). A sum of £3 6s. 8d. was paid by Canon John Westcote (see above), supervisor of his will, between Michaelmas 1412 and Michaelmas 1413 for his tomb (probably for permission for him to be buried in the cathedral), and 5s. was paid in the same period for stone for his tomb (D&C 2668).

Wyliet, John

Chancellor of Exeter Cathedral. Died by 14 December 1383 (Le Neve, p. 9). The bells of the cathedral were rung for him, probably at about that season (D&C 3550, f. 27v). Buried in the cathedral nave by 1396 when Chancellor Robert Bosoun (see above) was licensed to be buried on the south side of his grave (D&C 3550, f. 103r).

Wylle, Roger atte

Of Exeter; citizen. Died by 11 April 1377, when Bishop Brantingham arranged for the settlement of a dispute about the place of his burial, the Franciscan friars of Exeter having asserted that he chose to be buried with them (*Reg. Brantyngham*, i, 154).

Williams, Agnes

Parish of St Petroc, Exeter. Wife of Peter Williams (see below). Buried in the hospital of St John between 1492 and 1520 (DRO, ECA, Book 53A, f. 94v).

Williams, John

Canon of Exeter Cathedral. Died 1 May 1546 (Le Neve, p. 65). Allegedly buried in the cathedral beneath a ledger stone still existing in the nineteenth century but too worn to be fully deciphered (Oliver, *Lives of the Bishops*, p. 242).

Williams, Peter

Parish of St Petroc, Exeter. Husband of Agnes Williams (see above). Buried in the hospital of St John between 1492 and 1520 (DRO, ECA, Book 53A, f. 94v).

Willys, Richard

Brother of the hospital of St John. Buried before the altar of St Katharine in the church of the hospital between 1520 and 1535 (DRO, ECA, Book 53A, f. 95r).

Wynard, John (Wynnard)

Son of William Wynard (see below) (Oliver, *Monasticon*, p. 404). In his will, dated 1 May 1459, he asked to be buried in the Franciscan Friary, Exeter, 'in a certain new chapel there, next to my father' (PRO, PROB 11/5, f. 193r).

Wynard, William (Wenard)

Recorder of Exeter; married layman. Died between 31 January and 5 November 1442 (see below). In his will, dated 31 January 1442, he asked to be buried in the Franciscan Friary, Exeter, 'in a certain new chapel there' (PRO, PROB 11/1, f. 104r).

Wyndesore, —

Wife of Baldwin de Wyndesore. The record of her funeral in Exeter Cathedral occurs in Christmas term 1308–9 (D&C 3673, f. 89r).

Wyndesore, William

Subdean of Exeter Cathedral. Died about 24 February 1487 (Le Neve, p. 6). The bells of the cathedral were rung for him between Michaelmas 1486 and Michaelmas 1487 (D&C 3779, f. 231r).

Wyndout, John

The bells of Exeter Cathedral were rung for him in Easter term 1398 (D&C 3773, f. 70r).

Wyse, Thomas

Canon of Exeter Cathedral. Died 30 June 1548 (Le Neve, p. 63). In his will, dated 10 May 1537, he asked to be buried in the cathedral if he died in Exeter (PRO, PROB 11/32 (10 Populwell)).

Wythericg, Nicholas de

The record of his funeral in Exeter Cathedral occurs in Christmas term 1305–6 (D&C 3673, f. 65r).

Wodelegh, Agnes

Parish of St Mary Major, Exeter. In her will, dated 14 March 1349 (modern style), she asked to be buried in the church of St Mary Major (DRO, 51/1/2/1).

Wolston, John

Clerk of the works of Exeter Cathedral (Orme, *Minor Clergy*, p. 4). Died early in 1460; a sum of 3s. 1½d. was paid between Easter and Michaelmas 1460 for lime, sand and stone for his tomb, probably in or near the cathedral (D&C 2702).

Worth, Elizabeth

Parish of St Mary Arches, Exeter; widow. In her will, dated 17 November 1506, she asked to be buried in the church of St Mary Arches (PRO, PROB 11/15, f. 102r).

Worth, Roger (Wirth)

Parish of St Mary Arches, Exeter; layman. A sum of £3 6s. 8d. was paid to Exeter Cathedral between August 1486 and August 1487 for licence for him to be buried in the cathedral (D&C 3779, f. 3v). In his will, dated 7 October 1487, he asked to be buried in Exeter Cathedral 'in an ambulatory' if he happened to die in Exeter (PRO, PROB 11/8, f. 116r). The bells of the cathedral were rung for him between Michaelmas 1487 and Michaelmas 1488 (ibid., f. 231v).

Wotton, —

Wife of Robert de Wotton. The record of her funeral in Exeter Cathedral occurs in Midsummer term 1306 (D&C 3673, f. 99v).

Wulward of Jacobschurch

  Lord of the manor of Jacobschurch between Exeter and Topsham, later belonging to the priory of St James. Died in the early 12th century, before 1129. His funeral was held in Exeter Cathedral (Chambers, 1933, f. 4v; Rose-Troup, 1937, pp. 421–2, 429).

Yerde, —

  Buried in the hospital of St John by 1492 (DRO, ECA, Book 53A, f. 94v).

Yonge, Peter

  Parish of St Olave, Exeter. Died by 1446. A dispute took place over the offerings at his funeral between the rector of St Olave and the hospital of St John, between 1437 and 1446 (British Library, Harley MS 862, ff. 14r–15r). Buried in the hospital of St John by 1492 (DRO, ECA, Book 53A, f. 94v).

Yorke, William

  Citizen and merchant of Exeter. In his will, dated 28 February 1510, he asked to be buried in the Franciscan Friary, Exeter (PRO, PROB 11/ 14, f. 288r).

Ypotecar' – see Espicer

Part II

Wills and Executors

Introduction to Part II

Wills

The oldest extant will from the South-West of England was made by Ælfwold, bishop of Crediton, in the early eleventh century.[1] It is a solitary example and gives little clue to how common such documents were. Not until the middle of the thirteenth century do more wills make their appearance in the region, suggesting that the practice of will making had become or was becoming usual among wealthy clergy and laity, especially in Exeter from which the earliest such wills are forthcoming. We possess these wills largely by chance, as we do Bishop Ælfwold's, since there are no systematic collections or registers of wills from this period, if indeed any existed. Most of those that remain are preserved in the archives of religious houses in Exeter, because the testators (those who made the wills) were benefactors of the houses concerned. The cartulary of St Nicholas Priory contains the will of Canon William de Wullaveston (1244), that of Exeter Cathedral the will of Thomas Boteler (1263), and that of St John's Hospital those of Bartholomew Pinchun (1244) and Nicholas de Durneford (1326). The cathedral archives also include loose originals or copies of the wills of Walter Gervas (1258), Rosamund Kymmyng (1295), and five members of the Collecote family (1269–1324), who all appear to have owned property that passed to the cathedral. The only other wills made before 1300, those of John de Doulys (1267) and Henry de Berbilond (1296), also relate to St John's and the cathedral respectively, and may once have belonged to their archives although both documents have spent long stretches of their history elsewhere.[2]

A much larger collection of Exeter wills begins to survive in 1271, when a practice began of registering them in the mayor's court and having them inscribed on the rolls that recorded the court's activities. The mayor's

---

[1] For the will, see *The Crawford Collection of Early Charters and Documents*, ed. A.S. Napier and W.H. Stevenson (Oxford, 1895), pp. 23–4, 125–33. There were two such bishops in the same period (E.B. Fryde, *et. al.*, *Handbook of British Chronology*, 3rd ed. (London, 1986), p. 215), the will-maker apparently being the second.

[2] That of Doulys is now in the British Library, and that of Berbilond was recently purchased for the cathedral archives from a private owner.

court had no jurisdiction over wills as such and the registrations were voluntary, not mandatory, so that they represent only some of the wills made in Exeter or relating to it. They were registered because their makers bequeathed real property – lands and tenements – in the city, and the makers (or their heirs) wished these bequests to be recognised by the mayor's court and preserved for posterity in its records. Some 651 wills were registered in this way between 1271 and 1540, but the only significant parts of the wills for registration purposes were the clauses that dealt with real property, and these alone were normally transcribed onto the court roll. One of the earliest examples, that of Emer de Ponte (Document 9), includes a few other phrases, and later wills sometimes state that the property being bequeathed has some religious or charitable purpose, so that the interest of the extracts is not wholly limited to property and its conveyance. But it was not until 1474 that the clerks of the court began to register the whole of the will, and by that time the registrations were less frequent. In consequence, the rolls provide us with only 22 complete will texts between 1474 and 1540.

During the twelfth century the Church laid claim to supervising the making and execution of wills, and by the mid thirteenth, when wills from Exeter begin to survive, its claim was well established.[3] The wills concerned were usually wills bequeathing moveable property – household goods, money, and livestock – not real property of an immovable kind. A testator could permissibly bequeath moveable property, whereas lands and tene-ments were subject to the rights of overlords and heirs and could not always be bequeathed in a will. In towns, however, those who held lands and tenements often possessed the power to bequeath or sell them and this was the case in Exeter, so that its wills often include such bequests, hence the registration of such wills in the mayor's court. The Church's regulations on wills were set out for the diocese of Exeter (which covered Cornwall and Devon) by Bishop Quinil in 1287, as part of a code of statutes about religious beliefs and practices that he drew up for the benefit of his clergy. He laid down that when people wished to make wills, the clergyman of the parish should help them do so in the presence of at least two witnesses, so that they could dispose of their property for the benefit of their souls and make provision for their wives and children. A person's will could be written down or it could be 'nuncupative', meaning that it was made verbally in front of the witnesses who could testify afterwards to what had

---

[3] On the history of wills up to about 1300, see F. Pollock and F.W. Maitland, *The History of English Law Before the Time of Edward I*, 2nd ed., reprinted, 2 vols (Cambridge, 1968), ii, 314–56, and Michael M. Sheehan, *The Will in Medieval England, from the Conversion of the Anglo-Saxons to the End of the Thirteenth Century* (Toronto, Pontifical Institute of Mediaeval Studies, Studies and Texts, 6, 1963).

been said. Executors should be appointed to carry out the will and, when the testator was dead, the executors should go to the local ecclesiastical authority to prove the authenticity of the will. If the authority gave approval of this, the executors should be told to make an inventory in writing of the dead person's moveable goods and livestock in the presence of further trustworthy witnesses. This was to include all that he or she owned at the time of death, including any debts – owed or owing, and was to be made within fifteen days of the death, if possible. The executors were then to attach their seals to the inventory, after which they could be given power to administer the goods and to carry out the bequests of the will.[4]

The officers who supervised this process were the usual Church authorities: the bishop, the archdeacons (of whom there were four in Exeter diocese), and those who ruled the various 'peculiars'. Peculiars were parishes that lay outside the normal system of Church government, and most of them in Devon and Cornwall belonged either to the bishop or to the cathedral.[5] If you were a testator who died owning property located in a single archdeaconry, which was true of most people, your will was administered by the local archdeacon in his court. The three Exeter wills in the present volume whose administration has been recorded belonged to this category, beginning with that of John de Doulys in 1257, and came before the court of the archdeacon of Exeter, presided over by the person who deputised for the archdeacon, called his 'official'. If you had property in more than one archdeaconry, or lived in a peculiar belonging to the bishop, or (at least in later times) were a clergyman, your will was proved before the bishop or his deputy, known as his 'commissary'.[6] In the peculiars belonging to the cathedral, wills were supervised by the cathedral clergy. Thus the will of Rosamund Kymmyng, who lived in Topsham, was proved before the cathedral canon who administered the parish. If your property lay in more than one diocese, it came under the jurisdiction of the archbishop of the province, who was the archbishop of Canterbury in the case of Exeter diocese. The archbishop also claimed jurisdiction when a diocese was vacant, and if the archbishopric was vacant at the same time, the claim passed to the prior of the archbishop's cathedral at Canterbury.

From at least the end of the fourteenth century some Church authorities were keeping copies of the wills proved before them: copies written in registers. There is a good series of registers of the archbishop of Canter-

---

[4] *Councils and Synods with Other Documents Relating to the English Church, II: A.D. 1205–1313*, ed. F.M. Powicke and C.R. Cheney, 2 vols (Oxford, 1964), ii, 1045–9.

[5] For a map of the medieval peculiars in Exeter diocese, see Nicholas Orme, 'The Church from *c.*1300 to the Reformation', in *Historical Atlas of South-West England*, ed. R. Kain and W. Ravenhill (Exeter, 1999), pp. 214–15.

[6] *Reg. Stafford*, pp. 379–423.

bury's prerogative court, beginning in 1383, now in the Public Record Office, and these contain several dozen Exeter wills before the Reformation.[7] A smaller number of copies of Exeter wills, chiefly of clergy, are preserved in the episcopal registers of the archbishops of Canterbury, now at Lambeth Palace,[8] and four wills from the city are included in the registers of the priors of Canterbury.[9] No wills appear among the records of the bishops of Exeter until the time of Bishop Stafford (1395–1419), whose episcopal register contains 60 examples over a period of about 22 years, while that of his successor Edmund Lacy (1420–1455) contains 38.[10] Both these registers include examples from Exeter itself. After Lacy's death, however, the copying of wills into the episcopal registers declined in frequency and was virtually obsolete by 1500. By the early sixteenth century it had given way to the keeping of copies of wills by the various Church courts which, by this time, administered them. Three of these courts are relevant to Exeter and its surrounding district. The court of the archdeacon of Exeter kept copies of wills by 1540. The dean and chapter's consistory court, which administered wills in the peculiars belonging to the cathedral (including Heavitree and Topsham), did so by 1547, and the bishop's principal registry, which handled the wills of clergy and those of people with property in more than one archdeaconry or other jurisdiction, by 1555.[11] These, however, are merely the earliest dates of the records that survived in about 1900, and the practice of keeping copies in all three courts may have been older than this.[12] All the early wills that existed in the three court archives were destroyed or lost following the bombing of the reposi-

---

[7] *Index of Wills Proved in the Prerogative Court of Canterbury*, ed. J.C. Challoner Smith, 2 vols, British Record Society, Index Library, 9 (1893), 11 (1895). The wills are now kept at the Public Record Office's Family History Research Centre in Islington, London.

[8] J.C. Challoner Smith, 'Calendar of Lambeth Wills', *The Genealogist*, new series, 34 (1918), pp. 53–64, 149–60, 219–34; 35 (1919), pp. 45–51, 102–26.

[9] *Sede Vacante Wills*, ed. C. Eveleigh Woodruff, Kent Archaeological Society, Kent Records, 3 (1914). Three of these wills are duplicates of wills in the registers of the Prerogative Court of Canterbury.

[10] *Reg. Stafford*, pp. 379–423; *Reg. Lacy*, ed. Dunstan, IV, 1–63.

[11] *Calendar of Wills and Administrations Relating to the Counties of Devon and Cornwall Proved in the Court of the Principal Registry of the Bishop of Exeter, 1559–1799, and of Devon Only, Proved in the Court of the Archdeaconry of Exeter, 1540–1799*, ed. E.A. Fry (Plymouth, The Devonshire Association, 1908), pp. v–xv; *Calendar of Wills and Administrations Relating to the Counties of Devon and Cornwall Proved in the Consistory Court of the Bishop of Exeter, 1532–1800*, ed. E.A. Fry (Plymouth, The Devonshire Association, 1914).

[12] In 1846 George Oliver printed extracts from three clergy wills of the 1530s that may have come from an earlier register of the bishop's principal registry (*Monasticon Dioecesis Exoniensis*, p. 164).

tory in Exeter where they were held in 1942. Some remains of them survive in transcripts made before their destruction by Olive Moger and Sir Oswyn Murray, which are now preserved in the Devon Record Office and the West Country Studies Library, both in Exeter. Virtually all these transcripts are of wills dated later than 1540, and they therefore lie outside the scope of the present volume.

Devon and Exeter are less well provided with medieval wills than some other regions of England, notably East Anglia where there are large collections from the courts of the bishop of Norwich and his archdeacons. Nevertheless over 600 Exeter wills survive in the various sources mentioned above, either completely or in extracts in the mayor's court rolls (Document 23). The eighteen wills included in the present volume represent the earliest examples from the city, in a period (from 1244 to 1349) when little else survives by way of personal records relating to its inhabitants. Thirteen are wills of laymen, four of laywomen, and three of male clergy, the latter of whom were all staff of the cathedral. Of course a will was not wholly a document of personal statements and choices. It followed a set form, or forms, and was drawn up as much by its scribe – usually a priest or clerk – as by the person who nominally made it. Wills were religious as well as legal documents, a point underlined by the frequent presence of the parish clergyman when they were made. Many were drawn up close to the point of death, as can be seen by comparing the date when the will was made with that of its subsequent 'probate' when the executors brought it to the Church court. Even those made in health were usually preoccupied with the death and afterlife of their makers, giving much attention to funeral arrangements and charitable bequests for securing the passage of the soul to heaven as quickly and easily as possible.

A will might bequeath real property, moveable property, or a mixture of the two. Wills concerned with real property are more typical of the towns than of the countryside, reflecting (as has been mentioned) the greater freedom of urban dwellers to bequeath such property compared with their rural counterparts. One of our wills, that of William de Wullaveston, is solely concerned with disposing of his real property to charity and is not dissimilar in format to a charter conveying lands and tenements. Indeed it opens with a phrase often found in such charters: 'Let all the faithful in Christ to whom this present writing comes know that . . .' It differs from a charter in being a provisional grant, post-dated until after the maker's death rather than having immediate effect, and in appointing executors to give effect to the grant when the maker was dead. Wills conveying moveable property, or a mixture of moveable and real, usually begin with an invocation of God: 'In the name of the Father and of the Son and of the Holy Spirit, amen', or a similar phrase. This is followed by an identification of the person who was making the will, a statement that he or she was of sound mind (in case the will should be challenged), and a notification of the date on which the will was made. Will makers normally adopted an autobiographical manner, 'I make my will', and used the present tense. Wullaveston's in contrast is written in the perfect tense, 'I have made', which reflects a practice found elsewhere in the early and mid thirteenth century but not afterwards.[13] Three of the wills translated below (those of Bartholomew Pinchun, John de Doulys, and Adam de Collecote) are phrased in the third person, 'he bequeaths . . .' The last two of these are so detailed that they can hardly be nuncupative wills written down later on. Rather they seem to follow an alternative convention for writing a will that adopts the standpoint of the writer rather than the will-maker. This convention, like the use of the perfect tense, died out in the course of the thirteenth century.

After the opening phrases testators bequeathed their most intimate selves: their souls and bodies. The soul was commended to God and sometimes also to the Virgin Mary and other favourite saints, while the body was consigned to burial: often with an indication of where that was to be. Arrangements for funerals, graves, and tombs were sometimes made at this point. Next came the disposal of property, real or moveable, the sequence of which was not uniform but was likely to include bequests for religious purposes and gifts to relatives or friends. Religious bequests would include donations to the poor, to clergy, or to religious houses, usually in return for prayers. Occasionally a horse or gown was given as a 'mortuary' payment to the testator's parish priest or church, and a small sum for tithes or offerings that might have been forgotten during life. Moveable property included clothes, jewellery, bed furnishings, livestock, food, household utensils, and tools. There was a widespread custom in England that half of a man's moveables should pass to his wife, or a third if there were surviving children who had not been provided for already. The children also received a third share, or a half if there was no wife.[14] The remaining half or third share was free for testators to dispose as they wished. Wills usually ended by nominating the executors who were to carry out the testators' wishes, and sometimes also named supervisors to oversee the work of the executors.

All the testators represented in this volume gave money to clergy and for religious purposes, but some variations appear in their preferences. Most seem to have expected to be buried in the cathedral cemetery, though Emer de Ponte chose one of the friaries and Agnes de Wodelegh followed a new fashion for burial in a parish church. Apart from funerals and burials, however, the early Exeter wills suggest that the cathedral was somewhat remote from its townspeople, except for Walter Gervas who endowed

---

[13] Sheehan, *The Will in Medieval England*, p. 194.
[14] Pollock and Maitland, *History of English Law*, ii, 348–56.

prayers to be said there. Instead the testators display attachments to other churches in the city. Emer de Ponte and Lucy de Collecote favoured the Franciscan Friary, and Bartholomew Pinchun and John de Doulys the hospital of St John. Several other wills made a selection of small donations to the two friaries, St John's, and the leper hospital of St Mary Magdalene outside the walls, but the priory of St Nicholas occurs only in the wills of Henry de Berbilonde and Peter Soth. The suburban priories of Cowick, Polsloe, and St James are not mentioned at all. The Collecote family and William Mounteyn seem to have lived near the parish church of St Mary Steps and gave it their allegiance, while Agnes de Wodelegh patronised St Mary Major. Walter Gervas endowed his own chantry priest to pray for him in the chapel of the Virgin Mary on Exe Bridge, and both priest and chapel lasted until the Reformation. Two wills remembered the prisoners in the Exeter gaols, and two the bridges in and around the city. The bequest of money to poor people on the day of the funeral was also a common practice.

These early Exeter wills belonged to relatively important people, and their contents reflect the standard of living of prosperous citizens and their wives. The three cathedral clergy were similar in status and wealth, two being canons and the third a vicar-choral who was less well paid but possessed a good deal of private property. Oddly the citizens' wills and those of their wives give us little or no indication of the trades they may have followed. We see them chiefly as the holders of lands and tenements, the rents of which formed a large part of their income. The wills contain a good deal of evidence about this property: houses in Exeter itself, gardens and closes just outside, and occasionally lands in other parts of Devon. It is interesting that our four testators who were women all used surnames that were different from those of their husbands, although in three cases the husbands were still alive. Instead they appear to have used their fathers' names, no doubt to signify that they had inherited real property of their own and were at liberty to dispose of it. Wealthy women in towns had more freedom of this kind than most of their counterparts elsewhere in society.

The wills are rich in mentions of moveable goods. Such items, of course, are mentioned selectively, and care is needed in arguing from them about their owners' whole possessions and culture. For example no lay person's will refers to a book, yet we know by chance that an Exeter citizen named Baldwin de Windesore caused a copy of the romance of Guy of Warwick to be written in 1301, testifying to an interest in reading by at least one such person of this class.[15] Fortunately in one case we can supplement what appears in the will with a document that lists the rest of the testator's

---

[15] *Index Britanniae Scriptorum*, ed. R.L. Poole and Mary Bateson, 2nd ed. (Cambridge, 1990), p. 104.

possessions. This is the inventory of 'all the goods' of Lucy de Collecote, made by her executors in 1324 and one of only two such documents to survive from Exeter at such an early date (Document 21). She was a member of a property-owning Exeter family, the widow of an apothecary, William de la Trewe, and appears to have died at an advanced age. Her inventory lists many clothes, furnishings, and items of household equipment, and even conveys some sense of the rooms in her house, including a chamber where she slept, a hall, and a kitchen.

Wills are also valuable for the light that they throw on the lives of individuals and their relationships with other people. Some of the families whose members made these early wills had originated in the countryside, and had gained or increased their wealth by coming to Exeter. The Collecote family probably took their name from a small rural settlement of the same name (it means 'the cold cottage'), and there are two possible candidates for the place in Devon: Chollacott in Whitchurch and Coldacott in Sampford Courtenay. Adam de Collecote, the earliest member of the family to leave a will, owned property at Kenn near Exeter. John de Doulys took his surname from Dawlish, and had family connections with the Teignhead area as well as property at Monkokehampton. Henry de Berbilond held land in Poltimore and Silverton, and he or his family probably originated from a farm in Silverton parish, now known as Babylon.[16] The widest affiliations, not surprisingly, were those of the cathedral canons who often moved to Exeter from elsewhere through the patronage of bishops. Here Thomas Boteler provides a good example, with his bequests to places in Gloucestershire and Oxfordshire, from which he apparently drew his origins. Wills mention family members, and it is possible to construct a genealogy for the Collecotes that covers three generations. We are also made aware of the presence of servants, who were often remembered with gifts, and of the will-maker's links with clergy: cathedral clergy, parish rectors, chaplains, monks, and friars, depending on his or her interests. The increasing complexity of thirteenth-century Exeter, with its newly-established parish churches and religious houses, probably meant brisk competition among their members for the favour of those with money to give.[17]

The Accounts of the Executors of Andrew Kilkenny

With their detailed inventories and records of expenditure, executors'

---

[16] Nicholas Orme, 'Henry de Berbilond, d. 1296, a Vicar Choral of Exeter Cathedral', *Devon and Cornwall Notes and Queries*, 37 part 1 (Spring, 1992), pp. 1–7.

[17] On the apparent growth of complexity in the city, see also above, p. 37.

accounts have long been recognised as an important source of religious and social history. Unlike wills, which raise considerable problems of interpretation, they offer a more complete record of possessions and wealth as well as showing how dead people's estates were disposed of.[18] In addition, where the will has also survived, they enable some assessment to be made of the extent to which the testator's intentions were carried out. Most wills left considerable discretion to the executors, especially in handling the residue of the estate after the bequests had been made, which was often disposed of in a formulaic instruction that it be used for the good of the testator's soul. Executors' accounts provide valuable evidence of how precisely this was done, what types of provisions were made for the soul of the departed, and the charitable giving that was often part of this. As mentioned above, the duties of executors were codified in canon law during the thirteenth century.[19] Their first duty was to organise the funeral and burial of the deceased together with prayers and masses for their soul. After making an inventory of the deceased's goods and paying their debts, they assigned the portions due to surviving wives and children. Then debts owed to the deceased were collected, legacies were paid, and any other instructions (such as the foundation of an obit or chantry) were carried out, after which the residue of the estate was distributed. Finally the executors were required to present their accounts to the official in charge of the court that administered the will and to be discharged of their duties. The format of executors' accounts broadly follows this pattern.

Unfortunately there are very few such accounts from the medieval period. Most of those from England south of the Humber (the ecclesiastical province of Canterbury) were destroyed in the Great Fire of London. The best surviving collection, of about a hundred, is at York (relating to the northern archbishopric), which includes a broad range of testators: clerical and lay, male and female, wealthy and those of modest means. Many were published by the Surtees Society in the nineteenth century and all have recently been translated.[20] Chronologically, however, the majority of surviving accounts in England date from the fifteenth century, and there are not many older ones. One of the oldest and most complete are the accounts of Walter Merton, bishop of Rochester (d. 1277), who was coincidentally the patron

---

18 C. Burgess, 'Late Medieval Wills and Pious Convention: testamentary evidence reconsidered', in *Profit, Piety and the Professions in Late Medieval England*, ed. M.A. Hicks (Gloucester, 1990), pp.14–33.

19 Sheehan, *The Will in Medieval England*, pp. 215–19.

20 *Testamenta Eboracensia*, ed. J. Raine and J.W. Clay, 6 vols, Surtees Society, 4, 30, 45, 53, 79, 106 (1836–1902); *York Clergy Wills 1520–1600: I, Minster Clergy*, ed. C. Cross, York, Borthwick Institute of Historical Research, Borthwick Texts and Calendars, 10 (1984); *Probate Inventories of the York Diocese 1350–1500*, ed. P.M. Stell and L. Hampson (York, 1998).

of Andrew Kilkenny, dean of Exeter (d. 1302).[21] Kilkenny's own accounts, translated in this volume (Document 22), are another early example and form part of a remarkable small group of such records from Exeter, the others being those of Bishop Bitton (d. 1307) and Bishop Stapledon (d. 1326).[22] The Kilkenny accounts can also be compared, as illustrations of the property and affairs of a cathedral cleric, with ten examples relating to cathedral canons in the York collection and with a handful of similar records elsewhere, including those of Dean Mamsfield (d. 1328) and Chancellor Cotte (d. 1384) at Lincoln, and Chancellor Nassington (d. 1364) at Lich-field.[23]

The accounts of the executors of Andrew Kilkenny are contained in an eight-membrane roll measuring 213mm by 2709mm, which has survived in good condition. They are written in a clear early fourteenth-century script. Unfortunately no copy of the dean's will survives, though it can be partially reconstructed from the accounts. These are set out in two parts: income and expenditure. The first, in twenty-nine sections, is an inventory of the dean's wealth and possessions – the earliest such document that we possess from Exeter, anticipating that of Bishop Bitton by five years. The second, also in twenty-nine sections, consists of financial accounts describing the implementation of Kilkenny's will and the disposal of his estate by the executors. Both parts are remarkable for the detail they contain, which enables the activities of the executors to be traced over successive years from 1302 to 1315. The bulk of the accounts cover the nine years from the dean's death on 4 November 1302 to October 1311 when the executors presented them for audit. The accounts were periodically added to for another four years as the final distributions from the estate were made, though these were mainly small sums; the last dated payment was in June 1315. There were two executors at first: William Kilkenny, a relation of the dean and a canon of Exeter Cathedral, and Walter de Tottonia (or Totnes), a chaplain of lower status. But it appears that Walter died or withdrew during the long period of administering the will, and that William wound up the process as sole executor.

Andrew Kilkenny belonged to a notable clerical dynasty that can be traced for over a century. Its founder and most prominent member was

---

[21] *The Early Rolls of Merton College Oxford*, ed. J.R.L. Highfield, Oxford Historical Society, new series, 18 (1964).

[22] *Accounts of the Executors of Richard, Bishop of London, 1303, and of the Executors of Thomas, Bishop of Exeter, 1310*, ed. W.H. Hale and H.T. Ellacombe, Camden Society, new series, 10 (1874); *Reg. Stapeldon*, pp. 562–79.

[23] Lincoln, Lincolnshire Archives Office, Dean and Chapter, Dii/60/9, Div/14/1; *Catalogue of Muniments and Manuscript Books of the Dean and Chapter of Lichfield and of the Lichfield Vicars*, ed. J.C. Cox, William Salt Society, 6 part 2 (1886), pp. 225–30.

William Kilkenny (d. 1256), bishop of Ely and chancellor of Henry III.[24] Andrew's early career is obscure; he first appears in records in 1275 as an already successful cleric and senior diocesan administrator.[25] Though it is doubtful if he belonged to Bishop William's household, since he would have been too young, he certainly regarded him as a benefactor and remembered him in his own chantry foundation. He may have grown up under the patronage of another member of the dynasty, Henry Kilkenny (d. by 1280), executor of Bishop William and canon of both Chichester and Exeter.[26] No details of Andrew's education are known, but from 1275 he was usually styled *Magister*, probably because he had studied at university. In that year he was appointed to the important legal and administrative office of official principal of the diocese of Rochester by its bishop, Walter de Merton. After Merton's death in 1277 and a very brief period in royal service, he moved to the diocese of Exeter in 1278 to work for Bishop Bronescombe, whom he was serving as a similar official in 1280.[27] Soon afterwards, while still engaged in the administration of Merton's estate, he attracted the attention of Archbishop Pecham of Canterbury who recruited him to his service as dean of the court of Arches, the archbishop's important church court in London, from 1282 to 1286. This post did not sever his connections with Exeter, however. On the contrary Bronescombe's successor as bishop, Peter Quinil, appointed him as a canon of the cathedral in 1282, precentor in 1283, and dean in 1284, and after 1286 he appears to have been usually resident in Exeter.[28] Unlike many successful thirteenth-century clerics Kilkenny does not seem to have been a pluralist on a large scale (i.e. someone who held several church benefices at once), although he briefly occupied two Devon rectories before becoming canon of Exeter and had a prebend in the collegiate church of Darlington (Durham) in 1291.[29]

When Kilkenny's death took place in 1302 he was a very wealthy member of the higher clergy with an estate valued at £916 18s. 0¾d; few below

---

[24] D&C 1927; A.B. Emden, *A Biographical Register of the University of Oxford to A.D.1500*, 3 vols (Oxford, 1957–9), ii, 1048–9.

[25] His career is outlined in *The Early Rolls of Merton College Oxford*, ed. Highfield, pp. 39, 58.

[26] *The Register of John Pecham, Archbishop of Canterbury 1279–92*, ed. Decima Douie, vol. ii, Canterbury and York Society, 65 (1968), pp. 108–9; J. Le Neve, *Fasti Ecclesiae Anglicanae 1066–1300, 5: Chichester*, ed. Diane Greenway (London, 1999), p. 60.

[27] *Calendar of Patent Rolls 1272–81*, p. 264.

[28] *Reg. Bronescombe*, ed. Hingeston-Randolph, pp. 343–4.

[29] Ibid., pp. 119, 180; *Taxatio Ecclesiastica Angliae et Walliae Auctoritate P. Nicholai IV circa 1291*, ed. T. Astle, S. Ayscough, and J. Caley (London, Record Commission, 1802), p. 83.

the episcopate equalled his wealth.[30] Nearly a quarter of this, over £200, was in cash and plate: £160 in cash and the rest in plate. Twenty-five silver or gilt vessels are accounted for. His next most valuable possessions were his books, a collection of sixty-three volumes valued at £66. This was the working library of a senior diocesan administrator. It was dominated by the standard texts of canon law (the *Decretum* and *Decretals*), civil law (the *Digest, Inforciatum*, and *Parvum Volumen*), and commentaries upon them, together with liturgical books, collections of sermons, a little theology, and some history. Three volumes were partly written in the dean's own hand and were probably formularies: collections of model legal documents. Kilkenny's interest in learning is also reflected in his patronage of scholars, who included four of his kin. His other possessions are listed in detail. They give an impression of the dean's lifestyle as comfortable and well-provided. They reveal the importance of the generous hospitality that the resident cathedral clergy were expected to give, illustrated by the large quantities of table linen, the canopies for guests in the hall, and the alms dish kept there for holding portions of the meal that were set aside for the poor. The ancillary rooms of the deanery – kitchen, bakehouse, pantry, and cellar – were well equipped to provide this hospitality.

The majority of Kilkenny's wealth came from the income from his estates: some attached to the office of dean and some belonging to the chapter, the latter of which as a resident canon he was entitled to 'farm' or administer. The dean's office had been endowed at its foundation by Bishop Brewer in 1225 with revenues from three churches: Braunton and Bishop's Tawton in north Devon and Colaton Raleigh in east Devon.[31] Its annual income was valued at £62 13s. 4d. in the 1291 valuation of Pope Nicholas IV,[32] but the accounts suggest that this was a considerable underestimate, less than half of what the dean usually received in practice and less than that of Braunton, the most valuable church. In 1302 Braunton was valued at £211 15s. 1d. (although £122 of this consisted of arrears), Bishop's Tawton at £29 17s. 2d., its two dependent chapelries of Swimbridge and Landkey at £25 13s. 11d. and £30 16s. respectively, and Colaton Raleigh at £21 18s. 10½d. In addition the dean farmed two chapter estates, St

---

[30] Four fifteenth-century York canons matched or surpassed Kilkenny's wealth: Thomas Dalby, Thomas Greenwood, William Duffield, and Martin Collyns, worth £1,542 6s. 10d., £899 1s. 1d., £1,317 18s. 1¼d., and £1,437 15s. 5¾d. respectively (*Probate Inventories of the Diocese of York*, ed. Stell and Hampson, p.35; *Testamenta Eboracensia*, iii, 64–5, 125–52; iv, 279–308).

[31] Audrey M. Erskine, 'Bishop Briwere and the Reorganisation of the Chapter of Exeter Cathedral', *Devonshire Association Transactions*, 108 (1976), pp. 159–71.

[32] *Reg. Bronescombe*, ed. Hingeston-Randolph, p. 465.

Sidwell's Exeter, which included holdings in Heavitree, valued at £55 14s. 6½d. and Winkleigh worth £34 5 0¾d. He also held or administered a third unidentified estate at *Ynnyngeston* worth £18 17s. 4¾d. The dean's potential income was over £300 a year, but the accounts make clear that not all of this was actually received and that considerable sums were written off as losses or bad debts.

As was to be expected of a high-ranking cleric, Dean Kilkenny had a substantial household: one large enough to reflect his status and wealth and dispense hospitality on a generous scale.[33] Twenty-six of its members can be identified from the executors' accounts, mainly through their surnames, which are likely to indicate their occupations. Unusually the people concerned are mostly lower-ranking servants, who are generally hard to identify in medieval records, while the senior staff of the dean's household remain comparatively obscure. The household probably had about thirty members, its size being typical of the wealthier higher clergy just below the rank of bishop. Of those listed in the accounts, twenty were based at the deanery at Exeter and the remainder on his estates. The Exeter household included a porter, marshal, palfreyman, baker, brewer, cook, and six grooms from the lower ranks, and a chaplain and chamberlain from the upper. Five other men were based on the dean's estates and chapter farms and are simply called servants. They probably acted as estate managers or reeves.

A particularly important aspect of the executors' accounts is the way that they chart the dispersal of such a large estate over several years. Legacies made in observance of the dean's will accounted for £84, a relatively small proportion of his total wealth. From these his will can be at least partly reconstructed. They show that the dean made a conventional range of bequests to the cathedral and some of its clergy, to members of his household, and to a group of other individuals connected with him. Of greater interest are the much larger sums distributed in other ways, which were probably not specified in the will but left to the discretion of the executors. They suggest that the executors, especially the dean's kinsman, William, had very wide powers of discretion. The first major item of expenditure listed is Kilkenny's funeral and burial, costing £34 3s. Most of this was spent in an orthodox fashion on prayers and masses said for his soul and on £12 15s. worth of bread as alms to the poor. More unusual are the details of the construction of his tomb, which can still be seen in a much-mutilated form in St Andrew's chapel in Exeter Cathedral. It consisted of a large Purbeck marble slab incised with a quatrefoil cross and an inscription around the edge, the latter inlaid with brass letters. Only the

---

[33] Canons' households and hospitality are discussed in D.N. Lepine, *A Brotherhood of Canons Serving God* (Woodbridge, 1995), chapter 6.

outlines of the cross and of some of the lettering can now be identified.[34] Also of interest are the accounts of the expenses incurred in the establishment of a chantry in Kilkenny's memory. Together with the surviving foundation deed of the chantry (Document 30), these expenses provide an unusually detailed picture of the process of setting up such a foundation. The deed sets out the aims of the chantry: to provide prayers for the souls of Dean Andrew and other members of the Kilkenny family and to benefit the cathedral by increasing the number of its clergy and religious services. The executors spent £32 16s. 8½d. on founding the chantry, half of which was used to purchase its endowment. The endowment consisted of the church of West Anstey in north Devon, and two acres of land there (reflecting a legal requirement that a church could not be acquired without some land in addition). When clergy acquired possession of a church they were able to divert some of its revenues, with the bishop's permission, to another religious purpose, which in this case was the payment of a chantry priest and the expenses of running a chantry. The rest of the cost was incurred in the negotiations to acquire the church and in obtaining a royal licence to acquire it.

A substantial proportion of the estate was distributed among the dean's kin, though their precise relationship to him is usually difficult to trace. John de Briggeham and his sisters received nearly £70 for their maintenance and other expenses over five years from 1302 to 1307. Philip de Kilkenny (d. 1346) was another major beneficiary, receiving more than £58. He is the last known member of the Kilkenny clerical dynasty and benefited from the dean's executors in the form of payment for his university education at Oxford and subsequently overseas. Philip went on to have a successful career, if not quite on the dean's scale, as rector of Kettering (Nhants.) and as a member of the council of the abbot of Peterborough.[35] The executors also paid out money, under the heading of the dean's kin, to people from places with which he had been connected, such as the parishes of the churches belonging to the deanery. Small sums were given to named individuals from these places, often repeatedly in separate payments. Larger sums were allocated for distribution to poor parishioners, sometimes in the form of clothing and shoes and sometimes in the remission of debts.

The accounts show clearly how much of the dean's estate was distributed to places with which he had personal ties, particularly the estates and churches that had given him income and status, the decanal property of Braunton, Bishop's Tawton, and Colaton Raleigh, and the chapter estates

[34] V. Hope, 'Two Incised Slabs with Indents in Exeter Cathedral', *Transactions of the Monumental Brass Society*, 10 part 2 (1964), pp. 102–6.
[35] Emden, *Biographical Register of Oxford*, ii, 1048.

he farmed: Winkleigh and St Sidwell's. This also included the church of West Anstey, purchased to fund his chantry, whose chancel was rebuilt. Very little was distributed elsewhere, particularly outside the diocese, which suggests that after the mid 1280s the dean's career was almost exclusively focused in the diocese of Exeter. As would be expected from a long-serving resident dean, the cathedral and its clergy were treated generously with total grants of about £50. As well as his foundation of a chantry and an annual 'obit mass' to be held on the anniversary of his death, both inside the cathedral, there were payments to the minor clergy and the fabric, and gifts of £6 13s. 4d. and 100s. towards the cost of the new reredos behind the high altar. The city of Exeter was also the object of charitable giving for the benefit of the dean's soul to its parish clergy, poor, and prisoners. In contrast the other religious houses in the diocese were mostly either ignored or treated less generously. Only three received more than small token sums: the nunneries of Polsloe and Cornworthy, and most of all the Franciscan friars of Exeter. The dean (or his executors) had considerable respect for the ministry of the Franciscans, establishing an obit mass in their church for fourteen years and giving sums of 20s. to the community, 40s. for their 'new fabric', and £10 for needy members of their order.

The details of the accounts allow some insight into the personal devotion of the dean. In many respects his piety was conventional, as can be seen in the foundation of his chantry and obit and the prayers and masses said for his soul, although the accounts enable us to see precisely what provisions were made and how much they cost. However two features stand out. One is the dean's devotion to St Andrew. Kilkenny was presumably drawn to this saint by sharing his name, and he was almost certainly responsible for establishing St Andrew's chapel in the cathedral – a chapel that was being built while he was dean and which was largely equipped and decorated by him. As well as founding his chantry at its altar, he also endowed a procession there in 1299 to take place on the eve of the feast of St Andrew.[36] The other notable feature is the acquisition by the dean's executors of written indulgences from 'various bishops', offering remission of penance to those who prayed for his soul. The documents thus acquired were then copied and placed in 'various churches' to advertise them. This practice seems to have been fairly widespread in the case of eminent people during the early fourteenth century, and although evidence about it is hard to find, there are several such grants of indulgence in the registers of the bishops of Lincoln from this period.[37]

---

[36] D&C 394.
[37] These are discussed in R.N. Swanson, 'Prayers for the Dead in the Diocese of Lincoln in the Early Fourteenth Century', *Journal of Ecclesiastical History*, 52 (2001), pp. 197–219.

The accounts are remarkably thorough and complete, and the mass of detail they contain is one of their most important features. It ranges from the livestock and equipment on the dean's estates, which included ten peacocks and peahens, to the extensive negotiations, litigation, and travel undertaken by the executors in the recovery and disposal of the dean's assets, together with their expenses. Both the 2d. spent hiring a feather bed for two weeks, so that a chamberlain could sleep in the dean's room during his final illness, and the 14s. 4d. spent on a search of the rolls of the exchequer to clear the accounts of the dean when he had been in royal service as a tax collector, are itemised. Such information throws valuable light on the social history of the fourteenth century as well as on the personal history of a leading member of the higher clergy.[38]

[38] A full analysis of Andrew Kilkenny's career and the executors' accounts will appear in a forthcoming article by David Lepine.

3–21. Early Exeter Wills, 1244–1349

3. Bartholomew Pinchun, layman, 1244

(Source: DRO, Exeter City Archives, Book 53A, f. 16r. Latin text, adopting the convention of reported speech.)

The testament of Bartholomew Pinchun on the morrow [10 October] of St Denis the martyr, in the year of the Lord 1244. First he bequeaths his soul to God and his body to the cemetery of St Peter. Also he owes John le Granger 22½d. of debt. Also he bequeaths to God and the hospital of St John within the East Gate of Exeter all his rent against the wide part of his house which was formerly that of Adam Pinchun, his father, which Roger Beyvyn holds, next to the well [*fontem*], for his soul and for the souls of his ancestors and descendants [*successorum*]. Also he bequeaths his surcoat of russet to Henry de Moleheywil. Also he bequeaths to the master of the hospital his thigh-boots [*hocreas*]. Also he bequeaths to Robert the clerk his coat of russet. Also he bequeaths a carpet [*tapetum*] to Henry de Mole-heywil. Also he bequeaths a blanket to James the cook. Also he bequeaths a sheet to Guignet [*Guigneto*]. Also he bequeaths another sheet with a blanket to the poor infirm people of the house of St John. Also he bequeaths a pair of *crinium* [?] to John le Granger. Also he bequeaths his debt which Martin Durlyng owes him, namely 20s., and all the other debts that are owed to him to God and the hospital of St John. Also to Henry, chaplain of the house, his chest and his short gown [*waudecorsum*] of russet.

4. William de Wullaveston, canon of Exeter Cathedral, 1244

(Source: British Library, Cotton MS Vitellius D.ix, f. 104r. Latin text, copied into the cartulary of St Nicholas Priory, Exeter.)

Let all the faithful in Christ to whom this present writing comes know that I, William de Wllaueston, canon of Exeter, being sound and unimpaired by the grace of God, making my testament with a good memory, have assigned, ordained, and conceded (in case anyone should affect anything

139

of me that is human after my death) that from the 18s. of annual rent which I bought from the prior and convent of Bruton [Somerset] to be taken from the chapter of Exeter each year from the house in which I am accustomed to dwell in St Martin's Street, Exeter, the chapter is to retain to itself 10s. annually with which to hold the office of the dead in a solemn way on the day of the anniversary of my obit every year in the [cathedral] church of Exeter, as it is done for Master Isaac of good memory of the same church of Exeter and archdeacon of Totnes. And on the same day of my obit every year the Friars Preachers are to receive and have 2s. from the same rent, by the hands of the stewards of the said chapter, and the Friars Minor the same, and the monks of St Nicholas and the brothers of the Magdalene [hospital] of Exeter 1s. for a pittance so that they may have a memory of me in their prayers and benefits. In perpetual memory and fuller evidence of my testament and assignment and concession I have attached my seal to this present writing made on this [matter] [f. 104v], having constituted as principal executors or proctors of the same the religious men of the Friars Preachers and the priors of Blessed Nicholas, Exeter, who shall be [in office] for the time, so that they, always having God before their eyes, may faithfully carry out all the things stated above. Dated at Exeter in the year of the Lord 1244.

5. Walter Gervas, layman, 1258 [?]

(Source: Exeter Cathedral Archives, D&C 2097. Latin text. There is a copy by John Hooker in ECA, Book 52, ff. 272r–275v, printed in Hooker, 1919–47, iii, 598–603. Although the document is dated 1257, Walter Bronescombe, apparently mentioned as bishop, did not become so until the spring of 1258.)

In the name of the Father and the Son and the Holy Spirit. I, Walter son of Nicholas Gervas, whole in mind and sound in memory, make this my testament in the year of the Lord 1257 on Saturday in Easter week [*albis*]. First I commend my soul into the hands of my creator and redeemer, and I bequeath my body to the earth to be buried in the cemetery of SS Peter and Paul, Exeter, next to the body of my father, wherever it shall happen to me to die, and with my body I bequeath my horse by the name of 'Proved Friend' [*Provudfrend*]. Furthermore I wish that to begin with all the debts and crooked dealings and services due that can be reasonably shown be paid under the oversight of my executors after the forty days in which my wife and my funeral expenses have been honourably paid from my common property. I bequeath to my wife the third part of my goods and I reserve to myself two parts, except for my mills with the garden and other appurtenances between the two waters of Exe outside the West Gate of Exeter, with all the land from the mill of Sir John de Curtenay to the city wall and descending by the water as far as *Crikineputte*, which mills with the appurtenances and my great cellar with all the shops [*seldis*] and rents which are called Nine Chimneys [or Forges: *caminorum*] which my mother yet holds, I bequeath to the Exe Bridge in this form, that the wardens of the said bridge together with the mayor of the city shall provide annually one chaplain in perpetuity who shall celebrate divine service in the chapel on the said bridge for the souls of myself, Margaret my wife, my father and mother, and all deceased [people], and there shall be provided for such a chaplain 50s. from the aforesaid mills and the said rents. I will also that my anniversary be kept from the said mills and rents, so that on the appropriate day every year in perpetuity there may be a distribution of 50s. of bread, and on the same day from the aforesaid mills and rents I bequeath half a mark to the Friars Preachers of Exeter and half [a mark] to the Friars Minor for a pittance, and 5s. each year for the support of a lamp continuously burning before the body of Christ in the church of St James in the city of Exeter, in the parish where I first received the sacraments. Furthermore I will that the church of St Peter, Exeter, on the day of my obit shall receive from the said mills and rents half a mark that they may keep my anniversary, and so that this provision may be strengthened I will that the same wardens of the said Exe Bridge shall pay these sums and provide the priest, [and] that if they are negligent my heirs shall have the power to procure and present the aforesaid chaplain and to claim the right over the said donation, [and] that if both parties are negligent, the dean of Exeter with the [cathedral] chapter shall have the aforesaid power, so that he takes on the duty of each thing with regard to the souls [involved]. Furthermore I constitute as the executors of this my testament those written below. First I entreat our venerable father, Lord W., by the grace of God bishop of Exeter and Master John, chancellor of York, when he shall be in the region of Devon either with the [cathedral] canons or with W. de Bykele, knight, and Master John Toryz and Th. Gervas, that they assist in perfecting and completing my testament, seeking and obtaining my debts, as protectors and defenders of justice, under whom I constitute as executors and distributors John de Hokeston, Robert le Wetene, [and] Walter Fraunceys, who shall faithfully carry out and distribute with the counsel and knowledge of the above-mentioned executors, [providing] that if any one or ones of the above-mentioned subtract or dissent from these present [arrangements], the rest shall nevertheless proceed, with the counsel of Friar Henry, so that all things are expedited more quickly. Furthermore I entreat you all – I, Walter, sometime your friend – that the same grace and standard may be shown to me as you would wish to be shown to you at the dreadful [day of] judgment. Farewell.

6. Thomas Boteler, archdeacon of Totnes, 1263

(Source: Exeter Cathedral Archives, D&C 3672, pp. 339–41. Latin text, copied into the cathedral cartulary. Some words seem to have been omitted by mistake, especially in the third and fourth sentences.)

[p. 339]

In the name of the Father and the Son and the Holy Spirit, amen. In the year of the Lord 1263, on the feast of All Saints [1 November], I, Thomas archdeacon of Totnes, have ordained concerning my goods as follows. First I commend soul to God and body to the ground in the church of Blessed Peter before the altar of St Edmund, if it pleases [my] brethren to be buried where I wish. So that a priest may be supported with my goods, I assign my house in which I live for the support. Also I assign to the brothers of Blessed Thomas of Acon, London, my houses which were formerly those of Stephen in the town of Exeter. Also let all my debts be paid. Also to Constance, my sister, two oxen and two cows and 40s. Also to Felice, my sister, two oxen and two cows and 40s. Also to Iseud, the wife of William de la [p. 340] Grene, one ox. Also to Iseud, the wife of John de Haddon, one jewel of [worth or weighing] 40s. Also to Joan de Eston, one jewel of 40s. Also to Agnes, wife of Hugh de Cauz, one jewel of 40s. Also to Lucy de Wedon, one gold *garbaudechina* [brocade?]. Also I will and ordain that chalices be made from all my silver vessels, each of the weight of 20s., of which one is to remain in the chapel of *Turmerton* [Farmington, Gloucs.?], one in the church of Southrop [*Suthtrop*, Gloucs.], one in the church of *Eaton* [Wood or Water Eaton, Oxon.?], one in the church of *Westwelle* [Westwell, Oxon.?], and one in the church of *Northlegh* [North Leigh, Oxon.?], for the soul of my mother. Also to William le Botiler of *Turmerton*, eight oxen with a plough and one cart with iron tyres [*carectam ferratam*]. Also to William Curteys, 10 marks. Also to Ralph the marshal [*marescallo*], 40s. Also to Richard de Gurfenne, 100s. Also to Henry de Wynchecumbe, 100s. Also to William, son of Huon [*Huonis*], 100s. Also to Thomas de Mandevile, 5 marks for a horse. Also to Ralph de la Burg', 20s. Also to Oswald, 20s. Also to William, my vicar of Bosham [*Bothelham*, Sussex], 40s. Also to the fabric of the church of Bosham, 100s. Also to Sir William, my brother, the *Decreta* with my *Decretals*. Also to Lady Benedicta, my sister, my psalter and 40s. Also to Sapientia de Assefoul, one jewel of 40s. And to Sarra, the sister of her husband, 20s. Also to Master John de Blakedon, one jewel of 100s. Also to Robert Barat, 40s. Also to Master Gervase, 10 marks. Also to Sir Roger Prigge, 10 marks. Also to William, my chaplain, 5 marks. Also the house which Sir William de Bisman inhabits to provide 40s. every year on my anniversary for the use of the poor. Also from my [share of] commons [as a canon] for the whole year [after my death], two parts of the bread and the whole of the money to the Friars Minor of Exeter, the third part of the bread to the Friars Preachers. All the residue of my goods I commend to the discretion of my executors whom I constitute as follows: Sir William, my brother, the principal; William de la Hole; and Master Gervase when he may be available.

Memorandum that on the vigil [5 January] of the Epiphany in the year of the Lord 1263 [1264, *modern style*] I, Th[omas] archdeacon of Totnes, bequeath my house in which John Leaute dwells in the South Street of Exeter together with my house in which I dwell to the dean and chapter of the church of Exeter for the perpetual support of one perpetual chaplain celebrating in the early morning [p. 341] for my soul and the souls of all the faithful departed at the altar of St Edmund in the aforesaid church. And if it should happen that the said dean and chapter refuse the said legacy with the said obligation, I give [and] bequeath each house aforesaid with the aforesaid obligation as is aforesaid to the prior and convent of St Nicholas, Exeter, in the presence of the warden of the Friars Minor of Exeter, Brother [or Friar] John le Botiller, Master John de Blakedon, Master Gervase, and Sir William the chaplain.

7. John de Doulys, layman, 1267

(Source: British Library, Additional Charter 27523. Latin text, probably the original document, sealed on three tags, with remains of the seals. There is a copy of the opening bequests in the Cartulary of St John's Hospital, Exeter (DRO, Exeter City Archives, Book 53A, f. 6r). Like the will of Bartholomew Pinchun, this is cast in the form of reported speech. The paragraphing in this edition follows modern practice, not that of the original document.).

This is the testament of John de Doulys, made on the Tuesday [25 October] after the feast of St Luke the Evangelist in the year of grace 1267. In the name of the Father and the Son and the Holy Spirit, amen. First he bequeaths his soul to God and his body to be buried in the cemetery of Blessed Peter, Exeter. Also he bequeaths to the hospital of St John Baptist the house in which he dwells with the curtilage and all other appurtenances, and the house which he had from Richard Hureward and the chamber which he had from Mary Strange and the curtilage which was that of Alexander Pollard, with two houses and their appurtenances and with 10d. [rent] to be taken annually from two other houses, with the whole tenement which was that of the said Alexander Pollard.

Also he bequeaths to the Kalendar brethren [*fratribus Kalendar'*] of Exeter all the rent which he had from Richard le Masun towards the South Gate. Also he bequeaths [3?]s. of annual rent which he had from the house of John de Dunsford towards the North Gate for the lights of two churches, namely St Kerrian and St Cuthbert: to the church of St Kerrian 2s., to the church of St Cuthbert 12d. Also he bequeaths to the repair and protection of the well of St Sidwell one acre of land which he had from the heirs of Philip the Irishman [*Hiberniensis*] and a half acre which he had from John Fynamur, saving however to his wife while she lives, from all the [property] stated above, her dower or free bench if she keeps chaste and chooses this. Also he bequeaths all [his] farms of land outside the East Gate and rents of the city of Exeter or outside to the poor of Exeter diocese for his soul, on condition that his wife accepts the half part. Also he bequeaths to his wife the half part of all his goods, wherever they are.

Also he bequeaths his farm at Monkokehampton which he holds of Robert de la Mare with the corn, stock [*instauro*], term [of tenure], and rent and all other appurtenances, saving always [his] wife's part, for his soul, namely to the poor of Exeter diocese as above. Also he bequeaths all his part of the corn of Braunton [*Braunton*] for his soul to the poor, as above. Also he bequeaths all the part of his corn outside the East Gate and of Gabwell [*Gabewill*, in Stokeinteignhead] and of the *oisera* [?] of Teignmouth [*Teingemue*] for his soul, as above. Also he bequeaths his lectern [*lectrinum*] that he had at Monkokehampton to the poor for his soul, namely divided as above.

Also he bequeaths his gown of camlet with a hood to Richard his nephew of Upcott [*Oppecote*], his gown of burnet with a hood to William de la Lynche, his gown of bluet furred with squirrel to Walter his young male servant [*iuuenculo*], his robe of bluet furred with the bellies of rabbits to Richard de la Lynche, clerk. Also he bequeaths to his sister Alice, one gold brooch [*forinaculum*] of gold. Also he bequeaths to her daughter Clarice, one mark of silver. Also he bequeaths to her daughter Matilda 20s., to her son Richard 20s. Also he bequeaths to the children of Edmund de Afford, 20s. Also he bequeaths to each child of his brothers and sisters of Teignhead [*Tinhude*], 20s. Also he bequeaths to the children of William, his uncle, one cow with a calf; to the son of John his uncle, the clerk, one mark. Also he bequeaths to Thomas, his servant at Okehampton, 5s. Also to Adam and his brother serving there, one mark. To Nicholas de Fareford, his surcoat [*herigaudium*] of bluet. To William, called the Poor who sojourns [*stat*] in the parish of St Cuthbert, another of his surcoats. To William Longe outside the East Gate, his third surcoat. Also he bequeaths to the poor all his footwear. To Richard Marchepeys, his best hood of bluet. Also he bequeaths to Anger 3s. for service. Also he bequeaths to Clarice Sigrinne, if she remains in his service while he lives, 2s., and if not, nothing.

Also to Richard the clerk, his nephew, half a mark. To Roger Gosehee, half a mark. Also to William, the chaplain of St Kerrian, half a mark. To his clerk, 6d. To the Friars Preachers, half a mark. To the [Friars] Minor, half a mark. To each chapel of Exeter, 1d. To the lights of St Martin, 12d. Also he bequeaths to bridges, sick people, and other needy people as above, and also to [his] relations [*parentibus*], all his other goods not named nor bequeathed, according to the disposition of [his] executors. Also he bequeaths to John, son of Gregory, 20s. To carry out faithfully the performance of this he constitutes for himself executors, namely John de Castro, Henry de Staneweye, Nicholas de Kenton, William le Steymur.

[dorse]

This testament was proved before the official of the lord archdeacon of Exeter on the day of the apostles Simon and Jude [28 October] in the year of the Lord 1257. In the probate of which testament the same official affixed the seal of the officialty [*officialitatis*] of Exeter.

8. Adam de Collecote, layman, 1269

(Source: Exeter Cathedral Archives, VC/3053. Latin text. This text is presented in the third person, like Pinchun's. The testator was the father of Henry de Collecote, below.)

In the name of the Father, the Son, and the Holy Spirit, amen. This is the testament of Adam de Collecod made on the Monday [2 December] next after the feast of St Andrew in the year of the Lord 1269. First he bequeaths his soul to God and his body to holy burial. Also he bequeaths all his tenement on *La Hille* with its appurtenances to Rose his wife, on condition of rendering 4s. every year by her or her assigns to hold an obit for him, his father, and his mother throughout the parish churches of Exeter. Also he bequeaths to her the utensils, both copper pots and also pottles [*potellis*] and cups and other utensils, with the whole stock of the house, with one cask of cider [*cisar'*] with two full troughs. Also to the light of [the church of] Blessed Mary Steps, 2s. Also to Matillis, his maidservant, 5s. Also he bequeaths to Henry, his brother, 5s. Also to the children of the same Henry, four sheep. Also to Juliana, his sister, 6s. 8d., and to her [children?], three sheep. Also to the clerk of Blessed Mary Steps, 2d. Also he bequeaths to Geoffrey le Smale 4s. 6d in which he is in debt [*tenetur*] to him. Also he bequeaths to Yungge, 6d [?]. Also he bequeaths to Geoffrey de Keneford, 12d. Also to Edward Peytewin, 12d., and to Adam his brother, 12d. Also to Henry, son of Robert de Kenelod, 6d., and to John his servant, 6d. To

Beat[rice], his [John's?] wife, 6d. Also to Alice Pagaham, 6d. Also he bequeaths to four children whom he raised from the font [i.e. as godfather] in the parish of Kenn, four sheep. Also to Lucy, the daughter of Henry de Collecod, 6d. Also he bequeaths to Sir John, chaplain of St Mary Magdalene, 2s. Also to the brothers of St [Mary] Magdalene 12d. from the shop [*selda*] from which they had 12d. before. Also to the Friars Preachers, 12d. Also to the Friars Minor, 12d. Also to the bridge of Exeter, 6d. Also to the new bridge, 4d. Also to the bridge of Teign [*Teng'*], 6d. Also to Richard his relative, 2s. Also to Walter Deleit [?], 10s. from the money in which he is in debt to him. Also he bequeaths to Henry his son, two oxen which he has at Kennford, and one to his wife which is also there. Also to Robert Jesse, 2s. Also to [poor people?] on the day of his obit, 20s. And the residue was to be disposed according to the arrangement of his executors. He constitutes as his executors John, chaplain of St Mary Magdalene, Henry his son, and Robert Jesse. Also Geoffrey the tailor [*sutor*] is freed in respect of the money in which he is in debt to him. Also Simon the White [*albus*] in respect of the money in which he is in debt to him.

9. Emer de Ponte, layman, 1290

(Source: DRO, Exeter City Archives, Mayor's Court Roll, 18–19 Edward I, m. 14d. Latin text. The text is an incomplete copy of the original, and parts of the right-hand edge of the document are lost.)

In the name of the Father and the Son and the Holy Spirit, amen. I, Emer [*Emerus, also* Emerycus *in the title*] de Ponte, on the day of the Exaltation of the Holy Cross [14 September] in the year of the Lord 1290, make my testament in this manner. First I bequeath my soul to God <and> my <body> to be buried in the church of the Friars Minor of Exeter. ...50s. [*sic, probably following a long omission*]. Furthermore I ordain and constitute as executors of this testament Lord P[eter], bishop, John de Elmynistr', <and?> Master Richard Pater, warden [or Master Richard, father warden] of the Friars Minor of Exeter as counsellor and supervisor. And if there shall be any further residue [of my goods] I commit it to the ordinance and disposition of the said executors following what they may see best to be expedient for my soul, so that, with the exception of the settlement of all <my> debts on this side of the sea and beyond the sea, everything may remain to the Friars Minor of Exeter where my body rests, to celebrate <masses> for my soul and the <other?> souls [and] for the repair of their church. Also I bequeath to Richard the cook, one gown of brown camlet, furred with squirrel.

[The will was proved in the mayor's court of Exeter on the Monday next after the feast of St Hilary 19 Edward I [15 January 1291] by William, rector of the church of St Pancras Exeter, and Richard the cook.]

10. Henry de Collecote, layman, 1294

(Source: Exeter Cathedral Archives, D&C 2121. Latin text; sealed on a tag, so possibly the original or an authenticated copy. Printed in *Reg. Bronescombe*, ed. Hingeston-Randolph, pp. 435–6. The testator was the son of Adam de Collecote, above, and the father of Walter de Collecote, below.)

In the name of the Father and the Son and the Holy Spirit, amen. I, Henry de Collecote, of good and sound memory, on the Saturday [11 December] next after the feast of St Nicholas, in the year of the Lord 1294, make my will in this manner. First I bequeath my soul to the Lord and my body to be buried in the cemetery of the Blessed Peter of Exeter, in the place where my father and mother rest. Also I bequeath to the rector of the church of Blessed Mary Steps, for tithes forgotten, 4s. Also I bequeath 100s. for expending on poor people and for doing other funeral rites on the day of my burial. Also I bequeath to Juliana, widow of Walter de Karswill', and Cecily, her daughter, 20s. Also to Isot, daughter of the aforesaid Juliana, 5s. and a silver bowl which I had of the gift of Walter de Karswille, her father. Also I bequeath to Christine, my daughter, one mark and two shops [*seldas*] which are situated in St John's Lane, which I hold on lease [*firmam*] from John le Cok, for the remainder of the lease. Also to Matill', daughter of Margery de Doulys, 10s. Also to Lucy, daughter of Henry de Collecote, 4s. Also to Christine, her sister, 2s. Also to Henry, son of Robert the dyer [*tinctoris*], 12d. Also to Henry, son of Walter de Lenge, 6d. Also I bequeath to the Friars Preachers, 2s. Also to the Friars Minor, 2s. Also I bequeath to the brothers of St Mary Magdalene, Exeter, 13d. Also to Thomas de Criditone, chaplain, 5s. Also I bequeath to John Bythevalle, my best gown [*robam*]. Also I bequeath to Reginald de Venella, my second-best gown. Also I bequeath to Richard de Pouderham, my surcoat [*supertunicam*] of white russet with a hood and 12d. Also I bequeath to Richard, my taverner, my surcoat of cameline with a hood. Also to William, my servant, my surcoat of miniver [*griseo*] and a small lead trough. Also I bequeath to Henry, my servant, a coat of cameline and a surcoat of serge. Also to John de Keneford, my servant, a coat of white russet and 6d. Also to Adam Spear', a coat of serge. Also to Matill', my servant, 12d. Also to Matill' Golde, 12d. Also to Susanna Sank', 2s. Also I bequeath to John Belringer from the money that he owes me, 5s. Also I bequeath to Christine de

Keneford, two bushels of barley. Also I bequeath to Walter, my son, my coffer and sword, and if he dies under age, I will that Hugh, my son, have them. Also I bequeath to Master Adam de Brumel, my surcoat [*herigaudium*] and my white short gown [*wardecors*]. Also I bequeath to Philip Chabbel, my red short gown. Also I bequeath to Edelot de Elnecumbe, a gold ring and a silver brooch [or buckle: *firmaculum*]. Also to Hugh de Heleweye, a gold ring. Also to Walter Tantefer, a gold ring. Also to Sir Robert Beneit, a gold ring. Also to Hugh, my son, two gold rings.

The rest of all my moveable goods, not bequeathed or named in this my testament, I bequeath to Joan my wife and to my children begotten on her. Also I bequeath to Joan my wife, all my tenement in which I dwell, while she lives, so that after her decease it may revert to Walter, my son, and if he does not survive his mother, I will that it revert to all my heirs, except for one room in the front part and one cellar with another room situated between the shop belonging to the church of Blessed Mary Steps and the tenement of Robert Gesse. Also I bequeath to Margaret, my daughter, the aforesaid cellar with the other two rooms. Also I bequeath to Hugh, my son, all my tenement in which William Maynard dwells. Also I bequeath to Alice, my daughter, all that tenement in which Walter Scote dwells, and 4s. of annual rent to be taken from the tenement of Laurence the skinner [*Pellipar'*]. Also I bequeath to Walter, my son, 1d. of annual rent to be taken from the tenement in which John de Paynestone dwells, outside the west gate of the city of Exeter on the island. Also to Mariot, my daughter, all my tenement in Smithen Street [*Smithenestrete*] which I bought of Susanna Sank'. Also I bequeath to Walter Scote, chaplain, my girdle of silk. Also to Elias, chaplain, a girdle of leather with silver bars. Also to Sir Roger Huberd, 2s. Of this my testament I constitute as my executors Thomas de Criditon, chaplain, Joan my wife, and John Bythewalle.

This testament was proved before us, the official of the lord archdeacon of Exeter, on Ash Wednesday [16 February] in the year of the Lord 1294 [1295, *modern style*]. And the administration of the same testament was committed to the executors named in the aforesaid testament.

11. Rosamund Kymmyng, married woman, 1295

(Source: Exeter Cathedral Archives, D&C 2122. Latin text; possibly a copy. Printed in *Reg. Bronescombe*, ed. Hingeston-Randolph, pp. 433–4.)

In the name of the holy and indivisible Trinity, amen. I, Rosamund Kymmyng, the wife of John Smurch, in good and sound memory, blessed be God, make my testament in the form that follows. First I bequeath my soul to God and my body to be buried in the cemetery of Blessed Margaret at Topsham. Also I bequeath to the light of the aforesaid church, 3d. Also to the parish chaplain of the said church, that he may commend the memory of my soul in his prayers, 4d. And to the parish clerk, 2d. Also I bequeath a cloak and my surcoat of bluet to be sold, and with the money received Elias, chaplain of Alphington, is to celebrate divine service for the health of my soul and that of all the faithful departed. Also I bequeath to the rector of the church of Exminster, for tithes forgotten, 12d. Also I bequeath to Matillis, the daughter of Bartholomew de Deneford, my best gown [*rochetam*] and my mantle of green. To Meliora of Topsham, 6d. Also to Matillis, the widow of Maundevyle, 6d. Also to Beatrice, my sister, a surcoat of green and my red coat. And I bequeath to Cecily, my servant, 6d. And I bequeath to the light of the church of Blessed Michael of Alphington, a lamb. Also to Henry, son of Beatrice my sister, a lamb. And to John of Alfyngtone, clerk, 4d. Also I bequeath to Matillis, the daughter of Bartholomew de Deneford, a basin and a ewer. And to Christine, the daughter of Umfred Ocle of Exeter, a heifer. Also I bequeath to John Bythewalle, 12d.

Also I give and bequeath to the dean and chapter of Exeter and their successors in perpetuity, all that tenement with all its appurtenances which is situated outside the south gate in the suburb of the city of Exeter, between the tenement which was formerly William Peuerel's and the tenement of Richard le Arcedyakene in longitude, and extends itself in latitude between the king's highway leading towards *Crulledech* and the tenement of the aforesaid Richard le Arcediakene.

And I give and bequeath to Bartholomew de Deneford, his heirs, and assigns in perpetuity, half an acre of land with its appurtenances lying outside the south gate of the aforesaid city, by Southernhay, between the land of Emeric Coffyn and the land of Robert Tauntefer. And I give and bequeath to the same Bartholomew, his heirs, and assigns in perpetuity, all that tenement with its appurtenances which is situated in the aforesaid city in the highway which is called Bullhill Street [*Bolehillestrete*] between the tenement which was John Tauntefer's and the highway leading towards Preston Street [*Prustenestrete*] in latitude, and it extends in longitude from the tenement of Robert de Wodeleghe to the aforesaid highway of Bullhill Street. And I give and bequeath to the said Bartholomew, his heirs, and assigns in perpetuity 3s. of annual rent to be taken from the whole tenement, with its appurtenances, which Katharine de Venella holds and inhabits in the aforesaid city, which tenement is situated between the tenement of Sir Henry de Ralegh' and Sir John de Boneuyle and the tenement of John de Tresympel. And I give and bequeath to the same Bartholomew, his heirs, and assigns in perpetuity, 18d. of annual rent to be taken from the whole tenement, with its appurtenances, which Walter the dyer [*tinctor*] holds and inhabits outside the west gate of the aforesaid city between the mill dam and the king's highway leading towards north Exe Island [*North-exhilond*], together with all the right which may arise by reason of the said rent. And I bequeath and constitute that the residue of all my goods not bequeathed, belonging to my part, be applied to pious uses for the health of my soul, by the disposition of my executors, as shall seem best to be done.

I make, ordain, and constitute as my executors Sir Elias, chaplain of Alphington, Bartholomew de Deneford, and John Bythewalle. Made and dated at *la Pole* in the manor of Topsham, Friday in the feast of St Katharine the Virgin [25 November], in the year of the Lord 1295.

These are the debts that are owing to me. John Pykard, for one horse sold and given to him in Whitsun week, 16s. Also, the same owes for one feather bed, 4s. Also, 15s. which was paid for him to Robert de Newetone for a contract for a boat.

This testament was proved before us, Master Robert de Veteri Terra, farmer of the church of Topsham, Sunday next [11 December] after the feast of St Nicholas, in the year of the Lord 1295, and pronouncement was made for the same, and the aforesaid oath [being made] for the faithful making of an inventory and the return of an account, the execution of the testament was committed to Bartholomew de Deneforde and John Bythewalle, the above-named Elias not pursuing [his claim]. In testimony of which, the seal of the official of the lord bishop of Exeter is attached to these presents.

12. Henry de Berbilond, vicar choral of Exeter Cathedral, 1296

(Source: D&C ED 50, probably a copy of the original. Latin text. The translation was previously printed in Nicholas Orme, 'Henry de Berbilond, d. 1296, a Vicar Choral of Exeter Cathedral', *Devon and Cornwall Notes and Queries*, 37 part 1 (Spring, 1992), pp. 1–7.)

In the name of the Father and the Son and the Holy Spirit, amen. The Monday next [8 October] before the feast of St Denis the Martyr in the year of the Lord 1296, I, Henry de Berbilond, vicar in the church of the Blessed Peter of Exeter, being in good and sound mind, make this my testament in this manner. First I bequeath my soul to God, the Blessed Mary, and all the saints, and my body to be buried where my friends shall best provide. Also I bequeath to buy wax and for the [funeral] obsequies and to dispense to the poor on the day of the making of my burial, £10, and more if necessary at the discretion of my executors. Also I bequeath to the fabric of the [cathedral] church of Exeter, 20s. of silver. Also to the fabric of the church of the Holy Cross of Crediton, half a mark. Also I bequeath to each chaplain obliged to come together at the divine office for my soul in the church of St Peter, Exeter, 3d. Also to each clerk of the second form, 2d. Also to each boy of the choir, 1d. Also to the Friars Preachers of Exeter, 3s. Also to the Friars Minor of the same town, 3s. Also to the poor of the hospital of St John, Exeter, 12d. Also to the lepers of the Blessed Mary Magdalene of Exeter, 12d. Also to the prisoners of Exeter, 2s. Also to the fabric of the [priory] church of Blessed Nicholas, Exeter, 3s.

Also I bequeath to the 24 vicars of the church of the Blessed Peter of Exeter, all my tenement which I held by gift and remission of Henry Wyger and Thomas his brother, heirs of Sir John Wyger, knight, deceased, which tenement is situated next to the cemetery of the Blessed Peter of Exeter between the tenement of Thomas de Chaggeford and Joan his wife on the west side and the tenement in which a certain Herbert le Pessour dwelt on the east side in latitude, and extends in length from the said cemetery to the tenement of Walter le Paiuur, goldsmith, towards the High Street of Exeter, on condition that the aforesaid vicars, on the day of the obit of Sir Gilbert de Tytinges, formerly canon in the church of the Blessed Peter of Exeter aforesaid, shall pay 12s. in silver to the stewards of the canons of Exeter in their exchequer each year at the first hour to perform the obit of the said Gilbert in perpetuity, willing and ordaining furthermore that each canon personally present shall have and receive 4d. for the obit, and that which remains shall be distributed [to the minor clergy] in the choir following the manner and custom of the aforesaid church of Exeter. Also I will that the aforesaid vicars shall pay and distribute 6s. in the choir by the hand of the steward of the vicars on the day of my obit every year in perpetuity, following the custom of the aforesaid church, among the same vicars at my obit for my soul, to be held and performed by them in perpetuity. Otherwise I will that the aforesaid tenement with all its appurtenances shall revert to my heirs following the form of the statute of the lord king made on this matter, in full right, until it shall happen that the aforesaid canons and vicars or their successors shall come by some means to restore the aforesaid condition.

Also I bequeath to Peter de Tytinges and Joan his wife, the administration of my lands which were formerly William Podyng's in the manor of Poltimore, together with the wardship, marriage, and custody of the body of Joel, son and heir of the aforesaid William Poding and all the other heirs of the same William, for the aforesaid Peter and Joan his wife and their heirs or assigns to have and to hold, as is fully contained in the charter of Stephen de London made to me, Henry, concerning the aforesaid matters.

Also I bequeath to William Podyng my nephew and Margery his wife, my farm and term of land at Landscore [in Poltimore parish] which I hold of William de Asperton and Mazelina his wife, to have and to hold according to the form of the letter made between the aforesaid William and Mazelina and myself. Also I bequeath to the same William and Margery, all my vessels and utensils together with the carts and other rural implements there, with one chest and waggon there. Also all my timber at Ratsloe except for four pieces of wood which I will to be brought to Woodbury to construct a door for the grange there, at my expense. Also I bequeath to them one colt which I had from Walter Tauntifer and one short gown [*wardecors*] of fur. Also I bequeath to them six ordinary oxen from Landscore, five ordinary cows from the cows that are at Woodbury, six bullocks from Landscore, and twenty sheep from the same place. Also I bequeath to them my best bed in which I lie, my third best tablecloth [*mappam*], two towels, the second-best brass pot, with one small posnet [*pocinetum*] lying at Exeter. Also one linen sheet for winnowing, which is at Landscore. Also I bequeath to them five quarters of rye and five quarters of oats to sow their land of Ratsloe and Landscore. Also I bequeath to Margery, the wife of the aforesaid William, my best gown and 40s., on condition that she require nothing from the goods which once belonged to John de Sechev[i]ll her father or Mabill' her mother, which have come into my hands; if she requires them, I will that all the preceding legacies be cancelled for the future.

Also I bequeath to Richard, son of Alan de Yhiuelegh, to help him that he may be instructed in some craft, 40s. Also I bequeath to Hamo my nephew, 20s. and one blanket with one sheet. Also to Clar', my aunt, one surcoat of white bluet [*blueto*] with a hood and one silver *cyrat'* [comb?] and one blanket with one linen sheet. Also to Sir Nicholas, rector of the church of Thorverton, my best cloth. Also I bequeath to Joan, the wife of Peter de Tyting, my second-best cloth. Also I bequeath to Walter de Yhalde-forde, my nephew, all my term [i.e. lease] of the field which I hold of Nicholas de la Brigg in Salterton by indenture. Also to him I bequeath one surcoat of furred serge and half a mark of silver. Also I bequeath to William his brother, 2s. Also to John the smith, brother of the same, 2s. Also I bequeath to Alice de la Holte, 3s. Also to the bridge of Bishop's Clyst, 3s. Also to the bridge of Exeter, 12d. Also to the bridge of Thorverton, 12d.. To the bridge of *Hederdig* [probably Ellerhayes, Killerton], 12d. Also to the bridge of Stoke [Canon], 12d. Also I bequeath to the church of Silverton, one pair of vestments with all the apparel and my worn surplice, on condition that my executors receive from the same church a pair of worn vestments in which I may be buried. Also I bequeath to each of my god-children, 6d. Also to Margaret, my laundress, two hangings [*tapent'*] and two sheets. Also to each of my servants at Woodbury, besides their wages, 6d. Also to each of my servants at Landscore, 6d. Also I bequeath to Sir John, chaplain of Woodbury, my tabard of white camlet with the hood. Also to William, my reeve there, my tabard of black bluet. Also to Royse la Daye, my bed which I have at Woodbury. Also I bequeath to Margery de

Ponte, my niece, 3s. Also I bequeath 50s. to celebrate an annual for my soul. Also I bequeath to John de Yaldeford, my servant, 3s. Also to Henry, son of Walter, formerly clerk of Silverton, 12d. Also to John Bregh, 12d., John Grep, 6d., Alex' de Hedfelde, 6d. Also I bequeath to the church of Woodbury a surplice and a pair of coral [beads, i.e. a rosary]. Also to little Henry de Braneys, 6d.

Also I bequeath to Sir Andrew [de Kilkenny], dean of the church of Exeter, my maple-wood cup with the silver foot. Also to Sir John de Gorkelegh, one silver spoon with a knob [*nodo*]. Also to Sir John de Oxton, one spoon with a knob. Also to Robert de Asperton, one spoon with a knob. Also to Master Elias de Criditon, one spoon with a knob. To Thomas de Teynton, one spoon with a knob. Also to Henry de Middleton, one spoon with a knob. To John de Evelegh, one spoon. To John de Mar', one spoon. To Roger de Stok, one spoon. To John de Glasney, one spoon. To Nicholas Strange, one spoon. To Robert de Kedelonde, one spoon. To every other vicar [choral], one spoon, and to John Mountein, one spoon. Also I bequeath to Sir William de Niweton, chaplain, my chest with the red key and 20s., on condition that he takes on himself the task of executing my will. Also I bequeath to Master Elias de Criditon, one chest and 20s. on the same condition. Also I bequeath to Vincent de Oxton, clerk, 40s. on condition that he returns an account of the testament of Robert Peyngne, deceased, in my name together with Sir William [de Niweton], chaplain, and the above-named Master Elias, and takes on himself the task of executing my will. Also I bequeath to the church of the Blessed Mary Major of Exeter, a candle of one pound of wax.

The rest of all my goods not bequeathed, [I bequeath] to the disposal and discretion of the aforesaid Sir William de Niweton, chaplain, Master Elias, and Master Vincent de Oxton, whom I ordain, make, and constitute my executors and commit by this part, so that they dispose and ordain from my unbequeathed goods as best sees expedient for the salvation of my soul, and may they take care to do so effectively on peril of their souls.

Also in addition I bequeath to Sir Nicholas de Thorverton, one *moertium* [mortar?]. Also I bequeath to the children of Wyon de Lask, 10s. Also to the daughters of Robert de la Pitte of Silverton, 4s. Also to the children of Walter Bythelake, 2s. Also to Rose, the sister of Margery de Ponte, 3s. Also to Roger, the servant of W. de Asperton, 3s. Also I bequeath to Margery, the wife of William Podyng, all the wooden cups and the dishes that are in my house at Exeter. Also to John, son of Mabell' de Sechevil, 3s. Also to the bridge [i.e. Pynes Bridge, Upton Pyne] on the other side of the Creedy towards the house of Sir W[*recte* Her]bert, 2s. Also to Peter, son of Peter de Tyting', 12d., and to Isobel, daughter of the same Peter, half a mark. Also to Philip, son of Henry de Berbilond, my nephew, 5s. Also I bequeath to John, son of Philip de Sechevil, £4 of silver, on condition that he exacts nothing from me or my executors concerning the goods of the aforesaid Philip his father, which came to my hands and those of Peter de Tytinges; otherwise I will that she shall have or receive nothing of the aforesaid bequest.

13. Margaret de Collecote, married woman, 1305

(Source: Exeter Cathedral Archives, VC/3018. Latin text. Formerly sealed on a tongue, so possibly the original or an authenticated copy.)

In the name of the Father and the Son and the Holy Spirit, amen. I, Margaret de Coldecote, wife of John de Beare, tanner of Exeter, Friday [7 May] next after the feast of St John before the Latin Gate, in the year of the Lord 1305, ordain and make my testament in this manner. First I bequeath my soul to God and my body to be buried in the cemetery of the Blessed Peter of Exeter. Also I bequeath to John Beare, my husband, my tenements which I had enfeoffed on the part of my father by myself before the solemnisation of the marriage between me and him was first held, to have for the whole of his life. Also I bequeath to the same John, one brass pot with a bowl [*patella*]. Also I bequeath to him, one coffer. Also I bequeath to the same John, one carpet with two sheets, one cloth with one dish, and one chest. Also I bequeath to Sir Elias, chaplain, one towel. Also I bequeath to John Bithewalle, 8d. Also I bequeath to Lady Elena Palmere, my best surcoat [*supertunicam*] with one gold ring. Also I bequeath to Walter my brother, one carpet with two sheets, one cloth with a towel, and one purse of silk. Also I bequeath to Alice my sister, one gown [*rochetum*] with my best hood. Also I bequeath to Mariot my sister, one carpet with one sheet. Also I bequeath to Edith my sister, 2s. with one cloth. Also I bequeath to the said Alice, one veil of silk with one *lrecca* [brooch?]. Also I bequeath to Juliana Palmere, 12d. Also to Cecilia, daughter of the said Juliana, 6d. Also to Elena, wife of John Jolif, 6d. Also I bequeath to Christina my sister, one coat of perse with a hood. Also I bequeath to Alyue, mother of Sir Elias, chaplain, one smock. Also to Alice my sister, I bequeath my other smock. Also I bequeath to Agnes, the mother of my husband, one pelisse. Also I bequeath to Matillis Silvertounce, one worn surcoat of perse. Also I bequeath to make my funeral, 5s. and my best coat. Accordingly I ordain and make my executors of this my will John de Beare, my husband, and John Bithewalle.

14. Walter de Collecote, layman, 1316

(Source: Exeter Cathedral Archives, VC/3057. Latin text. Formerly sealed on a tongue, so possibly the original or an authenticated copy. The testator was the son of Henry de Collecote, above.)

In the name of the Father and the Son and the Holy Spirit, amen. I, Walter de Collecote, son and heir of Henry de Collecote, make my testament in this manner, on the Tuesday [14 September] in the feast of the Exaltation of the Holy Cross in the year of the Lord 1316. First I bequeath my soul to God and my body to sacred burial. Also I bequeath to the rector of the church of Blessed Mary Steps, Exeter, that he may pray for me, 12d. Also I bequeath to Richard de Okehampton, parish chaplain of the same place, 3d. Also I bequeath to Sir Geoffrey de Esse, chaplain, 3d. Also I bequeath to Sir Henry de Middelcote, chaplain, 12d. Also I bequeath to Alice my sister, half a mark. Also I bequeath to Adam Uppehill[e], half a mark. Also I give and bequeath to Walter, son of Adam Uppehille, 2d. of annual rent arising from a certain garden which the aforesaid Adam Uppehille holds next to his tenement of *Uppehill[e]*, and 1d. of annual rent, with the relief [*relevio*] when it occurs and all other appurtenances appertaining, from a certain tenement which was formerly that of John de Peyniston in Exe Island [*Exylond*], between the tenement formerly of Henry de la Hurne and the tenement formerly of Sir Henry de Kenelond, chaplain, to have and to hold to him and to his heirs or assigns in perpetuity. Also I bequeath one half mark of annual rent, when it falls due, of a certain tenement at *Uppehill[e]* in which William [de la Trewe] the apothecary inhabits, when the term [of the lease] of the said William is complete, to Henry de Middelcote, chaplain, and Adam Uppehille, my executors, to be sold, made, and disposed for my soul as they may see most expeditious in God, which aforesaid Sir Henry and Adam Uppehill[e] I make, ordain, and constitute my executors to treat faithfully all and singular the things that have been mentioned before.

15. Lucy de Collecote, married woman, 1324

(Source: Exeter Cathedral Archives, VC/3050, 3552. Latin texts; probably copies of the original. VC/3050 is legibly written but has lost a large area on the top right; VC/3552 is complete but very faded. The whole text can be reconstructed, with a few gaps, by utilising both copies.)

In the name of God, amen. I, Lucy de Collecote, widow of William de la Trewe, make my testament on the Friday [4 February] next after the feast of the Purification <of Blessed Mary the Virgin?> in the year of the Lord 1323 [1324, *modern style*]. First I bequeath my soul to God my creator and all his saints, and my body to ecclesiastical burial. Also I bequeath to Joan, my daughter, my best brass pot, my smaller brass posnet, one basin, one ewer, and my best bowl. Also I bequeath to Henry, my son, my best brass posnet, one basin, one ewer, and one pan. Also I bequeath to Joan, my daughter, my best green gown. Also to Mariot, my sister, one quilted surcoat and one coat of indigo-blue [*indeblueto*] and one cap furred with miniver. Also to the said Joan, my daughter, one piece of cloth of indigo-blue, containing nine ells. Also I bequeath and will that my executors sell all my tenement situated within the west gate of the city of Exeter, which is called *Uppehille*, which I had by the bequest of the said William, formerly my husband, and therewith to make, ordain, and dispose for the soul of the said William, formerly my husband, and for my soul what to these my executors shall seem and be thought most salubrious and best to expedite for the souls of the aforesaid. Also I bequeath to Joan, my daughter, all my tenement which is situated in the city of Exeter between the tenement that John de Lercome holds on the east side and a certain place that Isabel de Gatepath holds on the west side, to have and to hold all the said tenement with all its appurtenances to the said Joan and her heirs and assigns, by the services due and accustomed by law to the chief lord of the fee, with hereditary right in perpetuity. Also I bequeath to Christine my sister, one surcoat of cameline. Also to Henry my son, one hood, one set of bed furnishings [*supellectilia*], one blanket [*lodicem*], two best linen sheets for one bed, two cloths namely the second best and the second worse, [and] two towels namely one double and the other <single?>. Also to the said Joan, my daughter, one double towel and four other towels, two cloths, two sets of bed furnishings, and my best feather bed. Also to the said Henry, my son, one feather bed. Also to Master Henry, rector of the church of Blessed Mary Steps, Exeter, for tithes forgotten, 3s. Also to Sir William, the parish chaplain of the same church of Blessed Mary, 12d. Also to the parish clerk of the said church, 6d. Also to John Beyvyn, clerk, for his labour spent on my affairs, 12d. Also I will and bequeath that the Friars Minor of Exeter shall have, from the money raised from the sale of the aforesaid tenement bequeathed above, six marks of silver to support the fabric of the church of the same friars. Also I bequeath to Adam le Yunge and Alice his wife, all that house of mine which is situated between my kitchen and the tenement of Sir Elias, chaplain, to have and to hold to them and their heirs and their assigns in hereditary right in perpetuity, on condition that they pay annually in perpetuity for the anniversary of the said William, <formerly my husband?>, 12d., namely 3d. for three masses for his soul, 3d. for bread for the poor, and 3d. for three masses at my anniversary and 3d. for bread for the poor. Also I bequeath to a certain woman who was the nurse of Henry my son, one green surcoat. Also to Christine Palmer, one courtepy of russet, one hood of russet, and one woman's smock. Also to Lucy Jesse, one woman's smock. Also to Agnes Keda, one woman's smock. Also to Matilda Limerig', one woman's smock. Also I bequeath to the aforesaid Joan, my daughter, all my lands which I have in the suburbs of the city of Exeter, outside the East Gate of the said city, wherever they lie, to have and to hold to her and her heirs and assigns by hereditary right in perpetuity. Also to Rose Don, a gold ring with a garnet stone. Furthermore, all and singular the rest of my goods, by whatever name they consist, either in things or found in the hands of debtors, I bequeath to my executors that they may make, ordain, and dispose therewith as they shall believe to be best and more healthful for the health of my soul. I wish furthermore that all the goods bequeathed above to my son Henry shall remain in the keeping of Adam le Yungge until the coming of the said Henry. If, however, the said Henry does not come to his fatherland, then I will and bequeath that all the said goods so bequeathed revert to my daughter Joan. Also I will and bequeath that Joan, the daughter of John Tremenet of Hennock [*Hanek*] have ten marks of money coming from the tenement bequeathed to be sold above, as an aid to her marriage. Furthermore I bequeath to Mariot, my sister, one kerchief [*cuuerecher*] of silk. Moreover to execute this my testament I make, ordain, and constitute as my executors Thomas le Spicere, citizen of Exeter, and Sir Henry de Middelcote, chaplain, so that they may have full and free power to make and exercise and dispose all and singular that they see and believe by themselves to be better and healthier for the health of my soul.

16. Nicholas de Durneford, married clerk, 1326

(Source: Devon Record Office, Exeter City Archives, DRO, ECA, Book 53A, f. 53v. Latin text, a copy of the original. The testator was connected with the consistory court of Exeter (*Reg. Stapeldon*, pp. 118–19).)

In the name of God, amen. I, Nicholas de Durneford, clerk, on the Sunday next [17 August] after the feast of the assumption of the Blessed Virgin Mary in the year of the Lord 1326, bequeath my soul to God and my body to be buried in the cemetery of the Blessed Peter of Exeter. Also I bequeath to Sir William [Vealde], rector of the church of St Martin, Exeter, 3s. 4d. for tithes not paid. Also I bequeath to William Godeknaue, the chaplain there, 6d. etc. Also I give and bequeath to John my son all my tenement in the North Street of the city of Exeter, which I had by the gift and feoffment of Nicholas the son of Henry de Lywerne, together with the reversion of

dower [*reversione dotis*] when it happens, to have and to hold all the aforesaid tenement with its appurtenances together with the reversion when it
happens, to the aforesaid John and his heirs of his body legitimately procreated, by hereditary right in perpetuity. And if the aforesaid John dies
without heirs of his body legitimately procreated, then all the aforesaid
tenement together with the aforesaid reversion shall remain to Robert my
son to have and to hold to him and to his heirs or assigns in perpetuity, etc.
Also I give and bequeath to Robert my son, after the decease of Joan my
wife, all my tenement which I had by the gift and feoffment of John Bonde
in Shutbrook Street [*Schutebrokstrete*], with a certain moor which is called
Wygamour and also one acre of land at *Chaldefeld* which I had by the gift
of the aforesaid John Bonde next to the land of William Steymour, together
with a certain piece of land which is called *Myleslond*, to have and to hold
the whole aforesaid tenement and the aforesaid lands with their appurtenances whatsoever to the aforesaid Robert and his heirs of his body
legitimately procreated, by hereditary right in perpetuity, etc. The rest of
all my goods not bequeathed here, after the debts have been paid, I wish
[and concede – *cancelled*] that they be equally divided according to the
demand of the law between the aforesaid Joan my wife and my aforesaid
children; and after the division is made that anyone may know what he
needs to seek. I will that all the goods remain in the custody of the aforesaid
Joan my wife and also all the aforesaid lands previously bequeathed to my
children, until they are of full age, so that she may maintain my aforesaid
children in food and clothing according to her ability in all things. And to
make and carry out this execution well and faithfully, I constitute as my
executors Joan my aforesaid wife and Walter Farcheyr, clerk.

The present testament was proved before us, the official of the lord
archdeacon of Exeter, in the hall of our house in the city of Exeter on the
sixteenth day of the month of September in the year of the Lord aforesaid
and pronounced by us for the same. And because Walter Farcheyr, named
as one executor in the said testament was not willing to undertake the
work of administration, we absolved him from the work, and the sole
administration was committed on the twenty-second day of the month of
October in the year of the Lord aforesaid to Joan, widow of the said deceased Nicholas, in the form prescribed by law. Dated and done on the
day, place, and year aforesaid.

17. Peter Soth, layman, 1327

(Source: Devon Record Office, Exeter City Archives, ED/M/276. Latin text. Copy of the original, sealed on a tag, with seal attached. For convenience, the will has been divided into paragraphs.)

In the name of God, amen. I, Peter Soth, son and heir of John Soth, make my testament at Exeter on the Friday [3 April] next before the feast of St Ambrose in the year of the Lord 1327, in this manner. First I bequeath my soul to God and Blessed Mary and my body to be buried in the cemetery of the church of Blessed Peter, Exeter. Also I bequeath to Sir John, rector of the church of St Kerrian, Exeter, for my forgotten tithes and my unpaid oblations, 20s. Also I bequeath to the fabric of the church of St Nicholas, Exeter, 5s. Also I bequeath to the Friars Preachers of Exeter, half a mark, and to the Friars Minor of the suburb of Exeter, half a mark. And to Friar John de Whatelegh, as a grant for a habit, 10s. And to the brothers and sisters of the house of Blessed Mary Magdalene, Exeter, half a mark. Also I bequeath, will, and concede that my funeral expenses be performed at the ordinance and disposition of my executors, as seems to them best for the health of my soul.

Also I give and bequeath to Martin le Keu of Bridford, 40d. of annual rent which I acquired from Jordan de Brittestowe from a tenement which was formerly that of Roger Russel in Waterbeer Street in Exeter, which Jordan recovered against Stephen de London in the court of the city of Exeter by judgment of the same court by reason of his lack of warranty, and 12s. of annual rent which I acquired from Henry de Trickote from a tenement which was that of Joan de Coleton in the High Street of the city of Exeter, between the tenement which was formerly that of Stephen de London and the lane which is called *la Smale Lane*, which the same Henry recovered against the said Stephen in the aforesaid court by the judgment of the same court by reason of his lack of warranty, to have and to hold the aforesaid 40d. and 12s. of annual rent with their appurtenances to the said Martin, his heirs and assigns, by capital demesnes of their fees by hereditary right in perpetuity. Also I bequeath to John Bolle, my nephew, all that tenement in which he lives next to the Friars Preachers of Exeter together with a certain tenement adjoining the same, to have and to hold to him and to his heirs or assigns by hereditary right in perpetuity.

Also I give and bequeath all my tenement where I now live with the garden [*herbarium*] and the new kitchen adjoining, with free ingress and egress in the street which is called Northgate Street [*Northyetstret*], together with one old hall with all its appurtenances in which John Soth my father dwelt while he lived, together with a certain solar [*solar'*] in the front of the same tenement, which my father acquired from Stephen de London, with a certain small upper room annexed above my porch, with two store-

rooms above, and a certain solar with shops built above it in the same
street. And 6s. 8d. of annual rent with its appurtenances arising from a
stall [*selda*] which William de Chaggeford holds in the High Street of the
city of Exeter. And 28s. of annual rent with its appurtenances arising from
a tenement which William le Brewer holds in the High Street of Exeter.
And all my tenement which John le Plumbour formerly inhabited, which I
had by bequest of Master John Wele in Exeter. And all my tenement with
the stalls and solars and the cellar in the High Street of the city of Exeter,
which is called *Marsheles Hous Bakere* with the *coffinus* [place for baked
meats, or strong-room?] which is called *Wylye* adjoining, and the appurtenances. And 8s. of annual rent arising from all that tenement which was
formerly that of Peter Lydene and afterwards John Horn acquired the
same tenement, which tenement is situated between the tenement of John
David and the tenement of John le Keu, spicer, in the High Street of Exeter.
And 18d. of annual rent which I acquired from Stephen de London arising
from a tenement which was formerly that of John le Mey in the High
Street of Exeter, together with the reliefs and escheats and the other
appurtenances from it when they occur. And all my tenement which was
formerly that of Richard de Poltymor, junior, knight, situated in the parish
of St Laurence, Exeter, except for 20s. of annual rent arising from the
same tenement which I gave to Sir Nicholas Daune to him and to his heirs
in fee. And all my tenement situated outside the East Gate of Exeter, in the
street which leads towards Polsloe, which tenement John Soth my father
acquired from Hamelin le Gaunt. And all my garden with the dovecote
situated outside the North Gate of Exeter, which garden with its
appurtenances John Soth my father and Isabel my mother acquired from
Christina Troune according to the metes and bounds made there, which
extends between John Eyr and the said Christina Troune, coheir of the
said John Eyr. And 20s. of annual rent arising from certain lands and
tenements in *La Tyghtehaye* and from other lands and tenements which
Sir William de Byry, chaplain, holds from me for the term of his life, together
with the reversions of the same lands and tenements when they occur. And
6s. of annual rent arising from a tenement and garden which John de
Norton, miller, holds from me for the term of his life outside the said
North Gate, together with the reversion of the same when it happens. And
26d. of annual rent arising from a certain cliff [*falasia*] outside the North
Gate next to the bank of the Exe, which Adam atte Broke holds from me
for the term of his life, together with the reversion of the same cliff when
it happens. And 18d. of annual rent arising from a certain garden which is
called *la Medehaye* outside the said gate, which the said Adam atte Broke
holds from me for the term of his life, together with the reversion of the
same garden when it occurs. And two cottages with the gardens adjoining,
situated on St David's Hill, and the reversion of the same tenement situated

on the hill when it occurs, which tenement John Sor holds of me in fee-tail. And one and a half acres of land situated outside the North Gate in the fee of Duryard [*Dureyurd*], which Joan Gaudechoun holds from me from year to year at will. And one *cophynum* [see above] which is called *Wylye*, which I had by the gift of Stephen de London and which John de Muluerton, baker, formerly held from me at will. And all my tenement which was formerly that of Alice de Bolehulle, situated in the High Street of the city of Exeter between the tenement which was formerly that of Stephen de London and the tenement which was formerly that of Nicholas Page, in latitude. And all my tenement in the High Street of the city of Exeter in which William de Ketene, chandler, now dwells and holds from me from year to year at will, together with a certain stall annexed to the same tenement which Robert de Silfertone holds from me at will. And 6d. of annual rent arising from a certain tenement which is called *la Cage* opposite the church of St James, Exeter, together with the demesne of the same tenement.

[All these I bequeath] to Geoffrey Gilberd, Martin le Keu of Bridford, and John Sor, my executors, together with the help of Alured Aylward, to sell and distribute for the health of the souls of John Soth, my grandfather, and Christine his wife; John Soth, my father and Isabel his wife; and for the health of my soul and the soul of John de Lerkebere my relation, following what seems best and most useful to them. Also I give and bequeath to Joan, my daughter, 26s. of annual rent going out of a tenement which Thomas le Specer now inhabits in the North Street of Exeter. And 24s. 8d. of annual rent going out of a certain tenement which Jordan de Brittestowe inhabited while he lived, in the South Street of Exeter. And 12s. of annual rent going out of a certain tenement which William Poleyn now inhabits, next to the church of the Holy Trinity, Exeter, to have and to hold to her and her heirs of her body by hereditary right in perpetuity. And if it happens that the aforesaid Joan dies without heirs of her body, all the aforesaid rents with their appurtenances shall remain to Martin le Keu of Bridford and to the heirs of his body in perpetuity. And if the aforesaid Martin dies without heirs of his body, then all the aforesaid rents shall remain to Geoffrey Gilberd and the heirs of his body in perpetuity. And if the said Geoffrey dies without heirs of his body, then all the aforesaid rents with their appurtenances shall remain to John Sor and the heirs of his body in perpetuity. And if the said John Sor dies without heirs of his body, then the aforesaid rents with their appurtenances shall remain to my right heirs in perpetuity.

Also I bequeath to John Sor, 100s. Also I bequeath to Baldwin, the son of the same John Sor, and Joan, the daughter of the same John Sor, 40s. Also I bequeath to Alured Aylward, clerk, two marks of silver for his service in making this testament and so that he may be of help to my aforesaid executors, so that he may maintain that this testament is my last will in all things, according to his ability and his powers. Also I bequeath to John de Tauistok, cordwainer, my gown which I had of the archdeacon of Totnes last year. Also I bequeath to John de Bannebury, servant of Martin le Keu, my gown which I had of Lady Joan de Carru last year. Also I give and bequeath to Sir Thomas de Stapeldon, all my plot [*placea*] in the South Street of the city of Exeter which Peter de la Grene formerly held from me and which, after the death of the said Peter, by reason of non-payment of the rent I recovered as chief lord of the same, by the name of gavel-lack [*gauelack*] and shortford in the court of the city of Exeter by judgment of the same court, to have and to hold the said plot with its appurtenances to the said Sir Thomas, his heirs and assigns, of capital demesnes of his fees by hereditary right in perpetuity. Also I give and bequeath the reversion of 5s. from the tenement which Geoffrey Gilberd holds from me in the parish of Blessed Mary Arches, Exeter, after the death of the aforesaid Gilbert to my right heirs when it occurs. Also I bequeath to Walter de Ferlegh, my servant, half a mark. Also I will, remit, and concede all the actions which I have against John Sor by reason of any receipt, debt, or account before the date of the feast of the Nativity of the Lord last past. Also I give and bequeath the reversion of 18d. from a tenement which John de Chuddelegh holds from me, next to the wall of the [cathedral] close near the court of the bishop of Exeter, to my right heirs when it happens. Also I wish and concede that the residue of all my goods shall be according to the ordinance of my aforesaid executors.

18. Ralph atte Lane, layman, 1330

(Source: Devon Record Office, Exeter City Archives, ED/M/294. Latin text. Sealed on a tongue, with seal attached.)

In the name of the Father and the Son and the Holy Spirit, amen. I, Ralph Attelane, being of sound memory and remembering death, from which no one should flee, make my testament in this manner, the sixth day of the month of March in the year of the Lord 1329 [1330, *modern style*]. First I bequeath my soul to God its creator, and my body to ecclesiastical burial. Also I bequeath to Sir William, chaplain of the church of St Sidwell, to pray for me, 6d. Also to the clerk of the place, 2d. Also I give, bequeath, and concede to Agnes my wife all my tenement that I inhabit, with the land adjoining and all its appurtenances, for the whole of her life, and after the decease of the same Agnes to William and Isabel, the children begotten between us, to their heirs and assigns in perpetuity, on condition that the same William and Isabel, their heirs and assigns, cause six masses to be celebrated for my soul and my benefactors in perpetuity on the day of my anniversary, and the same tenement lies between the tenement which was once that of Thomas Laghedene and the tenement which was once that of William Fynamour, outside the [East?] Gate of the city of Exeter. Also I bequeath to the same Agnes my tenement with its appurtenances which I have by the gift and feoffment of Robert Tylle, outside the aforesaid gate, for the whole of her life and to our children aforesaid after her death, observing the aforesaid conditions, and the same tenement lies between the tenement which was once that of William Germeyn and the land which was once that of Walter Hemery. Also I bequeath to Isabel my daughter, one garden and one virgate of land in *Chollefelde*. Also I bequeath to William my son, two selions [*sullines*] of land which lie in *Serlyshey*. Also I give, bequeath [and concede?] to Thomas my son and Cecily my daughter, my tenement which is situated between the tenement of the heirs of John Germeyn and my tenement, to their heirs and assigns in perpetuity. Also I give, bequeath, and concede to the aforesaid Agnes my wife, all my tenement which is situated between the tenement of William de Howeton and my tenement, namely to her heirs and assigns in perpetuity. Also I give, bequeath, [and concede?] to the said Agnes, one pot and one ewer of brass and two copper pans [*patellas*] on condition that they remain to my children, namely William and Isabel, after the decease of the same Agnes. Also to the same Agnes, one kiln [*fornacem*] of lead, with the same condition. Also I bequeath to the same Agnes, when my debts and legacies have been fully paid, all the rest of my goods wherever they are found or shall be found, for the support of her and of our children. Furthermore, I ordain, make, and constitute as executors of this testament William de Lutton and Agnes my wife aforesaid, giving full power to them and to each of them to ordain and do with my goods what shall seem expedient for the health of my soul.

19. Agnes de Wodelegh, married woman, 1349

(Source: Devon Record Office, 51/1/2/1. Latin text; either an original or a copy. Formerly sealed on a tag. The document is disfigured by a vertical strip of damp staining, rendering some words illegible. Such gaps are indicated by angle brackets, and any words within the brackets are conjectural. Paragraphing has been added for convenience.)

In the name of God, amen. I, Agnes de Wodelegh, make my testament on Saturday [14 March] next before the feast of St Gregory the pope in the year of the Lord 1348 [1349, *modern style*] in this manner. First I bequeath my soul to God and my body to be buried in the church of Blessed Mary

Major, Exeter. Also I give and bequeath all my tenement with the cellar adjoining and all and singular its appurtenances, in which tenement I live on the day of the making of these presents, to John White my husband, which tenement is situated in Guinea Street [*Gennestrete*] between the tenement which was that of Benedicta Steymour on the east side and the tenement which is now that of John Cryst on the west side and the tenement which was that of William de Smalecomb on the south side and the king's highway of Guinea Street on the north side, to have and to hold for the whole life of John himself, freely, quietly, well, and in peace by the services due and accustomed thereof by right. And after the decease of the same John I give and bequeath the whole of the aforesaid tenement with its appurtenances to David le Bruere and Petronilla his wife, the daughter of the aforesaid John le White and me, to have and to hold to the same David and Petronilla and the heirs of their bodies legitimately procreated, freely, quietly, well, and in peace, by the services due and accustomed thereof by right. And if the said David and Petronilla die without heirs of their bodies legitimately procreated, then I give and bequeath all the aforesaid tenement with all its appurtenances to Agnes the daughter of John White, to have and to hold to her and the heirs of her body legitimately procreated, freely, quietly, well, and in peace, by the services due and accustomed thereof by right. And if the said Agnes dies without heirs of her body legitimately procreated, I give and bequeath all the aforesaid tenement with its appurtenances to Master John atte Stappe to have and to hold for the whole life of John himself, freely, quietly, well, and in peace, by the services due and accustomed thereof by right. And after the decease of Master John himself I give and bequeath all the aforesaid tenement with all its appurtenances to the wardens of the church of Blessed Mary Major who are wardens for the time being there, that they may hold a day of anniversary for the said Agnes, John, David, Petronilla, Agnes, and John in perpetuity and use the residue of the profits of the aforesaid tenement for the repair of the said church, to have and to hold to the same wardens for the time being there, freely, quietly, well, and in peace by the services due and accustomed thereof by right.

Also I give and bequeath to the aforesaid John my husband all my tenement which is situated on St David's Hill with all my lands and gardens existing in the parish of St David with all their appurtenances, namely six acres of land which lie next to the new castle [*la Nywecastel*] on the west side, between the land of Richard de <Chusoldon?> which was formerly that of Walter Tauntefer on the east side, the west, the south, and the north, to have and to hold for the whole life of John himself, freely, quietly, well, and in peace by the services due and accustomed thereof by right. And a half acre of land which lies next to the aforesaid land between a certain way on the east side and the land of the aforesaid Richard which was formerly that of the aforesaid Walter on the west side, the south, and the north, to have and to hold for the whole life of John himself, freely, quietly, well, and in peace by the services due and accustomed thereof by right. And also one park [*parcum*] with one messuage and one garden adjoining which contain 2½ acres of land, which are situated on the south side of the court of the aforesaid Richard which was formerly that of the aforesaid Walter Tauntefer, to have and to hold for the whole life of John himself, freely, quietly, well, and in peace by the services due and accustomed thereof by right. And also one garden which lies outside the North Gate of the city of Exeter between the street which leads from Exeter towards Duryard [*Durhurd*] on the west side and a garden which was that of <Thomas?> le Fourbour on the east side and a garden which was that of Roger le Candeler on the north side and the water of Longbrook [*Langebrok*] on the south side, to have and to hold for the whole life of John himself, freely, quietly, well, and in peace by the services due and accustomed thereof by right. And after the death of the aforesaid John le White I give and bequeath all my aforesaid lands and tenements with the gardens and all their other appurtenances on the hill aforesaid and in the parish aforesaid to John atte Stappe my son, to have and to hold to him for the whole of his life, freely, quietly, well, and in peace by the rents and services due and accustomed thereof by right. And after the death of my son John aforesaid I give and bequeath to the aforesaid David and Petronilla his wife and my daughter all the aforesaid lands and tenements with the gardens and all the other appurtenances aforesaid, to have and to hold to them and to their heirs of their bodies legitimately procreated by the services due and accustomed thereof by right. And if the said David and Petronilla die without heirs of their bodies, then I give and bequeath all the aforesaid lands and tenements and the gardens with all their other appurtenances aforesaid to Agnes the daughter of John White, to have and to hold to her and to her heirs of her body legitimately procreated by the services due and accustomed thereof by right. And if the said Agnes daughter of the aforesaid John dies without heirs of her body legitimately procreated, then I will and concede that all the aforesaid lands and tenements and gardens with all their appurtenances aforesaid be sold by the last and surviving executors of the aforesaid, and that the money received thereof received and accepted be divided and distributed for the souls of my father and my mother and the souls aforesaid, when they depart from this light, and for my soul.

Also I give and bequeath to the wardens aforesaid, 5s. of annual rent <annually to be taken?> from all the tenement with its appurtenances which was that of Robert Mere, situated in Preston Street [*Prustestrete*] in the city of Exeter, opposite the tenement of Laurence Coterel to have and to hold the aforesaid 5s. of annual rent to the aforesaid wardens and their successors as wardens, freely, quietly, well, and in peace by hereditary right in perpetuity, supporting thereof each year the day of the anniversaries of the aforesaid Agnes, John, John, David, Petronilla, and Agnes in perpetuity. Also I bequeath for the making of <?> *de condend'*, 5s. Also I bequeath to the rector [*persona*] of the church of Blessed Mary aforesaid one penny on each day of the year following my death, to be received from my executors. Also I bequeath to the clerk of the aforesaid parish church, 12d. to pray for my soul. Also I bequeath to Agnes, daughter of John le White, one gown, my best < >, the brass < >, and two brass pans, and two beds, and one girdle of silk studded with silver. Also I bequeath 20s. to be distributed to the poor for my soul. Also I bequeath [money] from my goods to hold an annual in the aforesaid church at the altar of Blessed Thomas the Martyr as quickly as it can be arranged for my soul and for the souls of John my husband and of our benefactors, and for the souls of all the faithful departed. And I bequeath the residue of all my goods to my executors to employ for my soul, <having regard to?> the fear of God faithfully to carry out and execute everything and what is written above. I ordain, make, and constitute as my executors John White, my husband, David le Bruere, and Petronilla wife of the same.

20. William Mounteyn, layman, 1349

(Source: Exeter Cathedral Archives, D&C 2232. Latin text. Sealed on a tongue, so either the original or an authenticated copy. The document is damaged and what remains has been heavily stained with oak-galls, so that it is virtually impossible to recover the whole text.)

In the name of God, amen. I, William Mounteyn of Exeter, being in good memory, blessed be God, make my testament on the third day of the month of May in the year of the Lord 1349. First I leave my soul to God and his mother <together?>, and my body to be buried in the <cemetery?> of St Peter, Exeter, in the grave where my father lies in the same place. Also I bequeath for the making of my burial five <marks?>. And to relieve the poor, five marks, so that each one individually may have a halfpenny. Also I bequeath to John Mounteyn, my [brother], 20s. and my best robe, one silver cup without a <*signum*? i.e. mark>, and one feather bed with a <*lodicio*? i.e. blanket>, and one set of bedding. Also I bequeath to Richard, my brother, one mark of silver, and my second best gown, and one <hat?> called a houve [*huve*], and one feather bed. Also I bequeath to Christine White, 10s. and one feather bed. Also I bequeath to the light of the church of Blessed Mary Steps, Exeter, 40d. And to Sir William, the rector there, half a mark. Also I bequeath to the Friars Preachers of Exeter to celebrate for my soul, 5s., and to the Friars Minor of Exeter for prayers and for *dirige*, 5s. Also I bequeath to each prisoner in the gaol [*gayola*] of Exeter, 1d. And to each poor person in the East Gate, 1d. And to each poor <person?> in the hospital of St John, Exeter, 1d. And to Stephen de Mattacote, clerk, 2s. Also I bequeath the residue of all my goods to my executors written below to support a suitable chaplain to celebrate divine service in the church of Blessed Mary Steps, Exeter, <for one year?> after my decease for my soul and the soul of Agnes my <wife?>, and to support two chaplains if my goods are sufficient for this purpose. And to <perform?> this testament and funeral arrangements, I ordain, make, and constitute as my executors John de <Wre?>fford, John Sloman, and John Mounteyn, my brother. Furthermore to my said executors, 10s. Debts which are owing: from Joan Mendy 10s. 9d., Joan Jacob, widow of Walter Jacob, < > 17s. 8d., and < >.

21. Inventory of the Goods of Lucy de Collecote, 1324

(Source: Exeter Cathedral Archives, D&C VC/3050, 3052. Latin text. These are two copies of the inventory, both probably copies of an original, of which the former is much the more legible and forms most of the basis of this translation. The original text is continuous, but it is here divided into sections for ease of consultation, and titles have been added to indicate the approximate contents of each section.)

This is the inventory of all the goods of Lucy de Coldecote, deceased, found at the time of her death by the sworn executors of the testament of the same Lucy and by very many trustworthy neighbouring men specially sworn by the same executors for this purpose, with an estimation faithfully made of the value on the Thursday [9 February] next after the feast of St Agatha the Virgin 1323 [1324, *modern style*], and continuing for some days.

[Clothes and soft furnishings]

First in money found, 1d. Also one green robe without a hood, worth [*precium*] 10s. Also one surcoat of peacock colours [*pounacis*], worth 6s. Also one tunic of indigo-blue [*indeblueto*], worth 2s. 6d. Also one hood of motley colour [*melleto*], furred with miniver, worth 4s. 6d. Also one surcoat of cameline, furred with old miniver, worth 4s. Also one green surcoat, furred with strandling [*strallyng*], worth 3s. Also one green tunic, worth 2s. 6d. Also one courtepy of grey russet [*grisanco russeto*], with a hood, worth 6s. Also one cloak of light-blue [*alboblueto*], worth 2s. Also one tunic of black burnet [*burneto*], worth 8d. Also one red hood, worth 2d. Also one fur of miniver for one hood, worth 40d. Also five smocks [*camisie*] for women, namely one worth 5d., another 5d., the third 4d., the fourth 3d., and the fifth 1d. Also one girdle, worth 1d. Also four pieces of striped [*stragulata*] bedding [*superlectilia*], namely one worth 12d., another worth 10d., the third worth 6d., and the fourth worth 3d. Also three carpets [*tapeta*], namely one worth 16d., another worth 4d., and the third worth 2d. Also two white blankets [*lodic'*], one worth 6d. and the other worth 3d. Also eleven sheets [*lintheamenta*], of which seven are worth 6d. each, one worth 4d., and three worth 2d. each, of which the total is 4s. 4d. Also three feather beds, namely one worth 18d., another worth 16d., and the third worth 12d. Also four cushions [*pulvinar'*], worth 12d. Also twelve pillows [*auricular'*], worth 12d. Also one piece of canvas [*caneuatus*] for a bed, worth 2d. Also three chests, namely one worth 8d., another 6d., and the third worth 3d. Also six coffers, namely one worth 2s., another worth 12d., the third worth 6d., the fourth worth 4d., the fifth worth 3d., and the sixth worth 1d. Also two coffers for trussing [*ad trussand'*], worth 14d. Also one strong-box [*forcer'*], bound with iron, worth 10d. Also one green strong-box, worth 3d. Also one leather strong-box, worth 2d. Also one piece of kerchief [*cuuercher*] of silk, worth 12d. and another piece of kerchief of silk, worth 8d. Also a half piece of kerchief of silk, worth 6d Also one old kerchief, worth 2d. Also one kerchief of linen, worth 2d. Also 59 barbettes [*barbet'*] of silk and one barbette of linen, worth 5s.

[Gold and silver]

Also 15 gold rings, namely five worth 2s. each, four worth 8d. each, three worth 6d. each and one worth 4d., and two broken rings worth 6d. of which the total is 15s. Also eight buckles [or brooches: *firmacula*] of silver, namely three buckles worth 9d., two buckles worth 4d., and three buckles worth 3d. Also four bags [*loculi*] of silk, namely one worth 6d., one worth 2d., and two worth 2d. Also one *wytweban* of silver with a case [*casu*] of silk, worth 1d. Also eight silver spoons weighing 7s., worth 6s. 6d. Also one silver cup weighing 17s. 10d., worth 16s., and one silver cup weighing 7s. 2d., worth 6s. 6d.

[Utensils and household goods]

Also three pieces of samite [*samit*], worth 9d. Also one quarter of borax [*boreys*], worth 3d. Also one case of silk for corporal cloths [*corporalibus*], worth 6d. Also one old piece of muslin [or fine linen: *sindon*], worth 3d. Also one balance [*bilanx*] for weighing, worth 1d., and another balance, worth ½d. Also two ewers [*lavator'*], worth 14d. Also two basins [*pelues*], namely one worth 5d. and the other worth 4d. Also one very small ewer, found in the custody of Sir Elias the chaplain, worth 2d., because it was pledged to him. Also two very small ewers of tin worth 2d. Also 119 pins for kerchiefs, worth 1d. Also various leaden weights for weighing, worth 1d. Also flax [*linum*], worth 3d. Also two shafts [*seftes*] for weighing, worth 9d. Also two sieves [*cribra*], worth ½d. Also one iron candlestick [*candelabrum*], worth 3d. Also two pitchers [*picher'*] of tin, weighing seven pounds, worth 10d. Also one small mortar of brass, weighing seven pounds, with a pestle of iron, worth 14d. Also one little stool [*scabellum*] of straw [*stramine*], worth ¼d. Also three lanterns, worth 3d. Also two *purle* [purses?] of leather for carrying money, worth 2d. Also *sem[in?]elini* [seed-bags?], worth 2d. Also one bag [*mala*], worth 2d. Also one chelle [*chylla*] of brass [*enea*], worth 2d. Also woollen yarn [*filum laneum*], worth 3d. Also five cups of wood, worth 16d. Also two cups of wood, worth 1d. Also silver, weighing 44d., worth 40d. Also broken silver enamel [*daumayll*], with various stones and glass, worth 4s. 6d. Also one little box [*skybettus*] of leather, worth 1d. Also 19 silver-gilt buttons, weighing 9d., worth 9d. Also four silver rosaries [*pater noster'*], weighing 30d., worth 3s. Also 252 little buttons of silver enamel, worth 2s. Also broken pieces of a *serte* [headband?] of silver, with stones, worth 4d. Also three drinking cups, bound with iron, worth 6d. Also 786 dies [or counters: *printe*], of various forms and various colours, worth 4s. 10d. Also one little table [*tabula*] for the dies [*princtis*] and one little pyx of wood with a lock [*serata*], worth 3d. Also six cloths, namely one 4½ ells in length, worth 16d., another 5 ells in length, worth 15d., the third 4½ ells in length, worth 14d., the fourth 4 ells in length, worth 12d., the fifth 4 ells in length, worth 6d., and the sixth 3 ells in length, worth 2d. Also two double towels [*tualle*], namely one worth 10d. and the other worth 9d. Also seven short [*curte*] towels, worth 2s. 4d. Also three tablecloths [*sauenap*] of linen, worth 3d. Also two iron *ferra* [pots?] for ginger [*zinizyber*], and one small bowl with tongs [*tenal'*], worth 2d. Also eight pounds of mustard [*senap'*], worth 2s. Also one very wide girdle, worth 2d. Also two arrows [*quarrell'*], worth 2d.

[Furniture and tools]

Also one chair of wood, worth 1d. Also six bankers [*bankar'*], one worth 4d., another worth 4d., and four worn ones worth 4d. Also one folding table [*mensa plicabil'*], worth 3d. Also one tin salt-cellar [*salar'*], worth ¼d. Also four tables with three pairs of trestles [*trestell'*], worth 12d. Also nine little tables [*tabule*], worth 16d. Also seven benches [*formuli*] of wood, worth 7d. Also one pair of cords for trussing [*ad trussand'*], worth 3d. Also four sacks, worth 4d. Also one cloth [*pannus*] for holding one sack, worth 1d. Also one jar [*olla*] of brass, weighing 26 pounds, worth 4s. 4d.

Also one pot [*urciolus*] of brass, weighing 14 pounds, worth 28d. Also one pot of brass, weighing eight pounds, worth 16d. Also three bowls [*patille*], namely one worth 6d., another 3d., and the third with tongs, worth 8d. Also two tripods, worth 3d. Also two spits [*verua*] of iron, worth 2d. Also two gridirons [*craticle*] of iron, worth 2d. Also one andiron, worth 8d. Also one knife for the kitchen, and one *ferot* [small piece of iron], worth 1d. Also all the wooden dishes [*disce lignei*], worth 3d. Also two mortars of stone for the kitchen, with two pestles, worth 2d. Also one wooden bushel [*bussel*], worth 2d. Also one cask [*tina*], worth 2d. Also two casks, worth 2d. Also one ladder, worth 3d. Also one empty cask [*doleum*], worth 6d. Also two barrels [*barrel'*], worth 8d. Also one rake [*rastellus*], worth 2d. Also two tubs [*cuue*], worth 5d. Also two muck forks of iron [*furce ad fimum*], worth 2d. Also one axe [*secur'*], worth 2d. Also one axe for a *cem'us* [mason?] with a trowel [*trolle*], worth 2d. Also one hoe [*sarpa*], worth 1d. Also in the custody of Sir William Spycer, chaplain, one gold ring worth 2s. and four silver buckles worth 2s., in pledge to him. Also in honey [*mel*], worth 3d.

The said executors furthermore declare publicly, openly, and distinctly that if they should happen to find any other item or items of goods of the said deceased person in future, whether in things or in the hands of debtors, wherever and in whatever circumstances they may be found, by whatever name they shall be valued, they will faithfully construct an inventory of all the goods found in this manner, and exhibit the inventory to a judge who is competent on this matter at the appropriate place and time, rendering an account in this respect concerning all the aforesaid goods which shall happen to be found in future, fully and faithfully debiting the value, and to augment the inventory of the aforesaid goods above, as concerning right and deed they were bound by the oath prescribed in this matter, and if in the passage of time in the future it shall appear evident that any of the aforesaid goods contained in the inventory were alien, put into the said inventory, and valued through ignorance, all such goods shall be withdrawn from the aforesaid inventory upon that account, and the executors shall be properly exonerated concerning them.

22. Inventory and Accounts of the Executors of Dean Andrew Kilkenny, 1302–15

(Source: D&C 2846. Latin text. The document is a roll of eight membranes, drawn up by or on behalf of the dean's executors, William de Kilkenny and Walter de Tottonia, and kept and added to over a period of some thirteen years.)

[m. 1]

The Account of the Executors of the Will of Sir Andrew, Formerly the Dean of the Church of Exeter

[Part I: Assets and Income]

Money and Silver Vessels

First they account for £139 8s. 1½d. found in cash and £21 16s. received from the servant and reeve at Braunton before the inventory was made. And in small change [*argento fracto*] 28s. 8d. by weight. And 30s. 4d. in small and black pounds Tournois [*turonensis parvorum et nigrorum*] with cauldrons by number [*cum caudronibus per numerum*]. And 3s. 3d. in weight for fittings for a belt [*harnesis ad unam corrigiam*]. And 59s. 4d. for one silver-gilt bowl [*cuppam*] of the same weight in money [*eiusdem ponderis per pecuniam*]. And 38s. for another silver-gilt bowl of the same weight in money. And 39s. 6d. for another gilt bowl of the same weight. And 41s. 1d. for another silver-gilt bowl of the same weight. And 38s. 10d. for another gilt bowl of the same weight. And 74s. 10d. for another gilt bowl of the same weight. And 49s. 2d. for another gilt bowl. And 27s. for one mazer with a silver base [*pede*]. And 37s. 6d. for one silver cup [*cipho*] with a gilt base of the same weight. And 40s. 3d. for another gilt cup with a base of the same weight. And 39s. 6d. for another gilt cup with a base. And 22s. for another gilt cup with a base. And 19s. 7d. for another

171

gilt cup with a base. And 31s. 8d. for another silver [*albo*] cup with a base. And 28s. 4d. for another silver cup with a base; for 60s. for one silver jug [*picherio*]. And 18s. 9d. for another silver jug. And 13s. 4d. for another silver jug. And 21s. 8d. for a silver salt cellar. And 24s. 7d. for one silver basin. And 25s. for another silver basin. And 16s. 9d. for one silver piece [of plate]. And 18s. 6d for another silver piece. And 17s. 10d. for another silver piece. And 14s. 11d for another silver piece. And 20s. for another silver piece. And 13s. 4d. for one mazer with silver-gilt base. And 6s. 8d. for one mazer with silver-gilt base. And 2s. for one mazer without a base and another smaller mazer without a base. And 2s. for another mazer. And 4s for another mazer with silver-gilt base. And 12s. 9d. for < > gilt spoons with knobs [*coclearis cum nodis deauratis*] of the same weight. And 11s. 8d. for twelve plain [*planis*] spoons. And 16s. 8d. for < > plain spoons. And 7s. 6d. for six plain spoons. And 4s. 2d. for five spoons. And 5s. for six old spoons with knobs [*cum nodis*]. And 15s. 2d. for one gilt chalice. And 20s. for another silver chalice. And 8s. for another silver chalice. And 10s. 4d. for two silver cruets.

Total £211 13s. 2½d. Also total of pounds Tournois 30s. 4d. And nothing remains. Six large rings, one gold buckle [*firmaculum*], and two silk purses are not valued [*non apprec'*].

Books

Also they account for 5 marks for one *Old Digest*. Also 60s. for one *Afforciatum* [i.e. *Inforciatum*]. And 53s. 4d. for one *New Digest*. And 40s. for one *Parvum Volumen*. And 53s. 4d. for one *Codex*. And 7 marks for one fine and good *Decretals*. And 53s. 4d. for a *Decreta* in old lettering [*de antiqua littera*]. And 26s. 8d. for another *Decreta* in old lettering. And 40s. for another old *Decreta*. And 40s for one *Decretals* with manuals [*manualibus*]. And 40s. for a *Summa Innocentii*. And 60s. for one new *Digest* with an old text and a new commentary [*apparatu*]. And 30s. for a *Liber Institutionum* with the *Authentica*. And 30s for a *Summa Gaufredi*. And 53s. 4d. for an old *Codex* with a new commentary. And 10s. for a *Summa* of Azo. And 16s. for an old *Summa Gaufredi* with a certain tractate *De Ordine Judicario*. And 4s. for a *Summa Reymundi*. And 18d. for a *Summa Egidii*. And 10 marks for one Bible. And 10s. for a short compend- ium [*summula*] *De Exposicione Verborum*. And 30s. for a *Liber Sentenc- iarum*. And 13s. 4d. for the *Letters* of Augustine with the book *De Spiritu et Anima* and *Liber Arbitrium* in one volume. And 20s. for Augustine *De Videndo Deo*. And 26s. 8d. for one glossed psalter. And 26s. 8d. for another glossed psalter. Also 12s. for the *Constitutions* of Boniface with a tractate of elections and a repertory of canon law [*tractatu eleccionum et repertorio in iure canonico*] in one volume. And 8s. for a book of Papias. And 30s. for a book of history [*libro hystor'*]. And <50s.? > for a new missal. And 20s.

for one antiphoner with a psalter. And 53s. 4d. for one portiforium. And 5s. < > for one old and worn portiforium. And 20s. for a book that is called *Legenda Sanctorum*. And 6s. 8d. for one gradual. And 5s. for one troper. And 3s. for another troper. And 10s. for a good psalter. And 2s. for a *Summa* that is called *Fareta*, with other quires written by the deceased. And 2s. for one book of various sermons without boards [*asseribus*]. And 2s. for another book of various sermons with boards. Also 12d for a book of various quires partly written by the deceased. And 12d. for a *Summa* of John [*Johannis*] Velet *De Divinis Officiis*. And 2s. for one book of sermons with the *Testamenta Duodecim Patriarcharum*. And 2s. for two martyrologies. And 12d. for the *History of St Richard* and *De Corpore Christi*. And 2s for *Repeticiones in Iure Ciuili*, with many quires written by the deceased. And 12d for a *Summa* called *Margareta* on the commentary of Innocent. And 2s. for the *Brocardica* of Azo. And 12d. for four quires of cases of the *Decreta*. And 4d. for three small quires of an exposition of the Bible. And 3s. for a certain *Summa* by John of Spain [*Hyspani*] on the *Decretals*. And 12d. for a *Summa* of Seneca [*Senece*]. And 4s. for a *History of the English*. And 18d. for expositions on various *Decretals*. And 2d. for certain *Letters of the Blessed Thomas*. And 12d. for statutes of the king with various papal books. And 3s. for a *History of the Britons*. And 6d. for a certain book of various prayers [*oracionum*]. And 2s. for the book of Boethius *On the Consolation of Philosophy*. And 12d. for a canon of the mass. Also a register [*in margin*: note register and portiforium] of St Sidwell kept back [*reservatur*] by the [cathedral] exchequer. Also one portiforium that ought to be returned to the chapel of St Theobald [in Colaton Raleigh parish]. Also a *Summa Reinfredi* with other short compendia [*summula*] in the same volume, of 30s.

Total £66 11s. And nothing remains. The register of St Sidwell and the portiforium.

Spices

Also they account for 9s. 2d. for 88 pounds of almonds, price 1¼d. per pound. And 2s. 8d. for <25½> pounds of rice, price 1¼d. per pound. And 18s. for 12 pounds of sugar [*cykure*], price 18d. per pound. And 5s. 7½d. for 2¼ pounds of ginger [*zingibis*], price 2s. 6d. per pound, with 14s. 7d. for 2¼ pounds of saffron, price 6s. 6d. per pound. And 10d. for mace. And 2d. for one pound of sermountain [*ciremonteine*]. And 2½d. for 1¼ pounds of peony seeds. And 7d. for zedoary. And 18d. for *cumfofr'* [comfrey?]. And 4s. 4½d. for 3½ pounds of pepper, price 15d. per pound. And 2s. 4d. for 1¼ pounds of galingale [*galigan*] and cinnamon [*canella*]. And 10d. for 10 pounds of cumin. And 1d. for dill [*anisio*]. And 1d. for licorice [*likoriceo*].

Total 61s. 1d.

Cloths

Also they account for 8s. for a quarter part of a cloth for a groom's livery [*de secta garcionis*]. And 42s. for 18 yards of cloth of lupin flower [*flour de vesce*], price 2s. 4d. per yard. And 13s. 4d. for one surcoat and a cloak with a hood of cameline of tripe [*tripe*]. And 2s. 4d. for 7 ells of linen, price 4d. per ell. And 2s. for one piece of perse containing [enough?] for two hoods. And 2s. for 8 ells of green carde cloth, price 3d. per ell. And 6s. for 24 ells of broad linen [*linei ampli*], price 3d. per ell. And 2s. for half a bolt [*bolt*] of [cloth of] Aylsham [*Eylisham*]. And 7s. 6d. for two bankers [*bankariis*] of *pauiot* [peacock?]. And 8s. for one long and broad banker. And 20d. for one banker with white roses and crosses. And 2s. for one banker with shields and castles. And 2s. for one broadcloth with shields. And 6s. for three narrow and old bankers. And 2s. for one purse of Lombardy [*Lumbardia*]. And 1d. <for one?> red leather purse. And 12d. for one cap [*pileo*] lined with miniver [*menifer*]. And 3d. for one cap lined with black lambskin. And 12d. for three caps. And 2s. for four pillows [*pulvinaris*] for a bed. And 5 marks for three surplices and two rochets with a cope of new silk with a new amice. And 16s. for one furred lining [*forura*] of strandling [*stranling'*] for a surcoat, with half a furred lining of squirrel [*scurellus*] and a new hood of byse [*bise*]. And 12d. for one old red silk cloth.

Total £9 11s. 10d.

Tablecloths with Towels

Also they account for 3s. 6d. for one tablecloth [*mappa*] seven ells long, price 6d. per ell. And 8s. 8d. for two tablecloths in one piece thirteen ells long, price 8d. per ell. And 3s. 6d. for one tablecloth seven ells long, price 6d. per ell. And 5s. for two tablecloths in one piece, ten ells long, price 6d. per ell. And 5s. for one tablecloth ten ells long, price 6d. per ell. And 10s. 10d. for two tablecloths in one piece thirteen ells long, price 10d. per ell. And 5s. for one tablecloth six ells long, price 10d. per ell. And 2s. for one tablecloth six ells long, price 4d. per ell. And 4s. for one tablecloth twelve ells long, price 4d. per ell. And 4s. 2d. for one tablecloth ten ells long, price 5d. per ell. And 20d. for one tablecloth five ells long, price 4d. per ell. And 5s. for one tablecloth twelve ells long, price 5d. per ell. And 5s. 3d. for two tablecloths nine ells long, price 7d. per ell. And 16d. for one tablecloth four ells long, price 4d. per ell. And 6s. for one [m. 2] tablecloth twelve ells long, price 6d. per ell. And 2s. 8d. for one tablecloth eight ells long, price 4d. per ell. Also 12d. for an old and worn tablecloth eight ells long. Also 5s. for two towels [*tuall'*] in one piece fifteen ells long, price 4d. per ell. And 2s. for four towels in one piece eight ells long, price 3d. per ell. And 2s. 4d. for one towel seven ells long, price 4d. per ell. Also 4s. 4d. for two towels in one piece thirteen ells long, price 4d. per ell. And 2s. 4d.

for two towels in one piece seven ells long, price 4d. per ell. And 2s. 4d. for one towel in one piece seven ells long, price 4d. per ell. And 2s. 4d. for two towels in one piece seven ells long, price 4d. per ell. And 2s. 4d. for two towels in one piece seven ells long, price 4d. per ell. And 2s. 6d. for two towels in one piece seven and a half ells long, price 4d. per ell. And 2s. 4d. for two towels in one piece seven ells long, price 4d. per ell. And 2s. for three towels in one piece eight ells long, price 3d. per ell. And 3s. for four towels in one piece twelve ells long, price 3d. per ell. And 2s. 4d. for two towels in one piece seven ells long, price 4d. per ell. And 15d. for two towels in one piece five ells long, price 3d. per ell. And 12d. for one unlined [*simplici*] towel three ells long, price 4d. per ell. And 18d. for two towels in one piece six ells long, price 3d. per ell. And 12d. for one unlined towel three ells long, price 4d. per ell. And 9d. for one towel three ells long, price 3d. per ell. And 4d. for one towel two ells long, price 2d. per ell. And 4d. for another towel two ells long, price 2d. per ell. And 4d. for another towel two ells long, price 2d. per ell. And 4d. for another towel two ells long, price 2d. per ell. And 6d. for a towel three ells long, price 2d. per ell. And 6d. for another towel three ells long, price 2d. per ell. And 6d. for another towel three ells long, price 2d. per ell. And 12d. for two towels in one piece six ells long, price 2d. per ell. And 12d. for two towels in one piece six ells long, price 2d. per ell. And 4d. for one long old towel seven ells long. And 18d. for one sanap [*sasnap*] six ells long, price 3d. per ell. And 18d for another sanap six ells long, price 3d. per ell. And 8d. for one canvas eight ells long. And 12d. for one canvas six ells long, price 2d. per ell. And 12d. for another canvas six ells long. And 6d. for another canvas six ells long. And 9½d. for one canvas seven ells long, price 1½d. per ell. And 4d. for one canvas eight ells long. And 3d. for two sanaps. And 1d. for one sanap. And 2d. for one sanap. And 6d. for three canvas towels. And 9d. for three canvas towels. And 3d. for two cloths for a dresser [*ad dressator*']. And 1½d. for one *portitor* [portable cloth?]. And 6d. for one towel three ells long. And 4d. for one canvas 2½ ells long.

Total £6 10s. 8d.

In the Parchment Room and Others

Also they account for 4s. for four cushions for the altar. And 18s. for six dozen parchments, price 3s. per dozen. And 4s. for two dozen parchments. And 2s. for eighteen membranes of parchment. And 18d. for a dozen parchments. And 5s. 6d. for one brass mortar with a pestle. And 2s. for one lamp [*lanterna*]. And 6d. for another stone lamp. And 3d. for another old lamp. And 12d. for another lamp with branches [*cum turellis*]. And 12d. for six sacks for spices. And 12d. for two cushions of deerskin [*corio ceruino*]. And 12d. for three cushions with shields. And 6s. for five wild animal skins [*pellibus ferarum*]. And 12d. for four pairs of gloves. And

12d. for one cap of green cord [*capello de laqueo viridi*]. And 12d. for two caps. And 5s. for one black chest. And 5s. for another white chest. And 5s. for one chest in the exchequer. And 4s. 6d. for one old large chest. And 12d. for one chest in the chapel. And 6d. for two chests. And 4s. for two chests for harnessing [*ad hernesii*]. And 18d. for one green strong-box [*forcerio*]. And 6d. for one black strong-box. And 12d. for one green coffer. And 4d. for one small coffer. And 18d. for two lampstands [*abstonsis*]. And 3s. 6d. for seven pounds of new wax for torches and candles. And 15d. for 2½ ells of green sindon. And 2s. 1d. for 2½ ells of black sindon. And 2s. 6d. for four ells of buckram in two pieces. And 6d. for 1½ ells of buckram. And 2s. for one silk purse called a pautener. And 12d. for one piece of quadruple samite [*katersamite*]. And 8d. for one cord for a cap. And 1d. for another black cord for a seal. And 4d. for green and black silk. And 14d. for two silk purses. And 4d. for four ivory handles [*manubriis eburneis*].

Total £4 16s.

In the Chapel

Also they account for 2s. for one silk cloth for a paten. And 4½d. for eight seal cords [*laqueis*]. And 8s. for one leather belt with a buckle [*hernes'*] of silver. And 4s. for two striped cloths for a paten. And 18d. for one cloth for a lectern. And 3s. for one case for a corporal. And 3s. for another case [decorated] with an eagle [*aquila*]. And 5s. for one amice with shields. And 6s. 8d. for one case for a corporal. And 12d. for one gold plated pyx. And 2d. for another pyx. And 8d. for another pyx in a black bag. And 13s. 4d. for one complete set of old vestments with a lined [*duplex*] chasuble. And 40s. for a complete set of vestments with a lined amice, lined stole and lined maniple. And 2d. for one box for bread [i.e. wafers]. And 2s. 6d. for one surplice with a rochet. And 6d. for three short altar towels. And 12d. for one altar frontal. And 8d. for a canvass for the altar with one towel to cover the altar and three towels with two tassels [*pendiculis*]. And 2d. for two cruets. And 18d. for one small latten [*laton*] ewer. And 12d. for another latten ewer with towel. And 3d. for one ash-blower [*ciniflone*]. And 6d. for one set of scales [*libra siue statera*]. And 18d. for an ivory comb. And 6d. for another ivory comb. And 4d. for one pound of candle wax.

Total £4 19s. 4½d.

Arms and Other Things

Also they account for 11 marks for arms, which begin thus in the inventory, 'Also for one hauberk', and the inventory is concluded thus, 'Also caps with a tester [*cappes cum testario*] and a surcoat over armour [*camisia super armatura*]'. And 6d. for one shield [*targia*]. And 2s. for six battleaxes [*hachebek'*]. And 3d. for three lances. And 1d. for two lances without iron. And 10d. for one fork for a chimney [*furca ad caminum*]. And 6d. for one knife. And 6s. for three sacks for cloth. And 18d. for one cart cover [*barhude*]. And 15d. for another cart cover. And 8d. for another cart cover. And 8d. for another cart cover. And 2d. for another cart cover. And 10s. for one saddle. And 12d. for another saddle. And 4s. for two sumpter-saddles [*sellis summariis*]. And 18d. for three saddles. And 4d. for a sumpter-saddle. And 2d. for another old sumpter-saddle. And 6d. for a saddle. And 4s. for one long thick rope. And 8d. for old [pieces of] iron [*ferris*] with girdles and a stirrup. And 8d. for two saddle cloths [*husciis*]. And 12d. for one large and broken rope. And 2s. for one pair of saddle bags [*besazes*]. And 12d. for another pair of small saddle bags [*basaces*]. And 3d. for [m. 3] one pair of new ropes for trussing [*ad trossand'*]. And 4d. for one rope. And 4d. for one pair of old braces [*braces*].

Total £9 8s. 8d.

Lead, Iron, et cetera
Also they account for 11s. 11d. for 6½ fotmals of lead, price 22d. per fotmal. Also for 10s. 9½d. for 310 pounds of iron, price 3s. 6d. per hundred. And 8d. for old iron. And 1d. for one lock. And 4s. 7d. for five and a half stones for collecting fat in the kitchen, price 10d. per stone. And 8s. 8d. for eight *sep* [separate?] stones, price 13d. per stone. And 8d. for one brass vessel for holy water. And 12d. for twenty-four white metal cups [*ciphis albis*]. And 4d. for one chair. And 18d. for one knife with a black handle [*manubrio*]. And 4d. for peacock feathers [*pennis pavonum*]. And 20d. for a crowbar for digging stones [*crowa ad lapides fodend'*].

Total 42s. 2½d.

Horses
Also they account for 30s. for one horse. And 20s for another horse. And 13s. 4d. for another blind horse. And 2s. for another blind horse. And 2s. for one draught horse [*affero*]. And 6¼d. for one hide of a draught horse.

Total 67s. 10¼d.

In the kitchen
Also they account for 12s. 1d. for one brass pot [*olla*], weight 58 pounds, price 2½d. per pound. Also 8s. 8d. for one pot, weight 52 pounds, price 2d. per pound. And 23s. 4d. for one brass *campaner* [bell-shaped?] pot, weight 112 pounds, price 2½d. per pound. And 3s. 4d. for one pot, weight 20 pounds, price 2d. per pound. And 5s. 10d. for one pot, weight 28 pounds, price 2½d. per pound. And 2s. 8d. for one pot, weight 16 pounds, price 2d. per pound. And 16d. for one posnet [*poscenet*], weight 8 pounds, price 2d. per pound. And 10d. for another posnet, weight 5 pounds, price

2d. per pound. And 3s. for one pan without hoops [*sine ligatura*]. And 2s. for another hooped [*ligata*] pan. And 3s. for two dishes. And 12d. for one frying pan [*patella ad friand'*]. And 4d. for another similar dish. And 10d. for three andirons. And 12d. for two brasiers. And 2d. for one iron for roasting meat. And 9d. for a tripod. And 12d. for one iron dish for collecting fat. And 6d. for another similar dish. And 2d. for one scoop with a hook [*scupar' cum hamo*]. And 1d. for one small old dish. And 6d. for one axe for wood [*securi ad busta*]. And 4d. for another axe for meat [*securi ad carnes*]. And 4d. for two knives. And 4d. for one grater with a bowl [*micatorium cum scafa*]. And 2s. for one mortar. And 12d. for another mortar. And 4d. for another mortar. And 8d. for two tubs with lids [*cinis cum opercul'*]. And 2d. for two benches. And 4d. for one barrel of vinegar. And 12d. for two mills. And 2d. for two buckets. And 2d. for three large dishes. And 4d. for dishes and plates. And 2d. for two barrels with large bore-holes [*magnis foraminibus*].

Total 79s. 9d.

In the Bakehouse
Also they account for 2s. for three large tubs [*cuuis*]. And 2s. 11d. for seven small tubs. And 12d. for four trundle-wheels [*trendell'*]. And 3d. for one broach [*braka*]. And 8d. for one sieve. And 4s. 4d. for three troughs for dough [*alueis ad pastum*]. And 12d. for one cask and one tub for sifting flour [*cuna ad bolitand'*]. And 2s. 6d. for six sacks. And 12d. for one large sack. And 8d. for one cooking pot. And 2d. for two sieves. And 6s. for one large trough for meat. And 4d. for one dresser [*drescator'*]. And 2d. for another dresser. And 4d. for two old tubs.

Total 23s. 4d.

In the Hall
Also they account for 2s. 6d. for one new table [*mensa*]. And 6d. for one table. And 4d. for another table. And 6d. for one table with legs. And 6d. for boards for the head of a bed [*asseribus ad capud lecti*]. And 7d. for fourteen canopies. And 4d. for four benches and three chairs. And 4d. for six new dishes with saucers. And 8d. for one vessel [*vase*] for alms. And 16s. for two basins. And 2s. for one ewer. And 4d. for another ewer.

Total 24s. 7d.

In the Pantry
Also they account for 8d. for three baskets [*paneriis*]. And 3d. for eight candlesticks. And 8d. for two large knives. And 2d. for two benches. And 2d. for one salt-cellar. And 2d. for two salt-cellars.

Total 2s. 1d.

In the Cellar

Also they account for 45s. for five casks of cider [*dol' cisere*], price 9s. per cask. And 33s. 4d. for one cask of old wine. And 30s. for another cask of old wine. And 45s. for one cask of new wine. And 18d. for two pewter [*stagn'*] pitchers. And 12d. for two pewter pitchers. And 8d. for four pewter pitchers. And 6d. for other pitchers. And 3d. for fifteen wooden cups. And 10d. for two kegs containing three gallons [*costrell' continentis iii lageni*]. And 8d. for two two-gallon kegs. And 6d. for two two-gallon kegs. And 4d. for two one-gallon kegs. And 3d. for two old three-gallon kegs. And 8d. for two large barrels for trussing [*ad trossand'*]. And 5s. for fifteen barrels for ale. And 12d. for a barrel of verjuice. And 20s. for five barrels of mead. And 10d. for one barrel with some old mead. And 12d. for one gallon of honey. And 6d. for one barrel with a small quantity of oil. And 15d. for three taps [*clepsedr'*]. And 4d. for one case for carrying candles [*casu ad candell' portand'*]. And 8s. 8d. for thirteen empty casks, price [m. 4] 8d. per cask. And 13s. for thirteen empty casks. And 12d. for two empty casks. And 5d. for two tankards [*tankard'*]. And 6d. for four quarters of charcoal. And 2s. for five casks for salt and one tub, price 4d. each. And 14d. for four quarters of lime, price 3½d. per quarter. And 7d. for six boards of ash [*asseribus de fraxino*]. And 12d. for six boards. And 2d. for two boards. And 18d. for fifty boards of oak [*bord quercinum*]. And 3d. for one old spit [*hostio*]. And 46s. 8d. for timber. And 12d. for two old spits. And 4s. for fifty horse shoes. And 12d. for old iron. Also 1d. for one small chest for the said iron. Also 4d. for two halters [*capistris*]. Also 6d. for one chest.

Total £13 14s. 3d.

Oxen with Other Goods Found

Also they account for 40s. for eight oxen. Also 4s. for timber. Also 23d. for five weak boards and other small pieces, and the rest of the same price. Also 26s. 8d. for iron found. Also 20s. for furze [*jampnum*]. Also 2s. for firewood. Also 8d. for two carts without wheels. Also 12d. for one pig. Also 6d. for stockfish [*stokfys*]. Also 21s. 8d. for 20 quarters of salt, price 13d. per quarter. Also 10d. for two winnowing fans for corn [*vannis ad bladum*]. Also 1d. for one pitchfork [*furcam ad bladum*]. Also 5d. for one bushel and a half measure. Also 2s. for one peacock [*pauone*] and one peahen [*paua*]. Also 3d. for one hook for a well [*hamo ad puteum*]. Also 3d. for laths. Also 6d. for two knives of [?] [*cultellis de parme*]. Also 50s. for the deceased's palfrey. Also 4 marks for two horses. Also 13s. 4d. for one horse. Also 8s. for one horse. Also 8d. for two ladders.

Total £12 18s. 1d.

At St Sidwell

Also they account for 2d. for one old bushel. And 2d. for six sieves [*cribr'*] with one basket [*corbillo*]. And 3d. for one worn sheet for winnowing [*panno ad ventand'*]. And 1d. for one pitchfork. And 6d. for one large rope. And 2d. for one box with a little firewood [*trunco cum modica busta*]. Also 4d. for two ladders at Heavitree. And 4d. for two pairs of ropes for trussing. And £50 for corn in the granges at St Sidwell and Heavitree. And 104s. 9d. in money received from the servants at St Sidwell before the making of the inventory. Also five [livery] robes and other clothing [*indumenta*] that follow in the inventory, not valued, [that] were distributed among those of the [deceased's] kin. And 3s. for one silk belt with an [ink]horn and a pencase [*cornu et pennar'*]. And 5d. for two pulleys [*poleys*]. And 2d. for one small table with legs. And 1½d. for one pair of baskets. And 2d. for six baskets. And 4d. for six boards of ash. And 2d. for two old ladders. And 3s. 6d. for timber at St Sidwell.

Total £55 14s. 6½d., except for the said robes and other clothing which are not valued.

Winkleigh

Also they account for £8 4s. 3¾d. received in arrears from Walter de Lollardesdon, servant there, for the year of the Lord 1301. And £22 2s. for which the said Walter is held [liable] from the sale of the tithe of corn sheaves [*garbarum*]. And 2s. rent paid at the feast of the Nativity of the Lord in 1302 at the house of the same. And 40s. for corn in the grange there. And 5s. for one cask [*pipa*] of cider. And 10d. for two tubs. And 8d. for three baskets and one bushel and a half of wood [*bussello et dimidie ligneis*]. And 12d. for one pan [*patella*]. And half a mark for one large pot. And 4s. for another pot. And 2s. for one cooking-pot [*cacabo*]. And 3s. for one basin with a ewer. And 4d. for one axe. And 4d. for one sheet for winnowing [*lintheamen ad ventandum*]. And 4d. for one tub. And 18d. for one chest. And 4d. for one muck fork and another pitchfork and one barrow. And 10d. for one mortar. And 2d. for two ladders. And 3s. for iron. And 12d. for one dish for a press with a pipe and another small timber for the same [*disco ad pressor' cum fisulla et alio paruo meremio ad idem*]. And 12d. for one large beam in the hall. And 2d. for one gridiron [*craticula*].

Total £34 5s. 0¾d.

[Bishop's] Tawton

Also they account for 18s. for nine large beams [*trabibus*] of new timber there. And 4s. for old *silis* [sills?]. And 18d. for one long dresser and another smaller one. And 10 marks for corn in the grange. And £22 4d. for which

Richard de Doune, servant there, is held [liable] from the sale of corn in the fields in the autumn of the year 1302.
   Total £29 17s. 2d.

Landkey
Also they account for 20 marks for corn in the grange there. And £17 9s. 4d. for which the said Richard was held [liable] from the sale of corn in the fields in the autumn of the year aforesaid [1302].
   Total £30 16s.

Swimbridge
Also they account for 2d. for one basket there. And 1d. for one hanging saw [*sera pendente*]. And £25 13s. 8d. for which the said Richard was held [liable] from the sale of corn in the fields in the autumn of the year aforesaid [1302].
   Total £25 13. 11d.

[m. 5]

Braunton
Also they account for £122 13s. 7½d. of the arrears of Richard de Doune, servant of the deceased there, on his last account for Braunton, [Bishop's] Tawton, Landkey, and Swimbridge. And £44 8s. 4d. in which the same Richard was held [liable] from the sale of the tithes at Braunton in the year of the Lord 1302. And £30 from corn in the grange there. Also 40s. for three casks of cider, price per cask with wood [*ligno*]13s. 4d. And 18d. for three quarters of fine salt [*minuti salis*]. And 3s. 6d. for seven tubs, price 6d.each. And 20d. for four barrels. And 12d. for one empty cask. And 6d. for one small *trendell'* [trundle-wheel or windlass] and one bowl [*gata*]. And 2s. 8d. for two empty casks. And 4d. for one barrel. And 2s. 6d. for one chest with a lock. And 6d. for one chest in the chamber. And 4d. for one chest at Knowle [*Cnolle*]. And 4d. for one small chest without a lid. And 5s. for one draught horse. And 12d. for one worn out cart [*carecta*]. And 12d. for one wagon [*plaustro*] without wheels. And 4s. for three peacocks and one peahen. And 3d. for two capons. And 5d. for one cock and four hens. And 10s. for one large brass pot. And 7s. 6d. for another pot. And 6s. 8d. for another pot. And 2s. 8d. for one posnet. And 2s. for one pan. And 2d. for one small pan. And 1½d. for one iron pan. And 18d. for one ewer. And 8d. for another ewer. And 5s. for one cauldron [*caldar'*]. And 6d. for one gridiron. And 8d. for one basin. And 4d. for one mortar with a *pila* [pestle?]. And 4d. for two tripods. And 6d. for two axes. And 6d. for two pitchforks and two muck forks and one pick-axe [*picoys'*]. And 5d. for one sickle for furze [*falce ad iampnum*] and one meadow

sickle [*falce ad pratum*]. And 10d. for two wooden bushels with iron hoops [*bussellis ligneis ferro ligatis*]. And 4d. for one tub [*tina*]. And 2d. for one bucket. And 10d. for one sheet for winnowing. And 1d. for one banker. And 6½d. for one sumpter-saddle. And 4d. for another saddle. And 1d. for one *tondio* [beater?] and one bowl. And 4d. for two chargers [i.e. dishes] [*chargores*]. And 6d. for one sack. And 4d. for another sack. And 14½d. for forty dishes, thirty plates and thirty saucers. And 18d. for one old *chitel* [kettle?]. And 13s. 4d. for a certain quantity of oats produced from one holding [*crofta*] there. And 5s. for hay, by estimation six bales [*trossarum*]. And 12d. for one receptacle for dung [*sterquilinio*]. And £8 8d. for arrears of the reeve of Braunton.

Total £211 15s. 1d.

Colaton [Raleigh]

Also they account for 3s. for one cooking pot [*cacabo*] there. And 3s. 8d. for one brass pot. And 2s. 2d. for another bronze pot. And 16d. for one posnet. And 16d. for one large pan. And 10d. for another small pan. And 4d. for one small pan. And 6d. for one gridiron. And 2d. for one tripod. And 1d. for one iron pan. And 16d. for one basin. And 16d. for one ewer. And 3d. for twelve dishes, ten plates and eleven saucers. And 2s. for two new tables. And 2d. for one table four feet long. And 8d. for one saw. And 1d. for one iron fork. And 4d. for one mortar. And 42s. for six casks of cider, price for each with the wood [*ligno*] 7s. And 4s. for one cask of cider with the wood. And 12d. for two small tubs. And 5d. for one tub. And 1d. for another tub. And ½d. for two candlesticks. And 6d. for one pick-axe and one handle [*hachetapik et i lancea*]. And ½d. for one rod without iron for raising corn [*pertica ad bladum levand' sine ferro*]. And 16d. for one pot with honey. And ½d. for one muck fork. And 12d. for one beehive [*rusca*]. And 4d. for four large pieces of timber with two trundle-wheels for barrows [*trendell' ad ciueras*]. And 12d. for one large piece of wood [*magno ligno*]. And 4s. for eighteen tables of ash. And 8d. for one empty cask. And 4d. for one vat [*fat*]. And 1d. for one hoe. And 3s. for four thousand tiles. And 6s. for one thousand old *ferri* [nails?]. And 4s. for another thousand. And 3s. 4d. for another thousand *ferri*. And 2d. for one coop for capons [*cista pro caponibus*]. And 12d. for one cask with the vicar and another with Robert de Middelton. And 45s. for nine quarters of corn, by estimation, from tithes in the grange, price 5s. per quarter. And 25s. for five quarters [of corn] from the demesne, price 5s. per quarter. And 100s. for twenty-five quarters of rye, by estimation, price 4s. per quarter. And 64s. for sixty-four quarters of oats, by estimation, price 12d. per quarter. And 3s. 4d. for two quarters of *selprith*, by estimation. And 6d. for 1½ bushels of beans [*fab'*], by estimation. And 2½d. for one bushel of vetch [*vescarum*]. And 4d. for one long pulley [*poley*]. And 2d. for one wooden bushel. And 2d. for four baskets. And 12d. for one windlass [*vernula*] for constructing a house. And 4d. for one board for the head of a bed [*tabula ad capud lecti*]. And 6d. for two ladders. And 4d. for another two ladders. And 12d. for firewood in the cellar. And 3s. for timber and other firewood. And 6d. for one large box and another smaller one. And 6d. for forage [*furag'*]. And 6d. for six hens. And 8d. for four geese. And 7d. for seven geese. And 35s. for seven quarters of wheat, by estimation, at St Theobald, price 5s. per quarter. And 2s. for half a quarter of rye. And 37s. 6d. for an estimated twenty-five quarters of oats, price 18d. per quarter. And 21s. for eighteen quarters of oats from the demesne, price 14d. per quarter. And 5d. for two bushels of peas [*pis*]. And 4d. for one bushel of beans. And 4d. for one sack. And 7d. in money found in a box there with seven pounds Tournois. And 1½d. for one iron fork.

Total £21 18s. 10½d.

Ynnyngeston [not located]

Also they account for 3s. for one draught horse there. And 2s. 6d. for another draught horse. And 2s. for two draught horses. And 2s. for another draught horse. And 50s. for ten plough oxen, price per ox 5s.. And 10s. 6d. for three oxen for slaughtering [*mactand'*], price 3s. 6d. per ox. And 4s. for one bull. And 8s. for two cows. And 14s. for four cows, price 3s. 6d. each. And 6s. for two mares. And 9s. 4d. for seven pigs, price 16d. each. And [m. 6] 3s. 4d. for four sheep [*multon'*], price 10d. each. And 8s. 4d. for ten ewes, price 10d. each. And 4s. 8d. for twenty-eight geese, price 2d. each. And 4s. for four peacocks. And 18d. for eighteen capons. And 6s. 4d. for two brass pots. And 2s. for one posnet. And 2s. 2d. for one pan. And 12d. for another pan. And 7d. for another pan. And 3d. for one iron pan. And 3s. for one basin and ewer. And 2d. for one tripod. And 1d. for one gridiron. And 2d. for one dresser. And 3s. for one chest [*cofero*]. And 3d. for two chests. And 2½d. for one wooden bushel. And 5s. for four empty casks. And 10d. for two tubs. And 1½d. for two sieves. And 3d. for one bowl [*gata*]. And 4d. for one axe. And 1½d. for another axe. And ½d. for one sickle [*fausiculo*]. And 5d. for thirty dishes, plates, and saucers. And 2d. for two candlesticks. And 7s. 6d. for ten pieces of iron, each piece eighteen pounds, price ½d. per pound. And 5s. 10d. for fourteen pieces of iron, each piece ten pounds, price ½d. per pound. And 5s. for two cart wheels lined with iron. And 3d. for one wheelbarrow [*cinera cum rota*]. And 18d. for one cart with all the equipment [*caruca cum toto apparatu*]. And 4s. for a complete animal fold [*tota falda*]. And 3d. for two muck forks. And 2d. for one shovel. And 2d. for two pitchforks. And 12d. for three sumpter-saddles with saddle pads and girdles. And 6d. for three pairs of ropes for trussing. And 2d. for two pairs of baskets for dung [*ad fimum*].

And 4d. for six hair ropes for draught animals [*funibus crineis ad affr'*]. And 2d. for one sheet for winnowing. And 10d. for ten sacks for sand. And 5s. for iron. And £7 8d. for corn in the grange and stacked [*tassat'*] outside. And 10s. 6d. for three and a half acres of wheat, price 3s. per acre. And 12s. for four acres of rye, price 3s. per acre. And 11s. 3d. for four and a half acres of palm-barley [*palmal'*], price 2s. 6d. per acre. And 4s. for two acres of winter oats [*aven' yiemal'*], price 2s. per acre. And 6s. 7¾d. in arrears [owed] from Geoffrey atte Wode, the deceased's servant there.

Total £18 17s. 4¾d.

Debts in the Hands of Various Debtors
Also they account for £30 of debts in the hands of various debtors. And £9 17s. 1d. of similar debt.

Total £39 17s. 1d.

Desperate [i.e. Unrecoverable] Debts
Also they account for £24 3s. 11¾d. of desperate debts in the hands of various debtors.

Total £24 3s. 11¾d.

Found after the Making of the Inventory
Also they account for 40s. from a bond owed by Robert de Upphaye. And 5d. for two pairs of ropes for trussing. And 5d. for two small troughs [*alueis*] and three small bowls. And 12d. for a certain old pail [*perta*]. And 5d. for two baskets with covers. And 9d. for one hamper [*hanaperio*], one old sack, one old chair and one rope. And 5½d. for two small troughs and one basket with a cover. And for one brass pot weighing 32 pounds, price 2d. per pound. And £50 2s. 6¼d. and six pounds Tournois for all the profits from the deceased's prebend in the year after his death, except for the bread distributed among the Friars Minor, the hospitals of St John and St Mary Magdalene, and the prisoners. And 23s. 6¼d. from the deceased's share of the money from *Lanslader*. And 10s. for the deceased's share of the non-residence of Master Peter de Insula. And 2s. 11¼d. from the offerings of [the chapel of] St Theobald. And 9s. 3¼d. from the deceased's share of the non-residence of the chancellor, Master Henry de Somersete. And 6d. for two old empty casks. And 26s. 10d. arrears from John Daysse received after the inventory had been drawn up. And £6 13s. 4d. arrears from Richard Rossel, servant at St Sidwell, received in the same way. Also one silk belt found after the making of the inventory, which is not valued. Also 2s. 7½d. received from the vicar of Harberton by Kilkenny.

Total £63 0s. 4d.

Increases

Also they account for 4s. 4d. increase from the sale of one gradual and troper. And 8d. increase from the sale of carde. And 4d. increase from one purse of Lombardy. And 1d. increase from one red purse. And 1d. increase from one cap lined with black lambskin. And 2d. increase from two chests. And 12d. increase from one green strong-box. And 6d. increase from one surplice with a rochet. And 4d. increase from one shield and five lances. And 6d. increase from three sacks for cloth. And 1d. from one lock. And 3d. from one andiron [*andir'*] and an iron for roasting meat. And 2d. from four pewter pitchers. And 1d. from other pitchers and cups. And 8d. increase from one ewer. Also at Colaton [Raleigh] 12d. increase from one pot valued at 3s. 8d.. And 2d. increase from one posnet. And 4d. increase from the sale of one pan valued at 16d. and another pan valued at 10d. and one basin with a ewer valued at 2s. 6d.. And 7s. increase from the sale of six casks and one cask of cider at Colaton [Raleigh] that were estimated in the inventory at 46s. [Also for 2s. 7½d. received from the vicar of Harberton – *cancelled*.]

Total 16s. 9d.

Also they account for 100s. 4¾d. received in arrears from Guy, servant at Braunton, after the inventory had been drawn up. Also 2s. increase from the sale of one book of Papias.

Total 102s. 4¾d.

[Total of the totals £911 15s. 8d. – *cancelled*.]

Total of all the totals and all debts [*totius oneris*] £916 18s. ¾d.

Total of pounds Tournois 30s. 4d., which is accounted for below and nothing remains.

And nothing remains.

Res [the residue or the real property?] is not valued [*non appreciatur*], as shown above.

[Part II: Expenditure]

Expenses About the Funeral

Also they account for offerings on the day of the deceased's burial and in payments for the obit among the canons, vicars, and others of the choir and to other chaplains, £4 9s. 8d. For 60 pounds of wax bought, 35s., price 7d. per pound. For measures [*methis*] for the same, 2½d. For payment to Geoffrey de Gidelonde for making candles, and for his service for four years before the death of the deceased, 15s. For one metal chalice, 4d. For shoes and slippers [*pinzonis*], 18d. For saying psalters, 13s. 10d. For candles for the same, 9d. For expenses about the burial, both carpentry and metalwork [*tam in carpentar' quam in latonis*], one coffin of stone, one chest of lead, and other necessaries, 28s. 8d. For payment to the custors of the cathedral [*custoribus*] for bell ringing, 10s. Also for the same and for celebrating masses in the city, 3s. For bread bought and distributed among the poor, £12 15s. 11d. For one stone placed over the deceased and the expenses of a messenger going to buy the same, 13s. 4d. For the expenses of a cart to seek the same stone at the quarry [*quarreram*], 10s. For the wages of Master John the artist [*pictoris*] for drawing [*pertractand'*] a cross on the said stone and lettering around it, and for the wages of two masons cutting them [*ad ingrauand'*] for fifteen days, 6s. 10d. For paving [*pauimento*] made around the stone, 4d. For metal bought for the cross and lettering, 17s. 1d. For the wages of John le Horner for making and putting the cross and letters on the stone, £4. Also for mastic [*mastico*] bought for this work, 4s. 2d. Also paid to the Friars Minor for a pittance on the day of burial, 6s. 8d. Also to the same afterwards, 12d. Also to the rectors and priests of the city for celebrating trentals for the deceased, 45s. Also for doing the same at Crediton, 30s. Also delivered to the porter of the lord bishop, 6d. For painting [*depinguenda*] one table [*tabula*] in front of [*coram*] the altar of St Andrew, 13s. 4d. For whitewashing [*dealbanda*] in the chapel of St Andrew, 10½d.

Total £34 3s.

[m. 7]

Expenses of the Executors and Household

Also they account for the expenses of the executors from the Sunday [4 November] next after All Saints 1302 to the Sunday [11 November] in the feast of St Martin next following, namely in food and drink about the funeral [or corpse: *funus*], and for their other expenses for the store of the household [*instauro domus*], 57s. 11¾d.

Total 57s. 11¾d.

Also Expenses of the Executors and Household

Also they account for the expenses of the executors and household from the Sunday [11 November] in the feast of St Martin to the Sunday [21 December] next after the feast of St Thomas the Apostle, namely for six weeks, 61s. 3¼d. Also they account for one part of the spices [*speciorum*] named above [and?] for their expenses on several occasions, [cost 61s. 1d. – *cancelled*], 41s. 11d.

Total 103s. 2¼d.

Also Expenses of the Executors and Household

Also they account, as expenses of the executors, for 7 pounds of new wax for torches and candles, price 3s. 6d. Also for their expenses for one pound of wax for candles, price 4d. Also for their expenses for four oxen, 20s. Also for one pig, 12d. Also for stockfish, 6d. Also for 10 bushels of salt, 15d. Also for their expenses for one barrel of vinegar, 4d. Also for the expenses of them and of the household for three casks of cider, 27s. Also for one barrel of verjuice [*viridi succo*], 12d. Also for three barrels with mead, 12s. Also for one barrel with a certain quantity of old mead, 10d. Also for one barrel with a certain quantity of oil, 6d. Also for the expenses of the executors and others of the household for their horses and the horses of the deceased before they were sold, namely in shoeing, 13s. 4d. Also from the murrain [*morina*] of one palfrey, 60s. Also they account for the expenses of the executors for six hens, 6d. Also for four geese, 8d.

Total £7 2s. 9d.

Expenses

Also they account for money distributed in the choir among canons, vicars and other ministers of the church thirty days after the death of the deceased, 15s. 8d. For bread distributed among the poor on the same day, 61s. 1d. Also for the Friars Minor on the same day, 4s. For money distributed among the canons, vicars and other ministers of the church on the anniversary of the deceased in the first year, namely the year of the Lord 1303, 23s. 2d., and each canon received 8d., each vicar 4d., and each priest and other minister 2d. Also among the rectors and chaplains of the city of Exeter, the hospitals of St John and Magdalene, and those continuing sick in the city, 12s. 11d. For the anniversary of the same [deceased] at Crediton on the same day, 7s. 8d. Also at Polsloe on the same day, 6s. 8d. Also to the Friars Minor on the same day, 6s. 8d. For wax bought, 6s. 6d. For candles made therewith, 3d. For bread distributed among the poor on the same day, £8 4s. 5d. Also for money distributed in the choir among the canons, vicars, and other ministers on the anniversary in the second year after the death [1304], 25s. 5d., and each received the sums as above. For 12 pounds of wax bought, 6s. 6d. For candles made therewith, 6d. Also to the Friars Minors for a pittance on the same day, 6s. 8d. For bread for the use of prisoners on the same day, 23½d. For money distributed in the choir among the canons, vicars, and others as above for the third year [1305], 24s. 7d., who received as above. For 5½ pounds of wax, 3s. 2½d. For making candles, 6d. Delivered to the Friars Minor on the same day, 6s. 8d. Also for bread for prisoners, 22½d. Also for money distributed in the choir among the canons and others as above and to the priests of the city in the fourth year [1306], 26s. 3d., and they received as above. For 10 pounds of wax, 6s. 8d. For making candles therewith, 6d. Also to the Friars Minor on the same day, 6s. 8d. For bread to prisoners, 2s. 6d. Also for money distributed in the choir among the canons and others as above in the fifth year [1307], 26s. 5d., and they received as above. Also for 12 of pounds wax, 8s. 6d., price per pound 8½d. Also for making candles therewith, 6d. For a gift to the Friars Minor, 6s. 8d. For bread for prisoners, 4s. 2d. Also for money distributed in the choir among the canons as above in the sixth year [1308], 26s. 4d., and they received as above. For 3½ pounds of wax bought, 2s. 4d., price per pound 8d. For candles made therewith from wax in store, 4d. Also to the Friars Minor, 6s. 8d. For bread for the use of prisoners, 3s. 1¾d. For money in the choir among the canons, vicars, priests, and others on the anniversary of the deceased in the seventh year [1309], 26s. 11d., and they received as above. For 6¾ pounds of wax bought, 4s. 9d., price per pound 8½d. For bread for the use of prisoners on the same day, 10¼d. Also to the Friars Minor on the same day, 6s. 8d. For making candles, 6d. Also for money distributed to the canons and vicars in the choir on the eighth anniversary [1310], 20s. 11d., and they received as above. Also for 6 pounds of wax bought, 4s. For candles made, 4d. Also to the Friars Minor on the same day, 6s. 8d. For bread for prisoners on the same day, 12¼d. Also for money distributed in the choir among the canons, vicars, chaplains . . . [*unfinished; no total*].

Costs of the Priests

Also they account for the stipend of Sir Adam de Braunton celebrating [mass] for the soul of the deceased in the first year [1303] after his death, 40s. And for the stipend of the same for the second year [1304], 53s. 4d. And for the stipend of Sir Henry de Tottonia [Totnes] celebrating for the same deceased in the third year [1305], 53s. 4d. And for the stipend of Sir Nicholas Piring celebrating for him, 10s. Also for a chaplain celebrating at Harberton for him, 40s. Also for a chaplain celebrating at Ugborough for him for the fourth year [1306], 20s. Also for Sir H[enry] de Totton' for the same year, 53s. 4d. Also for a chaplain celebrating at Ugborough for him for the fifth year [1307], 20s. Also for Sir H[enry] de Totton' for the same year, 53s. 4d. Also for each chaplain celebrating at Ugborough for him for the sixth year [1308], 13s. 4d. Also for Sir H[enry] de Totton' for the same year, 53s. 4d. Also for Sir H[enry] de Totton' celebrating for the deceased for the seventh year [1309], 53s. 4d. Also for the same Sir H[enry] de Totton' celebrating for the deceased for the eighth year [1310], 53s. 4d. Also to the same chaplain celebrating for the deceased for the ninth year [1311], 53s. 4d. [m. 8] Also for a chaplain celebrating for the same for the next six years £16, and he receives 4 marks a year. Also for distribution in the choir [of Exeter Cathedral] on his obit day for the said period, £7 7s. Also for wax bought and candles made for the said period, 28s. 3½d. For bread for distribution among prisoners and other poor people for the same period, 19s. 0½d. Also for the Friars Minor and Preachers of Exeter for the same period, 8s. 8d.

Total £54 13s.

New Expenses after the Ninth Year

Cancelled because it is written in another part at the end. [*This section has been cancelled, and is identical with the section of the same name printed below.*]

[m. 2d]

Costs of the Land and Church of West Anstey

Also they account for the purchase of two acres of land at West Anstey with the advowson of the church of the place, £16 13s. 4d. Also paid to Richard de Regny for carrying out the negotiation for the same, 40s. For expenses about the taking of seisin of the said land with the advowson, 5s. 2d. For two writs for levying a fine upon the said advowson, 12d. For one attorney in the plea for the said fine, 6s. 8d. For other expenses made upon the same plea, 10s. For one writ of the king for an inquisition *ad quod dampnum*, etc., of the said land with the advowson, 9d. For the expenses of a messenger for the same writ, 6d. For the expenses of a certain groom going to West Anstey with the charter concerning the new sealing, 2d. For the expenses of Master W[illiam] de Kilkenny to London and staying there for thirty-five days for the royal licence to be had for the appropriation of the said church made to the dean and chapter of Exeter and returning, with allowance for two horses, 108s. 0½d. For the charter of the lord king about the licence for the appropriation of the same, 22s. 4d. For seal cords and wax for the same, 7d. For writing a letter to the lord bishop of Exeter about the appropriation, 6d. For the expenses of the executors on four occasions to put the dean and chapter of Exeter in possession of the said land with the said advowson, 34s. 3¾d. For a gift [*exennio*] sent to Sir William Martin on the aforesaid occasion, 17¼d. For two casks of wine given to the same on the said occasion, £4 2s. For letters carried to the abbot of Tavistock about the same negotiation, 3d. For a fine being levied in the court of the king for the said land and church, 6s. 8d. For the expenses about the inquisition of the said land and aforesaid advowson, 3s.

Total £32 16s. 8½d.

Expenses with Certain Debts Paid

Also they account for 40s. paid to William de Kilkenny for his expenses going to his home region [*versus partes suas*] immediately after the death of the deceased. Also to Philip his brother for the same, 12s. Also to Geoffrey Wood [*de Bosco*] for his *forma* [form: *sense unclear*] which was owed to him, 2s. Also to the canons of the church of St Peter, Exeter, for the palfrey of the deceased, 100s. Also to the same for a cope owed by the deceased according to the custom of the church, 66s. 8d. Also for a procession [*processionem*] to the altar of Blessed Andrew [in Exeter Cathedral], 2s. Also paid to Sir Robert, warden of the work of St Peter for the new fabric, for the dignity of the deanery, £6 7s. 4d. Also paid for a tenth granted in subsidy to the church of Rome for the second term of the second year, 63s. 8d. For the acquittance, 2d. Also paid to the exchequer of Blessed Peter [i.e. Exeter Cathedral] for the arrears of the pension for Mortehoe, 45s. Also paid to Philip Rurde 13s. 4d. which was owed to him. Also to the same for one cask of wine, 43s. 4d. Also for one fotmal of lead bought before the death of the deceased and sent to *Ynnyngeston*, 2s. Also paid to Adam the apothecary for mustard powder [*puluere sen'*] 6d., which was owed to him. Also paid to the lord king for the deceased for a debt found in the Pipe [Office] [*invento in pipa*], 40s. Also to William de Coleton for his service in business for the deceased while he lived, 13s. 4d. Also to the vicar of Colaton [Raleigh] for cider, 7s. Also paid to Sir Henry [de Somersete], dean, for defects of houses, £10. Also to Master William Kilkenny £34 for his prebend of Crediton which the said deceased received for three years while he lived. Also to the same £10 13s. 4d. for one horse which belonged to the said Master W[illiam], which the said deceased sold while he lived and received part. Also for 2½ marks for two parts of a cask of wine delivered to the same deceased while he lived by the said Master William. Also 60s. paid to the same Master William for defects of the farm of Winkleigh.

Total £87 18s. 7d.

Expenses for the Negotiations of John de Brychham and the Expenses of his Sisters and Certain Things Given to the same J[ohn]

Also they account for the expenses of Master William in negotiations with John de Brigeham to London, there, and in the county of Cambridge, £8. Also delivered to Robert Urry for linen clothes bought from him, 12d. Also to William Maudit for shoes [*ad sotular'*], 6d. Also for shoes for William of the kitchen [*coquina*] and for making his surcoat, 6¼d. For shoeing one horse, 5d. Also for the expenses of Robert Urri to go to the region of Cambridge for negotiations with J[ohn] de Briggeham, 12d. Also for the expenses of Henry de Otery and the said John to go to London for negotiations of the said John and returning to Exeter, 16s. 10d. Also for their expenses going to *Lym* [Lyme Regis, Dorset?] and returning, 6d. Also for various royal writs for pleas of the said John de Briggeham, 2s. Also delivered to his attorney for pleas before the justice of the [King's] Bench, 6s. 8d. For expenses made by H[enry] de Otery in negotiations and pleas with the said John both in London and in the county of Cambridge, and in clothing and food for his sisters from the time of the deceased's death to the feast of Easter in the year of the Lord 1306, £39 10s. 11½d. For the expenses of the said John going to the region of Cambridge, 6s. 8d. For shoes for his groom, 4½d. Also delivered to the said John going to the said region together with Henry de Otery, 13s. 4d. For food for his sisters from the feast of St Michael [29 September] in the said year [1306] until the feast of St John the Baptist [24 June] next following, 60s. 8d. Also paid to the said Henry for his work in the negotiations of the said John, 40s. Also delivered to the said John for the use of his sisters from the Monday [28 November] next before the feast of St Andrew in the said year [1306], 20s. Also to the same for his expenses going to his [home] region, 6s. 8d. Also for the expenses of Walter the chaplain going to London and the region of Cambridge together with the said John on the feast of St Scholastica [10 February] in the year of the Lord 1307, 20s. 1d. Also for one cloth bought for the use of the said sisters, 73s. 5¼d. For three furred linings for their use, 11s. ¼d. For three yards of sindon, 2s. 6d. Also delivered to the same sisters for other necessities, 10s. For an allowance of one horse for the use of the said John, 2s. 8d. Also they account for the gift to the said John de Brigheham of the arms of the deceased, which are valued in the inventory at 11 marks.

Total £69 14s. 5¾d.

Legacies Paid

Also they account for payment to the new fabric of the church of St Peter, Exeter, £6 13s. 4d. Also to the nuns of Cornworthy, 40s. Also to the daughter of Guy de Wasseborne, a nun there, 20s. Also to the nuns of Polsloe, 20s. Also to the new fabric of the Friars Minor, Exeter, 40s. And to the same, 20s. Also to the same brothers for distribution among the needy of the order, £10. Also to Walter de Totton', chaplain, 100s. Also to Sir Robert de Asperton, 20s. Also to Master Elias de Criditon, 20s. Also to Geoffrey Wood [*de Bosco*] and his children, £6 13s. 4d. Also to Sir Gervase, chaplain, 40s. Also to Sir W., vicar of [m. 3d] Colaton [Raleigh], 20s. Also to Sir Gilbert, chaplain of Landkey, 20s. Also to Nicholas de Wytherigge, chaplain, 40s. Also to Master Roger the mason [*cymentarius*], 26s. 8d. Also to Master John Pollard, 100s. Also to Master William, his brother, 40s. Also to the hospital of Blessed John, Exeter, 20s. Also to the hospital of St Mary Magdalene, Exeter, 20s. Also to Master Roger de Wytherigge, 20s. Also to William, son of Walter de Wytherigge, 13s. 4d. Also to John, son of William de Holecumbe, 100s. Also to Geoffrey Corbin, 40s. Also to Walter de Witherigge, 40s. Also to Richard the marshal [*marescallo*], 20s. Also to Hubert, 20s. Also to Henry de Otery, 20s. Also to John de Bynnelegh, 10s. Also to John the cook [*coco*], 5s. To William the palfreyman [*palefredario*], 5s. To Nicholas Baret, 5s. To John the baker [*pistori*], 5s. To William Maudit, 5s. To Robert the brewer [*braciatori*], 5s. To Elias the porter [*janitori*], 5s. To Robert Urry, 10s. To John Daysse, 40s. Also to the abbot and convent of Torre, one mark. To the abbot and convent of Buckfast, 20s. Also to the Friars Minor of Bodmin, 6s. 8d. Also to Brother Bartholomew of the same convent, 6s. 8d. [Also to Brother Bartholomew of the same convent, 6s. 8d. – *cancelled*.] Also they account for the delivery to the vicar of the deceased of a complete set of clothes of the same deceased, value 5 marks, and for a surplice and rochet given to the church of Colaton [Raleigh]. Also to the same a lantern, value 12d., according to the custom of the church. Also they account for the delivery of one horse, value 26s. 8d., to Walter de Wytherigge. And to Geoffrey Corbin one horse, value 26s. 8d. Also to Lord Thomas the bishop one silver cup, weight 41s. 1d. Also to Master Thomas de Bredestret one silver cup with a gilt base, weight 37s. 6d. Also to the altar of Blessed Mary in the church of St Peter, Exeter, one alb with an amice, stole, and maniple [*phanon*] which are not valued.

Total £84 7s 11d

Given in Money on the Instructions of Master William

Also they account for a gift of 48s. to the vicars of the church of St Peter Exeter, that is 2s. to each one, newly bequeathed [*noue legati*]. Also to the priests and clerks of the second form [secondaries] 28s.; 12d. each. Also to the choristers 7s.; 6d. each. Also to John the cook, 16s. 8d. To Hubert, 15s. To William de Holecumbe, 20s. To his wife, 10s. To Gervase de Coleton, half a mark. To Eve, sister of John le Tanner, 2s. To William Kalstyn, 2s. To Margery, wife of Nicholas the tailor [*cissoris*], 2s. Also to the said Eve, 12d. To Diana, daughter of William de Holecumbe, for her marriage, 66s. 8d. To Margery, wife of Nicholas the tailor, 3s. Also to the mother of Richard de Doune, 2s. To William de Chedlyngton for the marriage of his daughter, 40s. To Joanna, daughter of William de Holecumbe, 4s. Also to Eve, sister of John le Tanner, 6d. Also to each pregnant mother, 12d. Also to each mother of Harbertonford, 2s. Also to William de Holecumbe, 13s. 4d. Also to Walter Beaupl' for the marriage of his daughter, 40s. Also to John le Tanner, 10s. Also to Brother Roger de Columpstok, 3s. Also to Brother John de Cruce, 8s. Also to each Friar Minor from Scotland [*de Scocia*], 4s. Also to Margery, wife of Nicholas the tailor, 2s. Also to Eve, her sister, 18d. Also to Henry de Lyncoln, cleric, of the deceased's kin, 6s. 8d. Also to William de Chedlyngton for the marriage of his daughter, 40s. Also to Richard Proute, 2s. Also to the same, 6d. Also to John, son of William of Cornwall [*Cornubiens'*], 12d. Also to Alice, sister of John le Tanner, 3d. Also to Brother J. Pycot, 4s. Also to Walter Wytherigge, 40s. Also to Adam de Wyterigge for the marriage of his daughter, 13s. 4d. Also to John le Blunt for the marriage of his daughter, 40s. Also to Henry de Alyngton, 5s. Also to William Kynesman, 7s. Also to John the cook and John the baker and six grooms for shoes, 4s., at 6d. to each of them. Also to Robert the brewer, 5d. Also to Robert Bozon, 40s. for his work in the business of the deceased. Also to Master John Pollard, 30s. 4d. in pounds Tournois. Also to a pauper of Braunton, 6d. Also to the son of Paine de Slapton, 2s. Also to Robert le Heyward de Braunton, 5s. Also to Geoffrey Corbyn, 40s. Also they account for a gift to Christine de Kerly of the deceased's kin for her maintenance [*poutura*] per week for a full year, namely 1310, 13s., at 3d. per week. Also for one surcoat bought for the same purpose, 8s. 6d. Also for shoes bought for the same purpose, 5d.

Total £31 12s. 11d.

Also Given in Money
Also given to Eve, sister of John le Tanner, 2s. Also to Anger, brother of William of Cornwall, 20s. Also to John, son of the said William, 20s. Also to Joan his sister, 2s. Also to Adam Cryspyn, clerk, for his help, 20s. Also given for the repair of the chancel of Winkleigh, 5s. Also to William the palfreyman, 6s. 8d. Also to Brother John de Kylkenny for his expenses coming to England from overseas, 20s. To John, son of Roger of Cornwall, 10s. Also to the nuns of Polsloe, 6s. 8d. Also 2s. given for the funeral [*exequias*] of Hubert. Also to his wife and sick children, 15d. Also to John Daysse for his [livery] robe for the last year that he was with the deceased, 13s. 4d. Also to John le Blunt, 3s. Also to the said Eve, 2s. Also to the wife of William de Chedlyngton and her daughter for her marriage, £4. Also to Brother John de Kilkenny to buy him clothes, 20s. Also to William Maudit, 6s. Also to William le Sopere of Witheridge for the marriage of his daughter, 40s. Also to John le Tanner, 4s. Also to Alice his sister, 12d. To Tibba her sister, 2s. Also to Roger de Doune, brother of Richard de Doune, 30s. Also to William of the kitchen, 10s. Also to Alice, sister of John le Tanner, for her marriage, 13s. 4d. Also to Simon de Lytelwere, 30s. for all the charges he has against the executors of the deceased. Also to Alice, sister of John le Tan- [m. 4d] nere, 12d.

Total £18 11s. 3d.

Expenses of Master Philip de Kilkenny
Also they account for one *forma* [form: in which sense?] for the use of Philip de Kilkenny, 2s. 6d. For tailoring his clothes and necessaries for the same, 15¼d. For his shoes, 6d. Also paid to him to go to Oxford, 60s. Also to his groom for his expenses returning with a horse, 16d. For shoes for the same horse, 4d. Also paid for the use of the same Philip, 26s. 8d. Also for his expenses returning to Exeter, 6s. 8d. For footwear [*calciamentis*] for him, 2s. 2d. Also delivered to the same Philip to go to Oxford in the second year after the death of the deceased [1304], 32s. 8d. Also for the use of the same, 40s. Also to his messenger for the said money, 6d. Also to the same [Philip] in the third year [after the deceased's death, 1305], 40s.

To his messenger, 6d. Also to Master Philip de Kilkenny on the Sunday next after the Epiphany in the year of the Lord 1305 [9 January 1306], 40s. Also to the same on the Monday [1 May 1307] next before the feast of the Invention of the Holy Cross in the following year, 40s. Also given to Master Philip de Kilkenny for his maintenance at university overseas [*ad exhibicionem suam in scolis in partibus transmarinis*], £10 in the year of the Lord 1308. Also the aforesaid Master Philip had the books written below to sell, the price of which he spent at university at his graduation [*incepcione*] in arts, namely one *New Digest*, price 50s. One *Codex*, price 53s. 4d. Also one *Summa Innocentii*, price 40s. [Also a *Decreta*, price 40s. – cancelled.] Also a *Parvum Volumen*, except for the three books of the *Codex*, price 26s. 8d. Also the *Decretals*, price 40s. Also a *Summa Gaufredi*, price 30s. Also a *Summa* of Azo, price 10s. Also he had a complete *Corpus Juris* of the deceased, with *Decreta* and *Decretals*, price £21 in the summary of the inventory. Also Brother Robert, monk, of Okehampton, has by the conveyance [*tradicione*] of the deceased [one psalter glossed, price 26s. 8d. Also Master Roger de Otery has a *Summa Reynfredi* with other short compendia [*summulis*] in one volume by the conveyance of the deceased, price 30s., books of the deceased which he had not demanded back, as it is believed – *cancelled*.]

   Total £58 15s 1¼ d

Necessary General Expenses

Also the same executors account for the expenses of Walter, priest, to London with Master Philip de Kylkenny, two grooms and three horses, and staying there for two days, together with Henry de Otery with a groom and his horse, and for the expenses of the said Philip from there to Oxford with a groom and two horses, and for the return of the same groom and horse to London, and for the expenses of the said W[alter] and H[enry] to Canterbury and going to the archbishop and returning to London and staying there for five days with three grooms and four horses for negotiations of the deceased, 38s. 4¾d. with the hire [*locacione*] of two horses. For five pounds of wax bought at Canterbury for one candle offered for the deceased, 2s. 6d. For making the same candle, 2½d. Also for 8 pounds of wax bought at Chichester [*Cycestr'*] for two candles made there and to be offered for the deceased, 4s. For making the said candles, 4d. For the expenses of the same Walter to London, Canterbury, and Wingham to seek the archbishop for negotiations of the deceased for seventeen days, 12s. 5d. For the hire of his horse, 4s. Also for the expenses of the said Walter going to the said places afterwards on two occasions for the same negotiations, 33s. 6d., with the expenses of Henry de Otery from London and returning to London, and the hire of horses.

   Total £4 15s. 4¼d.

Also General Expenses for Negotiations of the Deceased

Also they account for the fee [*salar'*] of Master John Wele for his work in negotiations of the deceased, 6s. 8d. For the fee of Master Robert de la Pitte for the same, 6s. 8d. For the fee of Ralph de Stokes, proctor, 5s. For copies of documents [*instrumentorum*] in a case against the dean, 5d. For 7¼ pounds of wax bought for bodies of the dead, 4s. 8½d. Also delivered to Sir Thomas Bastard for two weeks after the death of the deceased, 8d. Also delivered to Gervase de Doderigge staying at Colaton [Raleigh] for ten weeks after the death of the lord [i.e. the dean], 5s. Also to the groom of St Theobald for eight weeks, 16d. Also to Henry de Totton' for his work about writing the inventory, 6s. 8d. For the service of other clerics in negotiations of the deceased on several occasions, 8s. 6d. Also for making silver spoons for distribution among the canons, 7s. Also to a laundress [*lotrici*] for her service, 16d.

Total 53s. 11½d.

Expenses

Also they account for the hire of a feather bed for two weeks before the death of the deceased for the use of his chamberlain during the night, 2d. For one hooped [*liganda*] pan, 4d. For expenses of John de Holecumbe going to his [home] region, 3d. For the expenses of one messenger with letters sent to the lord bishop, 5d. For another messenger sent to Dunkeswell, 1d. For two small keys for a chest, 2½d. For roofing [*coopertienda*] the dean's hall, 5d. For the hire of two horses to bring vessels [*vasa*] from Colaton [Raleigh] [to] Exeter, 2d. For canvas bought for a frontal for the altar of Blessed Andrew, 10½d. For making the same, 1d. For writing letters of indulgence of various bishops, 2s. 2d. For copying them [m. 5d] in large letters, illuminating [them], and putting them in various churches, 4s. 4d. For parchment for them, 14d. For buying one cup, 1d. For the expenses of Robert Urri of Blandford [*Blaneford*, Dorset] going to Exeter, 3d. For the hire of one horse for the use of Walter the priest going to Braunton and for his expenses, 14¾d. For parchment for various rolls and letters on [several] occasions, 10½d. For the expenses of Gervase de Doderigge going to Braunton, 3d. For letters sent to Winkleigh, 3d. For letters sent to Richard de Doune on two occasions, 7d. Also for parchment, 5½d. Also for parchment, 7d.

Total 15s. 2¾d.

Also Expenses

Also they account for obtaining a distraint [*capcione impetranda*] against certain debtors of Braunton and for various writs of the king to recover debts, 3s. 4d. For shoes for William Maudit, 6d. For shoes for Henry de Wytherigge, 6d. Also for shoes for the said William, 6d. For one robe of linen for the use of Robert Urry and for shoes for him, 18d. For shoes for the same, 6d. For shoes for William Kalstyn, clerk, 5d. Also for shoes for the same, 5d. For expenses for the same for thirteen days, 13d. Also for shoes for the same, 5d. For his expenses going to Paignton, 2d. For shoes for the same on two occasions, 10d. For cloth for one tunic [*tabardum*] for John de Bryggeham, 6s. 6d. For linen cloth and shoes for William of the kitchen, 15d. Also paid for a grant [*subsidium*] in a suit about the restitution of the houses of Walter de Tremur, 66s. 8d. Also paid for a grant for the making of peace [*reformacione pacis*] between the dean and chapter and the Friars Preachers, £10. Also for securing one writ which is called '*pone*' in a plea against Simon de Lytelwere, 9d. For the expenses for a messenger for this, 12d. For making essoin before the sheriff [*vic'*], 5d. For the service of John de Hakeworth in two pleas against the same Simon, 5s. For the serving [*citacione*] of a certificate against the same, 2d.

Total £14 11s. 11d.

Costs of the Inventory

Also they account for the expenses of the executors about making the inventory at Colaton [Raleigh], 7½d. For their expenses at *Ynnyngeston*, 10s. 1d. Also for their expenses for the same purpose at Braunton, 22½d. For expenses about repairing and building [*emendand' et operiend'*] the lord's house and grange at Winkleigh, 31s. 10¾d. [For the expenses made by the executors to repair the said houses, 60s. – *cancelled*]. Also for shoeing the horses of the deceased and of the executors at the time that they acted together, 2s. 2d. For expenses about negotiating and selling the corn at Braunton, [Bishop's] Tawton, and Landkey, about repairing the buildings, recovering debts, and other business [*necessariis*], £7 11s. 7¼d. For the service of servants there for two years after the death of the deceased, 71s. 10d.

Total £13 10s. 1d.

Distribution of Alms

Also they account for alms given to poor scholars on the eve [*vigilia*] [20 November] of the Blessed Edmund, 17d. For bread for the use of prisoners on the feast of Blessed Peter *in Cathedra* in the year of the Lord 1302 [22 February 1303], 13¼d. For making the obit of Master Henry de Kilkenny, 2s. For bread for the use of prisoners on the Friday [2 March] next after the feast of St Matthias in the same year, 20½d. For bread given to the same on the Friday [9 March] before the feast of St Gregory in the same year, 21½d. For bread for the same on the Friday following [16 March], 21½d. For bread for the same on the Friday [23 March] next after the feast of St Benedict, 20¾d. For bread for the same on the Friday [13 April] before Palm Sunday, 21d. For bread for the same before Easter, 21d. For bread for the same in Easter week, 16d. For bread for the same at the feast of the Nativity of the Lord in the year of the same 1305, 14½d. For bread for the same at the octave [3 June] of the Ascension, 23d. For bread for the same on the Thursday [5 August] after Lammas Day [*Gulam Augusti*], 16d. For bread for the same on the feast of All Saints [1 November], 22d. Also for alms given to a certain blind pauper, 6d. For bread for prisoners at the feast of the Nativity of the Lord in the same year 1306, 10s. 9d. For bread for the use of the same on the day of St James next following [25 July], 4s. 2d. Also given to the chest [*truncum*] in the church of Blessed Peter Exeter for the furtherance [*promocione*] of the said land for the soul of the said deceased, 6s. 8d. Also for bread bought for the use of prisoners on the day of the Assumption of the Blessed Mary [15 August] in the year of the Lord 1311, 14d. Also for bread bought for prisoners on the eve [1 February] of the Purification of the Blessed Mary in the year of the Lord 1310, 18d.

Total 47s. 5d.

Also Distributions among those of the Kin

Also they account for distribution among those of the kin of the deceased on Wednesday next after the feast of the Translation of St Thomas [8 July] in the year of the Lord 1304, £22 6s. 8d. For their food [*pastu*] on the same day, 7s. 2d. For hire of one horse for the same business, 6d. For distributions made among them in the same year, 101s. 8d. For distributions made among them on the feast of the Nativity of St John the Baptist [24 June] in the next year [1305], £8 4s. 10¾d. For expenses about the same, with the hire of one horse, 12¾d. For distributions made among poor parishioners of Braunton at the same time, £12 9s. 8d. For distributions made among poor parishioners of [Bishop's] Tawton, Landkey, and Swimbridge, £6 15s. 6d. Also for expenses about this, 8s. 9¼d. For distributions made among poor parishioners of Colaton [Raleigh], 65s. 4d. For expenses about this, 15d. For distributions among poor parishioners of Winkleigh, 56s. 2d. For distributions made among poor parishioners of Heavitree, 53s. 4d. Also for 240 ells of cloth bought for distribution among the poor, £4 10s. 6d. For expenses about buying the said cloth, 16¼d. For eighteen pairs of shoes for the poor, 4s. 10d. For making distributions to those of the kin of the deceased on the Thursday next before the feast of the Invention of the Holy Cross [28 April] in the year of the Lord 1306, £14 11s. 3d. For clothing [*indumento*] for a certain pauper, 3s. 8d. Also to William Kastyn, clerk, and to his brother who are kinsmen of the deceased, £6 from the goods at *Ynnyngeston*. Also to Andrew [m. 6d] de Wythcheleghe and his children, £4. Also to Geoffrey atte Wode, for the advancement [*promocione*] of his children, all the residue of the goods at *Ynnyngeston*, namely £8 10s. 9d., by order of Master William. For money distributed with the said cloth, 3s. 9d. For clothing [*indumento*] bought for seven paupers, 17s. 8d.

Total £103 15s. 9d.

Remissions [of Debt] with Certain Allowances

For remission [of debt] made to poor parishioners at [Bishop's] Tawton, Braunton, Landkey, and Swimbridge, £7 14s. 3d. For remission made at Winkleigh, 3s. 8d. For remission made at Heavitree, 19s. 10d. For remission made to Reginald de Heyswylle, 6s. 4d. For remission made to purchasers [*emptoribus*] of corn at St Sidwell and Heavitree, 46s. 8d. For remission made to Master Walter de Stapeldon 100s., which the deceased had not demanded back, as it is believed. Also to John le Tanner, 12d. For allowance made to the reeve of Braunton for his autumn livery for two years [*pro liberacione sua de ii annis per autumpni*] while he was in the service of the deceased, 26s. 3d. For allowance made to the same for John Messore, 4s. 8d., which is remitted to him because of poverty. Also to Nicholas Baret, 6s. Also for remissions of debt made to poor parishioners of Winkleigh, debtors of the deceased, [£6 17s. 11d. – *cancelled*] 108s. 8¾d. [For remission made to Richard de Doune, servant at Braunton, [Bishop's] Tawton, Landkey, and Swimbridge, for all in which he is held [liable] to his lord the deceased in his last account, £45 12s. 1¼d. – *cancelled*.] Also to Walter de Tottonia, chaplain, £4 for his work spent on the business of the deceased, both in the life and after the death of the same. Also for remission made to John Knyllebole of half a mark, because of his poverty, for which he is held [liable] to the deceased. Also for an allowance made to Richard Rossel, servant of the deceased at St Sidwell, 60s., namely for ten years at 6s. each year, of which the 6s. each year [is] in addition to his last account which was in default because of a decrease in rent, which happened afterwards. Also to the same Richard 26s. 8d. for his wages for the last year that he was in the service of the said deceased.

Total £32 10s. 8¾d.

Ecclesiastical Ornaments Given

Also they account for the gift outside the will to the altar of Blessed Mary of one case for corporals, price 6s. 8d. Also a cloth for the lectern, price 18d. Also to the altar of Blessed Andrew where they celebrate for the deceased, one set of vestments, two blessed [*benedicta*] towels and one not blessed for the altar, and one for the hand [*ad manus*], which are not valued. Also for two cruets, price 2d. Also to the church of Crediton one cushion, price 12d. Also for one cloth for a paten, price 2s.; one silk case for corporals with eagles, price 3s. Also to the chapel of St Leonard in the parish of Harberton one missal, price 60s. Also to the church of Colaton [Raleigh] one antiphoner, price 20s., and one surplice and one rochet which are valued with the vestments delivered to the vicar of the deceased. Also to the church of Bridestowe one complete set of vestments with a lined chasuble of red and white sindon, price 13s. 4d. Also to the altar of Blessed Andrew in the church of St Peter [Exeter] one case for corporals, price 3s., and one silk cloth, price 12d.

Total 111s. 8d.

Given outside the Will

Also they account for the gift to the dean of one strong-box, price 6d., and one cap lined with miniver, price 12d. Also to Sir G de Knouile one basin [*bacini*], price 8s. Also to Master J[ohn] Pollard one old portiforium, price 5s. Also to Master W[alter] de Stapeldon two cloths in one piece, [price] 8s. 8d., length thirteen yards, price per yard, 8d. Also to the same one cloth, [price] 5s., length ten yards, price per yard, 6d. Also to the cellarer of Torre [Abbey] two empty casks, price 12d. Also to the archdeacon of Barnstaple three peacocks and one peahen, price 4s. Also to Richard the marshal old horseshoes with two halters and one small chest, price 17d. Also to the same one pair of saddle bags [*bezases*], price 12d. Also to William the palfreyman one old saddle, price 12d. Also to Master Roger the mason one old box, price 6d. Also they account for having delivered to the clerk of the exchequer one saddle, price 10s. Also they account for a gift to John the cook of two knives, price 3d. Also to the same one axe for meat, price 4d. Also to the same one scoop [*scupar'*] with a hook, price 2d. Also one mortar, price 6d. Also to the wife of Nicholas the tailor one small tub, two barrels for ale, and one barrel, price 22d. Also for one purse which is called a *pautener* with images, given to a certain knight, price 2s. Also for one belt of silk found after the making of the inventory, given to the sister of John de Brigeham, which is not valued. Also one silver spoon given to Richard le Blund, monk, weight 11½d. Also to Master John de Cowyk one cloth, price 20d. Also one belt of silk with an [ink]horn and pencase given to a certain clerk of the king, price 3s. Also one mortar at Colaton [Raleigh] given to the vicar there, price 4d. Also one large piece of wood given to the bridge there, price 12d. Also one empty cask given to the vicar there, price 8d. And there remains there a windlass [*vernula*] for the use of future deans, price 12d. Also one board for the head of a bed, price 4d. And firewood in the old cellar, price 12d. And two boxes, price 6d. Also they account for twenty-eight spoons, weight 25s. 10d., reworked into a new design [*redactis in novam formam*] and given to the canons. Also two thousand tiles of stone [*lapidum de tegul'*] given to future deans, price 12d. Also one table given to Sir Hugh de Ralegh, price 12d. Also to John the baker one wooden bushel and a half measure, price 5d. Also given to the dean two barrels full of mead, price 8s. Also five tables at Colaton [Raleigh], price 9d., remain for the use of the dean. Also they account for a quarter part of one livery cloth for a groom for the said year, price 8s., and two pieces of broadcloth [*panni integri*] of lupin flower [*flur de vez*], eighteen ells long 42s., price per ell 2s. 4d. Also for one piece of blue perse, enough for two hoods for the use of women, price 2s., given to those of the kin. Also to Brother Robert, monk, of Okehampton, one glossed psalter, price 26s. 8d., which the deceased did not claim back [*repetisset*], as it is believed. Also to Master John de Colepitte one book of histories, price 30s., for his work for the deceased when alive, paid to him because he did not previously [*prius*] wish to receive anything for his service.

Total £10 8s. 3½d.

Losses

Also they account for losses from silver vessels with one mazer, sold for 21s. 10¼d. Also for losses from the sale of three striped bankers, 12d. Also for losses from the sale of cloth and towels, 25s. 4d. Also for losses from the sale of parchment, 11s. 10d. Also for losses from the sale of skins of wild animals [*pellium ferarum*], 4d. Also for losses from gloves sold, 1d. Also for losses from two chests for harnessing, 12d. Also for losses from green sindon, 6d. Also for losses from black sindon, 11½d. Also for losses from five ells of buckram, 6d. Also for losses from one piece of quadruple samite, 6d. Also for losses from one pyx with gold plate, 1d. Also for losses from seven battleaxes [*hacheabekis*], 8d. Also for losses from one fork for a chimney, 4d. Also for losses from one rope, 1d. Also for losses ·from one chair, 1d. Also for losses from one brass pot valued at 12s. 1d. in the inventory, 15d. Also for losses from the sale of trundle-wheels [*trendellorum*], one bucket, and trestles [*trestellorum*] together, 2d. Also for losses from the sale of barrels for ale, 5d. Also for losses from the sale of taps, 2d. Also for losses from the sale of twenty quarters of salt, 20d. Also for the loss from one sack, damaged by a carter, price 12d. For the loss from one old wine cask valued at 30s. in the inventory, 3s. 4d. For the loss from two casks of ale valued at 18s. in the inventory, 4s. 8d. For the loss from furze, 5s. Also for the loss from one horse valued at 13s. 4d. in the inventory, 2s. 6d. Also at Colaton [Raleigh] for the loss from one small dish, 1d. Also for the loss from one small dish, 2d. Also for the loss from tubs and one sack, 8d. Also for the loss from one beehive, 4d. Also for the loss from timber for a barrow with trundle-wheels for the same, 2d. Also for the loss from all the hay [*feni*] there, 5s. 4d. Also for the loss from all the corn there, 27s. 2d. Also for the loss from all the corn at St Theobald, 15s. 6d. Also for the loss from one sack there, 1d. Also for the loss from the sale of the corn at St Sidwell and Heavitree, £13 6s. 8d. Also for the loss by estimation from corn in the grange at Braunton, [Bishop's] Tawton,

Landkey, and other things, £28 3s. 7d.

　　Total £48 5s. 0¾d.

Desperate Debts

Also desperate [unrecoverable] debts which extend to the sum of [£27 3s. 11¾d. – *cancelled*] £29 4s. 5¾d., namely Master R[oger] de Otery for 25s., Master R[ichard] de Plympstok 40s., Sir Robert Beaupel 70s. 9d., Robert de Upheye one mark, John de Reueton and his associates 40s., Walter de Colmpton 9s. 9d., Alice widow and executor of Roger de Middelton 44s. 11d., John de Estcolmp £8 8¾d., [m. 7d] Ralph de Dodescumb 13s. 4d., Master William de Dytton £8 6s. 8d.

　　Total £29 4s. 5¾d.

Also Desperate Debts

Also there remains £45 12s. 1¼d. in the hands of Richard de Doune from his arrears to be paid, from which because of poverty he has not hitherto been able to make satisfaction, for which he has been imprisoned for a long time, but it is awaited until better fortune shall come [*quousque ad pinguiorem venerit fortunam*], of which there is no hope.

　　Total £45 12s. 1¼d.

New Expenses after the Ninth Year

Also they account for payment to Master Philip de Kilkenny for his expenses and other costs [*necessariis*] to return overseas, 102s. Also for his use while staying at Oxford on the feast of Easter [7 April] in the year of the Lord 1314, 40s. Also paid to Christine de Kerly 8s. 4d. on the Monday after the octave of Epiphany [13 January] in the year of the Lord 1311 for her maintenance [*poutura*] to the end of the year. Also to Cecily de Kilkenny, of the kin of the deceased, 5 marks on the feast of the Holy Trinity [10 June] in the year of the Lord 1315. Also for expenses made searching the rolls of the exchequer of the lord king to account with the exchequer for a tenth collected by the deceased for the king, 14s. 4d.

　　Total £11 11s. 4d.

Expenses About the Chancel of West Anstey with the Stipend of the Chaplain There

Also they account for the payment of £7 3s. 4d. to Henry de Otery for the stipend of the chaplain of West Anstey and for the chancel newly constructed there.

　　Total £7 3s. 4d.

New Expenses After the Ninth Year

Also in citations taken by the [rural] dean of Aylesbeare [*Ayll'*] against the executors of Master Ralph de Pole and making certificate, 12d., with citations and certificates against Richard Rossel. For the fee of William de Nywenham in these cases, 2s. For examining witnesses against the said executors and for copies of attestations, 20d. Also for an allowance made to Guy de Braunton, 40s., which he paid to Margery daughter of Walter de Ynnyngeston for her marriage. Also paid to Margery sister of John le Tannere, 12d. Also for the hire of one horse for the negotiations of the deceased, 8d. Also for various letters carried to Braunton for recovering the debts of Guy de Braunton, 10d. For offerings made at Hereford for the deceased, 21d. Also for remission made to the wife of Guy de Braunton for the arrears of his last account, 40s. 4¾d.

Total £4 9s. 3¾d.

Total of all expenses £856 7s. 5¼d.
Total of all costs [*oneris*] £916 18s. 0¾d.

And there remains with the executors £60 10s. 7½d., from which in books and other things for sale which cannot be sold as valued, £26 7s.10d. And so there remains in money £34 2s. 9½d.

Also there remains from the revenues of the church of West Anstey, beyond costs applied to the building of the chancel and houses and the stipend of the chaplain there, 14 marks.

From which the executor, having full and general power from the deceased for ordaining and distributing his goods, assigns to the new fabric for a new reredos [*tabule*] of Blessed Peter [at Exeter Cathedral], 100s. Also to three [m. 8d.] scholars of the kin of the deceased, studying at Oxford, £12 in money together with some of the books of the deceased, so that each is matching in the faculty in which he is studying [*congruit in facultate quam audit*]. Also one part of the said goods for the repair of books, vestments, and houses of whoever shall be vicar of West Anstey, and for missals, chalices, and vestments and towels for the altar of St Andrew in the church of Exeter, in front of which altar the body of the deceased lies. And the whole of the residue for distribution among poor kin of the deceased and in other works of charity. And so the said executor went away quit and absolved of the administration of the said goods.

[Total of all expenses £857 7s. 6¼d. – *cancelled*.]
Afterwards [*post*], the total of all expenses £856 7s. 5¼d.

23. A Register of Surviving Exeter Wills, 1244–1540

The following wills are those that survive wholly or in part, made by people who had dwellings and property in Exeter and by some (but not all) of those living elsewhere whose wills mention Exeter. In one of the principal sources, the Mayor's Court Rolls of Exeter, all that usually remains of the will is the portion that deals with the disposition of real property, which was the reason for the registration of the will in the court. Only after 1474 was it usual to register the whole of the will on the court roll.

The dates of the wills given here, as far as possible, are those at which they were made (while their makers were still alive), but there are two categories of wills (marked with stars) whose dates are those at which they were proved in court (when their makers were dead). The first of these comprises many of the wills proved in the Prerogative Court of Canterbury (now in the Public Record Office, London), the published catalogue of which gives only dates of proof not dates of making. It has not been possible to check all the latter dates, although they are usually stated in the wills themselves. The second category consists of most of the extracts of wills registered in the mayor's court, where dates (as noted above) are those of registration and where (before 1474) it is rare for the dating clause of the will to be transcribed.

1297*   Adyn, Gunhilda (MCR 24–25 Edw I, m. 31)

1349*   Ayllyswille, Margery, widow of Robert (MCR 22–23 Edw III, m. 24)

1482   Aiscough, Robert, archdeacon of Exeter (PRO, PROB 11/7, f. 45r–v (6 Logge))

1349*   Ayshford, Robert de, clerk (MCR 22–23 Edw III, m. 36)

1429*   Aldryngton (Allerton), Richard, canon of Exeter Cathedral (PRO, PROB 11/3 (12 Luffenam))

1351*   Aleyn, Peter (MCR 24–25 Edw III, m. 36)

1352*   Alre, William de (MCR 25–26 Edw III, m. 53)

1517   Andrewe, Thomas (MCR 23–24 Hen VIII, m. 7; PRO, PROB 11/18, f. 238v (30 Holder); codicil 1529 PROB 11/23 (14 Jankyn))

Archdeacon – see Lercedekne

1394*   Archer, Henry (MCR 17–18 Ric II, m. 33)

1504*   Arundell, John, bishop of Exeter (PRO, PROB 11/14 (14 Holgrave))

1479   Arundell, Lady Katherine (Cornwall Record Office, Arundell Deeds, ARB 217/4)

Ashburton – see Stok

1510*   Atkynson, Thomas (PRO, PROB 11/16 (28 Bennett))

1313*   Attareweende, Christine (MCR 6–7 Edw II, m. 33)

Attelane – see Lane

1490   Atwyll, Philip; will registered 1491 (MCR 6–7 Hen VII, m. 42)

1385   Audley, James, Lord (Lambeth Palace Library, Reg. Courtenay, f. 121v).

1396*   Audley, Nicholas, Lord (MCR 20–21 Ric II, m. 12)

1509   Austell, Thomas, treasurer of Exeter Cathedral (PRO, PROB 11/18, f. 58r–v (8 Holder))

1323*   Austyn, Walter (MCR 17–18 Edw II, m. 9)

1289*   Austyn, Walter (MCR 17–18 Edw I, m. 1)

1376*   Avenel, William, rector of Sutton Courtenay (Berks.) (MCR 50 Edw III–1 Ric II, m. 6)

1415*   Baigge, John (MCR 2–3 Hen V, m. 38)

1369*   Bailly, Warin (MCR 42–43 Edw III, m. 46)

1301*   Baker (Pistor), Lucy, daughter of Jordan (MCR 29–30 Edw I, m. 10)

1336*   Bakere, Lucy le (MCR 9–10 Edw III, m. 38)

1483   Baker, Richard, citizen; will registered 1485 (British Library, Add. Charter 27631; (MCR 2 Ric III–1 Hen VII, m. 18)

1380*   Baker, Walter (MCR 4–5 Ric II, m. 9)

1313*   Baker, William le, of St Nicholas (MCR 6–7 Edw II, m. 42)

1317*   Bakhouse, Walter atte (MCR 11–12 Edw II, m. 8)

1396*   Baly, Joan, wife of Roger Hurdyng, smith (MCR 19–20 Ric II, m. 24)

1534   Bannaster, Thomas, chaplain of Polsloe Priory (extracts only, in Oliver, *Monasticon*, p. 164)

1375*   Baret, John, of Sutton (Devon) (MCR 48–49 Edw III, m. 47)

1350*   Baret, Thomas (MCR 23–24 Edw III, m. 17)

1357*   Barnstaple, Vincent de, rector of Stokenham (Devon) (MCR 30–31 Edw III, m. 37)

1415   Barton, Thomas, canon of Exeter Cathedral (*Reg. Stafford*, pp. 411–15)

1457   Batte, John alias Richard (D&C 2538/2)

1396*   Battushull, Meralde (MCR 19–20 Ric II, m. 29)

1426*   Batyn, John (MCR 4–5 Hen VI, m. 21)

1331*   Bayoun, Margaret, wife of John (MCR 4–5 Edw III, m. 37)

1397*   Beare, Joan (MCR 20–21 Ric II, m. 53)
1349*   Beauchamp, Elizabeth, wife of Richard (MCR 22–23 Edw III, m. 33)
1338*   Beauforest, Cecily (MCR 11–12 Edw III, m. 13)
1322*   Beauforest, John de (MCR 16–17 Edw II, m. 3)
1346*   Bedford, Peter de, formerly of Kingston-on-Hull (MCR 19–20 Edw III, m. 39)
1472   Benet, Edward, smith (DRO, ED/M/862)
1480   Benet, Joan (DRO, ED/M/879)
1295   Berbilond (Berbelaunde), Henry de, vicar choral of Exeter Cathedral (D&C ED 50; will registered 1296 (MCR 24–25 Edw I, m. 5); above, pp. 150–4
1410   Bernard, Roger, rector of St Paul, Exeter, and vicar choral of Exeter Cathedral (*Reg. Stafford*, p. 396); will registered 1411 (MCR 12 Hen IV, m. 24)
1349*   Bernehous, John, annuellar of Exeter Cathedral (MCR 22–23 Edw III, m. 43)
1337*   Bernevyle, Alice (MCR 10–11 Edw III, m. 37)
1332*   Byllysdon, Robert de (MCR 5–6 Edw III, m. 32)
1382*   Bynnecote, Nicholas (MCR 6–7 Ric II, m. 4)
1372*   Byrch, Geoffrey (MCR 45–46 Edw III, m. 43)
1308*   Bythewall, Alice (MCR 1–2 Edw II, m. 14)
1315*   Bythewall, Wynard (MCR 8–9 Edw II, m. 22)
1537   Blackall, Roger, layman (PRO, PROB 11/28, f. 217r)
1423*   Blakelond, John (MCR 1–2 Hen VI, m. 24)
1527*   Bodley, John (PRO, PROB 11/22(24 Porche))
1350*   Boghelegh, John (MCR 23–24 Edw III, m. 18)
1376*   Boghewode, William (MCR 49–50 Edw III, m. 25)
1393*   Boghner, Philippa, wife of Thomas (MCR 16–17 Ric II, m. 21)
1388*   Bole, Eleanor, wife of Walter de Brankscombe (MCR 11–12 Ric II, m. 50)
1331*   Bole, John le (MCR 4–5 Edw III, m. 19)
1327*   Bole, Thomas, clerk (MCR 20 Edw II–1 Edw III, m. 32)
1317*   Bolle, John, tucker (MCR 11–12 Edw II, m. 4)
1436   Bolter, John, precentor of Exeter Cathedral (*Reg. Lacy*, ed. Dunstan, IV, 27–30)
1349*   Bonde, Elias (MCR 22–23 Edw III, m. 15)
1344*   Boly, Juliana, widow of William (MCR 17–18 Edw III, m. 46)
1340*   Boly, William (MCR 14–15 Edw III, m. 2)
1503*   Bonde, Thomas (PRO, PROB 11/13 (24 Blamyr); Canterbury Cathedral Archives, Register F, f. 184v)
1494   Bonvyle, John, esquire, of Shute (Devon); will registered 1495 (MCR 10–11 Hen VII, m. 29)
1367*   Bonevyle, Sarah, wife of Hugh (MCR 41–42 Edw III, m. 15)

Bosco – see Wood

1352*   Bosse, Robert (MCR 26–27 Edw III, m. 3)

1392*   Bosun, Joan (MCR 16–17 Ric II, m. 8)

1263   Boteler, Thomas, archdeacon of Totnes (D&C 3672, pp. 339–
       41); above, pp. 142–3

1316*   Bovy, Alexander de (MCR 9–10 Edw II, m. 22)

1308*   Bovey, Beatrice de (MCR 1–2 Edw II, m. 30)

Bovy, John – see Morton

1349*   Bovys, Cecily, daughter of John (MCR 22–23 Edw III, m. 51)

1308 *   Boylond, Robert de (MCR 2–3 Edw I, m. 2)

1349*   Bozoun, Robert (MCR 22–23 Edw III, m. 25)

1319*   Bradecroft, Joel de (MCR 12–13 Edw II, m. 19)

1499   Bradeworthi, John, citizen (D&C 2538/1)

1326*   Bradeworthi, Richard de, chaplain (MCR 19–20 Edw II, m. 46)

1349*   Bradworthy, Robert de (MCR 22–23 Edw III, m. 39)

1350*   Bradworthy, Robert de (MCR 23–24 Edw III, m. 44)

1393   Brantingham, Thomas, bishop of Exeter (PRO, PROB 11/1, f.
       24v (4 Rous); *Reg. Brantyngham*, ii, 742)

1399   Braybroke, Nicholas, canon of Exeter Cathedral (Lambeth Palace
       Library, Reg. Arundel, i, f. 165); will registered 1401 (MCR
       2 Hen IV, m. 40)

1335*   Brewer, William le (MCR 8–9 Edw III, m. 19)

1321*   Brydeford, Joan, wife of Martin de (MCR 14–15 Edw II, m. 13)

1326*   Bridistou, Jordan de, clerk (MCR 19–20 Edw II, m. 33)

Bridge – see Ponte

1358*   Bridport, Robert de (MCR 31–32 Edw III, m. 43)

1349*   Brigge, William, vicar choral of Exeter Cathedral (MCR 22–23
       Edw III, m. 20)

1523*   Brigeman, John (PRO, PROB 11/21 (17 Bodfelde))

1434*   Brigon, John (PRO, PROB 11/3 (22 Luffenam))

1369*   Brittestowe, Nicholas (MCR 42–43 Edw III, m. 26)

1404   Brokelond, Henry, canon of Exeter Cathedral (*Reg. Stafford*, p.
       382)

1382*   Bromhull, Joan, wife of John (MCR 5–6 Ric II, m. 32)

1414   Broun, Richard, canon of Exeter Cathedral (Lambeth Palace
       Library, Reg. Arundel, ii, f. 202v)

1361*   Brown, Robert (MCR 35–36 Edw III, m. 8)

1513*   Browne, Robert, alias Sherman (PRO, PROB 11/17 (14
       Fetiplace))

1454   Brownyng, William, canon of Exeter Cathedral (*Reg. Lacy*, ed.
       Dunstan, IV, 59–61)

1367*   Brounewylle, Joan, daughter of T. Nyweton (MCR 40–41 Edw
       III, m. 4)

1537   Bruckeshaw, John, annuellar of Exeter Cathedral (extract only, in Oliver, *Monasticon*, p. 164)

1353*   Bruges, Amyas de (MCR 26–27 Edw III, m. 29)

1322*   Bruscote, John de (MCR 15–16 Edw II, m. 43)

1346*   Buckerell, Henry de (MCR 19–20 Edw III, m. 50)

1312   Buffet, William (MCR 6–7 Edw II, m. 5)

1499   Bulwyke, Philip, possibly an Exeter will (PRO, PROB 11/12, f. 151v (19 Moone))

1426*   Burgon, John, rector of Doddiscombsleigh (Devon) and prebendary of Crediton College (MCR 4–5 Hen VI, m. 18)

1312   Burrydge, John de, chaplain (MCR 5–6 Edw II, m. 27)

    Butler – see also Boteler

1509*   Butteler, John (PRO, PROB 11/16 (19 Bennett))

1309   Cadbury, Joan, widow of William de (MCR 2–3 Edw II, m. 44)

1480   Calwoodlegh, Thomas, 'junior', esquire (DRO, Chanter XII (ii), Reg. Fox, f. 126r)

1492   Calwodley, Thomas, esquire; will registered 1493 (MCR 8–9 Hen VII, m. 24)

1393*   Camelford, Thomas, rector of St Mary Steps, Exeter (MCR 16–17 Ric II, m. 32)

1521   Carewe, Isabel, of Antony (Cornwall); requested burial in Exeter (Truro, Royal Institution of Cornwall, Henderson MS 66, p. 165)

1387*   Carpenter, Joan, wife of Henry (MCR 10–11 Ric II, m. 20)

1534   Carslegh, Peter, canon of Exeter Cathedral (PRO, PROB 11/25, f. 230v (F.31 Hogen))

1350*   Casse, Alexander, butcher (MCR 23–24 Edw III, m. 18)

1316*   Caticote, William de (MCR 9–10 Edw II, m. 45)

1416   Catrik, John, later bishop of Exeter (d. 1419) (Lambeth Palace Library, Reg, Chichele, i, ff. 328v–329v; *Reg. Chichele*, ii, 178–82)

1333*   Chagford, Joan, wife of William de (MCR 6–7 Edw III, m. 31)

1314*   Chaillou, Matilda, widow of Jordan (MCR 7–8 Edw II, m. 46)

1514   Chalmore, John (PRO, PROB 11/18, f. 34v (F.5 Holder))

1291*   Chamberleyn, John (MCR 19–20 Edw I, m. 7)

1357*   Chekston, Juliana (MCR 30–31 Edw III, m. 27)

1474   Choun, John; will registered 1474 (MCR 13–14 Edw IV, m. 34)

1307*   Christchurch, Ralph de, carpenter (MCR 34–35 Edw I, m. 33)

1347*   Chudleigh, John de (MCR 20–21 Edw III, m. 34)

1452*   Chudleigh, Simon, rector of St Mary Major, Exeter (MCR 30–31 Hen VI, m. 21)

1426*   Clerk, John, grocer (MCR 4–5 Hen VI, m. 28)

1418   Clyfford, Thomas, canon of Exeter Cathedral (*Reg. Stafford*, p. 422)

1347*   Clopton, Walter de, canon of Exeter Cathedral (MCR 20–21
              Edw III, m. 1 (MCR 20–21 Edw III, m. 22)
1350*   Clotere, Christine (MCR 24–25 Edw III, m. 10)
1383*   Cobbelegh, Thomas (MCR 6–7 Ric II, m. 14)
1297*   Coccyng, William (MCR 24–25 Edw I, m. 28)
1347*   Cok, John le, spicer (MCR 20–21 Edw III, m. 34)
1403*   Cock, John (MCR 4 Hen IV, m. 16)
1431   Cokworthy, John, clerk, probably canon of Exeter Cathedral
              (*Reg. Lacy*, ed. Dunstan, IV, 22–3)
1396*   Cole, William, of Plymouth (MCR 19–20 Ric II, m. 23)
1335*   Colebrook, Clarice, wife of John de, skinner (MCR 8–9 Edw
              III, m. 32)
1363*   Colbrok, Margery (MCR 37–38 Edw III, m. 6)
1349*   Colbrok, John de, layman (MCR 23–24 Edw III, m. 12)
1269   Collecote, Adam de (D&C, VC/3053); above, pp. 145–6
1294   Collecote, Henry de (D&C 2121); above, pp. 147–8
1305*   Collecote, Hugh de (MCR 32–33 Edw I, m. 33)
1324   Collecote, Lucy de (D&C, VC/3050, 3552); will registered 1324
              (MCR 17–18 Edw II, m. 18); above, pp. 155–7
1305   Collecote, Margaret de, wife of John Beare (D&C, VC/3018);
              above, p. 154
1424   Colecote, Nicholas, rector of St Laurence, Exeter (*Reg. Lacy*, ed.
              Dunstan, IV, 1–3)
1316   Collecote, Walter de (D&C, VC/3057); above, p. 155
1430*   Collys, John (MCR 8–9 Hen VI, m. 18)
1452   Colles, Walter, precentor of Exeter Cathedral (*Reg. Lacy*, ed.
              Dunstan, IV, 57–9)
1423*   Colyn, John, merchant of Culmstock (Devon) (MCR 1–2 Hen
              VI, m. 24)
1490   Colyns, Arnulph, canon of Exeter Cathedral (PRO, PROB 11/8,
              f. 273r–v (34 Milles))
1519   Colshill, Elizabeth – see Speke
1495   Colshyll, John, citizen; will registered 1496 (MCR 11–12 Hen
              VII, m. 40; PRO, PROB 11/10, f. 207r (26 Vox))
1518   Colshill, John (PRO, PROB 11/19, f. 81r (11 Ayloffe))
1540*   Colsell, William (PRO, PROB 11/28 (12 Alenger))
1362*   Comb, Iseult, daughter of Master William, clerk (MCR 35–36
              Edw III, m. 25)
1364*   Comb, William, clerk (MCR 38–39 Edw III, m. 9)
1438*   Cook, Thomas, rector of St Kerrian, Exeter (MCR 16–17 Hen
              VI, m. 45)
1450*   Cook, William (MCR 29–30 Hen VI, m. 11)
1394*   Coos, Raymond (MCR 17–18 Ric II, m. 28)

1494   Coryngdon, John, canon of Exeter Cathedral (PRO, PROB 11/
         10, f. 184r (23 Vox))
1323*   Cornel, Clarice (MCR 16–17 Edw II, m. 44)
1402*   Coscumbe, Margery, widow of William (MCR 4 Hen IV, m. 10)
1450*   Cosyn, John, of West Teignmouth (Devon) (MCR 29–30 Hen
         VI, m. 10)
1349*   Coterel, Laurence (MCR 22–23 Edw III, m. 41)
1315*   Cotiller, Joan, widow of Walter le (MCR 8–9 Edw II, m. 33)
1371*   Courtenay, Emmeline (MCR 44–45 Edw III, m. 43)
1391*   Courtenay, Margaret, countess of Devon (PRO, PROB 11/1 (2
         Rous))
1487   Courtenay, Margaret, Lady, of Powderham (Devon) with Exeter
         bequests (Lambeth Palace Library, Reg. Morton i, f. 129v;
         Reg. Morton, ii, 86–7)
1466   Courtenay, Matilda, Lady, wife of Sir Hugh Courtenay of Hac-
         combe (Devon), requesting burial in Exeter (PRO, PROB 11/
         5, f. 161r (21 Godyn))
1485*   Courtenay, William, knight (MCR 1–2 Hen VII, m. 12)
1421   Courtour, Philip (DRO, ED/M/682)
1339*   Crediton, Alured de, fisher (MCR 12–13 Edw III, m. 15)
1368*   Criditon, Christine, wife of William (MCR 42–43 Edw III, m.
         9)
1316*   Crediton, John de (MCR 9–10 Edw II, m. 48)
1303*   Criditon, Joan, widow of Richard de (MCR 30–31 Edw I, m.
         32)
1380*   Criditon, William (MCR 4–5 Ric II, m. 14)
1483   Cremell, William; will registered 1484 (MCR 1–2 Ric III, m.
         28)
1290*   Crendon, Thomas de (MCR 17–18 Edw I, m. 31)
1320*   Cretynges, Stephen de (MCR 13–14 Edw II, m. 21)
1402   Crockere, Ralph (DRO, ED/M/568)
1332*   Crosse, Alice atte (MCR 5–6 Edw III, m. 26)
1361*   Crosse, Joan atte, widow of William Kydelond, chandler (MCR
         34–35 Edw III, m. 21)
1520*   Crugge, William (PRO, PROB 11/19 (26 Ayloffe))
1316*   Cullompton, Matilda de (MCR 9–10 Edw II, m. 48)
1503*   Dagnall, Marion (Canterbury Cathedral Archives, Register F, f.
         212r)
1504*   Danaster, John (PRO, PROB 11/14 (5 Holgrave))
1349*   Daune, Joan (MCR 22–23 Edw III, m. 26)
1436*   Dauney, William, esquire (MCR 14–15 Hen VI, m. 41)
1349*   Davy, John (MCR 22–23 Edw III, m. 27)
1361*   Davy, John, son of Roger (MCR 35–36 Edw III, m. 28)

1495   Davy, Simon (Oliver, *Ecclesiastical Antiquities*, i, 80)
1517   Davy, Thomasia, widow of Simon, tailor; will registered 1517 (MCR 8–9 Henry VIII, between mm. 48 and 49)
1521*   Davies, Richard, possibly an Exeter will (PRO, PROB 11/20 (13 Maynwaryng))
1349*   Degher, William, priest (MCR 22–23 Edw III, m. 35)
1398*   Dene, Robert (MCR 21–22 Ric II, m. 27)
1398*   Dygon, Richard (MCR 21–22 Ric II, m. 45)
1497   Dynham, Jane, widow of Sir John Dynham, knight (PRO, PROB 11/11, f. 87r (10 Horne))
1336*   Direwyn, Amicia, wife of William (MCR 9–10 Edw III, m. 21)
1314   Direwyne, alias Exeter, Master John, canon of Exeter Cathedral (MCR 7–8 Edw II, m. 1314)
1391*   Dirwin, Robert (MCR 14–15 Ric II, m. 26)
1367*   Dirkyn, John (MCR 40–41 Edw III, m. 37)
1324*   Dyrkyn, Richard (MCR 17–18 Edw II, m. 40)
1400   Dodyngton, John, canon of Exeter Cathedral (*Reg. Stafford*, pp. 370–1)
1351*   Dollyng, John, baker (MCR 24–25 Edw III, m. 20)
1410*   Doly, Roger (MCR 11 Hen IV, m. 38)
1319*   Don, John, carpenter (MCR 12–13 Edw II, m. 31)
1267   Doulys, John de (London, British Library, Add. Charter 27,523); above, pp. 143–5
1510   Doun, William, yeoman (DRO, ED/M/964)
1416*   Drewe, Richard (MCR 4–5 Hen IV, m. 12)
1453   Druell, John, archdeacon of Exeter (Lambeth Palace Library, Reg. Kempe, f. 290r)
1473   Duke, William, citizen (DRO, ED/M/864A)
1351*   Durnford, Alice (MCR 24–25 Edw III, m. 23)
1326   Durneford, Nicholas de (DRO, ECA, Book 53A, f. 53v); above, pp. 157–8
1326*   Duryer, Alice de (MCR 20 Edw II–1 Edw III, m. 9)
1464   Dyer, Martin, canon of Exeter Cathedral (DRO, Chanter XII (i), Reg. Nevill, f. 141v)
1369*   Eglyshale, Adam (MCR 42–43 Edw III, m. 48)
1349*   Eglosheyl, Robert de, rector of St Paul, Exeter (MCR 22–23 Edw III, m. 21)
1323*   Eyr, Ancelin le, of Brentwood (MCR 17–18 Edw II, m. 6)
1413   Ekerdon, William, canon of Exeter Cathedral (Lambeth Palace Library, Reg. Arundel, ii, f. 175; *Reg. Stafford*, pp. 402–3)
1308*   Ermyte, Nicholas (MCR 1–2 Edw II, m. 33)
1317*   Espicer, Adam le (MCR 10–11 Edw II, m. 48)
1290*   Espicer, Richard le (MCR 17–18 Edw I, m. 27)

Espicer – see also Spicer
1308*   Esse, Henry de (MCR 1–2 Edw I, m. 15)
1441   Estbrok, Thomas, subdean of Exeter Cathedral (*Reg. Lacy*, ed. Dunstan, IV, 36)
1291*   Exeter, William de, clerk (MCR 19–20 Edw I, m. 12)
1359*   Exeter, William de, canon of York (MCR 32–33 Edw III, m. 51)
        Exeter – see also Direwyne
1516   Faryngdon, Elizabeth, widow of John, esquire; will registered 1517 (MCR 8–9 Hen VIII, m. 36)
1361*   Ferour, Hugh (MCR 35–36 Edw III, m. 6)
1435   Fylham, William, canon of Exeter Cathedral (*Reg. Lacy*, ed. Dunstan, IV, 32–3)
1411*   Fyllegh, John (MCR 13 Hen IV, m. 8)
1316*   Fynamour, Adam (MCR 9–10 Edw II, m. 36)
1347*   Fleyngemouth, Alice, widow of Adam (MCR 20–21 Edw III, m. 17)
1347*   Fleyngemouth, Joan, daughter of Adam de Forde alias (MCR 20–21 Edw III, m. 31)
        Fleyngemouth – see also Forde
1463   Flower, John, canon of Exeter Cathedral (DRO, Chanter XII (i), Reg. Neville, f. 138r–v)
1404*   Foke, Christine (MCR 6 Hen IV, m. 3)
1356*   Fourbour, Joan, daughter of Thomas le (MCR 30–31 Edw III, m. 5)
1349*   Forbour, Thomas le (MCR 22–23 Edw III, m. 20)
1356*   Fourbour, Thomas, son of Thomas le (MCR 30–31 Edw III, m. 5)
1327*   Forde, Joan atte (MCR 20 Edw II–1 Edw III, m. 25)
1349*   Ford, Roger atte, skinner (MCR 22–23 Edw III, m. 29)
1332*   Forde, William atta (MCR 5–6 Edw III, m. 45)
        Forde – see also Fleyngemouth
1304*   Fosse, Margaret de la (MCR 32–33 Edw I, m. 9)
1289*   Fosse, Mariot de la (MCR 17–18 Edw I, m. 2)
1290*   Fosse, Matilda de la (MCR 18–19 Edw I, m. 5)
1349*   Froggwille, Laurence (MCR 22–23 Edw III, m. 34)
1508   Frost, William; will registered 1509 (PRO, PROB 11/16 (17 Bennett); MCR 1 Hen VIII, m. 11)
1475   Fulford, William, archdeacon of Barnstaple (PRO, PROB 11/6, f. 196v (26 Wattys))
1356*   Fursdon, Thomas de (MCR 29–30 Edw III, m. 50)
1417*   Gardyner, William (MCR 5–6 Hen V, m. 4)
1291*   Gaschoyng, Peter (MCR 18–19 Edw I, m. 15)
1306*   Gatepath, John de (MCR 34–35 Edw I, m. 3)

1326*   Gatepath, John de (MCR 19–20 Edw II, m. 38)

1320*   Gatepath, Richard de (MCR 14–15 Edw II, m. 8)

1316*   Gatepath, William de (MCR 10–11 Edw I, m. 10)

1472   Geffery, Richard; will registered 1476 (MCR 16–17 Edw IV, m. 9)

1310*   Germeyn, Adam, rector of St Paul, Exeter (MCR 4–5 Edw II, m. 2)

1331*   Germayn, Isabel, widow of Stephen (MCR 5–6 Edw III, m. 10)

1460   Germyn, John, chancellor of Exeter Cathedral (DRO, Chanter XII (i), Reg. Nevill, ff.140v–141r)

1326*   Germayn, Stephen (MCR 19–20 Edw II, m. 41)

1333*   Germeyn, Udo (MCR 7–8 Edw III, m. 2)

1314*   Germein, William (MCR 7–8 Edw II, m. 27)

1467*   Germyn, William, of Pinhoe (Devon) (MCR 6–7 Edw IV, m. 33)

1403*   Gervase, Beatrice, widow (MCR 5 Hen IV, m. 12)

1349*   Gerveys, Thomas (MCR 22–23 Edw III, m. 25)

1258?   Gervas, Walter (D&C 2097); above, pp. 140–1

1400*   Gervays, William (MCR 1 Henry IV, m. 22)

1302*   Gesse, Robert (MCR 29–30 Edw I, m. 29)

1427*   Gybbe, John, tucker (MCR 5–6 Hen VI, m. 43)

1412   Gybbes, Walter, canon of Exeter Cathedral (Lambeth Palace Library, Reg. Arundel, ii, f. 168r)

1537*   Gybbons, John, chancellor of Exeter Cathedral (PRO, PROB 11/27 (4 Dyngeley))

1487   Gyffard, John, apparently of Withycombe Raleigh, requesting burial in Exeter (Lambeth Palace Library, Reg. Morton, i, f. 130r; *Reg. Morton*, ii, 87–8)

1308*   Giffard, Robert, clerk (MCR 1–2 Edw II, m. 28)

1350*   Gilbert, Geoffrey (MCR 23–24 Edw III, m. 39)

1361*   Gylla, Robert (MCR 35–36 Edw III, m. 4)

1348*   Gist, Isabel, widow of John (MCR 21–22 Edw III, m. 43)

1381*   Gyst, John (MCR 4–5 Ric II, m. 25)

1425*   Glamvyle, Walter (MCR 3–4 Hen VI, m. 48)

1322*   Glasneye, John de, vicar choral of Exeter Cathedral (MCR 15–16 Edw II, m. 27)

1483*   Godde, William, sometime rector of Powderham (Devon) and prebendary of Glasney College (Cornwall) (PRO, PROB 11/7 (7 Logge))

1402*   Godman, Nicholas (MCR 4 Hen IV, m. 10)

1396*   Gold, Adam (MCR 19–20 Ric II, m. 46)

1335*   Golde, Clarice (MCR 8–9 Edw III, m. 27)

1429*   Golde, Roger (MCR 7–8 Hen VI, m. 43)

1376*   Goldsmith, Richard (MCR 50 Edw III–1 Ric II, m.12)

1290*   Gordet, Walter (MCR 17–18 Edw I, m. 45)

Gorgeys – see Thornbury

1416 Govys, John, rector of Holy Trinity, Exeter, and vicar choral of Exeter Cathedral (*Reg. Stafford*, p. 415)

1368 Grandisson, John de, bishop of Exeter (Lambeth Palace Library, Reg. Whittlesey, f. 103; *Reg. Grandisson*, iii, 1549–57)

1319* Gregory, rector of St Olave, Exeter (MCR 12–13 Edw II, m. 18)

1306* Grendel, Richard de (MCR 33–34 Edw I, m. 47)

1411 Grendon, Simon, citizen (*Reg. Stafford*, pp. 397–8); will registered 1413 (MCR 14 Hen IV, m. 15)

1362* Greneweye, Thomas (MCR 35–36 Edw III, m. 46)

1508 Guscott, Joan, widow (DRO, Exeter St Mary Arches, 332A/PF 248)

1336* Guz, John (MCR 9–10 Edw III, m. 30)

1331* Haccombe, Stephen de (MCR 4–5 Edw III, m. 17)

1416* Hakeworthy, Robert (MCR 4–5 Hen IV, m. 12)

1349* Halberton, Nicholas de (MCR 22–23 Edw III, m. 15)

1349* Halberton, William (MCR 22–23 Edw III, m. 20)

1417 Hals, Richard, treasurer of Exeter Cathedral (*Reg. Stafford*, pp. 416–17)

1347* Halscombe, William de, skinner (MCR 20–21 Edw III, m. 33)

1443 Halstowe, Henry, rector of St Stephen, Exeter (*Reg. Lacy*, ed. Dunstan, IV, 43–4)

1303* Hamelyn, John (MCR 31–32 Edw I, m. 32)

1318* Hamelin, John, glover (MCR 11–12 Edw II, m. 36)

1504 Hamlyn, Nicholas, merchant (PRO, PROB 11/14, f. 164r (21 Holgrave))

1337* Hamme, Richard atte, leather-dresser (MCR 10–11 Edw III, m. 27)

1474 Hamond, John; will registered 1477 (MCR 16–17 Edw IV, m. 32)

1492 Hanforth, Henry (Lambeth Palace Library, Reg. Morton, i, f. 130v; *Reg. Morton*, ii, 89)

1343* Hardewyne, William (MCR 16–17 Edw III, m. 29)

1349* Hardy, John, clerk (MCR 22–23 Edw III, m. 27)

1511 Harrys, Thomas, precentor of Exeter Cathedral (DRO, Chanter XIII, Reg. Oldham, f. 172r–v)

1348* Hauk, Roger, clerk (MCR 22–23 Edw III, m. 8)

1418 Haukyn, Laurence, precentor of Exeter Cathedral (*Reg. Stafford*, pp. 421–2)

1405* Haycombe, Robert (MCR 7 Hen IV, m. 10)

1358* Haycomb, Roger (MCR 31–32 Edw III, m. 27)

1323* Haye, John in the (MCR 16–17 Edw II, m. 32)

1349* Haye, Richard in the Haye, alias de Tavistock (MCR 22–23 Edw III, m. 28)

1355* Hayne, Reginald, baker (MCR 28–29 Edw III, m. 30)

1349*   Hayne, Robert (MCR 22–23 Edw III, m. 18)

1326*   Hemmeston, Elias de (MCR 19–20 Edw II, m. 45)

1538*   Hengescott, Tristram, possibly an Exeter will (PRO, PROB 11/ 26 (12 Crumwell))

1432   Hethman, John, citizen (DRO, ECA, ED/M/733)

1383   Hethman, Roger (DRO, ED/M/495); will registered 1393 ((MCR 16–17 Ric II, m. 32)

1520   Hewet, Richard, citizen and merchant (PRO, PROB 11/19, f. 81r (23 Ayloffe))

1415   Hyckelyng, Hugh de, precentor of Exeter Cathedral (*Reg. Stafford*, pp. 410–11)

1303*   Hydon, Clarice de (MCR 30–31 Edw I, m. 15)

1382*   Hydon, Richard (MCR 6–7 Ric II, m. 5)

1499*   Hyette (Yott), John, annuellar of Exeter Cathedral (PRO, PROB 11/11 (34 Horne))

1351*   Hille, Emma atte (MCR 24–25 Edw III, m. 49)

1402*   Hille, Roger atte (MCR 3 Hen IV, m. 34)

1350*   Hobbe, Richard (MCR 23–24 Edw III, m. 33)

1400   Hodell, William, layman (British Library, Add. Charter 27580)

1393*   Hoiggeslond, Geoffrey (MCR 16–17 Ric II, m. 35)

1534   Hoker, Robert; will registered 1538 (PRO, PROB 11/26 (10 and 16 Crumwell); MCR 30–31 Hen VIII, m. 5)

1506   Holond, Roger (PRO, PROB 11/15, f. 137v (17 Adeane))

1473*   Holand, Thomas (MCR 11–12 Edw IV, m. 17)

1400*   Holbrok, Thomas (MCR 1 Henry IV, m. 16)

1349*   Hole, Isabel, daughter of Richard and Margaret atte (MCR 22– 23 Edw III, m. 15)

1352*   Hole, Serlo atte (MCR 25–26 Edw III, m. 29)

1362*   Holle, John, draper (MCR 35–36 Edw III, m. 18)

1413*   Holte, John atte (MCR 14 Hen IV, m. 34)

1377*   Hooper, Alice, wife of John (MCR 50 Edw III–1 Ric II, m. 32)

1492   Hopton, David, archdeacon of Exeter (PRO, PROB 11/9, f. 60r– v (8 Dogett))

1399*   Hore, Roger (MCR 1 Henry IV, m. 5)

1349*   Horn, Alfred (MCR 22–23 Edw III, m. 22)

1337*   Horn, Clarice (MCR 10–11 Edw III, m. 36)

1318*   Horn, John (MCR 11–12 Edw II, m. 16)

1531   Horsey, William, canon of Exeter Cathedral (PRO, PROB 11/ 29, f. 198r).

1349*   Houton, Joan (MCR 22–23 Edw III, m. 27)

1510   Huddesfeld, Katherine, Lady, formerly Rogers (PRO, PROB 11/ 18, f. 30v (4 Holder))

1350*   Hugheton, Henry de (MCR 23–24 Edw III, m. 17)

1361*   Hugheton, Robert de (MCR 35–36 Edw III, m. 8)

1353*   Hugheton, Walter de (MCR 26–27 Edw III, m. 16)

1425   Hull, Henry (DRO, 48/13/10/1); will registered 1426 (MCR 4–5 Hen VI, m. 19)

1407   Hulle, Sir John (PRO, PROB 11/2A, f. 128v (17 Marche))

1416   Hunden, William, archdeacon of Totnes (*Reg. Stafford*, pp. 408–10)

1441*   Huntelond, Meliora, wife of Robert (MCR 19–20 Hen VI, m. 57)

1457*   Huntelond, Alice (MCR 36–37 Hen VI, m. 11)

1509*   Huntingdon, William (PRO, PROB 11/16 (15 Bennett))

1349*   Hurnell, John (MCR 23–24 Edw III, m. 5)

1348*   Jellen, Joan, wife of John (MCR 21–22 Edw III, m. 19)

1348*   Jobbe, William (MCR 21–22 Edw III, m. 39)

1384   Jon, Margaret, wife of William Jon, cook (D&C VC/3164); will registered 1387 ((MCR 11–12 Ric II, m. 9)

1382*   Jonyng, John (MCR 5–6 Ric II, m. 33)

1390*   Jurdan, Richard (MCR 13–14 Ric II, m. 36)

1330*   Kelly, John de, knight (MCR 3–4 Edw III, m. 32)

1486   Kelly, John; will registered 1487 (MCR 3–4 Hen VII, m. 10)

1457*   Kelly, Thomas, possibly an Exeter will (PRO, PROB 11/4 (11 Stokton))

1411*   Kersye, Richard (MCR 12 Hen IV, m. 50)

1336*   Ketene, William, chandler (MCR 9–10 Edw III, m. 50)

1335*   Keu, Martin le (MCR 8–9 Edw III, m. 27)

1322*   Keu, Richard le, of Bridford (MCR 15–16 Edw II, m. 30)

1320*   Keu, Sabina, widow of William le (MCR 14–15 Edw II, m. 9)

1328*   Keu, William le (MCR 3–4 Edw III, m. 28)

1350*   Kew, William le (MCR 23–24 Edw III, m. 27)

1319*   Kydelonde, John de (MCR 12–13 Edw II, m. 16)

1349*   Kydelond, William, chandler (MCR 22–23 Edw III, m. 22)

    Kydelond – see also Crosse

1291*   Kilrington, John de (MCR 18–19 Edw I, m. 43)

1295   Kymmyng, Rosamund, wife of John Smurch (D&C 2122); above, pp. 148–50

1290*   Kynelond, Emma de (MCR 18–19 Edw I, m. 2)

1474   Kirkeby, Thomas, treasurer of Exeter Cathedral (PRO, PROB 11/6, f. 218v (29 Wattys))

1318*   Knight, Henry (MCR 11–12 Edw II, m. 26)

1362*   Knolle, John, priest (a former or present annuellar of the cathedral) (MCR 35–36 Edw III, m. 27)

1315*   Lane, Jordan de la (MCR 8–9 Edw II, m. 18)

1329   Lane, Ralph atte (DRO, ED/M/294); will registered 1331 (MCR 5–6 Edw III, m. 1); above, pp. 162–3

1427*   Lange, John, clerk (MCR 5–6 Hen VI, m. 17)
1349*   Lange, Nicholas (MCR 22–23 Edw III, m. 34)
1419*   Lange, Ricarda, widow of John (MCR 6–7 Hen V, m. 36)
1347*   Langedone, John de, clerk (MCR 21–22 Edw III, m. 1)
1418*   Langedon, Thomas, alias Sharpe (MCR 5–6 Hen V, m. 37)
1414   Langeton, William, canon of Exeter Cathedral (*Reg. Stafford*,
            pp. 404–5)
1385*   Langkarn, John, clerk (MCR 8–9 Ric II, m. 45)
1373*   Lappeflod, Andrew de, rector of St Mary Major, Exeter (MCR
            46–47 Edw III, m. 25)
1336*   Lappeflod, Henry de (MCR 9–10 Edw III, m. 45)
1323*   Larkbeare, John de (MCR 16–17 Edw II, m. 34)
1416   Latymer, Lady Matilda (*Reg. Stafford*, pp. 415–16)
1349*   Launceston, William de (MCR 22–23 Edw III, m. 42)
1334*   Laurence, Robert (MCR 8–9 Edw III, m. 5)
1430   Lercedekne, Martin, canon of Exeter Cathedral (Lambeth Palace
            Library, Reg. Chichele, i, ff. 435v–437v; *Reg. Chichele*, ii,
            476–82)
1442   Lercedekne, Michael, treasurer of Exeter Cathedral (*Reg. Lacy*,
            ed. Dunstan, IV, 37–41)
1306*   Archdeacon, Richard (MCR 33–34 Edw I, m. 25)
1407   Lydford, John de, archdeacon of Totnes (*Reg. Stafford*, pp.
            389–90)
1422*   Lydeford, John (MCR 1–2 Hen VI, m. 9)
1339*   Lydford, Nicholas de (MCR 12–13 Edw III, m. 13)
1406   Lyf, Joan, wife of Richard atte More (DRO, 51/1/3/8)
1401*   Lymmere, Andrew (MCR 2 Hen IV, m. 30)
1428   Lyngham, Robert, rector of St Mary Major, Exeter (*Reg. Lacy*,
            ed. Dunstan, IV, 12–14)
1327*   London, Joan de (MCR 20 Edw II–1 Edw III, m. 18)
1324*   London, Stephen de (MCR 17–18 Edw II, m. 31)
1271*   Lorimer, Philip le (MCR 48 Hen III–2 Edw I, m. 19)
1399*   Losquyt, John, rector of St Kerrian, Exeter (MCR 1 Henry IV,
            m. 5)
1295*   Lovecok, Roger (MCR 23–24 Edw I, m. 3)
          Lucas – see Seyngler
1517   Luysshant, Gervase (DRO, Exeter St Mary Arches, 332A/PF 32A)
1332*   Luvenet, Joan, widow of John (MCR 5–6 Edw III, m. 45)
1351*   Mayde, Amice (MCR 24–25 Edw III, m. 34)
1475*   Mannyng, John (MCR 14–15 Edw IV, m. 31)
1361*   Mantel, Katherine, wife of Thomas (MCR 34–35 Edw III, m. 36)
1309*   Mark, Joan (MCR 2–3 Edw II, m. 35)
1442*   Marshall, John (MCR 20–21 Hen VI, m. 39)
1349*   Marshall, Laurence, chaplain (MCR 23–24 Edw III, m. 9)

1461   Martyn, Richard, canon of Exeter Cathedral (DRO, Chanter XII
          (i), Reg. Nevill, ff. 137v–138r)
1349*   Mathu, John, junior (MCR 22–23 Edw III, m. 44)
1350*   Mathu, John, senior (MCR 23–24 Edw III, m. 40)
1349*   Mathu, Katherine, daughter of John, clerk (MCR 22–23 Edw
          III, m. 25)
1336*   Maundevyle, Agnes (MCR 9–10 Edw III, m. 52)
1536   Maynwaryng, Nicholas, canon of Exeter Cathedral (PRO, PROB
          11/27, ff. 45v–46r (6 Dyngeley))
1412*   Mayowe, Henry (MCR 13 Hen IV, m. 37)
1349*   Merton, Henry de (MCR 22–23 Edw III, m. 30)
1510*   Meyston, John (PRO, PROB 11(31 Bennett))
1380*   Michel, Harvey (MCR 3–4 Ric II, m. 28)
1304*   Middlecote, John (MCR 31–32 Edw I, m. 43)
1358*   Midwinter, Matilda, daughter of Alexander (MCR 31–32 Edw
          III, m. 51)
1348*   Milioun, Christine (MCR 21–22 Edw III, m. 31)
1349*   Mille, John atte (MCR 22–23 Edw III, m. 16)
1464*   Mylton, Nicholas, rector of St Olave, Exeter (MCR 3–4 Edw IV,
          m. 43)
1454*   Myrfeld, Walter, skinner (MCR 33–34 Hen VI, m. 48)
1336*   Modbury, John de, physician (MCR 9–10 Edw III, m. 20)
1524   Mogryche (Mogryge), John, canon of Exeter Cathedral (PRO,
          PROB 11/21, f. 182v (23 Bodfelde); D&C 2418)
1490   Molyneux, Henry, canon of Exeter Cathedral (PRO, PROB 11/
          8, f. 359r–v (45 Milles))
1329*   Molton, Gervase, rector of St Edmund, Exeter (MCR 3–4 Edw
          III, m. 12)
1341*   Molton. Gervase de (MCR 15–16 Edw III, m. 4)
1366*   Molton, James de, Master (MCR 39–40 Edw III, m. 22)
1464*   More, John (PRO, PROB 11/5 (4 Godyn))
1320*   More, William atte (MCR 13–14 Edw II, m. 44)
1464   Morwell, Ralph, canon of Exeter Cathedral (DRO, Chanter XII
          (i), Reg. Nevill, f. 141r–v)
1457   Morton, John, alias Bovy, canon of Exeter Cathedral (DRO,
          Chanter XII (i), Reg. Nevill, f. 139r–v)
1311*   Mounteyn, Richard (MCR 4–5 Edw II, m. 26)
1336*   Mounteyn, William (MCR 10–11 Edw III, m. 2)
1349   Mounteyn, William (D&C 2232); above, pp. 166–7
1380   Mugge, William, canon of Exeter Cathedral (Lambeth Palace
          Library, Reg. Courtenay, ff. 201v–202r)
1507   Nans, John, canon of Exeter Cathedral (PRO, PROB 11/16, f.
          63v (9 Bennett))
1328*   Neldere, Ralph le (MCR 3–4 Edw III, m. 28)

1391   Nymet, John (DRO, ED/M/527); will registered 1392 (MCR 15–16 Ric II, m. 30)

1305* Nympton, Robert de, clerk (MCR 32–33 Edw I, m. 18)

1318* Nywenham, William de (MCR 11–12 Edw II, m. 27)

1348* Nyweton, Isold, widow of John de (MCR 21–22 Edw III, m. 49)

1349* Nyweton, John de (MCR 22–23 Edw III, m. 26)

1322* Nyweton, Ralph de, leather-dresser (MCR 16–17 Edw II, m. 4)

1311   Nywton, Robert de; will registered 1311 (MCR 4–5 Edw II, m. 46)

1361* Nyweton, William, *dominus* (priest or knight; possibly rector of Churchstow, Devon) (MCR 35–36 Edw III, m. 4)

1363* Noble, Robert (MCR 36–37 Edw III, m. 40)

1496* Nordon, William (PRO, PROB 11/10 (28 Vox))

1316* Norman, Alice (MCR 9–10 Edw II, m. 36)

1523   Norton, Richard, precentor of Exeter Cathedral (DRO, Chanter XIV, Reg. Veysey, ff. 31v–32r)

1505   Obley, William, citizen and merchant; will registered 1511 (MCR 2–3 Hen VIII, m. 26; 37–38 Hen VIII, m. 9)

1315* Offelegh, Richard de (MCR 9–10 Edw II, m. 12)

1296* Okampton, William de, clerk (MCR 23–24 Edw I, m. 28)

1327* Oke, John atte (MCR 20 Edw II–1 Edw III, m. 37)

1416* Oke, William (MCR 3–4 Hen V, m. 38)

1303* Okeston, Vincent de, clerk (MCR 30–31 Edw I, m. 20)

1516* Oldham, Bernard, treasurer of Exeter Cathedral (PRO, PROB 11/18 (24 Holder))

1518   Oldham, Hugh, bishop of Exeter (PRO, PROB 11/19, ff. 147v–148r (19 Ayloffe))

1361* Oliver, Richard (MCR 35–36 Edw III, m. 8)

1436   Orum, John, chancellor of Exeter Cathedral (*Reg. Lacy*, ed. Dunstan, IV, 23–6)

1355* Ottery, John de (MCR 29–30 Edw III, m. 12)

1315* Oxton, John de, vicar choral of Exeter Cathedral (MCR 9–10 Edw II, m. 7)

1324* Oxton, Michael de (MCR 17–18 Edw II, m. 33)

1311* Page, Nicholas (MCR 4–5 Edw II, m. 14)

1349* Page, Robert, skinner (MCR 22–23 Edw III, m. 16)

1286* Page, William (MCR 14 Edw I, m. 4)

1308* Palmere, Cecily, daughter of Juliana la (MCR 1–2 Edw II, m. 23)

1487   Palmer, John, baker (DRO, Holy Trinity Exeter, 1718A add./PFW 1–2)

1415   Palmer, Richard, canon of Exeter Cathedral (*Reg. Stafford*, p. 423)

1506   Parker, Thomas (PRO, PROB 11/15, f. 188v (24 Adeane))

1438   Parys, Maior, canon of Exeter Cathedral (*Reg. Lacy*, ed. Dunstan, IV, 33–4)

1362*   Parleben, John (MCR 35–36 Edw III, m. 8)

1494   Pascow, John, canon of Exeter Cathedral (PRO, PROB 11/10, ff. 115v–116r (15 Vox))

1418   Penels, Richard, canon of Exeter Cathedral (*Reg. Stafford*, pp. 420–1)

1415*   Pernell, Thomas (MCR 3–4 Hen V, m. 8)

1367*   Pestour, Lucy, wife of Roger (MCR 41–42 Edw III, m. 29)

1351*   Petherton, Andrew de, clerk (MCR 24–25 Edw III, m. 23)

1296*   Peverel, Hugh, knight (MCR 23–24 Edw I, m. 41)

1300*   Peverel, Thomas (MCR 27–28 Edw I, m. 28)

1506*   Pydiocke, John, prebendary of Crediton College (PRO, PROB 11/15 (21 Adeane))

1393*   Pyl, William, canon of Exeter Cathedral (MCR 16–17 Ric II, m. 15)

1244   Pinchun, Bartholomew (DRO, ECA, Book 53A, f. 16r); above, p. 139

1305*   Pynde, Joan (MCR 32–33 Edw I, m. 34)

1296*   Pynghe, Robert (MCR 23–24 Edw I, m. 27)

1296*   Pynge, Walter (MCR 23–24 Edw I, m. 27)

1377*   Pytman, Agnes, wife of John (MCR 1–2 Ric II, m. 10)

1402*   Pitte, Isabel, daughter of Simon atte (MCR 3 Hen IV, m. 50)

1464   Pyttes, John, canon of Exeter Cathedral (DRO, Chanter XII (ii), Reg. Bothe, ff. 50v–51r)

1302*   Planecumbe, Robert de (MCR 29–30 Edw I, m. 20)

1349*   Plegh, Fina, widow of Richard (MCR 22–23 Edw III, m. 30)

1348*   Plegh, Richard (MCR 22–23 Edw III, m. 1)

1483   Plente, John, canon of Exeter Cathedral (PRO, PROB 11/7, ff. 55v–56r (7 Logge)

1349*   Pocock, John (MCR 22–23 Edw III, m. 28)

1396   Polworthy, Andrew, baker (DRO, ED/M/551); will registered 1397 (MCR 20–21 Ric II, m. 23)

1406*   Poleworthy, T., baker (MCR 7 Hen IV, m. 37)

1457*   Pollyng, John (PRO, PROB 11/4 (11 Stokton))

1290   Ponte, Emer de; will registered 1291 (MCR 18–19 Edward I, m. 14d); above, pp. 146–7

1376*   Portysham, Richard (MCR 49–50 Edw III, m. 43)

1295*   Pot, Matilda (MCR 23–24 Edw I, m. 24)

1411   Poundestoke, William, canon of Exeter Cathedral (*Reg. Stafford*, pp. 403–4)

1414*   Prall, Richard (MCR 1–2 Hen V, m. 43)

1373*   Pricchere, Robert (MCR 46–47 Edw III, m. 19)

1343*   Proute, Matilda (MCR 16–17 Edw III, m. 52)

1357*   Qwynterel, William, son and heir of Abraham (MCR 30–31 Edw III, m. 38)

1322*   Radesle, Walter de (MCR 15–16 Edw II, m. 14)

1308*   Radeslo, Robert de (MCR 1–2 Edw II, m. 30)

1522*   Radway, Thomas (MCR 14–15 Hen VIII, m. 6)

1503   Rawlens, Robert (PRO, PROB 11/13, f. 240v (29 Blamyr); Canterbury Cathedral Archives, Register F, f. 212r)

1430   Redman, Thomas, canon of Exeter Cathedral (*Reg. Lacy*, ed. Dunstan, IV, 16)

1519   Reygny, William, canon of Chulmleigh and Crediton, and rector of Plymtree; probably died in Exeter (PRO, PROB 11/20, f. 83v (F.11 Maynwaryng))

1349*   Renebaud, Geoffrey (MCR 22–23 Edw III, m. 45)

1349*   Reva, John, vicar of Constantine (Cornwall) (MCR 22–23 Edw III, m. 37)

1313   Rewe, Thomas de; will registered 1313 (MCR 6–7 Edw II, m. 26)

1394*   Rye, John (MCR 17–18 Ric II, m. 16)

1410   Rygge, Robert, chancellor of Exeter Cathedral (PRO, PROB 11/2A, f. 160r (21 Marche))

1395*   Rygge, William (MCR 18–19 Ric II, m. 17)

1329*   Rixthyvele, Joan, widow of Henry atte (MCR 3–4 Edw III, m. 4)

1516   Robyns, John (PRO, PROB 11/19, f. 27v (4 Ayloffe))

         Rogers, Katherine – see Huddesfeld

1410*   Roos, John (MCR 11 Hen IV, m. 52)

1323*   Ropere, John le, of Bridport (MCR 16–17 Edw II, m. 36)

1428*   Ros, Joan, wife of William, widow of John Stapilton (MCR 6–7 Hen VI, m. 42)

1453   Rotherham, Richard, chancellor of Exeter Cathedral (*Reg. Lacy*, ed. Dunstan, IV, 61–3)

1341*   Rouland, William (MCR 15–16 Edw III, m. 6)

1462   Rowe, John, subdean of Exeter Cathedral (DRO, Chanter XII (i), Reg. Nevill, ff. 139v–140v)

1395   Row, William (DRO, ECA, Book 53A, f. 53r; ED/M/542); will registered 1395 (MCR 19–20 Ric II, m. 7)

1336   Rufford, Walter de, rector of All Hallows, Goldsmith Street, Exeter (MCR 9–10 Edw III, m. 36)

1536   Rugge, John, vicar of St Thomas, Cowick (Oliver, *Ecclesiastical Antiquities*, i, 57; Beatrix F. Cresswell, 'John Rugge, Vicar of St. Thomas by Exeter', *Devon and Cornwall Notes and Queries*, 17 (1932–3), pp. 163–7)

1497   Russell, John (DRO, 51/1/5/5)

1329*   Russel, Richard (MCR 2–3 Edw III, m. 38)

1497   Russell, Robert (DRO, 51/1/5/5); will registered 1503 (PRO, PROB 11/13 (22 Blamyr); Canterbury Cathedral Archives, Register F, f. 175v)

1329*   Russel, Walter, son of Richard (MCR 3–4 Edw III, m. 7)

1496   Ruygeway, Stephen, citizen; will registered 1499 (MCR 14–15 Hen VII, m. 47)

1316*   Sage, Aveline (MCR 10–11 Edw II, m. 5)

1319*   St Helen (Sancta Elena), William de, canon of Exeter Cathedral (MCR 12–13 Edw II, m. 29)

1309*   St Leonard, Nicholas de, clerk (MCR 2–3 Edw II, m. 48)

1454*   Salmon, John (PRO, PROB 11/4 (1 Stokton))

1514*   Sandeforth, Roger, canon of Exeter Cathedral (PRO, PROB 11/18 (1 Holder))

1291*   Sarger, Henry le (MCR 18–19 Edw I, m.15)

1314*   Sarger, Osbert le (MCR 7–8 Edw II, m. 51)

1382*   Scam, Henry (MCR 5–6 Ric II, m. 37)

1382*   Scobbe, John (MCR 5–6 Ric II, m. 49)

1415*   Scotesham, William (MCR 3–4 Hen V, m. 12)

1430*   Seyngler, Cecily, wife of Henry, widow of Stephen Lucas (MCR 8–9 Hen VI, m. 35)

1344   Seler, Richard le (MCR 1 Henry IV, m. 41d); will registered 1346 (MCR 20–21 Edw III, m. 1)

1387*   Serle, John (MCR 11–12 Ric II, m. 8)

1374?   Serle, Sara, wife of John (D&C VC/3103)

1331*   Sex, Thomas (MCR 4–5 Edw III, m. 50)

1410*   Shaplegh, John (MCR 11 Hen IV, m. 37)
         Sharpe – see Langedon

1426*   Shephurd, John, butcher (MCR 4–5 Hen VI, m. 21)
         Sherman, Robert – see Browne

1417   Shillyngford, Baldwin de, canon of Exeter Cathedral (*Reg. Stafford*, p. 417)

1388   Shillyngford, John de, canon of Exeter Cathedral (PRO, PROB 11/2A (13 Marche); *Reg. Stafford*, p. 387)

1425   Schute, John, archdeacon of Exeter (*Reg. Lacy*, ed. Dunstan, IV, 5–7)

1514*   Sydnor, William (PRO, PROB 11/18 (4 Holder))

1506   Sylke, William, precentor of Exeter Cathedral (PRO, PROB 11/15, f. 280r (22 Maynwaryng))

1524   Symon, John, mayor (PRO, PROB 11/22, f. 8r (1 Porch))

1319*   Skinnere, Matthew le (MCR 13–14 Edw II, m. 1)

1307   Skinner (Pelliparius), Richard (MCR I, m. 26)

1319*   Skinner, William (MCR 12–13 Edw II, m. 34)

1382*   Slegh, William, of Kenton (Devon) (MCR 5–6 Ric II, m. 41)

1349* Smale, John (MCR 22–23 Edw III, m. 26)

1328* Smalecombe, Agnes de (MCR 1–2 Edw III, m. 46)

1314* Smalecombe, John de (MCR 7–8 Edw II, m. 30)

1351* Smalecomb, William, vicar of Harberton (Devon) (MCR 24–25 Edw III, m. 20)

1288* Smith, Clarice, widow of Drogo the smith (MCR 15–16 Edw I, m. 29)

1431* Smyth, Roger, rector of Exminster (Devon) (MCR 9–10 Hen VI, m. 21)

1418* Smyth, Thomas (MCR 6–7 Hen V, m. 3)

1391* Smythesheghes, Thomas (MCR 14–15 Ric II, m. 46)

1448 Snetysham, John, chancellor of Exeter Cathedral (*Reg. Lacy*, ed. Dunstan, IV, 44)

1407 Somaister, Joan, widow of Richard Somaister of Netherexe (Antony House, Sir William Pole, 'Extracts from Deeds, Charters and Grants', no. 1978)

1369* Somaistre, John, dyer (MCR 42–43 Edw III, m. 46)

1374* Somer, William (MCR 47–48 Edw III, m. 29)

1353* Somery, John (MCR 26–27 Edw III, m. 15)

1509* Soper, Thomas, gentleman (PRO, PROB 11/16 (23 Bennett))

1349* Soth, Joan (MCR 22–23 Edw III, m. 26)

1327 Soth, Peter (DRO, ED/M/276); above, pp. 159–62

1518 Speke, Elizabeth, formerly Colshill, widow of Sir John Speke, knight, of White Lackington (Som.) (PRO, PROB 11/19, f. 136r (17 Ayloffe))

1517 Speke, Sir John, of White Lackington (Som.) (PRO, PROB 11/ 19, f. 70r (9 Ayloffe))

1311 Spenser, Henry le; will registered 1311 (DRO, ECA, Mayor's Court Rolls, 4–5 Edward II, m. 46)

1361* Spicer, John (MCR 35–36 Edw III, m. 8)

1361* Spicer, Katherine, wife of Thomas (MCR 35–36 Edw III, m. 4)

1361* Spicer, Thomas (MCR 35–36 Edw III, m.4)

1324* Spicer, William le (MCR 17–18 Edw II, m. 18)

   Spicer – see also Espicer

1349* Squier, Vincent (MCR 22–23 Edw III, m. 18)

1329* Squyer, Walter (MCR 2–3 Edw III, m. 18)

1418 Stafford, Edmund, bishop of Exeter (Lambeth Palace Library, Reg. Chichele, i, ff. 319r–321r; *Reg. Chichele*, ii, 153–60)

1394* Stayndrop, Thomas de, canon of Exeter Cathedral (MCR 17– 18 Ric II, m. 36)

1332* Stapledon, Richard de, brother of Bishop Walter (MCR 5–6 Edw III, m. 27)

   Stapilton – see also Ros

1314*   Stappe, Alice de la (MCR 8–9 Edw II, m. 1)
1321*   Stappe, John atte (MCR 14–15 Edw II, m. 39)
1291*   Stappe, Ralph de la (MCR 19–20 Edw I, m. 34)
1537   Stephyns, Henry, annuellar of Exeter Cathedral (DRO, 1049M/
        FW 33)
1346*   Steymor, Benedict (MCR 19–20 Edw III, m. 30)
1317*   Steymour, Philip le (MCR 10–11 Edw II, m. 26)
1271*   Steymur, William de (MCR 48 Hen III–2 Edw I, m. 23)
1326*   Steymour, William (MCR 20 Edw II–1 Edw III, m. 2)
1521*   Stynte, William, canon of Exeter Cathedral (PRO, PROB 11/20
        (22 Maynwaryng))
1432*   Stypyng, John (MCR 10–11 Hen VI, m. 47)
1328*   Stochaye, Robert de, knight (MCR 1–2 Edw III, m. 34)
1349*   Stoke, John de, canon of Glasney and rector of St Mellion,
        Cornwall (MCR 23–24 Edw III, m. 4)
1304*   Stok, Mazeline de, widow of William de Ashburton (MCR 32–
        33 Edw I, m. 3)
1431*   Stoklegh, John (MCR 9–10 Hen VI, m. 16)
1394*   Storre, John (MCR 17–18 Ric II, m. 51)
1320*   Strange, John, canon of Exeter Cathedral (MCR 14–15 Edw II,
        m. 8)
1349*   Strange, William (MCR 22–23 Edw III, m. 24)
1298*   Sude, Benedict, chaplain (MCR 25–26 Edw I, m. 26)
1349*   Sutton, John de (MCR 22–23 Edw III, m. 23)
1415*   Swan, Ralph (MCR 3–4 Hen V, m. 4)
1372   Swynesheved, John, canon of Exeter Cathedral (Lambeth Palace
        Library, Reg. Whittlesey, f. 125v)
1348   Tayller, John (MCR 22–23 Edw III, m. 13)
1492*   Taylour, John, chancellor of Exeter Cathedral (PRO, PROB 11/
        9 (23 Dogett))
1420   Talbot, John, citizen (DRO, ECA, Book 53A, f. 84r); will
        registered 1421 (MCR 9 Hen V–1 Hen VI, m. 13)
1400*   Tapper, William (MCR 1 Henry IV, m. 23)
1360*   Tauntefer, Thomas, rector of Clyst St Mary (Devon) (MCR 34–
        35 Edw III, m. 6)
1339*   Tauntefer, Walter (MCR 12–13 Edw III, m. 10)
1343*   Tauntifer, William (MCR 16–17 Edw II, m. 52)
1371*   Taverner, Richard (MCR 44–45 Edw III, m. 30)
1383   Taverner, Robert (DRO, 51/1/3/4); will registered 1386 (MCR
        9–10 Ric II, m. 54)
1351*   Taverner, Robert le (MCR 24–25 Edw III, m. 22)
1328*   Tavistok, Denise, wife of John de (MCR 1–2 Edw III, m. 21)
        Tavistock – see also Haye

1381   Vaggescombe, Robert, canon of Exeter Cathedral (Lambeth Palace Library, Reg. Courtenay, f. 200r)

1326*   Venella, William de (MCR 20 Edw II–1 Edw III, m. 8)

1318*   Verour, Walter le (MCR 1–12 Edw II, m. 17)

1535   Veysey, William, apparitor general of the bishop (DRO, Moger Wills, xxi, 7428)

1316*   Vyel, John (MCR 9–10nEdw II, m. 41)

1517*   Vygurs, William (PRO, PROB 11/19 (7 Ayloffe))

1325*   Vyk, William (MCR 18–19 Edw II, m. 17)

1506*   Vude, Richard (PRO, PROB 11/15, f. 184v (23 Adeane))

1302*   Wadekyng, Emma (MCR 29–30 Edw I, m. 43)

1331*   Waleys, Nicholas (MCR 4–5 Edw III, m. 25)

1465   Ward, John, canon of Exeter Cathedral (DRO, Chanter XII (ii), Reg. Bothe, ff. 51v–52r)

1391*   Warre, John, bishop of *Cumanagiensis* (MCR 14–15 Ric II, m. 44)

1412   Watelyngton, Roger, layman (*Reg. Stafford*, p. 398)

1369   Waterford, Nicholas (DRO, ED/M/432)

1422*   Waye, Elizabeth, wife of Henry atte (MCR 9 Hen V–1 Hen VI, m. 28)

1369*   Waye, Joan, daughter of John (MCR 42–43 Edw III, m. 25)

1477   Waye, Richard (DRO, ED/M/872)

1349*   Webbe, Thomas (MCR 22–23 Edw III, m. 27)

1387*   Webber, Estmund (MCR 11–12 Ric II, m. 8)

1472   Webber, Henry, dean of Exeter Cathedral (D&C 2365)

1389*   Webber, John (MCR 12–13 Ric II, m. 37)

1321*   Wele, John (MCR 14–15 Edw II, m. 36)

1295*   Wele, Matilda (MCR 23–24 Edw I, m. 1)

1465   Were, Robert (DRO, Holy Trinity Exeter, 1718A add./PFW 11)

1405*   Westcote, Beatrice (MCR 6 Hen IV, m. 44)

1411   Westcote, John, rector of St Petroc, Exeter, and canon of Exeter Cathedral (*Reg. Stafford*, pp. 418–19)

1332*   Wethergrave, Nicholas de (MCR 5–6 Edw III, m. 24)

1375   Whyker, John (D&C VC/3079); will registered 1375 (MCR 49–50 Edw III, m. 13)

1307*   Whyte, Juliana, widow of John (MCR 34–35 Edw I, m. 17)

1349*   White, Walter (MCR 22–23 Edw III, m. 21)

1338*   Whitebrother, John (MCR 11–12 Edw III, m. 11)

1346*   Whiteslegh, Thomas de (MCR 19–20 Edw III, m. 17)

1377*   Whythorn, William (MCR 50 Edw III–1 Ric II, m. 24)

1314*   Wycher, Matilda, widow of Robert (MCR 7–8 Edw II, m. 28)

1327*   Wyk, Beatrice, daughter of William de (MCR 1–2 Edw III, m. 2)

1375*   Wyke, William (MCR 48–49 Edw III, m. 32)

1327*   Wylde, Isabel la (MCR 20 Edw II–1 Edw III, m. 26)

1391   Wylde, Joan (DRO, ED/M/526); will registered 1393 (MCR 16–
        17 Ric II, m. 40)
1307*   Wilde, Nicholas le (MCR 34–35 Edw I, m. 34)
1418*   Wilford, John (MCR 5–6 Hen V, m. 30)
1397*   Wilford, Robert (MCR 20–21 Ric II, m. 17)
1476   Wylfford, Robert; will registered 1477 (MCR 17–18 Edw IV,
        m. 7)
1413   Wilford, William, citizen (*Reg. Stafford*, pp. 401–2)
1414*   Wilforde, William (MCR 1–2 Hen V, m. 41)
1511   Wilfford, William, esquire (DRO, ED/M/980)
1345*   Wille, Anastasia de la (MCR 18–19 Edw III, m. 27)
1350*   Wille, Isabel atte (MCR 24–25 Edw III, m. 9)
1377*   Wille, Isabel, widow of Roger atte (MCR 50 Edw III–1 Ric II,
        m. 31)
1401*   Wylle, John atte (MCR 3 Hen Iv, m. 5)
1377*   Wille, Roger atte (MCR 50 Edw III–1 Ric II, m. 31)
1459   Wynard, John (PRO, PROB 11/5, f. 193r (25 Godyn))
1442   Wynard, William, recorder of Exeter (PRO, PROB 11/1, f. 104r)
1348*   Winchester, John, priest (MCR 21–22 Edw III, m. 20)
1383*   Wyndesore, John (MCR 6–7 Ric II, m. 41)
1326*   Windsor, Walter de (MCR 19–20 Edw II, m. 28)
1332*   Wyntonia, Juliana, wife of William le Hopere (MCR 5–6 Edw
        III, m. 48)
1436   Wyse, Joan, wife of John (D&C VC/3182).
1537   Wyse, Thomas, canon of Exeter Cathedral (PRO, PROB 11/32
        (10 Populwell))
1310*   Wyther, Roger (MCR 3–4 Edw II, m. 34)
1352*   Withoun, Reginald (MCR 26–27 Edw III, m. 8)
1348*   Wyval, Christine (MCR 21–22 Edw III, m. 35)
1290*   Wockesweye, Stephen de (MCR 18–19 Edw I, m. 9)
1363*   Wode, Cecily atte (MCR 36–37 Edw III, m. 34)
1381*   Wode, William atte (MCR 4–5 Ric II, m. 22)
1349   Wodelegh, Agnes de, wife of John White (DRO, 51/1/2/1); will
        registered 1350 (MCR 23–24 Edw III, m. 21); above, pp.
        163–6
1371*   Wodelond, Walter de, knight (MCR 44–45 Edw III, m. 26)
1349*   Wolbeater, Matilda, widow of Nicholas le, butcher (MCR 22–
        23 Edw III, m. 20)
1309*   Wood (Bosco), Adam de, priest (MCR 2–3 Edw II, m. 20)
1506   Worth, Elizabeth, widow (PRO, PROB 11/15, f. 102r (13
        Adeane))
1487   Worth, Roger (PRO, PROB 11/8, f. 116r (14 Milles))
1369   Woterford, Nichola, widow (DRO, ED/M/432)

1317*   Wotton, Alice, widow of Robert de (MCR 10–11 Edw II, m. 42)

1244   Wullaveston, William de, canon of Exeter Cathedral (British Library, Cotton MS Vitellius D.ix, f. 104r); above, pp. 139–40

1399*   Ynndover, Thomas (MCR 1 Henry IV, m. 7)

1510   Yorke, William, citizen and merchant (PRO, PROB 11/14, f. 288r (36 Holgrave))

    Yott – see Hyette

1341*   Yunge, John le (MCR 15–16 Edw III, m. 10)

1348*   Yunge, Stephen le, priest (MCR 22–23 Edw III, m. 11)

1349*   Yunge, Walter, vicar choral of Exeter Cathedral (MCR 22–23 Edw III, m. 18)

Part III

Memory

Introduction to Part III

Remembrance in and around Exeter: 900–1200

There was a third important dimension to death in the middle ages: the wish to be remembered afterwards. This wish arose from motives both secular and religious. The desire not to be forgotten goes back to pagan times and to funeral monuments such as barrows and mounds. Beowulf, in the Anglo-Saxon poem, asks to have a mound built for him on a headland, so that travellers may see it and think of him.[1] Christianity added to this the idea that commemorating those who had died, by saying prayers or giving alms, was a deed of merit that would improve their spiritual standing in the next world. People were, no doubt, remembered and prayed for in Exeter from late Roman times, but the earliest written evidence of the fact comes from the late Anglo-Saxon period. The so-called 'Leofric Missal', formerly belonging to Exeter Cathedral, contains 17 notes of dates of people's deaths, implying that the cathedral clergy prayed for those concerned on the dates in question (Document 24). The notes were probably made before the end of the eleventh century, since they mention only the first bishop of Devon, Eadwulf (909–34), and his two most recent successors, Lyfing (1027–46) and Leofric (1046–72). Most of the other people named are clergy (none of them linked with a particular place or foundation), together with a few laymen and women. An interest in the wider world is shown by the inclusion of William the Conqueror, his queen Matilda, and Lambert of Spoleto, king of Italy (d. 898). There are also some year-dates of the deaths of English kings and bishops, in the manner of a series of annals.

The practice of recording dates of death at Exeter Cathedral continued, after they ceased in the Leofric Missal, in a copy of Usuard's *Martyrology* written at Exeter in the early twelfth century (Document 25).[2] The

---

[1] *Beowulf with the Finnesburh Fragment*, ed. C.L. Wrenn, 3rd ed., rev. W.F. Bolton (London, 1973), lines 2802–8.

[2] On the manuscript, see N.R. Ker, *Medieval Manuscripts in British Libraries*, 4 vols (Oxford, 1969–92), ii, 828.

Martyrology was a handbook listing the saints commemorated on each day of the year and, in later times, was read out daily to the clergy in the chapter house. Such a book constituted a calendar, and during the twelfth century its margins came to be used for noting names and dates of deaths. The earliest name is that of Bishop Leofric in 1072, and the next are those of his successor Osbern (1072–1103) and of some of the cathedral clergy of Osbern's reign. No attempt, however, was made to incorporate names (other than Leofric) from the Leofric Missal or from other late Anglo-Saxon sources, so that the evidence of the *Martyrology* effectively begins in Osbern's reign. It is not, unfortunately, a complete text. The surviving pages of the volume include only the days from 8 February to 10 October and 6 to 30 December, and the deaths recorded within these periods. Even here not all the names survive since some have been scraped out, presumably because they were no longer being honoured. The entries were first systematically transcribed by G.H. Doble (d. 1945) whose typescript of them is preserved in the cathedral library. His transcript contains a number of errors, some of which have found their way into Frank Barlow's edition of the acts of the bishops of Exeter from 1046 to 1257, a work that includes the first attempt to list in print all the dignitaries and canons of that period.[3]

The entries of deaths in the *Martyrology*, when they survive, are informative in up to five respects. These comprise people's names, descriptions of their status or rank, the calendar date of their death, the year of their death, and the way in which they were commemorated. Two kinds of commemoration seem to have existed. One was what might be termed 'ordinary', in which a dead person's name was inserted in the prayers of the normal round of worship on the appropriate day, and the other was what the *Martyrology* calls 'a solemn service'. This appears to have been a special act of worship, probably a mass dedicated to commemorating the dead person: similar to what, by the later thirteenth century, was called an 'obit mass'. The earliest names in the volume are forenames alone: Anglo-Saxon and Norman ones. Later names reflect the great name-change of the twelfth century, in which a smaller body of forenames became popular, mixing Anglo-Saxon, Norman, Biblical, and saints' names.[4] Surnames gradually became added, and were normal by the thirteenth century. The overwhelming majority of entries, as one would expect, were those of bishops and cathedral clergy. In the case of clergy it was usual to state their office (archdeacon, dean, or canon) and their ranking in holy orders (priest,

---

[3] Frank Barlow (ed.), *English Episcopal Acta: XI. Exeter 1046–1184; XII. Exeter 1186–1257*, 2 vols (Oxford, 1996), ii, 301–21.

[4] On this subject, see Robert Bartlett, *The Making of Europe* (London, 1994), pp. 270–80.

deacon, subdeacon, or acolyte). Not all clergy were priests in this period, and even some cathedral canons seem never to have progressed beyond the lesser orders.

Nearly all the twelfth- and thirteenth-century bishops of Exeter are listed in the *Martyrology*. The cathedral dignitaries and canons are less fully recorded and there was evidently no automatic right that this should be done. Clergy probably had to make a payment or give an endowment, and the erasure of some of the names may reflect the fact that these gifts had been exhausted: a practice that is known to have happened in confraternities elsewhere.[5] A minority of names, as in the Leofric Missal, are those of outsiders to the cathedral. They include a few important lay people, notably William Rufus, Adela the mother of King Stephen, and William Brewer, the great Devon landowner and benefactor of the thirteenth century. Other clergy, laymen, and laywomen are simply designated as 'our brother' or 'our sister', and were evidently less exalted people: inhabitants of Exeter or elsewhere in Devon who had been recognised as members of the cathedral's confraternity. This confraternity does not seem to have been an organised body, like a guild, but a privilege granted to individuals in return for their goodwill or the benefactions they had made. A few of the benefactions are recorded. Algar had built 'Christ Church': either the chapel of that name off the High Street or the parish church also known as Holy Trinity, both of which later belonged to the cathedral. Ailmer Laking and Robert Sclich had each given rent charges levied on local property.

The cathedral's arrangements for commemorating the dead were probably the most sophisticated in Exeter during the late eleventh and twelfth centuries, but they were not unique. The city included at least one guild by the late Anglo-Saxon period, perhaps the eleventh century, whose statutes survive. They provide that the guild members, who appear to have been prosperous people of Exeter or Devon, should meet three times a year for worship and fellowship, and arrange for psalters or masses to be said for their colleagues who died.[6] The Exeter Book, the great anthology of Anglo-Saxon poetry that Leofric left to the cathedral, contains outer leaves that were subsequently used as a register of documents, including some lists of members of guilds in Devon (Document 26). The lists are undated but seem to have been written down in about 1100, or a decade or two either side. Fourteen guilds are represented, all in the countryside

---

[5] Joelle Rollo-Koster, 'Forever After: the dead in the Avignonese confraternity of Notre Dame la Majour (1329–1381)', *Journal of Medieval History*, 25 (1999), pp. 115–140, especially pp. 115–16, 121, 129.

[6] Benjamin Thorpe, *Diplomatarium Anglicum Aevi Saxonici* (London, 1865), pp. 613–14, translated in *English Historical Documents c.500–1042*, ed. Dorothy Whitelock (London, 1968), pp. 558–9.

near Exeter. East of the city there are four in Woodbury parish (including one at Nutwell), two at Colaton Ralegh, and one each at Axmouth, Broadclyst, Clyst St George, and Sidmouth. To the west there is one at Bridford, two in Whitestone parish, and possibly a fourth, said to be based at *Legh* which may be Doddiscombsleigh. In each case the names of the guild members are given, ranging in number from 12 to 45, the names being entirely Anglo-Saxon or Scandinavian with the exception of a cleric named Isaac and a William, apparently a Norman, at *Legh*, where he is given a prominent place.

The makers of the lists observed some care in setting out the order of names. Priests (if any) are listed first, then laymen, and women usually last. Men or women with the same name are sometimes coupled together, but there are fewer women than men. Most of the people concerned cannot have been of high status, in view of the fact that Woodbury had four guilds and Colaton and Whitestone two, which must have gathered in a great many of the men of these parishes. Why were the names recorded? It seems that, at some point around 1100, the cathedral tried to generate goodwill and money by offering to include the names of local people in its prayers, or else responded to requests from local people for that to be done. Very likely a down payment or regular subscription was made in return for the prayers. It is not stated whether the members were living or dead, and either eventuality is possible. No mention is made of when any prayers would be said, so the guilds and their members may have been commemorated on some kind of cyclical basis, once a month or once a year. It was clearly intended to maintain the relationship with the guilds on a long-term basis, because empty spaces were left on the pages for the addition of more names and about a dozen more were subsequently included. In one case a name was erased, presumably through its owner leaving the guild or not paying his dues. There is also an untitled section containing a single entry in Latin, 'Ordeua, our sister', which looks as if a separate attempt was being made to record members admitted to the confraternity, mentioned above. It was not followed up, however, and the practice of enrolling these rural guilds does not seem to have endured for very long either, unless the records were transferred to some other documents now lost.

Remembrance in the City: 1200–1500

The earliest lists of people being commemorated in the city of Exeter, apart from the cathedral records, come from the twelfth and thirteenth centuries. They are both in calendar order: one relating to the parish church of St Martin (Document 27), and the other to the city guild of Kalendars (Document 28). The parish list is the smaller of the two and survives only in a transcript in the medieval cartulary of the hospital of St John, Exeter, taken, so the cartulary states, 'from an old missal of St Martin'. This appears to refer to the parish church of that name since the transcript includes a mention of its dedication in 1065. The list contains 25 names: five clergy, fifteen laymen, and five laywomen, with the dates on which their commemorations took place and the sums of money that were paid for this purpose. As has already been mentioned, Exeter had as many as 29 chapels by the end of the eleventh century, of which about 24 (including St Martin) were given parochial status in 1222 and came to be regarded as parish churches.[7] It is likely that many of these chapels and churches commemorated the dead and kept records of the fact in similar calendars, although no other such sources have survived. The guild of Kalendars, on the other hand, was a city-wide organisation, dating back to at least the twelfth century and therefore preceding the establishment of the parishes. It included clergy, laymen, and laywomen, and took its name from its custom of meeting on the 'kalends', the first day of the month, to celebrate mass with intercessions for the souls of its members, living and dead. There were similarly named guilds in at least two other southern English towns, Bristol and Winchester, with parallel functions.[8]

The Exeter guild possessed a small amount of property in the form of rent charges and tenements that had been bequeathed to it, but it was not wealthy and does not seem to have employed permanent priests to pray for the dead, like its counterpart in Bristol. During the thirteenth century its masses took place in the parish church of St Mary Major, presumably celebrated by its clergy members or by other clergy hired for the occasion. The guild was still an independent body in 1336, but by the end of the fourteenth century it had ceased to exist and its property had passed to the vicars choral of the cathedral, who went on celebrating the masses until the Reformation. Before this change took place, a list of the names of the deceased members was drawn up for recitation at the monthly masses, apparently in the early fourteenth century. It is written in a large script to assist legibility, like the script of a church service book, and gathers the names under months without specifying the days within the months. Whoever compiled the list appears to have used earlier written sources, probably calendars containing dates of death. This has given rise to some mistakes

[7] *Ordinale Exon*, ed. J.N. Dalton and G.H. Doble, 4 vols, Henry Bradshaw Society, 37–8, 63, 79 (1909, 1926, 1941), i, p. xxi; Frances Rose-Troup, *Lost Chapels of Exeter* (Exeter, 1923), pp. 10–11. The number 29 may include the cathedral itself.

[8] Nicholas Orme, 'The Kalendar Brethren of the City of Exeter', *Devonshire Association Transactions*, 109 (1977), pp. 153–69; idem, 'The Guild of Kalendars, Bristol', *Bristol and Gloucestershire Archaeological Society Transactions*, 96 (1978), pp. 33–52.

or obscurities in the names, due to faulty transcription, and to an order of names that at first sight appears to be random, linking important and unimportant people. In fact the order probably reflects the earlier sources, listing the deaths in the sequence in which they occurred during the month.

The list contains about 927 names of guild members, apparently stretching in time from the early twelfth to the early fourteenth century. They consist of a mixture of clergy, laymen, and laywomen, numbering 155, 409, and 363 respectively. The clergy are the easiest to identify, since their names are followed by indications of office or status. There are five bishops of Exeter: Leofric, William Warelwast, Robert Warelwast, Bartholomew, and William Brewer. Leofric may perhaps be there on historical grounds, but the presence of the next three bishops is a strong indication that the guild existed in their days: the twelfth century. The cathedral community is represented by a dean, a chancellor, a treasurer, eight archdeacons, eleven canons, and fourteen vicars choral. The rest of the clergy are described merely as priests or chaplains, and probably represent the men who served the parish churches and chapels of the city and its neighbourhood. Two 'deans' who are not known to have been cathedral deans were apparently rural deans of Exeter, and four clergy are identified in relation to specific churches: Azo chaplain of St Mary, Hugh priest of Kenn, John chaplain of St Paul, and Thomas chaplain of St Mary Major. There are also two anchorites and five clerks. While the parish clergy appear to have been involved with the guild throughout the twelfth and thirteenth centuries, the same was not true of the bishops and cathedral dignitaries. Nearly all those who were members – 13 of the 16 who were more than mere canons – belonged before the year 1200, and only three afterwards. It seems that as the Church's leaders grew in wealth and involvement in concerns outside the city, they ceased to be associated with a society primarily made up of local clergy and laity.

The laity are less easy to identify. The men are usually given only names and surnames, and although the latter are sometimes occupational names, it is hard to know if these denote current employment or are inherited names. In a very few cases an occupation is given in addition to a surname: Richard Bonde (dyer), Henry Criditon (carpenter), Richard Dyrkyn (apothecary), William Hog (tanner), John de Miluertone (baker), and Isabel de Tadiforde (seamstress). Some of the women in the guild are linked with their husbands – about 40 married couples can be identified – but the marital status of most of the women is not indicated. The probability is that some were widows. Seven mayors of the city appear to be represented: Roger Beyuin, Hilary Blund, Walter le Chaue, William Durling, William Gatepathe, Martin Prodomme, Walter Turbert, and Nicholas de Yuelcestre.

There are also seven of the city's provosts and three of its seneschals.[9] As most of these lived in the thirteenth century, it appears that the guild continued to attract support from the upper echelons of the city during this period, unlike the higher clergy. It must therefore have been the chief religious fellowship in Exeter between about 1100 and 1300, though its failure to collect large endowments or to survive the fourteenth century warns us against overestimating its significance.

When the vicars choral took over the duty of celebrating the kalendar masses in that century, they kept the list of names which now survives as part of a composite volume, formerly in the vicars' archives, containing documents relating to masses for the dead for which the vicars were responsible. The guild membership seems to have withered away at about the time that the guild was wound up, since there is no indication of a regular recruitment of new members after the 1330s. A number of new names, however, were inserted into the margins of the original list during the fourteenth and fifteenth centuries: some 74 in all. The latest are two cathedral canons who lived at the end of the fifteenth century: John Taylor and William Sylke. Those added included several husbands and wives and, in the case of Richard and Joan Heydon, the names of their seven children. The people concerned were probably being commemorated because they had given benefactions to the vicars choral, or had been admitted to some kind of confraternity with them – a relationship that was spiritual (as in the eleventh century) rather than expressed through a social organisation.

The guild of Kalendars, even at the height of its popularity, never accounted for all the commemoration of the dead in Exeter. Every local church and clergyman was potentially anxious to be involved in this process, in order to attract the goodwill and donations that accompanied it. The two or three dozen parish clergy who served the city churches were particularly appropriate to pray for the dead, given the small size of their parishes and the slenderness of their incomes. In the twelfth century, when there seems to have been a strong sense of belonging to the community of the city, some wealthy citizens left endowments sufficient to pay 1d. to every chapel in Exeter for prayers on their anniversaries. The calendar of St Martin mentions eleven such payments, one of which is credited to a grant by 'King William' and a second to Robert, archdeacon of Totnes (fl. 1170–1186).[10] A third was that of Peter of Palerna, made between 1209 and 1215, and now famous because his grant identifies the chapels and places them in topographical order, enabling us to locate them.[11] John de

[9] R.C. Easterling, 'Lists of Civic Officials in Exeter in the 12th and 13th Centuries', *Devonshire Association Transactions*, 70 (1938), pp. 455–494.

[10] DRO, ECA, Book 53A, f. 36r.

[11] D&C 2513, printed in Rose-Troup, *Lost Chapels of Exeter*, p. 47.

Doulys gave a single payment of the same kind in 1267,[12] and the device was still in being when Richard de Neweton made a permanent grant for the purpose in 1298.[13] By the fourteenth century, on the other hand, this sense of community seems to have declined, as did the Kalendars' guild, in favour of allegiances to individual churches and membership of diversified religious guilds. Bequests for prayers became more usually given to individual churches: both parish churches of the city and the local monasteries and friaries. Friars especially busied themselves in prayers for the dead, which their comparatively large communities enabled them to say in a short period of time, notably 'trentals' or groups of thirty masses.[14]

The task of listing all the benefactions for prayers in the churches of Exeter is beyond the scope of this volume. It would take a good deal of effort to compile a register of all that could be known, using the surviving Exeter wills, the numerous deeds endowing obits, and the five sets of churchwardens' accounts still extant from before the Reformation. Most money given for prayers was for the short-term only. Those who died, or their relatives, would pay for a single funeral mass, perhaps followed up by masses with prayers for the dead a month and a year after the death. Wealthier people might commission a month's worth of masses, or what was known as an 'obit' or 'anniversary': a mass of intercession said on the anniversary of the death for a number of years. In 1373, for example, the wardens of St Mary Major undertook to keep the anniversary of their late rector, Andrew de Lappeflod, in return for a sum of £4 in silver and a silver-gilt cup, and promised to distribute 3s. at the anniversary until the money ran out.[15] Only the very rich could afford to endow permanent obits on their anniversaries, and few even of them had the resources to found a chantry employing a full-time priest to say mass for their souls every day. The earliest chantry to be founded in the city was that of Walter Gervas in about 1258 in the chapel on Exe Bridge (Document 5), but it does not appear to have been followed by more than a handful of others. This emerges from the survey of chantries and permanent obits in the city, made in 1548 when the government of Edward VI suppressed them and confiscated their endowments. In that year (by which time, of course, the monasteries and friaries had disappeared) the commissioners in charge of the suppression identified only four chantries maintaining a full-time priest,

---

[12] See above, p. 145.

[13] DRO, 51/1/1/6.

[14] Compare the notes of obits taken by William Worcester from the calendar of Bodmin (Franciscan) Friary in 1478 (William Worcester, *Itineraries*, ed. J.H. Harvey (Oxford, 1969) p. 93).

[15] DRO, 51/1/2/7.

two religious guilds doing the same for their members corporately, about 45 long-term or permanent obits, and three other endowed masses.[16]

Remembrance at the Cathedral: 1300–1548

The remainder of the records in this part of the book relates to Exeter Cathedral in the fourteenth and fifteenth centuries, and we must now return to its role in the commemoration of the dead. During the thirteenth century this had come to centre on masses rather than on other kinds of prayers, reflecting the growth of the doctrine of transubstantiation. The consecrated bread and wine of the mass was now believed to become the real body and blood of Christ, and intercessions then made in His presence were considered to be the most effective kinds of prayer. The cathedral continued to pray for some people in its regular services after 1300, as we see from the fifteenth-century bidding prayer (Document 38), which lists the kings of England, bishops of Exeter, and a few other named persons. But no names were added to the *Martyrology* after 1282, and most of the names in that volume do not appear in later records. Instead commemoration was increasingly carried out through special masses endowed for particular people: daily masses (known as chantries) and annual ones (called 'anniversaries' or 'obits'). By the early fourteenth century nearly all the people mentioned in cathedral records as being commemorated were those who had set up a chantry or obit for themselves, or had had one established on their behalf.

The most ambitious form of commemoration was the chantry of one or more priests to say mass every day. Unlike the city of Exeter, where few such foundations were made, the cathedral attracted over twenty between the 1220s and 1530s, and the need of the chantry priests for altars at which to say mass was probably one of the motives for enlarging the second cathedral into the third between about 1270 and about 1340.[17] The earliest chantry in the cathedral was founded by a local knight, Sir John de Montacute, between 1224 and 1228, and a further thirteen were added between then and 1332, supporting a total of 21 chantry priests.[18] This was about the same number of priests as at Lichfield Cathedral, but far

---

[16] Nicholas Orme, 'The Dissolution of the Chantries in Devon, 1546–8', *Devonshire Association Transactions*, 111 (1979), pp. 106–7.

[17] On this subject, see Nicholas Orme, *Exeter Cathedral As It Was: 1050–1550* (Exeter, 1986), p. 16.

[18] On the history of the cathedral chantries, see Nicholas Orme, 'The Medieval Chantries of Exeter Cathedral', *Devon and Cornwall Notes and Queries*, 34 (1981), pp. 319–26; 35 (1982), pp. 12–21, 67–71.

smaller than the 40 or so at York Minster and the 74 at St Paul's London.[19] Chantries were relatively cheap to found up to the late 1340s, when the population was large and contained a substantial number of clergy seeking employment. Men would work as chantry priests for as little as £2 10s. or £3 a year, necessitating an endowment worth about twenty times as much in capital value. Most of the chantries founded at Exeter Cathedral during the late thirteenth and early fourteenth centuries were established by or on behalf of bishops or cathedral dignitaries, like Dean Andrew Kilkenny (Document 30). There were only two exceptions: the foundations of Mont-acute and another Devon knight, Sir John Wyger. The clergy who served the cathedral chantries were known as 'annuellars', a term that was used elsewhere in England of priests who were hired to say masses for a year at a time, but at Exeter meant ones with permanent appointments. The annuel-lars were not originally members of the cathedral foundation, but they soon became integrated with it and were required to attend cathedral services and submit to cathedral discipline, just as if they belonged to the foundation like the vicars choral.

The Black Death of 1348–9 dealt a severe blow at chantries throughout the kingdom. It reduced the population and also the number of clergy, which never again reached the high levels of the early fourteenth century. More opportunities opened up to become rectors or vicars of parishes, so the poorly paid work of the chantry priests became less popular, and many existing chantry endowments were unable to provide enough income for the higher wages required. Some of the Exeter Cathedral chantries were suspended after 1349, and the complement of annuellars fell to about a dozen. This situation lasted until the 1370s, when there was something of a revival of clergy numbers and a renewal of interest in founding chantries at Exeter. In 1379 Bishop Brantingham (1370–94) endowed one for himself, staffed by two priests, and three further chantries came into existence between then and 1408. After this foundations dwindled again, although there were further examples in 1472, 1518, 1525, and 1531. By the early sixteenth century the number of the priests had risen again to 18, three less than its height in the 1340s. The founders of chantries after the Black Death resembled those before it by being principally bishops and cathedral dignitaries. The knightly founders, as before, were two: the Courtenay earl of Devon in 1385 and Sir John Speke in 1518.

Obits cost less to endow than chantries, and were therefore a more widely achievable form of commemoration. In principle all that was needed for an obit was to provide an annual sum for a single priest to say a mass of intercession for a few pence, but the obits observed at Exeter Cathedral

---

[19] Kathleen Edwards, *The English Secular Cathedrals in the Middle Ages*, 2nd ed. (Manchester and New York, 1967), p. 288.

were more grandiose services, probably held in the cathedral choir and attended by many of the cathedral clergy, each of whom got a small payment for coming. Even so the expenses of a fourteenth-century obit, usually about 7s. a year, cost a seventh or less to endow than the price of a chantry. By 1305 some 56 obits were celebrated at Exeter Cathedral during the year, so that they occurred at the rate of about one each week, and by the early fifteenth century there were over 100. Here again Exeter's obits can be compared with one of the lesser English cathedrals like Hereford, which had about 50 in the fourteenth century, whereas St Paul's observed 111 in the same period, twice as many.[20] Their history at Exeter can be charted from two kinds of records: obit accounts and liturgical calendars, of which the accounts form the larger body of material. Obit accounts were financial records, kept at Exeter in the form of books not rolls. They recorded the celebration of each endowed obit during the year, together with notes of the attendances of clergy at the obit and the payments of money made to those who came.

We do not know when the practice of keeping such accounts began at Exeter, but it probably commenced in the late thirteenth century or just after 1300. The earliest surviving account begins at Midsummer 1305, and the present volume contains translations of this and its successors for the two years to Midsummer 1307 (Document 29). The series then continues, with a few gaps, to 1467.[21] The early obit accounts tend to be more interesting than the later ones, because they contain a wider variety of contents including non-standard receipts and payments. This variety gradually disappears during the early fourteenth century, and the accounts adopt an increasingly rigid and predictable form. They were drawn up in the cathedral exchequer by the two clerks of the exchequer (who were usually vicars choral or annuellars) under the supervision of the two stewards of the exchequer (who were canons). An account was produced for each quarter of the year, beginning at Christmas, Easter, Midsummer (St John Baptist Day), and Michaelmas. Within these quarters the clerks listed the obits roughly in the order that they took place but not always exactly so, presumably because delays in handling income or making payments might cause the records of obits to fall slightly out of their true order.

Several kinds of information about the obits are provided. They include the name of the person commemorated, the amount of money available for distribution, and sometimes an indication of the categories of clergy

---

[20] Edwards, *The English Secular Cathedrals*, pp. 46–7, 286.

[21] On the obit accounts, which survive from 1305 to 1365, in a broken series from 1371 to 1404, and fairly completely from 1414 to 1467, see Audrey M. Erskine, 'The Medieval Financial Records of the Cathedral Church of Exeter', *Journal of the Society of Archivists*, 2 no 6 (1962), pp. 262–3.

who were meant to be present. Some obits (perhaps the earliest ones) seem to have envisaged only canons as taking part, and provided payments merely for them. Others, like that of Andrew Kilkenny (Document 30), aimed to include all the clergy. In their case the accounts state the sums of money to be paid to each grade of the clergy, graduated according to rank. Typically a canon might receive 4d., a vicar choral 2d., an annuellar and a secondary clerk 1d., and a chorister ½d. Occasionally an obit founder specified the making of distributions to people and places outside the cathedral: the poor, the leper hospital of St Mary Magdalene, the priory of St Nicholas, the two friaries, or the parish clergy of Exeter. These sums too are noted, because the cathedral was responsible for paying them. The obit entries usually conclude with a list of the names of the dignitaries and canons present at the obit, together with the amount they each received, but the minor cathedral clergy are not named in this way.

The money available for the canons was scrupulously divided down to the last farthing. Occasionally a few pence would be withheld because they could not be shared out, or added so as to make up a round sum per person. By mentioning the names of dignitaries and canons, the accounts provide an excellent means of ascertaining which of them were involved in cathedral worship. Only about two thirds of the 24 canons normally resided in Exeter, of whom several might turn up at the obits for short periods but only a few were invariable in their attendance. A refinement of the system of distribution should also be noticed: a canon who died was regarded as still resident for one year after his death and continued to receive all the payments to resident canons, including obit distributions. This privilege was customarily used for charitable purposes: thus Thomas Boteler, archdeacon of Totnes (d. 1264), gave his entitlements to the Exeter friaries.[22] The accounts also contain a variety of information that was not concerned with obits. This is because they were 'canons' accounts' as much as obit accounts, and listed items of income to which the canons were entitled. One of these consisted of funeral offerings, which were divided among the canons like the obit payments. During the early fourteenth century it was customary for the accounts to record the name of the dead person if the offerings amounted to a couple of shillings or more, since this was enough to be shared in its own right. As has already been noted, however, the names include only some of the wealthy propertied people of Exeter who died at this time; it is not clear why.[23] The funerals of very poor people evidently produced only a few pence, and this money tended to be kept until there was enough to distribute. It was then recorded simply as 'for certain corpses', without saying whose they were. Before long, all

[22] See above, pp. 142–3.
[23] Compare the names in the list of wills, pp. 203–27.

the funeral information diminishes and it ceases to be recorded after the middle of the fourteenth century.

Another regular item in the accounts consists of the rents forthcoming from the property of the dean and chapter in Exeter. These were gathered by a special collector of rents, paid into the exchequer quarterly, and divided among the canons. Income from three Cornish churches – St Breward, St Erth, and St Eval – is also regularly noted, as are the 'pentecostal offerings' which had to be made by every household in the diocese at Pentecost (Whitsuntide). The offerings are sometimes subdivided into the money received from Cornwall and from Devon. During the early fourteenth century, the members of the chapter agreed to pay half their 'prebends' or basic entitlements of income towards the cost of building the cathedral, then currently in progress. This money too appears in the obit accounts. Each of the 24 canons was entitled to 20s. a quarter as his prebend, and half of this, making a total of £12, was paid by the exchequer clerks to the clerk of the works who supervised the finances of the building project. The clerks also received the money deposited in the various collecting boxes inside the cathedral, which amounted to a sum of £1 or more every quarter. Half of the profits from the boxes went to the treasurer, who had to maintain the furnishings and ornaments of the cathedral, and half to the canons, the treasurer (if he was a resident canon) also counting as a canon for this purpose.

A number of small payments are also mentioned in the accounts. Every year a sum of about 7s. 6d. was divided among the canons for wine on St Martin's Day, 11 November, perhaps as a way of marking the opening of winter. The income of the collecting boxes was also used to pay a number of minor expenses before it was distributed to the canons and the treasurer. These included certain costs of running the cathedral that were held to be the responsibility of the former rather than the latter. They included payments for wine for mass, coals (probably charcoal for incense), grease and ropes for the bells, some candles, and the repair of thuribles and vestments. Some modest fees were also paid on a quarterly basis to certain members of the cathedral staff. The laundress and seamstress (the only women to be employed) each received 5d. per quarter, presumably as a retaining fee, as did the *fossor* who was probably the gravedigger. A sum of 13d. per quarter was granted to the four custors or sacristans and to the cat, who was another recognised member of the staff. Thirteen pence a quarter amounts to a penny a week, which may have been used to purchase enough cats' meat to keep the cat on the premises while not too much to deter it from catching rats, mice, and pigeons.[24]

---

[24] On this subject, see Nicholas Orme, 'The Cathedral Cat', *Friends of Exeter Cathedral, Annual Report*, 51 (1981), pp. 11–13.

The obit accounts of 1305–7 provide us with a complete list of the 56 obit masses then being celebrated. To chart the history of the cathedral's obits in subsequent years, however, would require a detailed study of the whole series of accounts and lies outside the compass of this book. The accounts show the dates when new obits appeared and when existing ones were suspended or discontinued. Short suspensions were not unknown, when (for example) the income from an obit endowment consisting of urban tenements had to be used for repairs and was not then available to finance the obit. The disappearance of the accounts in the 1460s, moreover, means that they cannot be used to elucidate the history of obits for the remaining eighty years up to the Reformation. Nevertheless, we can attempt some audits of the obit masses at certain dates from a second source: liturgical calendars. At least five of these survive from the cathedral in the later middle ages, containing tables of the months of the year and their major festivals and saints' days, on which have been noted the names of people whose obits were commemorated on particular days. Two of them (Document 37) contain only a few names, but the other three are more comprehensive. One is part of a volume of cathedral statutes and represents the dean and chapter's official list of commemorations, observed by the canons and often by the rest of the clergy too (Document 32). The second is part of the volume of obit material, already mentioned, which belonged to the vicars choral (Document 33), and can be dated, like the official volume, to the early fifteenth century. By this time the vicars had become a chartered community in their own right, with the power to manage their own affairs and to hold property, and the volume contains their official list of the obit masses, many of which were additional to those of the dean and chapter and for which the vicars took sole responsibility.

The two obit calendars are working lists of obits, to which new entries were added by hand when necessary, sometimes in rather clumsy annotations. Both volumes, however, have a degree of status, having belonged to their respective bodies of clergy, and it is likely that they represent the exact list of obits commemorated when they were drawn up, with the correct dates of the commemorations. The same cannot be said of our third source: an eleventh-century psalter, prefixed by a calendar that was probably added to the volume in about the thirteenth century (Document 31).[25] During the thirteenth and fourteenth centuries obits were also noted in this calendar, the latest being probably that of Bishop Grandisson (d. 1369). The psalter is known to have been kept in the cathedral choir in the early Tudor period, so that it was a corporate not a private volume, but

---

[25] On the volume, see *Medieval Libraries of Great Britain: a list of surviving books*, ed. N.R. Ker, 2nd ed. (London, Royal Historical Society, 1964), p. 83 (BL, Harley MS 863).

the obits in it (86 in number) are even more roughly entered than in the other two texts. They are usually placed at the right-hand margins of the pages, at a distance from the dates at the left-hand margins, and in some cases their alignment with the dates is not very clear. Most of the dates to which they seem to relate turn out to be quite different from those in the other two sources, sometimes earlier, sometimes later, by as much as a week. Clearly this volume cannot have been an accurate working manual in the same sense as the others, and its purpose remains mysterious. It is useful in adding a few names of obits not found in the other calendars, but it is not a reliable source for the dates of any of the obits that it contains.

Let us return, then, to the two fifteenth-century calendars that bear a degree of authority, beginning with the dean and chapter volume. This contains 114 names, including most of the 56 obits celebrated in 1305–7 and a similar number of new foundations made between then and the early fifteenth century. The latter were mostly those of bishops or cathedral clergy, but (as in previous centuries) only a minority of such men endowed an obit. As before a few outsiders were commemorated. King Æthelstan (d. 939) enjoyed an obit due to his reputation as the founder of the minster at Exeter that later became the cathedral. A similar honour was accorded to Pope John XXII (d. 1334), no doubt because he was the patron and friend of Bishop Grandisson (1327–69), and to King Edward III, Queen Philippa, and the Black Prince, who had a close connection with Bishop Brantingham. Other non-members of the cathedral included relatives of Bishops Stapledon (1308–26), Grandisson, and Stafford (1395–1419), and the solitary magnates who chose to be buried in the building: Hugh Courtenay, earl of Devon (d. 1377), and his wife Margaret (d. 1391).

The calendar of obits kept by the vicars was evidently based on similar traditions, and includes most of the names that appear in the dean and chapter's calendar. Occasionally it delays the dates of obits by one day, presumably because the vicars were involved in the chapter's commemoration on the day itself and held their own remembrance on the next. The vicars' calendar comprises more names, 201 in all, including some additions to the list after it was first drawn up. It differs from the chapter's list by containing a number of less exalted people who had endowed obit masses to be celebrated by the vicars alone. Some of these were members of the minor cathedral clergy – about nine vicars, five annuellars, and two secondary clerks – but only a few of the minor clergy were commemorated in this way; most lacked the resources to establish even a permanent obit. Other people honoured by vicars' obits were members of the laity, some of whom appear to have been citizens of Exeter (such as Alan Sares and William Frost) and others gentry of the countryside (Sir John Damarel and John Fortescue, esquire). The presence of such people reminds us that the vicars owned fewer endowments than the dean and chapter, and had more incentive to seek support from wealthy people in the local community.

It is possible to trace the history of the dean and chapter obits up to the middle of the 1460s, when the obit accounts cease to survive. A list of those that were being observed on the eve of their disappearance has been extracted from the accounts of 1462, one of the latest years for which there is a complete and legible record (Document 34). This list contains 101 obits, some for more than one person, a similar number to the chapter's calendar of a few decades previously. The loss of the accounts after this date is evidently simply a matter of chance, because some drafts or copies of accounts from the year 1521 show that they were still being produced in a similar form at that date, and this probably continued until the Reformation.[26] The next opportunity to see the system in operation, however, does not arise until the point at which it was abolished. The process of abolition began in December 1547 with the enactment of the second Chantry Act by the first parliament of Edward VI. The act condemned the theology of purgatory and intercessory masses on which chantries and perpetual obits were based, gave the crown power to make an inventory of all the existing foundations and their endowments, and sanctioned the confiscation of the endowments as from the following Easter.[27]

In the spring of 1548 the cathedral was visited by five royal commissioners, who caused a list of the dean and chapter's obits to be drawn up on 15 May, including the payments made at them (Document 35).[28] A similar inventory may have been made of the vicars' obits, but this does not survive. The purpose of the list was probably to enable the crown to seize the obit endowments and sell them to private purchasers, but the plan may have encountered difficulties. Many chapter obit endowments had declined so much that they were being supplemented from the cathedral's own revenues. In the end although all the cathedral's chantry and obit property appears to have passed to the crown (including that of the vicars), only parts of it were sold and the majority remained in royal custody.[29] This was eventually returned to the cathedral by Elizabeth I in 1585 in two parcels: one to the vicars and another to the dean and chapter (Document 36). The grant to the vicars was made in return for a nominal annual payment of 4d., perhaps reflecting their relative poverty and the small amount of property involved. The dean and chapter, on the other

[26] D&C 3686, f. 47r–v.
[27] *The Statutes of the Realm, from Magna Carta to the End of the Reign of Queen Anne*, 10 vols (London, Record Commission, 1810–24), iv part i, 25–6.
[28] D&C 3686, f. 39r.
[29] See, for example, *Calendar of Patent Rolls, 1548–9*, p. 366.

hand, were made to pay a substantial annual rent of £145 in return for the large portfolio of lands and tenements restored to them.[30]

The list of obits drawn up in 1548 probably provides us with a complete and accurate record of those being held at that date by the dean and chapter. It refers to 122 obit masses, usually stating only the name of the principal person commemorated by the obit and not any subsidiary names, a deficiency that is partly supplied by the grant of 1585. At 47 of the masses, mostly foundations of the thirteenth century, a uniform sum of 5s. 6d. was divided among the clergy present, indicating that the payment had been standardised by the cathedral chapter at some point, possibly to keep obits in being which would otherwise have disappeared through the failure of their endowments. The rest of the obits involved widely varying payments, reflecting endowments that were still administered separately. Together the list and the grant provide a valuable summary of the obits founded after the disappearance of the obit accounts in the 1460s. They suggest that such foundations remained fairly popular among the cathedral clergy up to about 1500. Obits were instituted by, or in memory of, Bishops Lacy, Nevill, and Booth in the second half of the fifteenth century, and for a number of the cathedral dignitaries and canons of that period, including John Morton (briefly a canon in 1476–8) who became archbishop of Canterbury and a well-known cardinal and servant of Henry VII. A few foundations were also made by lay people, including ones by or for some citizens of Exeter – Vincent Hert, John Holland, and Peter Williams – the last of whom oddly chose burial for himself and his wife not in the cathedral but in the hospital of St John. There was even an obit for a Cornish gentleman, John Edgecombe. In contrast the early sixteenth century is poorly represented. True, Bishop John Arundell (d. 1504) was honoured by an dean and chapter obit; his successor Hugh Oldham (d. 1519) gave the vicars a sum of £80 to celebrate mass at his, Oldham's, tomb;[31] and John Veysey, who followed Oldham and was still in office in 1548, had apparently also established an obit by that date. But the dignitaries and canons of the period are represented only by John Mogryche (d. 1524) and John Ryse (d. 1531), and the wealthy laity by Sir John Speke, founder of the Speke chantry (d. 1518). It appears from this that obit foundations were either not as popular by the reign of Henry VIII as they had been previously, or that the cathedral clergy were less receptive to their establishment because there were so many already.

---

[30] Public Record Office, C 66/1254, printed in *Draft Calendar of Patent Rolls 27 Elizabeth I 1584–1585*, List and Index Society, 241 (1990), pp. 5–9; a later copy is printed in G. Oliver, *Lives of the Bishops of Exeter and a History of the Cathedral* (Exeter, 1861), pp. 488–93.

[31] In his will (PRO, PROB 11/19, f. 148r).

It is probable that the last obits took place at Exeter Cathedral in the spring of 1548. The second Chantry Act expressed disapproval of such things, and the medieval missal and other prayer books on which the commemoration of the dead was based went out of use in 1549. The First Book of Common Prayer, which appeared in that year, did not forbid prayers for the dead but failed to provide for them, and the Protestantism of Edward VI's reign ruled them out for the next few years. Obit masses became lawful again under Mary (1553–8), and at least one of the cathedral's senior clergy proposed to revive them. Thomas Southern, the treasurer, who made his will on 30 April 1556 and died in the following December, ordered that his funeral should be carried out 'according unto the old ancient custom of this church', and left cash to maintain an annual obit as long as the money lasted. He laid down that the traditional payments to ministers should be made, graduated according to rank, and even envisaged the return of the chantry priests to share in the distributions![32] But if his obit was ever established it could not have been held more than twice, for Mary died in November 1558 and during the next few months, under Elizabeth I, Catholicism was dismantled once again. In 1559 an act of parliament ordered that any endowments given for chantries and obits since the reign of Edward VI should pass to the crown.[33]

Elizabeth's wealthy subjects continued to share much of the mentality of their forefathers, including a liking to be remembered after their deaths. So did their successors under the Stuarts. They followed their ancestors in some of the arrangements that they made for this purpose, notably by setting up tombs and monuments and by endowing almshouses, schools, and distributions to the poor. They were able to have their charitable deeds recorded on boards and inscriptions, and even their names read out in church, in prayers of thanks for the foundations they had made. Memory continued to favour the rich, as it had always done. But no one after 1559 could lawfully have prayers of intercession said for their souls in public.[34] In this respect the leaders of the Reformation successfully uprooted and killed the plant that had grown so luxuriantly and for so long.

---

[32] PRO, PROB 11 (25 Wrastley).

[33] *Statutes of the Realm*, iv part i, 399.

[34] On the post-Reformation history of commemoration, see Peter Marshall, *Beliefs and the Dead in Reformation England* (Oxford, 2002), pp. 265–308.

24. Obits from the Leofric Missal, 10th and 11th Centuries

(Source: Oxford, Bodleian Library, MS Bodley 579, described in F. Madan and H.H.E. Craster, *A Summary Catalogue of Western Manuscripts in the Bodleian Library at Oxford*, 7 vols in 8 (Oxford, 1895–1953), ii part i, 487–9. The material is printed in *The Leofric Missal*, ed. N. Orchard, 2 vols, Henry Bradshaw Society, 113–14 (2002), pp. 57–68, 86–7). Latin text. The entries have been anglicised to the extent of removing Latin masculine and feminine endings. The 'æsc' sign for 'æ' has been retained, but 'thorn' has been rendered as 'th'. Some identifications have been added in square brackets.)

[ff. 39r–44v Month Dates]

31	January	Æglflæd
10	February	Leofric, bishop [of Exeter]
13	February	Godo the young [*iuuenis*], priest
16	February	Brihtric, deacon
19	March	Lifing, bishop [of Crediton]
3	April	Byrhtric
26	June	Eadric, priest
29	August	Ælfwin, bishop [of Wells]
9	September	William the elder [i.e. the Conqueror], king
12	September	Segiua
27	September	Mathilda [wife of William the Conqueror]
2	November	Ælwold, monk
9	November	Eadulf, bishop [of Crediton]
11	November	Landbert, most pious king [of Italy]
22	November	Ordlau, layman [*laicus*]
16	December	Ordulf
17	December	Ælfwerd, priest

[f. 53r Year Dates]

976	The death of King Eadgar
979	Here King Eadweard was murdered
985	The burial [*depositio*] of Adelwold, bishop [of Winchester]
988	The death [*obitus*] of Dunstan, archbishop [of Canterbury]
990	Here Æthelgar, [arch]bishop [of Canterbury], died
992	The death of Osuuald, archbishop [of York]
994	The burial of Sigeric, archbishop [of Canterbury]

25. Obits from the Martyrology of Exeter Cathedral, 1072–1282

(Source: Exeter Cathedral Library, MS 3518. Latin text. The source is the cathedral's early twelfth-century copy of Usuard's *Martyrology*, now extant only from 8 February to 10 October and from 6 to 30 December. Into this, in the margins, numerous obits were inserted up to the late thirteenth century. They are chiefly of clergy of the cathedral, but include a few national figures and some local people described as 'our brother' or 'sister' who were apparently members of a formal or informal confraternity linked to the cathedral. Forenames have been modernised where there are equivalent modern forms, and the Latin termination *–us* has been removed from other male forenames. Surnames are left in their original form. Significant phrases added to the names have also been included, in translation. In the original, year dates are in Roman numbers and day dates follow the Roman calendar; these have also been modernised. Calendar dates apply to all the persons opposite or below them until the next date, but year dates (representing death dates) relate only to the first person opposite.)

[The material for January and early February is lost]

[February]

[f. 1r]	10	1111	Ailward, deacon and canon
			John de Tor', succentor of the church of Exeter
[f.1v]	11	1072	Leofric, first bishop of the church of Exeter
		1227	Master Isaac, archdeacon of Totnes, priest and canon, for whom a solemn service is done.
	12	1232	Thomas Mauthut, subdeacon and canon, for whom a solemn service is done.
[f. 2r]	14	1154	William, treasurer and canon
			William Briweir, son of William Briwerr, for whom a solemn service is done as for a canon, who gave the chapter 5s. rent in the town of Crewkerne [*Cruk'*].
	15	1092	Aelric, priest and canon
[f. 2v]	16	1083	Brihtric, priest and canon
[f. 3r]	18	1213	Milo, deacon and canon
	19	1258	John, archdeacon of Totnes, deacon and canon
[f. 3v]	20		William de Glouceter, priest and canon
[f. 4r]	23	1189	Simon Iuuel, deacon and canon

	25	1118	Algar, priest and canon
[f. 4v]	26	1097	Our brother Vitalis de Kolintonia
			Our brother Algar; he built Christchurch [*ecclesia Christi*]
		1154	< *dulfus*> [Ralph?], archdeacon and canon
	27		Our brother Lambert
			Roger de Sydebiria, priest and canon

[March]

[f. 5r]	1	1160	Master Richard, son of Reinfred, deacon and canon
[f. 5v]	2		Alwin, deacon and canon
	3		Master John de Hallesworth, priest and canon
[f. 6r]	5		Master Henry de Kylkeni, priest and canon
	6	1090	Ailric Scott, priest and canon
	7		Master R[alph] Cole, for whom a solemn service is made as for a canon.
[f. 6v]	8		Adela, mother of Stephen, king of the English
	10		Robert.ii.vii
[f. 7r]	11	1104	Rotlamnus, archdeacon and canon
	13		Jordan, nephew of Bartholomew the bishop, our brother
[f. 7v]	14	1136	Ernald, archdeacon and canon
		1174	William de Cicestria, deacon and canon
	15		Mactildis de Meluis, our sister
	16		William de Hely, subdeacon and canon
			Walter de Nortona, our brother
[f. 8r]	17		Simon de Echeuik [?], deacon and canon
[f. 9r]	23	10< >	Osbert, deacon and canon
	24		Lady Beatrice, wife of William Briwerre, our sister
			Walter son of Peter, treasurer of Exeter, priest and canon
[f. 9v]	26	1171	Gervase, deacon and canon
	27		Simon de Sutwille, deacon and canon
[f. 9v]			Agnes, our sister
	28	1155	The venerable Robert [Warelwast], bishop of Exeter, nephew of the venerable William Warelwast
		1164	Philip de < >rrell, canon

[April]

[f. 10v]	1		Goscelin, priest, our brother
		1240	William Germin [or Gernun], subdeacon and canon
[f. 11r]	5		Constantine, deacon and canon

			John de Lamford, acolyte and canon
	6	1097	Alwin, priest and canon
		1122	Godwi, priest and canon
	7	1129	Vivian, subdeacon and canon
		1169	Baldwin Winton, deacon and canon
[f. 11v]	8	1092	Odmar, canon
		1198 [*sic, for* 1199]	King Richard
[f. 12r]	12	1123	Rotbert Araz, deacon and canon
	13		Robert de Cicestria, acolyte and canon, and Ralph de Hiliur [?], our brother
[f. 12v]	14	1158	Richard de Wanci, deacon and canon
		1221	Henry de Meluis, archdeacon of Exeter, deacon and canon
			Baldwin, son of Theobald, canon
	15		Master Constantine, deacon and canon
[f. 13r]			Gilbert de Tyding, priest and canon
	17	1228	William de Su[i]ndona, priest and canon
	18	1125	Gerald, deacon and canon
		1127	Edmar, priest and canon
[f. 13v]		11[61]	Theobald, archbishop of Canterbury, and Thomas de Cicestria, our brother
	19	[*erasure*]	John, treasurer of the church of Exeter, deacon and canon
			Master Oliver de Traci, chancellor of the church of Exeter, deacon and canon
	20	1112	Godo, priest and canon
[f.14r]	21	1232	Master Adam de Sancta Brigida, precentor of the church of Exeter, priest and canon, for whom a solemn service is done.
[f. 14v]	22	1108	F[re?]dricus, priest and canon, and William de Moltona, our brother
[f. 15r]	23		Ruffinus [?], subdeacon and canon
	24	1211	Richard, son of Drogo, subdeacon and canon
[f. 15v]	26		Peter de Meluis, priest of Bishop Bartholomew, our brother
[f. 16r]	27	1240	Master William de Arundell, priest and canon
	28	1227	Master Henry de Warwic, first chancellor of the church of Exeter, priest and canon
[f. 16v]	30	1157	Walter, archdeacon and canon
			Master Roger de Toriz, dean and canon

[May]

[f. 17r]	1	1118	Mathildis, queen of the English, wife of King Henry [I]

[f.18r]	5		Gilbert de S[t]riguil, deacon and canon, and Theophania, wife of Edmar de Moltona, our sister
			Johel de Fan< >, priest, for whom service is done as for a canon
[f. 18v]	7	1084	<*illegible*>, archdeacon; Alan, priest and canon
[f. 19r]	8		John de Exonia, treasurer, priest and canon, for whom a solemn service is done.
	9		Maut Prilla, our sister
[f. 19v]	10	1241	Daniel de Longo Campo, deacon and canon
	11		Of Turbertin and Almar, priests and canons
[f. 20r]	13	1117	Guibert, priest and canon
[f. 20v]			Harald, priest and canon
[f. 21r]	16	1114	Edward, priest and canon
[f. 21v]	18	1083	Lambert, priest and canon
[f. 22r]	19		Reginald Arceuesk, subdeacon and canon, for whom a solemn service is done.
	20	1095	Harald, priest and canon
	21		Master Richard de Bremmele, chancellor of Exeter, priest and <canon>
[f. 22v]	23		Hugh, archdeacon, deacon and canon, and Geoffrey, priest, our brother
			Hugh, archdeacon <*the rest illegible*>
	24		Master William de Shorenton, deacon and canon
		1238	Roger de Lymesy, priest and canon, for whom a solemn service is done
[f. 23r]	26		Lamfranc, archbishop of the church of Canterbury
[f. 24r]	30		Master Henry de Merlawe, priest and succentor <*further material cut off*>

[June]

[f. 24v]	1	1191	The venerable bishop of Exeter, John
[f. 25r]	2	1245	Master John de Beluaco, deacon and canon
	3	1190	Bernard, archdeacon, priest, and canon, and Thomas Basset, our brother
[f. 26r]	6		<*obit obliterated*>
[f. 26v]	8	<1176?>	Benedict, priest and canon, and Ailmer Laking who gave a rent of < >s. to Blessed Peter from his houses, and Juliana < >raleia, our sister
[f. 27r]	11	1138	William, son of Theodbald, deacon and canon
			Master Walter de < tone?>, priest and canon
[f. 27v]	13	1098	<*illegible*>, archdeacon
			Alnoth, deacon and canon
			Ralph, canon

[f. 28r]	15	1174	W. Giffart, priest and canon, and Robert Sclich who gave a rent of 2s. to Blessed Peter from his houses
	16		Henry de Cyrencestria, priest and canon, and Hugh de Pera, priest and canon
	17		John de Monte Acuto, our brother, for whom a solemn service is done, as for a canon
[f. 28v]	18	1224	Master Robert de Hareuis, subdeacon and canon
[f. 29r]	20		John de Monte Acuto, our brother, for whom is done [*unfinished; apparently a copy or repeat of the 17th*]
	21		Our sister Edith, wife of Conon. John de Monte Acuto, our brother, for whom is done a solemn [*unfinished*]
	22	1083	A< >, deacon and canon; Odo <*illegible*>
[f. 29v]	23	1216	Walter, archdeacon of Cornwall, deacon and canon
	24		Robert Couuer [?]
[f. 30r]	25	1183	Bartholomew, acolyte and canon
	26		Hugh, canon; also Richard, canon
[f. 31r]	28	1095	Restold, priest and canon, and Richard de Bagator, deacon and canon.
			John de Esse, archdeacon of Cornwall, priest and canon, for whom a solemn service is done.
[f. 31v]	30	< >2	Mark, subdeacon and canon

[July]

[f. 31v]	1	< >	Wio[m]ar, priest and canon
		< >33	<*illegible*>, acolyte and canon <*erasure*>
[f. 32v]	4	1114	Edgitha, our sister
		1135	Godwin, our brother
	22		Ascelin, [priest?] and canon
	5	< >27	Thur< >, priest and canon
			Master Laurence, subdeacon and canon, for whom a solemn service is done.
[f. 33r]	7		Simon, <archdeacon?>, for whom a solemn service is done.
	9		Cono<n?>, our [brother?]
			Alice Bauby, our sister
[f. 34r]	10	1182	Philip, son of Reinfrei, subdeacon and canon, and Reimund de Aqua, and Mary our sister
			William Decker
	11		Our brother Gilbert, son of Theobald

			Simon, archdeacon of Cornwall, deacon and canon, for whom a solemn service is done.
[f. 34v]	13		Ealditha, our sister, wife of <Rei?>nfred
[f. 36r]	19		William Dacus, for whom a service is done as for a canon.
[f. 36v]	21	< >71	<*illegible*> priest and canon

The venerable Serlo, first dean of the church of Exeter and priest, for whom a solemn service is done, as for a bishop.

[f. 37r]	24	1094	Robert, deacon and canon, and Beatrice, wife of Hosbert

Fairch<ild?>, our sister

[f. 38r]	27		Henry, archdeacon and canon, and Roger Baubi, our brother
[f. 38v]	30		Master Michael <d>e Bukintun, priest [and] canon, for whom a solemn service is done.
[f. 39r]	31		Alexander the fisher [*piscator*], our brother, for whom a solemn service is done, etc., <by?> the vicars.

[August]

[f. 39r]	1		Master John de Blakdon, precentor [*cantor*] and canon
		1153	Walth<er>, deacon and canon, and Teophania our sister
[f. 39v]	2		William the Younger [i.e. Rufus], king of the English
			Mary, abbess of Wilton
[f. 40r]	4		Our brother Rotbert Foliot
			Odo, archdeacon and <canon?>, and Henry, acolyte and canon
	6		<*illegible*>caretus <*illegible*>
[f. 40v]			William, treasurer, acolyte and canon
[f. 41r]	8		Master John de Bradelegh, archdeacon of Totnes, deacon and canon
			Richard and William, priests and canons
			William and John, deacons and canons
[f. 41v]	10		Simon, acolyte and canon
	11		Simon, acolyte and canon [*repeating the previous entry*]
[f. 42r]	13	1242	Master Roger de Winklegh, of good memory, second dean of the church of Exeter and priest, for whom a solemn service is done, as for a [bishop]

[f. 42v]	14		\<Eor?\>lidora, our sister
	15		William Martin, priest and canon
	16		Matildis, wife of Rodbert Dacus
	17		Aluured, \<arch\>deacon, priest, \<and\> canon
[f. 44r]	22	1164	Walter, son of Jocelin, priest and canon
			James de Sicca Villa, canon
[f. 44v]	23		John Lumbard, subdeacon and canon
	24		Simon, acolyte and canon
[f. 45r]	25		William Paz, deacon, our brother
[f. 46v]	30		Eorlitha, our sister, for whom a service is done as for a canon, and Jordan the white [*albus*], our brother
[f. 47r]	31	1253	Master John de Sancto Gorono, priest and canon

[September]

[f. 47v]	2	1248	William de Wllau[e]stona, priest and canon, for whom a solemn service is done.
[f. 48r]	5	1238	John de Neketun, subdeacon and canon
[f. 48v]	6	1137	William, priest and canon
[f. 48v]	7	1171	Peter, archdeacon of Cornwall, priest and canon, for whom a solemn service is done, as for a bishop.
[f. 49r]	8		Martin de Lytelbiri, priest and canon, and Algar, deacon and canon
[f. 49v]	9	1223	The venerable Simon, bishop of Exeter \<*illegible entry*\>
		1251	Master William de Molendina, priest and treasurer of Exeter
[f. 50r]	12		Robert de F[o]rnell, priest and canon
	13		Robert de Fornell, priest and canon [*repeated entry*]
[f. 50v]	14	1271	William Wome \<*and another name, erased*\>
[f. 51r]	15		\<*two entries erased*\> Robert Paul
	16	1139	Bartholomew, deacon and canon
[f 51v]	17		Serlo, subdeacon and canon
[f. 52r]	20	1136	Odo, archdeacon and canon
			Henry de Helingis, acolyte and canon
[f. 52v]	21	1247	Bartholomew, archdeacon of Exeter, priest and canon
	22	1258	Master William, our brother, of good memory
[f. 53r]	23		William, treasurer, acolyte and canon
[f. 53v]	25		Harold, son of Earl Godwin, king of the English, killed by Harold [*sic*], king of the Normans, and all his most victorious army triumphed. In which

war, furthermore, Earl Tostis, brother of the aforesaid king of the English, with the king of the Normans, was killed by the English.

[f. 54r] 27   1137   The venerable <William Warelwast>, bishop of Exeter

      28   1150   Godfrid de Mandauill< >, priest and canon
Johil, our brother
Algar Pavard, our brother

[October]

[f. 55r] 2   Roger the cordwainer [*corduanarius*], our brother
[f. 56r] 5   Richard, archdeacon of Totnes, priest and canon
      7   William, deacon and canon
               William de Puncherdon, priest and canon
[f. 56v] 8   <*erasure, followed by*> and Joan, the wife of Sampson Piper, our sister, who gave to the church of Blessed Peter a rent of 2s. in the manor of [*blank*]
               Master Thomas de Knolle, priest and canon
               Durand, deacon and canon
      8   Hugh de Rupibus, subdeacon and canon

[The rest of October, November, and early December are lost]

[December]

[f. 57r] 6   Master Adam de Belstede, subdeacon and canon, for whom a solemn service is done.
      7   Gilbert the reeve [*prepositus*], our brother
         1282   William Whytecnave, acolyte and canon, for whom a solemn service is done.
[f. 57v] 9   1103   Alfric, priest and canon
[f. 58r] 12   1230   Master Bartholomew, archdeacon of Winchester, deacon and canon of the church of Exeter
[f. 58v]   1227   Alan de Fornell, deacon and canon, and Richard de Nortun, priest, our brother
               Richard Waleraund, our brother
     14   The venerable Bartholomew, bishop of Exeter
[f. 59v] 16   <1>227 Master Roger de <Di>disam, priest and canon
     17   1231   <*erasure, referring to the next entry*>
               Eustace, priest and canon of Exeter, for whom a solemn service is done: a double obit
     18   <J>ohn, acolyte <and canon>

[f. 60r]	19	1091	<erasure>, priest and canon. Godric.
		1133	Godfrid, subdeacon and canon
[f. 61r]	23		Walter Cha[nte]mess, priest and canon
	24		Our brother, Walter the steward [*dapifer*] <erasure> Shaue, our sister [?]
			Peter Chacepork, chancellor of Exeter and canon
[f. 61v]	26	1257	The venerable Richard [Blundy], bishop of the church of Exeter
[f. 62r]	27	1257	Rob<ert> de Curtenay, canon of Exeter
	29	1191	Baldwin, son of < >
		1189	William, archdeacon <and canon>
[f. 62v]	30		Walter de Sancta Cristina, subdeacon and canon
	31		John Wiger, knight, for whom a solemn service is done, as for a canon.

26. Lists of Guild Members from the Exeter Book, late 11th or early 12th Century

(Source: Exeter Cathedral Library, MS 3501, f. 7r–v; facsimile in *The Exeter Book of Old English Poetry*, ed. R.W. Chambers, Max Förster, and Robin Flower (Exeter and London, 1933), f. 7r–v. Old English text, with one entry in Latin. All the personal names are transcribed in their original form, except that the Old English letters eth and wyn have been replaced by 'th' and 'w'. The æsc sign has been retained, as has 'u' when it is used instead of 'v' or 'w'.)

[f. 7r]

... at Woodbury [*Wudebirig*] ... These are their names that belong to the guild-ship:

Brihtwi, Wlnoth, Ealdwine, Leofric, Brihtmær, Alfric, Edmær, Edwine, Algar, Edwi, Wlword, Alword, Edwine, Godwi, Orgod, Atheleoue, Brihtmær, Godric.

At Woodbury there is another guild-ship:

Kytel, Theodric, Thurwurd, Ailnoth, Ailmer, Wulmer, Ailric, Alfgær, Sæwine, Alwine, Edric, <*erased name*>, Alwi, Alword, Hierding, Edmær, Godwine, Colswein, Brihtric, Edwine. [*Added names:*] Ælword, priest; Sæmer.

Of Colaton Raleigh's [*Colatunes*] guild-ship:

Ordric, priest; Almær, Ailwine, Alword, Athesta[n?], Godric, Algær, Alfric, Osmær, Hiathemær, Siric, Wulword, Ailric, Edric, Alfrid, Almær.

Of Broad Clyst's [*Clist tunes*] guild-ship:

Isaac, priest; Almær, Godwine, Alwine, Brihtric, Beoring, Hierding, Theodric and Theodric, Edrun, Gladwine, Aluwi, Leowine, Sæword, Toui, Hemming, Sæiuue [*for* Sæiuue?], Ailric, Alwine, Edrun, Ailword and Lifgiue, Edwine, Alfric and Alfric, Edwine, Edgiue, Wlfric and Wlfric, Wada, Godwine, Alword, Alwine, Hunewine, Ailword, Ailiue, Lifgiue, Ealdgith,

259

Lifgiue, Gunhild, Ailhild, Alwith, Edgiue, Lifgiue, Edgiue.

Of Alwine's guild-ship at Woodbury:

Alfstan, Leowine, Alfric, Ailwine, Athelhild, Ailric, Thureword, Algær, Sigær, Aluith, Edmær, Alword, Fræwine, Dirling, Leowi, Godwine, Edwine, Brihtwine, Ordric, Brungær, Alwine, Særic. [*Added names:*] Godwine, Algær, Hierding, Algær, Edwine, Vuiet, Alwine, Edgiue.

[f. 7v]

[No heading]

Ordeua, our sister [*soror nostra*]

Of Bridford's [*Bridafordes*] guild-ship:

Edwine, Wlfric, Sæwine, Sæmær, Edwine and Edwine, Alfric, Leowine, Ailric, Leofric, Alwine, Edmær.

Of Clyst St George [*Clist wike*]:

Waltere, priest; Edmær, Leowine, Sænoth, Swein, King, Ailword, Algær, Særic, Edwi, Edwine and Edwine, Edwi, Siword, Edwine, Ailmær, Dunning, Godwine, Snelling, Dirwine, Godwine, Sæwine, Edric, Bruning, Sæwi, Selewi, Ordgiue, Edgiue.

Of the guild-ship of *Lege* [*possibly* Doddiscombsleigh]:

Ailwine, priest; Tyrri, priest; Will[ia]m, Alfred, Gosfræg, Ailword, Edwine, Osged, Osword, Godric, Brihtric, Cola, Wunric, Ailsi, Alword, Alnoth, Algær, Leofric, Dirling, Brihtric, Bilehald, Lifgiue, Estmær, Limmær, Ailwine, Godric, Seyman, Roecgore, Siword. [*In the margin:*] Edwine, Godric.

Of Nutwell [*Hnutwille*, in Woodbury parish]:

Godric, Alwine, Edwine, Godwine, Godric, Wlfric, Alfric, Leofric, Dunewine, Algær, Edwine, Edgith.

Of Colaton Raleigh [*Colatune*]:

Alwine Treddason, Godric, Ailric and Beorn, Brihtmær, Almær, Ordric, Dirwine, Wurma, Dunning, Siword, Alfric.

Of Sidmouth [*Sidemutha*]:

Algar, Ailric, Wlwine, Wnking, Ailmær, Edwi, Brihtric, Alfric, Alwi, Luduwine, Kinsta, Wlfric, Ailric, Kipping, Edwine, Alfgiue, Edgith, Alfgiue, Edwine, Osword, Alfric, Alwi, Alwine, Leowine, Almær, Sceott, Leowine. [*In the margin:*] Alwric.

Of Halsford [*Halsforda*, in Whitestone parish]:

Ilberd, priest; Edwine, Alwine, Wlword, Limmær, Ailmær, Leofric, Edwine, Edwi and Edwi, Edwine, Leowine, Fugel, Edwine, Ealdwine, Edwine, Ailword, Ordulf, Sæword, Algær and Limmær.

Of Whitestone [*Hwita stane*]:

Edzi, Godric, Edwine, Leowine, Aluric, Ealdwine, Alwine, Sæwi, Sægar, Wlwi, Algar, Edwi, Kari, Wiking, Wnning, Siword, Alword, Ailwine, Leowine.

Of Axmouth [*Axamutha*]:

Godgith, Esgar, Edrid, Ailward, Ailwine, Leowine, Sænoth, Wiking, Herman, Edword, Sceggi, Atli, Sæword, Rotb[er]t, Siword.

27. Obit list of the Parish Church of St Martin, Exeter, 12th or 13th Century

(Source: DRO, Exeter City Archives, Book 53A, f. 36r. Latin text. The source, the Cartulary of the Hospital of St John, contains extracts which it describes as 'transcribed from an old missal of St Martin', evidently meaning the parish church, since the extracts include the dedication date of the church. The list here contains only dates and names; the source also includes information about payments of money made in connection with the obits.)

[16 January; Marcellus, pope]. Robert son of Gilda, archdeacon of Totnes.

[3 February; Blaise, martyr]. Peter de Palerna.

[22 February; Peter in cathedra]. Richard, son of Nicholas.

[12 May; Pancras]. Roger Lambert.

[4 February; morrow of St Blaise]. Sampson Rof.

[4 August; morrow of the Invention of Stephen]. Walter Tourbert and John Turbert, chaplains of the city of Exeter.

[11 August; morrow of St Laurence]. William Durling.

[6 October; St Faith]. Thomas Hid.

[29 October; morrow of Simon and Jude]. Mary, wife of Thomas Hid.

[25 November?; VII? Kal. Dec.]. Lady Alice Bauby.

[1 September; Giles, abbot]. Nicholas Gervase [*Gervasius*].

[11 November; morrow of Martin]. Christina, wife of Alexander the fisher [*piscator*].

[14 January; morrow of St Hilary]. Walter the chaplain, rector of All Hallows.

[4 July; morrow of the translation of Thomas, martyr]. Denise Blunda.

[Monday after Easter]. Nicholas Treydener.

[12 June; morrow of Barnabas]. Adam de Collecote.

[29 June; Peter and Paul the apostles]. John Persona.

[26 July; morrow of James]. Roger Baubi.

[7 July; translation of Thomas, martyr]. Vivian, rector of St Edmund.

[1 August; Peter ad vincula]. Alexander the fisher [*piscator*].

[4 August; morrow of the Invention of Stephen]. Jo[hn?] Yoreberu.

[9 August; vigil of Laurence]. William Long [*longus*].

[5 August; 5th day after Peter *ad vincula*]. Gilbert le Blond.

[29 September; Michael]. Rosa Pykout.

28. Obit List of the Exeter Guild of Kalendars, early 14th Century

(Source: Exeter Cathedral Archives, D&C 3675, ff. 7v–18v. Latin text. This list was drawn up in about the 1310s and 20s. Names were subsequently added to it; these are indicated at the end of each month. The list is in Latin, divided into months, which were presumably read out by a cleric at the appropriate monthly mass of commemoration for the souls of the guild's members. The Latinisation of forenames and surnames, however, is not consistent. Some forenames are not Latinised, while others are: usually in the nominative but occasionally in the genitive. Surnames are not normally Latinised, but there are a few such examples like 'iuxta murum' and 'super montem'. The names within each month appear, at first sight, in a random order, and while some appear individually, others are linked together. In part at least this order and linkage stem from earlier calendars in which the names were originally listed. From time to time the phrase 'our brother' or 'our sister' is included, but because of the linked names it is not always certain how many people are being referred to. Occasionally, it is hard to decide whether two adjacent names are independent forenames or a forename and a surname.

In this edition, capital letters and punctuation have been modernised, as have well-known Christian names like Alice and William. Less common names (including Isabel and Matilda which occur in variant forms) are given in the original, except that the Latin ending *–us* has been removed in the case of men's names. In the cases where Latin byenames and surnames have been translated, the Latin is indicated in brackets. It should be borne in mind that someone called 'baker', for example, might be a practising baker or someone who had come to be known as Baker, independently of his work.)

[January]

[f. 7v] The names of the brothers and sisters of the Kalendars who died in January.

Pray for William de Stanweye, dean of Exeter. Michael, chaplain, our brother; and Hodiern' wife of Other. Therri and Christina, mother of Adam the chaplain. Leowyn, priest and canon, our brother. Baldwin of Flanders [or the Fleming: *Flandrens'*] and Anguylla, our sister. Hugh de Molton and William, our brother[s?], and Edith our sister. Richard son of

Andrew and Aluoua de Botes, our sister. Osbert, priest. Theobald son of Ralph, and Hawis' [f. 8r] wife of Thurbert, and Gilla our sister. Algar and Hodiern', our sister. Richard Smalprut and Odeline, our sister. Robert, archdeacon of Totnes, and William the old [*senex*], priest. Aluoue, our sister. Baldwin Piper. William Paffard. Albrethe. Alice, wife of John de Fenton, and Haymer our brother. Robert Goseye and Emma our sister, and Mariot our sister. Clarice wife of Andrew Inhere. Thurstan and William Seph and Edith our sister. Algar, chaplain. Robert Haue, priest and chaplain. Alice de Molton, our sister, and Theobald, and Emma his wife. Thurbert Blund. Nicholas de Ponte, priest. Bricthiue, our sister. Osbert, priest. Ralph de Stokelegh, priest and our brother. Joan Beyuyn. Thomas de Lokynton. William of St Nicholas. Joan, wife of Jordan the baker [*pistoris*]. Roger de Dertheforde, priest and canon. Elias de Cyrecestria, priest and brother. Benedicta, widow of Richard Strange. Lucy de Langedene. William Hog le Tanner. Mariot Cristchurche and Alice Bithewalle. William de Sanforde, [f. 8v] priest, brother. Herwy the glover [*cerotekar*']. Floura Bastehaye. Sara Hog. Roger Bonde and Margery his wife. Ralph de Lideforde. Isabel Surrewa. Ralph Berwe. Nicholas Knouston. John Blaunmost. Denise Tetteborne. Richard Tiuertone and Alice Mounteyn. Matilda Prouta. John Bayli, mason. Emma Skinner [*pellipar*']. Alice Smalecombe. John Baker and Isabell', widow of Fisher [*or* the fisher: *piscatoris*]. John Bosse and Katherine his wife. Lucy Tiuerton and Agnes Walshe. Thomas Lokeys. Felicia Lywarne. Hayne Bakere and Joan his wife. Beatrice Lideforde.

[*Added:* Sir Richard Hacche who gave the making [*fabricam*] of a chalice to the Kalendar brothers. Robert. Alice. William. Margery. Geoffrey. Robert. Clement Browne.]

[February]

[f. 9r] Pray for John the clerk and Reimar. Edmer de Moltone. Geoffrey Furnell and Gille and Aluoue, our sisters. Wybert, priest, and William of Eu [*de Auco*], archdeacon. Matill' de Burlescumbe. Magtild' the wife of Quinel, and Hodiern' our sister[s?]. Godsweyn, brother. Ralph Pineldianus. Matill' By the wall [*iuxta murum*]. William son of Azo, priest. Wluric the anchorite [*anachorita*]. Leofric, bishop, and Mobert de Strete. Walter le Chawe. Roger de Hauk, and Gilbert, priest. Osbert Cornet. Ralph de Cam and Girard, our brother[s?]. Serlo, son of Wilburd, our brother. Theolad. Ralph de Camera and Theobald le Mercer. Henry Scherpe. Ralph Godchil. Odwyn Godchil and Gunnilde, daughter of Wynind. Richard Gape, priest, and Godith Gos, our sister. Joan, wife of Arnald. Richard de Lastappe. John de Holebrok. Robert Hobbe. Adam Cordwaner. Philip le Seler. Philip Long, priest and vicar. Stephen le Cordewener. Master John de Hallesworthi. William Pollard. [f. 9v] Margery Dounman. Margery de

Plymtone. Thomas le Mareschal. Agatha de la Putte. Felicia Bithewalle. Katherine Derherd. Richard de Plymton, vicar. Jordan Chayllo. Matilda Belebuche. Alice de Bolehille. William Nyweton, priest. John the baker [*pistor*] and Joan his daughter. Isabel Soth. Thomas le Wetene. Christina Honimom. Thomas the baker [*pistor*]. Alice de Tottonia. Lucy Arnold. Alice Bole. John Bole. Robert Aysperton.

[March]

[f. 10r] Pray for Master Richard son of Rumfrey and Thomas, our brother[s?]. Adam and Emma the wife of Richard Bere. Warin, priest, and Osmod, our brother[s?]. Richard Boschet. Matill' the wife of Dripling. Gilda de la Pesch[er]ie. Theophonia, widow of Laurence the tailor [*cissoris*]. Rimer and Rocelin and Alice and Gunill' de la Fenne. Rose la Crokere. Matill' and Ailward de Cam. Robert, bishop [the fourth, *added*]. Algar Oxewon. Philip de Sege. Richard le Grip, priest. Jordan. Ernald, archdeacon, and Matill' de Melhiwys. Guncelyn and Herius. Ang' le Palmere. William de Kerdyt. Almer, father of St Sidwell, and Osbert de Rouen [*Rotomago*]. William Setans and Beatrice, our sister, and Gilda and Joan, our sister[s?], and Nicholas Bisuthedone. William Sclich. Damaysele, wife of Asketil Yueling. Mazelin, wife of William de Moltone. Philip de Stokes and Gilbert, chaplain, and Emma Scote. Gilbert de Moltone. John de Wermunst[er?]. Nicholas Treydeners. [f. 10v] William Polyman. Roger Gosehe, vicar and chaplain. Petronilla, wife of Thomas de Crandon, and Thomas de Venelle. Gunnilda Aylwaker. William Pyge. Agatha, widow of Ralph le Bere. Richard Horn. Richard Dyrkyn, apothecary [*ypothecarius*]. William Caperon. Roger Godelep. Matild' de Mareys de Alfyintone. Henry le Yunge. Denise Hog de Cirencestria. Margery, wife of Richard Effelege. Peter de Hembiri, our brother. Alice de Tottonia. Sybil Barbour, our sister. David Seruintone.

[*Added:* Andrew Fursyn.]

[April]

[f. 11r] Pray for Gocelin, priest. Heriid and Matild' la Wyte, our sister[s?]. Philip the shoemaker [*sutor*] and Aubree, his wife. Godefrid and Helena, mother of Walter le Chawe. Godwin, priest. Vivian, canon. Moyses, priest, and Alward Hoc. Baldwin, canon, and Mazeline, and Isabele, wife of Walter Turbert. Hugh de Ralegh and Matill', sister, and Florence our brother. Gilbert, the carter [*caretarius*]. W. *de Cano* [dean?] of Exeter. Henry de Pomeray, brother, and Matill', our sister. Baldwin le Granger. Selina, our sister. Reginald, brother, and Matill', our sister. Anger, priest, and William, priest, and Robert, brother. Richard le Celer and Baldwin Dalfyn, brother[s?]. Alfred Custos and Aubree, sister. Alwyn Mody and

Roys, sister. Helewys, sister, and Alice, sister. Robert, son of Azo, and Rosemunda, sister. Richard de Ridon and Osbert, son of Algar. Algar, son of Listiled, and Aylward, priest, and Auicia, sister. Aceline, wife of Hog, and Christina, daughter of Azelin. Ailward, priest, and Gunnild' and Godith, our sister[s?]. [f. 11v] Walter, archdeacon, and Roys, our sister. Henry ata Wyke. Gricia de Waus. Nicholas de Yuelcestre. Robert Bone. William Maundewyle. Walter the dyer [*tinctor*]. Roger Rossel and Beatrice his wife. Alice Moggebrigge. Thomas le Whetene. Joan David. William de Gatepathe and Margery, his wife. Robert Cleyhangere, priest. Henry Luywerne, brother. Botill' de Sancford. Wyet de Fentone. Gilbert Faber. Isobell' de Beydone. Johel Due. Richard Bonde, dyer [*tinctor*]. Joan Wyctoe. Richard Lydeford. Sarra Hog.

[*Added:* Sir William Vises. Elizabeth Holle, mother of Henry Holle.]

[May]

[f. 12r] Pray for Arnulf of Flanders [or the Fleming: *Flandrens*'] and Theophania de Molton. Robert and David, priest[s?]. Alured Weliued and Goldiue, our sister. William, brother, and Albre and Alue, sister[s?]. Auice de Toriton' and Alurit the moneyer [*monetarius*]. Walter Lewerke and Seylda, sister. Nicholas Pole and Pleysante, sister. Leofrid, priest, and Alice, wife of B. Piper. Erenburga de la Porche. Robert By the wall [*iuxta murum*]. Turbert, priest, and Serlo, priest. Thomas, chaplain. Edith and Edwyn, brother. Audrea, our sister. Pagan, priest. Askelut, priest, and Mazelina, sister. Cecily Hauet. Semar, brother, and Aluoua, sister. Gyrard, priest, and Nicholas Terri, and William Howel. Matill' and Luweline, sister[s?]. Gille, sister. Matill', our sister. Hugh, archdeacon, and Geoffrey, brother. Ralph Babba. Roger the cook [*cocus*]. Richaude and Muriele, sister[s?]. Raulf, brother. Laurence the tailor [*cissor*] and Beatrice daughter of Denis [or Denise] La Blunde. Gouncelina, wife of Hamelin. Henry de Merlawe, priest. Anger, son of Remfrey. [f. 12v] Aceline, wife of the son of Semar. Roger Schipman. Alice Wodecok. Richard, clerk. Bartholomew, chaplain, and Joan de Coleton. Richard de la Bere. Baldwin Chil. Roger de Cristeschurche. Isabell' Oxon. Juliana, wife of Ralph the baker [*pistoris*]. John de Exon., treasurer [*thesaur*']. Isabella de Aula and Agnes, wife of Nicholas le Hoper. Ralph le Mercer. Richard de Hide. Margery Wonsome. Richard Proute. Elena Sowctele, sister. Elena Sude. Katherine Wonsom. Warin de Astyng. Joan, wife of the same. Richard Fichet and Isot, his wife. Warin Anstegh. Matilda Warin. Joan Warin.

[*Added:* Thomas Vye. John Hontelond. Floure Biriman.]

[June]

[f. 12r] Pray for Symon, priest. Emma, wife of Richard Boschet. Matill' de Vinea and Alice, wife of Henry the merchant [*mercator*]. William, priest, and Acelina, mother of Alan de Forneaus. Roger, priest. Godwyn de Lideford. Emma, sister, and Alice White [*alba*]. Walter the baker [*pistor*] and Damaysele, sister. Herman, priest. Moryn and Edward le Palmere. Ailmer at Laking and Reinfred [or Remfred], and Gilda by the wall [*iuxta murum*]. Alice, wife of the baker [*pistor'*]. William, son of Tithald, and Albredra, wife of Pagan. Osmoda, sister of Jordan. Sewi Cole. Robert Schlich. Rotland. Gilda and Matill', sister[s?]. Mahu de Boscho and Cristina, sister[s?], and Stephen, brother. Roger the cook [*cocus*]. Ric', daughter of Drian [*recte* Brian?], and Reinfred [or Remfred], brother. Emma and Gilda, sister[s?]. Baldwin, brother. Moyses, priest, and Martin Prodomme. Semar, brother. Bartholomew, nephew of Bishop William, and Matill', sister. Sewyl le Tanner' and Roger, priest, and Eua, our sister. [f. 12v] Ailwi, brother. Roger Pudding and Mariot de Yuelcestr'. Roger, priest, and Robert, priest, and Richeman, brother. Aliue and Godiue, sister[s?]. William de Asperton, priest. Margery Geruaise. Felicia de Tregoni. Pauline de Sancto David. Emma Hillari. John Paris. Alice Treideners. Richard de Purrigge. Thomas Cole. Agnes Marescal. Juliana, wife of Thomas the parchment-maker [*pergamenar'*]. Richard Brinnyng. Robert Blaunchecote. Richard Stranga. William the dyer [*tyntor'*] and Alice, his wife. Alice Kacchefrens. Richard Tetteborne. Alice Horn, sister. Clarice, widow of Richard Forst. Sabina Hembyri. William the skinner [*pelliparius*]. Joan Chakeforde. Margery, wife of John Treydeners. Henry de Criditon, carpenter [*carpentar'*].

[*Added:* John Yowe. Agnes, the wife of John Yowe, and Joan the wife.]

[July]

[f. 13r] Pray for Roger and Martin Puddyng, and Matill', wife of William Howell. Wyomar, priest, and Matill', wife of Thomas the dyer [*tinctor'*]. Albretha, sister. Godwin, priest. William, priest, and Acelin, priest. Roger, archdeacon of Barnstaple, and Helena, sister. Alice Baubi and Alice, sister[s?]. Ordric, priest, and Gilbert, priest. William, priest. Quenes of Flanders [*Flandrie*], and Ragenilla, sister[s?]. Philip, canon, and Mary, sister. Nicholas, brother, and Emma his wife. Wnfrid, our brother, and Herehit and Alci', sister[s?]. Goslin, brother, and Ealdith, our sister. Alwin, priest, and Reimund de Aqua. Emeline, daughter of Wele. Walter Schanke. Ralph, priest, and Henry de Walingeforde. Beatrice and Nicholas, clerk. Leofrid, brother, and Edith, sister, and Geoffrey Rufus. Geoffrey Howel, brother. Geoffrey Haileman. Beatrice, sister, and Walter de Lintone, brother, and Robert, son of Gunnild'. Alice, sister. Henry, priest, and Christiana, sister. Roger Baubi and Walter Turbet, and Stephen le Bulger. Richard Addaking and Gilbert the deaf [*surdus*]. Rannulf Peuerel. John de Modbiri. Isabell', wife of David the tailor [*cissor*']. John Quinel. Henry Hog. [f. 13v] Nicholas de Kenton, priest. Henry the taverner [*tabernar*'], and Joan his wife. Yolenta, widow of Crese. Margery, wife of Warin. Adam the writer [*scriptor*]. William de Criditon. Nicholas de Lana. Margery Goman. Clement, chancellor. Roger Beyuin. Robert Page. William Cherde, priest and brother. Matill' Spek. Vivian, priest and brother. David the tailor [*cissor*]. Mabill', wife of Adam le Spicer. Margery, daughter of Richard Strang'. Robert de Kydelonde. William Spicer. Simon de Exon, priest and vicar. William the fisher [*piscator*]. Margery. Roger le Machoun. Nicholas Page and Pauline, his wife. Henry Tricot. John de Wodebiri. Milla atte Beare. Roger Bonde and Margery, his wife. William Mortoun and Felicia, his wife. Stephen de London. Richard de Esselegh. Margaret, his wife. Elena Palmere. Agnes de Bamptone.

[*Added:* John Brovnwyll, senior, and John Brovnwyll, junior, and Joan his wife. John Holond, canon. Henry Gardener and Joan, his wife. Master John Gardener. Ricarda and Christiana, wives of William Gardener. Walter Weke. William Nydydon.]

[August]

[f. 14r] Pray for William, son of Durling, and Seffra Baron, brother[s?]. Isabell' and Matill' Cudele. Ralph son of Peter, and Mahaut, and Edith, wife of Wacelin. Thomas Greyn and Ralph the carpenter [*carpentar*'], and Beatrice, wife of Teob', and Thomas Witerel. Asketill de Bommine, and Roger Agnel, and William Trauers. Baldwin Lambrith. Hawis' and Osmod, *ux*' [wife, or wives] of Lambrith. Baldwin Iussel and Walter of Saint Omer [*de Sancto Odmaro*], and Robert de Insula. Richard Tinemento, and Simon de Piscina. Roger and Richard, priest[s?]., and Gilla de Cumba. Haym' and Richard Purs. Hillaria, sister. Anger and Adam, priest[s?]. William Treydeners. Edive on the hill [*super montem*]. Ailiue and Ameline, sister[s?]. Henry Palmere, and Matill', wife of Prille. Alured, archdeacon, and Robert the black [*niger*], brother. Rois. Alice and Hillaria. Pauline, sister. Gilbert Put, and Eva on the hill [*super montem*]. Sibill', wife of Dalfyn. Ailhille and Mary Fayrchil. Walter Long and Denise, sister of Walter la Chauue. Richard de Forneaus, priest. Hugh, priest of Kenn [*Ken*]. Margery. Hugh de Exon. Walter Herlewine and Richard Pipard, priest[s?]. Jocelin the white [*albus*] and Brithiue, sister. [f. 14v] William Brithrich, priest, and Turbert. Gilla and Alice de la Leye. Godefrid de la Fenne and Robert, brother[s?]., and Clarice Hann. Nicholas Gerueise and Alice, his wife. Walter Talegarth, brother, and Ragenilda, sister. William Milis, priest. Walter the tailor [*cissor*]. Philip the smith [*faber*]. Isabell' Grossa. Matilda de Tenta. Gilda, wife of Thomas le Celer. Robert Gesse. Arnulf le Sarger and Isabell', his wife.

Thomas Wyterel. Roger de Esse. Lucy Palmere. Ralph de Oteri. William Bola. Richard Russel. John de Bouistoc. Anastasea de la Tenta. John le Bera. Richard, son of Richard Stranga. Gonnot la Coyfestere. Hugh Herman and Helwyse, his wife. John the baker [*pistor*]. Rosamunda de Wychibroc. Elias de Criditon, priest and vicar. Osbert le Sargere. Clarice Baroun. Alexander de Toritone. Matill' Chaylo. Roger Strange, chaplain. Adam Spicer. Emma Skynnere. Simon de Membur'. Juliana Mountein. Joan Bollock. Reysanta de Bekelonde. Flour' Bafthehaye. Christina Lange. William Buf. James de Comba, chaplain and vicar.

[September]

[f. 15r] Pray for Walter Sturnel, priest. Peter Wymund, priest. Asketill, brother. Reineri and Laurence Busse. Ricinar. William, brother. Denise, sister, and Alfred, priest. Ralph son of Theobald. Richard, son of Grym, and Ralph, dean, brother, and Hawis', sister. William Buschet, priest, and Stephen, dean, and Alured le Bers. Alward on the hill [*super montem*]. Christina, wife of William the marshal [*mareschalli*]. William and Ralph, priest[s?], and Alured Quinel, brother, and Richard Trenchard. Richard Boschet and Walter on the hill [*super montem*]. Aylward the saddler [*sellarius*] and Seuar the baker [*pistor*]. Aldith, anchorite [*anachorita*]. John Swan. Adam the carpenter [*carpentar'*]. Roger de Clauile and Susanna, sister. Geoffrey and Alex', clerk[s?]. Pagan Wyggal. John of the Porch [*de porticu*] and Reymund, brother[s?]. Odo, archdeacon. Beatrice, sister. Alured the Irishman [*Hiberniens'*]. Richard [f. 15v] Milis. Godwin Luna. Ailward and Jordan Pope, brother[s?]. Sampson Piper and Liueue, and Roger, priest, and Alwe, sister. William, bishop, and Adelard, clerk, and William son of Robert. Ediue Criket and Aceline of the Porch [*de porticu*]. William Bure and William, son of Lambert, and Gelleinde de Hilmin'. Isabell' de la Graue, and Agnes, and Alice. Alice la Brewestore. Robert Poul, vicar. Henry of St Mary [*de Sancta Maria*], priest. Alice, widow of John le Futrer. William de Halis, priest. Katherine de Venella. Juliana de Venella, sister. John de Hylmist'. Ouger de Sancto Melano. Johel de Tetteborne. Peter de Chalouns. Deodatus de la Schute, chaplain. Nicholas Strange, priest and vicar. Elias de Hemstone, and Alice Willewerie. Robert Maynard. John Jakys. Isabel Pyn.

[*Added:* William Weston, canon of Exeter. Margaret Floyt, sister. Henry ata Wyke. Richard Waleuille and Agatha, his wife. Sir John Welly[n]gton, vicar. John Holle, father of Henry Holle. Lord John de Grandisson, bishop. Walter Foteryngay. John Downe, priest and vicar. Walter, bishop. John Eston and Agnes, his wife. John Eston and Joan, his wife. Robert Eston. William Eston and Joan, his wife. Ralph Henxe, clerk.]

[October]

[f. 16r] Pray for John Caperun. Ragenida, mother of Absalon. Gunnilda, widow of Warin. William Coc. William, deacon [*diacon'*]. John, chaplain of St Paul [*de Sancto Paulo*]. Joan, wide of Sampson Piper. Hawysia, mother of Walter de Clauile. Peter [and?] Reimfrei, deacon and canon. Agnes, wife of Laurence the tailor [*cissoris*]. Seger and Godiue and Matilda. Alice. Alured de Brente and Alice de Chadeleghe. Aszon, chaplain of St Mary [*S. Mar'*]. Edive and Osmund. Walter de Borlescumbe. Reymer. Geoffrey de Clist. Joel Thomas, chaplain of St Mary Major. Godric and Roger and Walter Ruffus. Hawys' and Wymarch, our sisters. Margery. John Paz, canon. Walter, priest. Segar, priest. Athelstan, king. Bartholomew Piper. Margery. Robert, chaplain. Reginald, chaplain. Absolon, priest. John M[er?]icius. Herbert the fisher [*piscator*], and Odelina, his wife. Juliana, wife of Henry the cook [*coci*]. Alice Horlock. Peter de Yuelcestr', chaplain and brother. Matill', wife of William de Karswille. Matill', wife of Thomas le Wetene. William de Harcumbe. Walter le Coteler. David de Wodebiri. Henry de [f. 16v] Berbelond, priest and vicar. Clarice Rok. Jordan de Wottone. John Petibon. John de Chuselgraue. Margaret Womseme, our sister. William de Smalecome, our brother. Sarra, wife of John le Lethre, our sister. Clarice, and Ralph de Lideforde. Beatrice, his wife. Joan Wythebrother. Thomas le Barboure. John de Miluirtoun, baker [*pistor*]. John Peyntrer. Felicia Mortone. Stephen Smalecombe. John Mounteyn, priest and vicar. Alice de Oteri.

[*Added:* Walter Trendelbeare. Master William Sylke, canon, doctor, and archdeacon of Cornwall. Master John Tayler, doctor and chancellor of Exeter. Master Henry Molynaux, canon. Master Thomas Erle, notary. Master Henry Helyar, notary. Thomasia Saris. Master William Cottehey. John Hall. For the souls of John Cottehey and Agnes, his wife, and Richard Hall and Margery, his wife. Richard Heydon and Alice his wife.

Richard Heydon, Joan his wife, Thomas, John, Richard, George, Matthew, sons of the said Richard and Joan, and also Joan and Sibilla, daughters of the said Richard and Joan, [and] for the souls of all their brothers, sisters, and benefactors and friends of memory.]

[November]

[f. 17r] Pray for Alestan and Alaeua. Gervase the merchant [*mercator*], and John the shield-maker [*scutarius*], and Ralph, brother[s?]. John Tubba, priest. Odo and Albreth. Osbert Blund. Pagan the doorkeeper [*ianitor*]. Christian, priest, and Wuluoue. Warin Clop, and Odeline, sister. Geoffrey Terri. Semar and his wife, and Osmund, and Herbert the reeve [*prepositus*]. Christina, wife of Alex' the fisher [*piscator*]. Robert de Goleuile. Robert de Buketon, priest and canon. Brictric le Tanner. Geoffrey, priest, and John Picot and Edith. Adam le Fulur. Alueua and Matill', wife [wives?] of Schildoun. Matill'. Walter de Granger. Edith, wife of Reymund. Richard Froda. Algar, priest. William Briwere, bishop. Adam *de famla episcopi* [of the household of the bishop?], and Richard de Stauerton. Brictmar, priest, and Theobald son of Renfrey, and Edith. Roger Frank and Alward, and Godiue, and Gille. William Horwode and Acelina, wife of William Durling, and Gode, sister[s?]. William Scildone. William Lumbard. Hugh Probus, priest. Margaret Gundewine. Sara de Hidone. Margaret Floylt. Alan de Canteley. Alanus de Ponte. [f. 17v] Helewyse, wife of Richard Horn. Agnes, widow of John de Coleton. Philip le Ganger. William de Werplesdone, priest and canon of Exeter. Thomas Fayreman. Robert Famegoz, vicar. Joan Piririg. John de Oxstone, priest and vicar. Alice ate Denes. Joan Wytebrother. Isabella de Tadiforde, seamstress [*sutrix*]. William de Wenella. Isobell' Priggele.

[*Added:* Sir Richard Mannyng.]

[December]

[f. 18r] Pray for Pagan, priest. Jordan son of Alg', and Pleysente, sister. Juliana, sister. Ediue and Rocelin, and Alex' the goldsmith [*aurifaber*]. Roger de la Lane. Philip the dyer [*tinctor*]. Aluoua, weaver [*textrix*] and Mauth, sister[s?]. Alan de Forneaus, and Reginald, priest, and William son of Walter, and Gille Peche. Richard Strange, and Richard le Mercer. Bartholomew, bishop, and Juliana, sister. Henry, priest. Peter de Moltone and Maysaute, sister. Denise Schanke, sister. John of Flanders [or the Fleming: *Flandrensis*]. Christopher and John, priest[s?]. Joan, wife of Roger son of Henry. Christina Cobi. Philip and Albrict, priest[s?]. Ralph le Cordewaner and William the saddler [*sellarius*], and Mauth', sister. Grim and Alward of St James [*de Sancto Jacobo*]. Hilary [*Hillarius*] Blund and Geoffrey, priest[s?]. Richard Wallwan', priest. Sabina, widow of Walter le Granger. Warin, brother. Master Baldwin son of Aubree, canon, and Alfric le Forbour, and Arnolf, brother. Herbert, priest, and Algar. Alice and Isabell'. Herbert, priest, and Brictiue, sister. Matill', wife of William Caperun. Henry Pelizun. John de Ponte, our brother. Walter de Topesham, priest. Thomas de Langden. [f. 18v] William Lyde, priest. William de la Hole, priest. Isabell' de Carswille. Aubrea Stur. Rosa Hobba. Thomas de Alfynton, priest and vicar. Henry de Mildelton, priest and vicar. Peter Gasquyn. Sir John de Bouy, chaplain. Joan Hawkyn, our sister. Joan Wytebrother. Christina de Gatepath. Lucy [*erased*]. Jordan le Marchel. Walter de Clopton.

[*Added:* Robert Olyver and Leticia, his wife.]

29. The Earliest Obit Accounts of Exeter Cathedral, 1305–7

(Source: Exeter Cathedral Archives, D&C 3673. Latin text. In the original accounts, the titles of the dignitaries and the names of the canons are not uniformly spelt, and are often highly abbreviated. In this edition, the titles are all spelt out in full and the names have been reduced to a common form, to facilitate identification and comparison of the material. The layout of the names in columns has been reproduced exactly.)

[f. 59r]

Here begins the term of St John the Baptist, in the year of the Lord 1305.

At the obit of John de Monte Acuto [17 June], 7s. 7½d.

Dean	Chancellor	W. de Kilkenny
Penitentiary	J. de Exonia	T. de Charleton
W. de Sancta Elena	H. Huse, deceased	
R. de Veteri Terra	Archd. of Barnstaple	
Archd. of Totnes	Treasurer	

At the obit of John de Esse [28 June], 8s. 4d.

Dean	Precentor	Archd. of Barnstaple
Archd. of Exeter	T. de Charleton	Treasurer
Penitentiary	J. de Exonia	
W. de Sancta Elena	Huse, deceased	
R. de Veteri Terra	W. de Kilkenny	
Archd. of Totnes	J. de Bruton	
Chancellor	J. Strange	

Rents. Memorandum that Robert, collector of the rents of the town, adding 6s. 8d. from St Eval [*de Sancto Uuelo*], paid 31s. of the payment at Easter. He also paid 20d. of arrears of the same rent, divided between sixteen canons resident in the term of the Nativity of the Lord [1304–5], each of whom received 2s. 0½d.

Dean	Chancellor,	J. Strange,
Archd. of Exeter,	by a vicar	by R., chaplain
by a vicar	J. de Exonia	T. de Charleton

272

Penitentiary,	R. de Cumbe,	Archd. of Barnstaple
by Luc'	deceased	Treasurer,
W. de Sancta Elena,	W. de Kilkenny,	by Elias
by <illegible>	by a vicar	J. de Bruton,
R. de Veteri Terra	R. de Molton,	by a vicar
Archd. of Totnes	by a vicar	

For the corpse of Alice de Dodderygg, deducting deductions, 3s. 1d., divided between 13 canons present, each of whom, adding 2d., received 3d. In a further dividend, to each ½d.

Dean	Chancellor	J. Strange
Penitentiary, by Luc'	J. de Exonia	Archd. of Barnstaple
W. de Sancta Elena	H. Huse, deceased	Treasurer
R. de Veteri Terra	T. de Charleton	
Archd. of Totnes	W. de Kilkenny	

The box. Memorandum that on Saturday next [26 June 1305] before the feast of the apostles Peter and Paul there was found in the box 26s. 9d. From which in expenses: for mats [*natis*] in the stalls, 4s. For wine for the whole term, 3s. 2½d. For coals, 11½d. For four belts [*baudreis*] for bells, 4d. For repairing thuribles, 2s. Also to the tailor [*cissori*] repairing vestments of the church for nine days, 18d. Also for grease for the bells for three feast days, 3d. For cord and thread, 12d. For sindon bought for copes and for other vestments, 12d. Also to the laundress, the seamstress, and the digger [*fossore*], 15d. Also for binding two books, 12d. Also to the subtreasurer and the clerk of the chapter, 8d. In placing and lighting candles for two feast days, 2d. To the custors and the cat, 13d. Total 17s. 10½d. and there remains 8s. 10d., of which to the chapter 4s. 5d. and to the treasurer the same amount.

[f. 59v]

Delivered to Robert de Asperton [clerk of the works] for the half-share [*medietatem*] of the canons' prebends from the aforesaid term of St John, £12.

For the corpse of Gervase le Pottere, deducting deductions, [no sum mentioned]

Penitentiary	Chancellor	Archd. of Barnstaple
W. de Sancta Elena	J. de Exonia	Treasurer
R. de Veteri Terra	H. Huse, deceased	
Archd. of Totnes	T. de Charleton	

At the obit of Laurence, canon [5 July], 7s. 7d.

Penitentiary	Chancellor	W. de Kilkenny
W. de Sancta Elena	J. de Exonia	Archd. of Barnstaple
R. de Veteri Terra	H. Huse, deceased	Treasurer
Archd. of Totnes	T. de Charleton	

For the corpses of Luke le Meler and the wife of Kerdewelle, 23½d., deducting deductions, divided among the aforesaid 11 canons, each of whom received 2d. and there remains 1½d.

At the obit of Simon, archdeacon of Cornwall [11 July], 7s. 9d.

Penitentiary	
W. de Sancta Elena	H. Huse [deceased]
R. de Veteri Terra	T. de Charleton
Archd. of Totnes	Archd. of Barnstaple
Chancellor	Treasurer
J. de Exonia	J. Strange

At the obit of R[oger] Baret [8 July], 10s.

Penitentiary	J. de Exonia
W. de Sancta Elena	H. Huse [deceased]
R. de Veteri Terra	T. de Charleton
Archd. of Totnes	Archd. of Barnstaple
Chancellor	J. Strange
Treasurer	

At the obit of Clement, chancellor [6 July], 8s.

Dean	Archd. of Totnes	R. de Molton
Penitentiary	Chancellor	J. Strange
W. de Sancta Elena	J. de Exonia	Archd. of Barnstaple
R. de Veteri Terra	H. Huse, deceased	Treasurer
W. de Kilkenny		

For certain corpses, deducting deductions, 8½d., divided among the 10 canons written below, each of whom received ¾d. and there remains ¼d.

Penitentiary	Chancellor	Treasurer
W. de Sancta Elena	J. de Exonia	T. de Charleton
R. de Veteri Terra	H. Huse [deceased]	

[the folio numbering omits f. 60 and continues as f. 61r]

At the obit of Serlo, formerly dean of Exeter [21 July], by H[enry de Somersete], dean, 10s.

Penitentiary	Precentor	J. de Bruton
R. de Veteri Terra	J. de Exonia	J. Strange
Archd. of Totnes	H. Huse, deceased	Archd. of Barnstaple
Chancellor	J. de Godeley	Treasurer

For John de Ridmore, deducting deductions, 16¼d., divided among 16 canons, each of whom received 1d. and there remains 1d.

Dean	Archd. of Totnes	R. de Molton	Treasurer
Penitentiary	Chancellor	J. de Bruton	
W. de Sancta Elena	J. de Exonia	J. de Berkeley	
R. de Veteri Terra	H. Huse [deceased]	J. Strange	
R. de Morcester	W. de Kilkenny	Archd. of Barnstaple	

At the obit of Roger, the second dean [14 August], 10s.

Dean	Archd. of Totnes	R. de Molton
Archd. of Exeter	Chancellor	J. de Bruton
Penitentiary	Precentor	J. de Berkeley
W. de Sancta Elena	J. de Exonia [*deleted*]	J. Strange
R. de Veteri Terra	H. Huse [deceased]	Archd. of Barnstaple
R. de Morcester	W. de Kilkenny	Treasurer

At the obit of John de [Sancto] Gorono [31 August], 10s.

Dean	Chancellor	T. de Charleton
Penitentiary	H. Huse, deceased	Archd. of Barnstaple
W. de Sancta Elena	R. de Molton	Treasurer
R. de Veteri Terra	J. de Berkeley	
Archd. of Totnes	J. Strange	

At the obit of William de Wollauinton [1 September], 16s.

Dean	Archd. of Totnes	T. de Charleton
Penitentiary	Chancellor	J. de Berkeley
W. de Sancta Elena	Precentor	Archd. of Barnstaple
R. de Veteri Terra	H. Huse, deceased	Treasurer
R. de Morcester	R. de Molton	

To the monks of St Nicholas 12d. To Brother John de la Mare for the Friars Minor 2s. To the Friars Preachers 2s., retained for a certain rent. To the lepers of the Magdalene 12d., by R[obert], collector of the rents of the town.

[f. 61v]

Gabriel. Costs of the feast of St Gabriel, celebrated on the Monday on the morrow of the decollation of the Blessed John the Baptist [31 August] in the year of the Lord 1304, forthcoming from the fruits of the church of St Breward [*Sancti Brueredi*] from the autumn of the year of the Lord 1304, which fruits were then sold for £11 1s. 6d., from which are distributed: to each canon, 17 canons being present, 2s. To each vicar similarly, 23 being present, 12d.; to each secondary present and within [*infra*] holy orders, namely 9, 6d.; to each boy of the choir within a certain *merum* [boundary?], 2d.; to the clerk of the chapter for his labour, 12d., and to the subclerk, 6d.; with deductions and expenses for the same day, namely in 22 pounds of wax purchased, 11s. 11d.; for making 30 pounds [of candles?] and wicks [*lic[i]nis*] and firewood, 16d.; for half a pound of incense, 8d.

Dean	Archd. of Totnes	R. de Molton
Archd. of Exeter	Chancellor	J. de Berkeley
Penitentiary	Precentor	J. Strange
W. de Sancta Elena	H. Huse, deceased	Archd. of Barnstaple
R. de Veteri Terra	T. de Charleton	Treasurer
R. de Morcester	W. de Kilkenny	

Tuesday in the morrow [1 September], on the anniversary of the Lord Walter, of good memory, bishop of Exeter, to each of the aforesaid canons 2s.; to each vicar, namely 23 present, 12d.; to each secondary, namely 9, within holy orders and present, 6d.; to each boy of the choir within a certain [boundary?], 2d.; to the clerk of the chapter for his labour, 12d., and to the subclerk, 6d. Also distributed to 500 poor, 41s. 8d., namely to each 1d. Sum of all the expenses of each day, £9 6s. 3d., and so remains 35s. 3d. divided between the aforesaid 17 canons, each of whom, adding 2d., received 2s. 1d.

At the obit of John de Necton [5 September], 10s., paid by the hand of Robert, collector of rents of the town.

Dean	Archd. of Totnes	R. de Molton
Penitentiary	Chancellor	J. de Berkeley
W. de Sancta Elena	H. Huse, deceased	Archd. of Barnstaple
R. de Veteri Terra	T. de Charleton	Treasurer

At the obit of Simon the bishop [9 September], 9s. 2½d. To each canon, 3d.

Dean	R. de Morcèster	H. Huse, deceased
Archd. of Exeter	Archd. of Totnes	T. de Charleton
Penitentiary	Chancellor	Archd. of Barnstaple
W. de Sancta Elena	R. de Molton	Treasurer
R. de Veteri Terra	J. de Berkeley	

At the obit of William de Molyns [10 September], 8s.

Dean	Archd. of Totnes	J. de Berkeley
Penitentiary	Chancellor	Archd. of Barnstaple
W. de Sancta Elena	H. Huse, deceased	Treasurer
R. de Veteri Terra	T. de Charleton	
R. de Morcester	R. de Molton	

On the same day, for a certain corpse, deducting deductions, 13d.; to each of those written above, 1d. Also, there remain ¼d. and a Tournois [coin] and a cauldron [*caldr'*].

[f. 62r]

Here begins the term of St Michael in the year of the Lord 1305.

For the corpse of Roger de Haydon, deducting deductions, 3s. 9d., divided among 11 canons present, each of whom received 4d. and there remains 1½d.

Dean	Archd. of Totnes	J. Strange
W. de Sancta Elena	Chancellor	Archd. of Barnstaple
R. de Veteri Terra	H. Huse, deceased	Treasurer
R. de Morcester	W. de Kilkenny	

For the corpse of Sir Andrew de Treluyk, deducting deductions, 5s. 8d., divided among 12 canons present, each of whom received 5½d. and there remains 2d.

Dean	R. de Morcester	W. de Kilkenny
Archd. of Exeter	Archd. of Totnes	J. Strange
W. de Sancta Elena	Chancellor	Archd. of Barnstaple
R. de Veteri Terra	H. Huse, deceased	Treasurer

For the corpse of Hugh Faukun, deducting deductions, 14d., divided among 10 canons present, each of whom, adding 1d., received 1½d.

Dean	Archd. of Totnes	Archd. of Barnstaple
Penitentiary	Chancellor	Treasurer
W. de Sancta Elena	Henry Huse, deceased	
R. de Veteri Terra	J. Strange	

At the obit of Bishop Peter, first founder of the new work, to each canon present in the choir, 12d., to each vicar, 2d., to each secondary, 1d., to each annuellar, 1d., to each boy, ½d., to the clerk of the chapter and other ministers of the exchequer, 12d., to the custors for ringing the bells, 4d., to Sir Robert de Aspertoun because [he is] master of the new work, 1[d.], to Master Roger the mason [*cementar'*], 1d. Total 18s. 2d.

Dean	Chancellor
Penitentiary	H. Huse, deceased
W. de Sancta Elena	J. Strange
R. de Veteri Terra	Archd. of Barnstaple
Archd. of Totnes	Treasurer

The new fabric. Delivered to Sir [Robert] de Asperton, master of the new fabric for the half-share of the canons' prebends from Michaelmas term in the year of the Lord 1305, £11 13s. 4d., besides which the stewards of the exchequer paid the same Sir Robert half a mark [6s. 8d.] and so the whole from the aforesaid Michaelmas term.

At the obit of Martin Derelyng [8 October], 10s. from two shops in North Street, [delivered] by Adam.

Penitentiary	Chancellor	Archd. of Barnstaple
R. de Veteri Terra	H. Huse, deceased	Treasurer
Archd. of Totnes	J. Strange	

[f. 62v]

The box. Found in the box, 22s. 8d. From which: in wine for the whole term, 3s. 7½d. Also in silk and white thread, 3½d. Also in wages of the tailor repairing vestments for 15 days, 2s. 6d. Also in wages of the seamstress helping him for four days, 3d. Also for ropes for the bells, 3s. 1¾d. For 30 ells of linen cloths for vestments of the boys, 5s. 5d., and there still remain 10 ells of the same cloth not cut. To the seamstress for 5 pairs of albs, newly made, 7d. Also for washing a picture [*tabula*] of St Peter, 6d. Also to the seamstress, the laundress, and the digger, 15s. [*recte* 15d]. To the custors and the cat, 13d. Also for coals, 11½d. For making 5 belts [*baudreis*], 5d. Also to the subtreasurer and the clerk of the chapter, 8d. Also for grease for the bells for four feast days, 4d. Also for the wages of a certain binder for binding a gradual, 6d. For placing and lighting candles for three feast days, 3d. Total 21s. 7d. and there remains 13½d., divided between the chapter and the treasurer, of which 6½d. [was paid] to Master Elias on behalf of the treasurer.

At the obit of Thomas de Herteford, formerly archdeacon of Totnes [11 October], 7s. 1½d.

Penitentiary	H. Huse, deceased	Archd. of Barnstaple
Archd. of Totnes	J. Strange	Treasurer
Chancellor	R. de Veteri Terra	

The old fabric. Delivered to Sir Robert de Asperton, £4 arising from the church of St Erth [*Lannudno*] for the old fabric.

The rents of the town. Memorandum that Robert, collector of the rents of the town, concerning the same rent of the payment made at the feast of St John [24 June], adding 6s. 8d. arising from the church of St Eval, paid 30s., divided among the canons resident in Easter term, namely 17, each of whom received 21d.

Dean, by a vicar	R. de Veteri Terra	R. de Molton, by a vicar
Archd. of Exeter, by A.	Precentor, by a vicar	J. de Bruton, by a vicar
	J. de Exonia, by A.	J. Strange
Penitentiary	H. Huse, deceased	Archd. of Barnstaple
W. de S. Elena, by A.	W. de Kilkenny	Treasurer
Archd. of Totnes, by A.	T. de Charleton	
Chancellor		

At the obit of R[obert] Tifford [19 October], 7s. 1½d.

Penitentiary	H. Huse, deceased	Archd. of Barnstaple
R. de Veteri Terra	W. de Kilkenny	Treasurer
Chancellor	J. Strange	

At the obit of Walter de Pembroke [20 October], 7s. 1½d.

Penitentiary	H. Huse, deceased	Archd. of Barnstaple
R. de Veteri Terra	W. de Kilkenny	Treasurer
Chancellor	J. Strange	

At the obit of Athelstan, king [27 October], 8s. 1d. To each canon 3d.

Penitentiary	H. Huse, deceased	Archd. of Barnstaple
R. de Veteri Terra	W. de Kilkenny	Treasurer
Chancellor	J. Strange	

[f. 63r]

At the obit of Henry [Marshal], bishop [26 October], 8s. 5½d. To each canon 3d.

Penitentiary	J. de Exonia	Archd. of Barnstaple
W. de Sancta Elena	H. Huse, deceased	Treasurer
R. de Veteri Terra	W. de Kilkenny	
Chancellor	J. Strange	

At the solemnity of the Holy Spirit made on Saturday next [30 October] before the feast of All Saints, in the year of the Lord 1305, for the healthful state of the venerable father Lord Thomas, by the grace of God, bishop of Exeter, there is accounted £16 arising from the church of St Eval in Cornwall, from which there is accounted in expenses for the annual wages of two [chaplains], £6 6s. 8d. Also at the obit of Gilbert de Tyting, 12s.

Also to the rector of the church of St James, 16d. Also to the farmer of St Sidwell for the diminution of the tithe in the area [belonging to] the Friars Minor, 4s. Also to the collector of the rents of the canons in the city for rent, 26s. 8d. Also the vicars of the church of Blessed Peter for various rents exchanged, 5s. 8d. Also to each of the canons written below and present at the solemnity, 2s., to each vicar present, 1s., to each secondary, 6d., to each boy of the choir, 2d., to each annuellar and chaplain of the town present in the choir, 1d. To the custors, 12d. to be taken equally among them. To the clerk of the chapter, 8d. To the submonitor [subclerk of the exchequer], 4d. and to the rest of the ministers each, 2d.

Dean	Chancellor	J. Strange
Penitentiary	J. de Exonia	Archd. of Barnstaple
W. de Sancta Elena	H. Huse, deceased	Treasurer
R. de Veteri Terra, by Ad.	W. de Kilkenny	

Expenses. To 24 vicars, 24s.; 11 secondaries, 5s. 6d.; the clerk of the chapter with the ministers of the same, 2s.; the Friars Minor, 2s.; 15 annuellars, 15d. Also to 17 chaplains from the city, 17d.; custors, 6d., because two are portioners [i.e. other clergy already covered]; boys of the choir, 2s. 4d. Total of expenses, £11 17s. 4d., and the remainder divided among the above written canons, £4 2s. 8d., each of whom received 7s. 6½d. and there remains [blank].

For a certain corpse, deducting deductions, 10d. divided between 11 canons present, each of whom, adding 1d., received 1d.

Dean	Chancellor	J. Strange
Penitentiary	J. de Exonia	Archd. of Barnstaple
W. de Sancta Elena	H. Huse, deceased	Treasurer
R. de Veteri Terra	W. de Kilkenny	

At the obit of John Nobil, formerly dean of Exeter [3 November], 15s. 10d. To each canon, 6d., each vicar, 3d., secondary, 1d., boy, ½d., annuellar, 1d.

Dean	Chancellor	J. Strange
Penitentiary	J. de Exonia	Archd. of Barnstaple
W. de Sancta Elena	H. Huse, deceased	Treasurer
R. de Veteri Terra	W. de Kilkenny	

At the obit of W. de Werplesdon, 10s.

Penitentiary	Chancellor	W. de Kilkenny	Treasurer
W. de Sancta Elena	J. de Exonia	J. Strange	
R. de Veteri Terra	H. Huse, deceased	Archd. of Barnstaple	

[f. 63v]

At the obit of Robert Gifford, canon of Exeter [12 November], 15s. To each canon, 4d., vicar, 2d., secondary, 1d., boy, ½d.

Penitentiary	J. de Exonia	Archd. of Barnstaple
W. de Sancta Elena	H. Huse, deceased	Treasurer
R. de Veteri Terra	W. de Kilkenny	
Chancellor	J. Strange	

At the obit of Walter de Lechlade [9 November], 6s. 10d.

Penitentiary	Chancellor	Archd. of Barnstaple
W. de Sancta Elena	H. Huse, deceased	Treasurer
R. de Veteri Terra	J. Strange	

For wine for St Martin [11 November], 7s. 6d.

Penitentiary	J. de Exonia	J. Strange
W. de Sancta Elena	H. Huse, deceased	Archd. of Barnstaple
R. de Veteri Terra	W. de Kilkenny	Treasurer

At the obit of Thomas Gapes [18 November], 7s.

Penitentiary	J. de Exonia	Archd. of Barnstaple
W. de Sancta Elena	H. Huse, deceased	Treasurer
R. de Veteri Terra	W. de Kilkenny	
Chancellor	J. Strange	

At the obit of John Rof [14 November], was paid by the collector of rents of the town 3s. 10d. and the residue cannot yet be collected, wherefore there are distributed among the canons and vicars, secondaries, choristers, and [*blank*]

Dean 1d.	Chancellor 1d.	J. Strange 1d.
Penitentiary 1d.	H. Huse, deceased 1d.	Archd. of Barnstaple 1d.
W. de S. Elena 1d.	J. de Exonia 1d.	Treasurer 1d.
R. de V. Terra 1d.	W. de Kilkenny 1d.	

At the obit of William Briwere, knight [23 November], 10s.

Dean	Chancellor	J. Strange
Penitentiary	J. de Exonia	Archd. of Barnstaple
W. de Sancta Elena	H. Huse, deceased	Treasurer
R. de Veteri Terra	W. de Kilkenny	

At the obit of William Briwere, bishop [24 November], to each canon, 4d., vicar, 2d., secondary, 1d., boy, ½d.; to each priest present and to other ministers of the church as the custom is. Total 12s. 1½d.

Dean	Chancellor	J. Strange

Penitentiary	J. de Exonia	Archd. of Barnstaple
W. de Sancta Elena	H. Huse, deceased	Treasurer
R. de Veteri Terra	W. de Kilkenny	

For the corpse of John Aleyn, deducting deductions, 3s. 7d. To each canon written below, 5d.

Dean	Chancellor	J. Strange
Penitentiary	J. de Exonia	Archd. of Barnstaple
W. de Sancta Elena	H. Huse, deceased	Treasurer
R. de Veteri Terra	W. de Kilkenny	

[f. 64r]

At the obit of John de Kantia [2 December], 7s. 9d.

Dean	Archd. of Totnes	W. de Kilkenny
Penitentiary	Chancellor	J. Strange
W. de Sancta Elena	J. de Exonia	Archd. of Barnstaple
R. de Veteri Terra	H. Huse, deceased	Treasurer

At the obit of Bartholomew, bishop [14 December], [no sum mentioned]. To each canon, 3d. and to the rest of the ministers of the church as is accustomed.

Penitentiary	Chancellor	Archd. of Barnstaple
W. de Sancta Elena	J. de Exonia	Treasurer
R. de Veteri Terra	H. Huse, deceased	
Archd. of Totnes	J. Strange [*erased*]	

At the obit of Eustace the Blind [17 December], 20s. by Robert, collector of the rents of the town. To each canon, 4d., vicar, 2d., secondary, [1d.], boy, ½d., and to the rest of the ministers as is accustomed.

Penitentiary	Chancellor	J. Strange
W. de Sancta Elena	J. de Exonia	Archd. of Barnstaple
R. de Veteri Terra	H. Huse, deceased	Treasurer
Archd. of Totnes	J. de Bruton	

To the monks of St Nicholas, 12s., the monks of Cowick, 6d., the canons of Marsh, 3d., the monks of St James, 3d., the bridge of Exeter, 12d. To a certain candle in the church of Blessed Mary Arches, 8d. (by Adam), the chapter, 4d., the fabric, 2d., the collector for his labour, 4d.

At the obit of Richard Blundi, bishop [23 December], 12s. 3d. To each canon, 4d., each vicar, 2d., each secondary, 1d., boy, ½d., and to the rest as is accustomed.

Dean	Chancellor	J. de Bruton
W. de Sancta Elena	J. de Exonia	J. Strange

R. de Veteri Terra	H. Huse, deceased	Archd. of Barnstaple
Archd. of Totnes	W. de Kilkenny	Treasurer

Rent. Memorandum that Robert, collector of the rents of the town, paid from the payment made at the feast of St Michael, adding 6s. 8d. which he received from the exchequer, 32s., divided among the canons resident in the term of St John, each of whom, adding ¾d., received 20¼d., which payment was applied to the payment of St Michael's [term].

Dean	Archd. of Totnes,	R. de Molton	Treasurer
Archd. of Exeter, by vicar	by Ad.	J. de Bruton, by vicar	
Penitentiary	Precentor, by vicar	J. de Berkeley, by vicar	
W. de S. Elena	J. de Exonia	J. Strange, by Ad.	
R. de V. Terra	H. Huse, deceased	Archd. of Barnstaple	
W. de Kilkenny	T. de Charleton, by vicar		

At the obit of W[illiam] de Stanweye [31 December], 12s. 11d. To each canon, 4d., vicar, 2d., secondary, 1d., boy, ½d., and to the rest of the ministers as is accustomed.

Dean	Archd. of Totnes	W. de Kilkenny	Archd.of
Penitentiary	Chancellor	J. de Bruton	Barnstaple
W. de S. Elena	J. de Exonia	T. de Charleton	Treasurer
R. de V. Terra	H. Huse, deceased	J. Strange	

[f. 64v]

Here begins the term of the Nativity of the Lord, in the year of the same 1305.

At the obit of Sir John Wyger [30 December 1305], 10s.

Dean	Archd. of Totnes	T. de Charleton
Penitentiary	Chancellor	W. de Kilkenny
W. de Sancta Elena	J. de Exonia	R. de Molton
R. de Veteri Terra	H. Huse, deceased	J. de Bruton
J. Strange	Archd. of Barnstaple	Treasurer

The new fabric. Delivered to Sir Robert de Asperton for the half-share of the canons' prebends for the term of the Nativity of the Lord, in the aforesaid year, £12 and so the whole for the same term.

The box. Found in the box on Thursday in the octave of the Epiphany [13 January 1306], 20s. 10¾d. From which: for coals, 12s. For mats for the stalls and elsewhere in the church, 3s. For repairing thuribles, 6d. For the wages of one tailor making two copes and repairing other vestments which were to be repaired in turn, that is for 27 days, 4s. 6d. paid at 2d. per day. For grease for the bells for the whole term, 3d. For lamps, 3d. For fastenings for two missals, 2d. Also for painting and decorating a certain receptacle for the candle of the priest celebrating mass on the day of the Purification [Candlemas], 6d. For canvas for copes, 7½d. For silk for copes, 8d. For black thread and *crecea* [yellow?], 2d. For making 11 amices and *hucris* [hoods?] of silk cloths, 3d. Also to the digger, the laundress, and the seamstress, 15d. For thread, 1d. For moulding candles for one double feast, 1d. Also to the custors and the cat, 13d. For wine for the whole term, 3s. 8¼d. Also for straw for two feast days, 2d. Also for one mat for the bishop, 1d. Also to the subtreasurer and clerk of the chapter, 8d. Total of the expenses, 18s. 0¾d., and so remains to the chapter, 17d., and to the treasurer the same amount.

For a certain corpse, 15d., divided among 12 canons each of whom received 1¼d.

Dean	Archd. of Totnes	W. de Kilkenny
Penitentiary	Chancellor	T. de Charleton
W. de Sancta Elena	J. de Exonia	Archd. of Barnstaple
R. de Veteri Terra	H. Huse, deceased	Treasurer

At the obit of R. the Leper, 10s.

Penitentiary	Chancellor	J. de Molton
W. de Sancta Elena	J. de Exonia	J. Strange
R. de Veteri Terra	H. Huse, [deceased]	Archd. of Barnstaple
Archd. of Totnes	J. de Bruton	Treasurer

At the obit of John de Somerset, by H[enry] the dean, 7s. 10d.

Dean	Archd. of Totnes	T. de Charleton	Treasurer
Penitentiary	Chancellor	W. de Kilkenny	
W. de S. Elena	J. de Exonia	R. de Molton	
R. de V. Terra	H. Huse, deceased	J. Strange	

Also on the same day, at the obit of Master J. de Cowyk, to each of the above written except for the dean, because he was not present at the mass, 2d. Also offered for the same [i.e. Cowyk's obit] 5s. 4½d., from which to each canon a sum of 5d. and there remains 4d. and four ballards [base coins].

[f. 65r]

At the obit of Hugh de Wylton [24 January], 7s. 7d.

Dean	Archd. of Totnes	T. de Charleton
Penitentiary	Chancellor	R. de Molton

W. de Sancta Elena	J. de Exonia	J. Strange
R. de Veteri Terra	H. Huse, deceased	Treasurer

For the corpse of William de Torre, baker, deducting deductions, 15¾d., divided among the above written canons, each of whom received 1¼d. and there remains ¾d.

At the obit of Adam de Yeuelcestr [1 February], 8s.

Dean	Chancellor	R. de Molton
Penitentiary	H. Huse, deceased	J. Strange
W. de Sancta Elena	J. de Exonia	Archd. of Barnstaple
R. de Veteri Terra	T. de Charleton	Treasurer
Archd. of Totnes	W. de Kilkenny	

At the solemnity of the Holy Spirit made on Thursday [3 February], the morrow of the feast of the Purification of Blessed Mary in the year of the Lord 1305 [1306, modern style], for the healthful state of Sir William de Puntyngton, are paid 18s. 4d., from which to each canon present in the choir written below, he receives 4d., to each vicar present similarly, 2d., to each secondary, 1d., to each boy of the choir, ½d., to the clerk of the chapter, 2d., to 15 poor, 15d., and that the residue be distributed among the same canons, each of whom received 7¼d. and there remains 1d.

Dean	Archd. of Totnes	T. de Charleton
Penitentiary	Chancellor	W. de Kilkenny
W. de Sancta Elena	J. de Exonia	J. Strange
R. de Veteri terra	H. Huse, deceased	Treasurer

At the obit of Richard de Brendiswo[rt]hy [4 February], for the choir, 7s. 4d. Also given to the poor, 25d.

Dean	Archd. of Totnes	H. Huse, deceased
Penitentiary	Chancellor	Treasurer
W. de Sancta Elena	J. de Exonia	
R. de Veteri Terra	T. de Charleton	

For the corpse of Nicholas de Wythericg, 17¼d., divided between 12 canons in residence, each of whom, adding 1d., received 1½d. and there remains ¼d.

Dean	Archd. of Totnes	W. de Kilkenny
Penitentiary	Chancellor	H. Huse, deceased
W. de Sancta Elena	J. de Exonia	J. Strange
R. de Veteri Terra	T. de Charleton	Treasurer

At the obit of Ysaac, archdeacon of Totnes [8 February], 8s.

Dean	Chancellor	J. Strange
Penitentiary	J. de Exonia	Archd. of Barnstaple
W. de Sancta Elena	T. de Charleton	Treasurer
R. de Veteri Terra	H. Huse, deceased	
Archd. of Totnes	W. de Kilkenny	

[f. 65v]

At the obit of Thomas Maudit [12 February], 9s.

Dean	Chancellor	W. de Kilkenny
Penitentiary	Precentor	R. de Molton
W. de Sancta Elena	J. de Exonia	Archd. of Barnstaple
R. de Veteri Terra	H. Huse, deceased	Treasurer
Archd. of Totnes	T. de Charleton	

For the corpses of two children of Robert de Nymeton, deducting deductions, 26d., divided among the underwritten canons, each of whom received 2d.

Dean	J. de Exonia	J. Strange
Penitentiary	H. Huse, deceased	Archd. of Barnstaple
W. de Sancta Elena	W. de Kilkenny	Treasurer
Archd. of Totnes	R. de Molton	
W., Precentor	R. de Veteri Terra	

For the corpse of Joan the seamstress, deducting deductions, 8½d., to each of the underwritten canons ½d. and there remains 2½d.

Dean	H. Huse, deceased
Penitentiary	R. de Molton
W. de Sancta Elena	J. de Bruton
R. de Veteri Terra	J. Strange
Archd. of Totnes	Archd. of Barnstaple
J. de Exonia	Treasurer

For the corpse of Richard Archedekene, deducting deductions, 3s. 5¼d., each of whom received 3¼d. and there remains 1d.

Dean	H. Huse, deceased	Archd. of Barnstaple
Penitentiary	W. de Kilkenny	
W. de Sancta Elena	R. de Molton	
R. de Veteri Terra	J. Strange	
Archd. of Totnes	Treasurer	
J. de Exonia		

For a certain corpse, deducting deductions, 12¾d., divided among the underwritten canons, each of whom received 1d. and there remains 1¾d.

Dean	Archd. of Totnes	J. de Bruton
Penitentiary	Chancellor	Archd. of Barnstaple
W. de Sancta Elena	H. Huse, [deceased]	Treasurer
R. de Veteri Terra, by vicar		R. de Molton, by vicar

At the obit of Ralph Cola [7 March], 8s. H Huse, last [payment].

Penitentiary	Archd. of Totnes	W. de Kilkenny	Archd. of Barn.
W. de S. Elena	J. de Exonia	J. Bruton	Treasurer
R. de V. Terra	H. Huse, deceased	J. Strange	
Chancellor			

At the obit of Master Thomas de Bodeham, 20s. arising from the house of the archdeacon of Totnes. To each canon present, 8d., each vicar, 4d., each annuellar and secondary, 1d., each boy of the choir, ½d.

Penitentiary	J. de Exonia	Treasurer
W. de Sancta Elena	W. de Kilkenny	Archd. of Barnstaple
R. de Veteri Terra	J. de Bruton	
Archd. of Totnes	J. Strange	

[f. 66r]

Rents of the town. Memorandum that Robert, collector of the rents of the town, counting 6s. 8d. which he received from the exchequer, paid from the rents of the town for the payment made at the feast of the Nativity of the Lord, 30s., divided among 12 canons resident in the term of St Michael, each of whom received 2s. 6d.

Dean	Archd. of Totnes	W. de Kilkenny
Penitentiary	Chancellor	J. Strange, by Ad.
W. de Sancta Elena	J. de Exonia	Archd. of Barnstaple
R. de Veteri Terra	H. Huse, deceased	Treasurer

Here begins Easter term in the year of the Lord 1306 [*a premature entry*].

At the obit of Robert de Warwest, bishop [22 March], total 8s. 3d. To each canon 3d.

Penitentiary	Archd. of Totnes	R. de Molton	Archd. of Barn.
W. de S. Elena	J. de Exonia	J. de Bruton	Treasurer
R. de V. Terra	W. de Kilkenny	J. Strange	
	[*erased*]		

Also for a certain corpse the same day, deducting deductions, 8½d., divided among the above written canons, each of whom received ¾d. and there remains ¼d.

For certain corpses, deducting deductions, 2s. 7½d., divided between

Dean	R. de Veteri Terra	W. de Kilkenny	Treasurer
Penitentiary	Archd. of Totnes	J. Strange	Chancellor
W. de S. Elena		J. de Exonia	Archd. of Barn.

Here begins Easter Term in the year of the Lord 1306.

The new fabric. Memorandum that in the aforesaid year, on Friday VI Ides [8] April, Sir Robert de Asperton received £12 for the half-share of the canons' prebends from the same Easter term.

For certain corpses, deducting deductions, 9s[*recte* 9d.]½d., divided between 12 canons each of whom, adding 1½d., received 1d.

Dean	J. de Exonia	J. Strange
Penitentiary	W. de Kilkenny	Archd. of Barnstaple
W. de Sancta Elena	J. de Bruton	Treasurer
R. de Veteri Terra	R. de Molton	

At the obit of Gilbert de Tyting [10 April], 9s. 1d. To each canon, 4d., and to the other ministers as is accustomed.

Dean	J. de Exonia	J. Strange
Penitentiary	W. de Kilkenny	Archd. of Barnstaple
W. de Sancta Elena	R. de Molton	Treasurer
R. de Veteri Terra	J. de Bruton	

[f. 66v]

At the obit of William de Suindon [16 April], 8s.

Dean	R. de Veteri Terra	J. Strange
Penitentiary	J. de Exonia	Archd. of Barnstaple
W. de Sancta Elena	W. de Kilkenny	Treasurer
R. de Molton		

At the obit of Adam de Brigida [20 April], 7s.

Dean	W. de Kilkenny	J. de Bruton	Treasurer
Penitentiary	J. de Exonia	J. Strange	
R. de V. Terra	R. de Molton	Archd. of Barnstaple	

At the obit of Robert de Euesham [18 April], 16s., from which to each canon, 4d., vicar, 2d., secondary, 1d., boy, ½d., custors, 8d.

Dean	W. de Kilkenny	Archd. of Barnstaple
Penitentiary	R. de Molton	Treasurer
R. de Veteri Terra	J. de Bruton	
J. de Exonia	J. Strange	

And remains 4s. 3½d. divided among the aforesaid canons each of whom, adding 1d., received 5¼d.

At the obit of Henry de Warwyke [28 April], 7s. 6d.

Dean	W. de Kilkenny	Archd. of Barnstaple
Penitentiary	R. de Molton	Treasurer
R. de Veteri Terra	J. de Bruton	
J. de Exonia [*deleted*]	J. Strange	

At the obit of Roger de Toryz [29 April], divided among the canons, vicars, secondaries, and boys present in the choir, each canon of which received 12d., vicar, 6d., secondary, 2d., each boy, 1d., the ministers, 12d., and that the residue shall be distributed among chaplains and clerks of the church and the city at the disposition of the stewards [of the exchequer].

Penitentiary	W. de Kilkenny	Archd. of Barnstaple
R. de Veteri Terra	J. de Bruton	Treasurer
J. de Exonia	R. de Molton	
T. de Charleton [*deleted*]	J. Strange	

In the box was found 29s. 10d. From which in expenses: for one belt [*baudr'*], 1d. For mending thuribles, 1d. Also to the tailor repairing copes for five days, 10d. For straw for three feast days, 3d. For grease for the bells for three feast days, 4d. For washing lamps, 1d. For wine for the whole term, 3s. 6d. Also to the custors and the cat, 13d. In placing candles for one feast, 1d. Also to the seamstress, the laundress, and the digger, 15d. For thread, 1d. Also for the same for banners, 1d. Also for making a plate for the door of the choir, ½d. Also for black and white thread to sew copes, ½d. For mending a key, ½d. Also to the subtreasurer and the clerk of the chapter, 8d. Total 8s. 6½d., and so remains to be divided between the chapter and the treasurer, 21s. 3½d.

[f. 67r]

At the obit of Daniel de Longo Camp [11 May], 8s. 3d.

Dean	Chancellor	J. de Bruton
Penitentiary	J. de Exonia	J. Strange
W. de Sancta Elena	T. de Charleton	Precentor
R. de Veteri Terra	W. de Kilkenny	Archd. of Barnstaple
Archd. of Totnes	R. de Molton	Treasurer

At the obit of Sir Reginald le Arceuesk [17 May], 8s. 1d.

Dean	Chancellor	J. de Bruton
Penitentiary	J. de Exonia	J. Strange
W. de Sancta Elena	T. de Charleton	Archd. of Barnstaple
R. de Veteri Terra	W. de Kilkenny	Treasurer
Archd. of Totnes	R. de Molton [*deleted*]	Precentor

For certain corpses, deducting deductions, 11d., divided among 14 canons each of whom, adding 3d., receives 1d.

Dean	Archd. of Totnes	T. de Charlton	Archd. of Barn.
Penitentiary	Chancellor	W. de Kilkenny	Treasurer
W. de S. Elena	Precentor	J. de Bruton	
R. de V. Terra	J. de Exonia	J. Strange	

For certain corpses, deducting deductions, 10½d., divided among 13 canons each of whom received ¾d. and there remains ¾d.

Dean	Archd. of Totnes	J. de Bruton	Treasurer
Penitentiary	Chancellor	Archd. of Barnstaple	
W. de S. Elena	J. de Exonia	T. de Charleton	
R. de V. Terra	W. de Kilkenny	J. Strange	

At the obit of Roger de Lymesie [24 May], 8s. 1d.

Dean	Chancellor	J. de Bruton
Penitentiary	J. de Exonia	J. Strange
W. de Sancta Elena	T. de Charleton	Archd. of Barnstaple
R. de Veteri Terra	W. de Kilkenny	Treasurer
Archd. of Totnes	R. de Molton	

Found on St Dunstan's day [19 May] in the red chest [*rubra archa*] and delivered to Sir Robert de Asperton on the vigil of Pentecost [21 May] for the new fabric, 19s. 11½d.

For certain corpses, deducting deductions, 14d., divided between 12 canons each of whom received 1d. and there remains 2d.

Dean	Archd. of Totnes	R. de Molton
Penitentiary	Chancellor	J. Strange
W. de Sancta Elena	J. de Exonia	Archd. of Barnstaple
R. de Veteri Terra	W. de Kilkenny	Treasurer

For certain corpses, deducting deductions, 10d., divided between 14 canons each of whom, with the addition of ½d., received ¾d.

Dean	Chancellor	W. de Kilkenny
Penitentiary	Archd. of Totnes	R. de Molton

W. de Sancta Elena	T. de Charleton	J. de Bruton
R. de Veteri Terra	J. de Exonia	J. Strange
Archd. of Barnstaple		
Treasurer		

[f. 67v]

Pentecostal offerings [of Devon], 61s. The underwritten canons received from the Pentecostal offerings, namely from 61s. from which to the subtreasurer, 12d., to the chapter clerk, 12d., to the subclerk, 6d., and to the custors, 6d. and there remains 58s. for dividing between the treasurer and the canons underwritten, of which the treasurer receives 29s. and the canons' residue [is] 29s., each of whom, adding 2d., receives 2s. 1d. Also the Pentecostal offerings of Cornwall, 20s., divided between the underwritten, each of whom receives 18d.

Dean	Chancellor	J. de Bruton
Penitentiary	J. de Exonia	J. Strange
W. de Sancta Elena	T. de Charleton	Archd. of Barnstaple
R. de Veteri Terra	W. de Kilkenny	Treasurer
Archd. of Totnes	R. de Molton	

For certain corpses, deducting deductions, 16¼d., divided between the underwritten canons, each of whom received 1¼d. and there remains 1¼d.

Penitentiary	Chancellor	J. Strange
W. de Sancta Elena	J. de Exonia	Archd. of Barnstaple
R. de Veteri Terra	T. de Charleton	Treasurer
Archd. of Totnes	W. de Kilkenny	

For a certain corpse, deducting deductions, 12d. To each canon 1½d. and there remains 1½d.

W. de Sancta Elena	T. de Charleton	Treasurer
R. de Veteri Terra	W. de Kilkenny	
J. de Exonia	Archd. of Barnstaple	

At the obit of John de Monte Acuto [17 June], 6s. 10d.

W. de Sancta Elena	J. de Exonia	Treasurer
R. de Veteri Terra	W. de Kilkenny	
Thomas, Chancellor	Archd. of Barnstaple	

For the corpse of John le Arblaster, deducting deductions, 10½d. To each canon underwritten, 1¾d.

W. de Sancta Elena	W. de Kilkenny
R. de Veteri Terra	Archd. of Barnstaple
J. de Exonia	Treasurer

The canons underwritten will participate in 20s.which escaped from the account of the term of the Nativity of the Lord and is being distributed between 15 canons then resident in that term, each of whom receives 16d.

Henry, dean, by vicar	Chancellor	R. de Molton, by vicar
J., penitentiary, by vicar	J. de Exonia	J. de Bruton
W. de S. Elena	H. Huse, dec.	J. Strange
R. de V. Terra	T. de Charleton	Archd. of Barnstaple
Archd. of Totnes, by vicar	W. de Kilkenny	Treasurer

[f. 68r]

Rents. Robert, collector of the rents of the town paid, adding 6s. 8d. which he received from the exchequer from the term of the Nativity, which is the payment for Easter term, 30s., divided between the next above-written canons, each of whom received 2s.

Here begins the term of St John the Baptist in the year of the Lord 1306.

At the obit of Laurence de Sancto Gorano [5 July], 6s. 2d.

W. de Sancta Elena	J. de Exonia	Treasurer
R. de Veteri Terra	W. de Kilkenny	
Chancellor	Archd. of Barnstaple	

At the obit of Master John de Esse [28 June], 10s.

W. de Sancta Elena	Chancellor	J. Strange
R. de Veteri Terra	J. de Exonia	Archd. of Barnstaple
Archd. of Totnes	W. de Kilkenny	Treasurer

The new fabric. Memorandum that Sir Robert de Asperton received £12 in the exchequer for the half-share of the canons' prebends from the term of St John the Baptist in the year of the Lord 1306, by the hands of Sir Walter de Totton.

At the obit of Clement the chancellor [6 July], 7s. 2d.

W. de Sancta Elena	J. de Exonia	J. de Bruton
R. de Veteri Terra	T. de Charleton	Archd. of Barnstaple
Chancellor	W. de Kilkenny	Treasurer

At the obit of Roger Barat [8 July], 10s.

W. de Sancta Elena	T. de Charleton	Archd. of Barnstaple
R. de Veteri Terra	W. de Kilkenny	Treasurer
Chancellor	J. de Bruton	
J. de Exonia	J. Strange	

For the corpse of Walter the cutler, 5s. 3½d., divided between 10 canons present, each of whom received 6¼d. and there remains 1d.

W. de Sancta Elena	T. de Charleton	Archd. of Barnstaple
R. de Veteri Terra	W. de Kilkenny	Treasurer
Chancellor	J. de Bruton, by vicar	
J. de Exonia	J. Strange	

At the obit of Simon, archdeacon of Cornwall [11 July], 7s. 4d.

W. de Sancta Elena	T. de Charleton	Archd. of Barnstaple
R. de Veteri Terra	W. de Kilkenny	Treasurer
Chancellor	J. de Bruton	
J. de Exonia	J. Strange	

[f. 68v]

For certain corpses, 14¼d., divided between 7 canons each of whom received 2d. and there remains ¼d.

W. de Sancta Elena	J. de Exonia	Treasurer
R. de Veteri Terra	T. de Charleton	
Chancellor	W. de Kilkenny	

For the corpse of Theobald the apothecary, deducting deductions, 12d. To each canon underwritten, adding ½d., he received 1¼d.

W. de Sancta Elena	T. de Charleton	Archd. of Barnstaple
R. de Veteri Terra	W. de Kilkenny	Treasurer
Chancellor	J. de Bruton	
J. de Exonia	J. Strange	

At the obit of Serlo the dean [21 July], by the dean, 10s.

W. de Sancta Elena	J. de Exonia	T. de Charleton
R. de Veteri Terra	J. de Bruton	Archd. of Barnstaple
Chancellor	W. de Kilkenny	Treasurer

For the corpses of W. Boyton and Ralph Carpenter, deducting deductions, 19¼d., divided between 7 canons each of whom received 2¾d.

W. de Sancta Elena	T. de Charleton	J. de Bruton	Treasurer
Chancellor	W. de Kilkenny	Archd. of Barnstaple	

For the corpse of Reginald the taverner, deducting deductions, 15d.

W. de Sancta Elena	J. de Exonia	J. Strange
R. de Veteri Terra	T. de Charleton	Archd. of Barnstaple
Archd. of Totnes	W. de Kilkenny	Treasurer
Chancellor	R. de Molton	

For the corpse of Nicholas de Karswylle, deducting deductions, 10d, whence adding 1d., each received 1d.

W. de Sancta Elena	J. de Exonia	J. Strange
R. de Veteri Terra	T. de Charleton	Archd. of Barnstaple
Archd. of Totnes	W. de Kilkenny	Treasurer
Chancellor	R. de Molton	

At the obit of Simon, bishop, 7s. 9d. To each canon, 3d.

W. de Sancta Elena	T. de Charleton	Treasurer
R. de Veteri Terra	W. de Kilkenny	
Archd. of Totnes	J. Strange	
Chancellor	Archd. of Barnstaple	

[f. 69r]

The box. Found in the box on Wednesday next after the feast of St Peter in Chains [3 August], 30s. 6¾d. From which, in expenses: for rushes for two stools [*scabella*] and for repairing them, 16d. For wine from the feast of Easter, 4s. 4½d. For payment to a smith mending the ironwork on one stall, 1d. For rushes bought for double feast days in the belfry, 3½d. For grease for the bells for four feast days, 4d. For buying 6 lamps, 3d. For buying coals, 4½d. For candles for placing around the church, 1d. For a *claue* [rivet?] for repairing the sepulchre, 1d. Also to the laundress, the seamstress, [and] the digger, 15d. For thread for the term, 1d. Also to the tailor mending copes and small capes [*capulas*] for one day, 2d. For black thread for the same, ½d. Also to the subtreasurer and clerk, 8d. Also to the custors and the cat, 13d. Total 11s. 1¾d. And so remains, divided between the treasurer and the chapter, 19s. 5d., from which the treasurer's share [is] 9s. 8½d. and the chapter's share the same.

At the obit of Henry Huse, celebrated on the Thursday next after the feast of St Peter in Chains [4 August], in the year of the Lord 1306, 24s. 2d. To each canon, 12d., vicar, 4d., annuellar and secondary, 2d., boy, 1d., clerks of the exchequer, 12d.

W. de Sancta Elena	J. de Exonia	J. Strange
R. de Veteri Terra	T. de Charleton	Treasurer
Archd. of Totnes	W. de Kilkenny	
Chancellor	R. de Molton	

The new fabric. Delivered to Sir Robert de Asperton by the executors of Master H. Huse for the soul of the same, 20s.

At the obit of Roger de Wynklegh [14 August], 7s. 3d.

R. de Veteri Terra	T. de Charleton	J. Strange
W. de Sancta Elena	W. de Kilkenny	Treasurer

Archd. of Totnes   R. de Charleton
Chancellor   R. de Molton

At the obit of John de Sancto Gorono [31 August], 7s. 2d.

W. de Sancta Elena	W. de Kilkenny	Treasurer
R. de Veteri Terra	T. de Charleton	
Archd. of Totnes	R. de Molton	
Precentor	J. Strange	

At the obit of William de Wollauynton [1 September], 16s.

R. de Veteri Terra	W. de Kilkenny	Archd. of Barnstaple
Archd. of Totnes	R. de Molton	Treasurer
Chancellor	R. de Charleton	J. Strange

To the monks of St Nicholas, 12d. by A. To the Friars Minor, 2s. by A. To the lepers of the Magdalene, 12d. by A. To the Friars Preachers, 2s., retained by the stewards for a certain rent which the same friars hold of the church – delivered to Robert, collector of the rents of the town.

At the obit of John de Necton [5 September], 10s., paid by the hands of Robert, collector of the rents of the town.

W. de Sancta Elena	W. de Kilkenny
R. de Veteri Terra	T. de Charleton
Archd. of Totnes	Archd. of Barnstaple
Chancellor	Treasurer

[f. 69v]

At the obit of William de Molendinis [10 September], 8s.

W. de Sancta Elena	Chancellor	Precentor
R. de Veteri Terra	W. de Kilkenny	Archd. of Barnstaple
Archd. of Totnes	R. de Charleton	Treasurer

Gabriel. Costs of the feast of St Gabriel celebrated on the Monday [5 September] next before the feast of the Nativity of Blessed Mary in the year of the Lord 1306, arising from the fruits of the church of St Breward from the autumn of the year of the Lord 1305, which fruits were then conveyed to Master Walter de Stapildon for £10, from which there is distributed to each canon present, 2s., to each vicar similarly present, 12d., to each secondary having a share in the mass of Blessed Mary the Virgin, constituted in holy orders and present, 6d., to each boy of the choir, 2d., to the chapter clerk, 12d., to the submonitor, 6d, deducting the expenses made for the same feast, namely for buying 18 pounds of wax, wicks [*lichinis*], and the making of 30 pounds of wax, 12s. 6d. For grease for the bells, 1d. Total 67s. 5d.

W. de Sancta Elena   W. de Kilkenny   Treasurer

R. de Veteri Terra	T. de Charleton	R. de Molton
Archd. of Totnes	J. Strange	
Chancellor	Archd. of Barnstaple	
Precentor		

On Tuesday [6 September] on the morrow, at the obit of Bishop Walter, to the above-written 11 canons present, vicars, secondaries, boys of the choir, clerk of the chapter, and submonitor as above. Total sum of the expenses of both days £8 3s. 11d. And so remains 36s. 1d., divided between the aforesaid 11 canons, each of whom received 3s. 3d. and there remains 4d. which the stewards have given by grace to Sir Roger de Sidebury and Martin Cumpanione.

For the corpse of the wife of Robert de Wotton, 2s. 11½d., divided between 7 canons present, each of whom received 5d. and there remains ½d.

W. de Sancta Elena	J., Penitentiary
R. de Veteri Terra	J. Strange
Archd. of Totnes	Treasurer
W. de Kilkenny	

At the obit of Bartholomew, archdeacon of Exeter [22 September], 10s. paid by the hands of Robert, collector of the rents of the town.

Penitentiary	Precentor	Archd. of Barnstaple
W. de Sancta Elena	W. de Kilkenny	Treasurer
R. de Veteri Terra	R. de Molton	
Archd. of Totnes	T. de Charleton	
Chancellor	J. Strange	

[f. 70r]

Here begins the term of St Michael, in the year of the Lord 1306.

For certain corpses, deducting deductions, 8½d., divided between 10 canons, each of whom received ¾d. and there remains 1d.

Penitentiary	Precentor	Archd. of Barnstaple
W. de Sancta Elena	W. de Kilkenny	Treasurer
R. de Veteri Terra	R. de Molton	
Archd. of Totnes	R. de Charleton	

Rents. Robert, collector of the rents of the town, paid from the rent of the town, adding 6s. 8d. which he received from the exchequer, 30s. from Easter term in the aforesaid year, which payment is called the payment of St John's [term], divided between the canons resident in the aforesaid Easter term, each of whom, adding ½d., received 25¾d.

Dean, by vicar	Chancellor	J. Strange
Penitentiary, by vicar	J. de Exonia, by vicar	Archd. of Barnstaple
W. de S. Elena	T. de Charleton, by R.	Treasurer, by himself
R. de V. Terra, by Ad.	W. de Kilkenny	
Archd. of Totnes	R. de Molton, by himself	
J. de Bruton, by R. his chaplain		

At the obit of Bishop Peter, first founder of the new work [4 October]. To each canon present in the choir, 12d., to each vicar, 2d., to each secondary, 1d., to each annuellar, 1d., to each boy of the choir, ½d. To the clerk of the chapter and the other ministers of the exchequer, 12d. To the custors for ringing the peal [*classici*], 4d. To Sir Robert de Asperton, 1d. because [he is] master of the new work, and to Master Roger the mason, 1d. Total 18s. 2d.

Penitentiary	Precentor	J. Strange
W. de Sancta Elena	W. de Kilkenny	Archd. of Barnstaple
R. de Veteri Terra	R. de Molton	Treasurer
Archd. of Totnes	R. de Charleton	
Chancellor	J. de Bruton	

At the obit of Martin Durlyng [8 October], 7s. 1d. from two shops in North Street, by Adam. Also 2s. from the same shops is placed in the Durlyng purse in the exchequer for the repair of the same shops when it is necessary. Paid to the bellman, 1d.

Penitentiary	Archd. of Totnes	Treasurer
W. de Sancta Elena	W. de Kilkenny	H., Dean
R. de Veteri Terra	R. de Charleton	

For certain corpses, deductions deducted, 20½d. and cauldrons, divided between 10 canons, each of whom received 2d. and there remains ½d. and three cauldrons.

Penitentiary	Archd. of Totnes	J. de Bruton
W. de Sancta Elena	W. de Kilkenny	J. Strange
R. de Veteri Terra	R. de Molton	

At the obit of Thomas de Herteford, formerly archdeacon of Totnes [11 October], 7s. 7d.

Penitentiary	Chancellor	J. de Bruton
W. de Sancta Elena	W. de Kilkenny	J. Strange
R. de Veteri Terra	R. de Molton	Treasurer
Archd. of Totnes	R. de Charleton [*erased*]	

[f. 70v]

For a certain corpse, deducting deductions, 16¾d., 2 pollards, and one Tournois coin, divided between 11 canons, each of whom received 1½d. and there remains 2 pollards, ¼d., and one Tournois coin.

Penitentiary	Archd. of Totnes	R. de Molton	J. Strange
W. de Sancta Elena	Chancellor	R. de Charleton [*erased*]	Treasurer
	W. de Kilkenny	J. de Bruton	
R. de Veteri Terra			

The box. Found in the box on Wednesday [19 October] next after the feast of St Luke the Evangelist, 27s. 1d. From which: for wine, 3s. 3¾d. For mats, 5s. 8d. For coals, 3½d. For grease for three feast days, 3d. For rushes for the belfries, 3½d. For placing candles for two feast days, 2d. For one new belt [*baudre*], 3d. Also to the laundress, the seamstress, and the digger, 15d. For thread, 1d. Also to the custors and the cat, 13d. Also to the subtreasurer and clerk, 8d. For washing lamps, 1d. For lamps bought, 3d. Total 13s. 7¾d. And so remains for dividing between the treasurer and the chapter 15s. 5¼d., from which 6s. 8½d. was delivered to the treasurer and the other half-share is placed in the exchequer in the accustomed place.

At the obit of Robert Tyffor, archdeacon of Exeter [19 October], 7s. 6d.

Penitentiary	Archd. of Totnes	R. de Charleton	Treasurer
W. de S. Elena	Chancellor	J. de Bruton	
R. de V. Terra	J. de Exonia	J. Strange	

At the obit of Walter Penbroc [20 October], 7s. 4d.

Penitentiary	Archd. of Totnes	J. de Bruton
W. de Sancta Elena	Chancellor	J. Strange
R. de Veteri Terra	J. de Exonia	Treasurer

At the obit of Athelstan, king [27 October], 8s. 1d. To each canon, 3d.

Penitentiary	Archd. of Totnes	W. de Kilkenny
W. de Sancta Elena	Chancellor	R. de Charleton
R. de Veteri Terra	J. de Exonia	Treasurer

At the obit of Henry, bishop [26 October], 8s. 7d. To each canon, 3d., and to the rest of the ministers as is accustomed at simple obits.

Penitentiary	Archd. of Totnes	W. de Kilkenny	J. Strange
W. de S. Elena	Chancellor	R. de Charleton	Treasurer
R. de V. Terra	J. de Exonia	J. de Bruton	

The new fabric. Sir Robert de Asperton received in the exchequer for the half-share of the canons' prebends from the term of St Michael, in the year of the Lord 1306, £12.

In wine for St Martin, 7s. 4d.

Dean	Chancellor	R. de Molton [*erased*]	Archd. of Barn.
Penitentiary	J. de Exonia	R. de Charleton	Treasurer
R. de V. Terra	T. de Charleton	J. Strange	
W. de Kilkenny			

Also on the same day and to the same canons, for the child of Thomas the barber [*barbitonsoris*], 12d., each of whom, deducting deductions, received 1d. and there remains 1d.

[f. 71r]

At the solemnity made on Monday [31 October] in the vigil of All Saints, in the year of the Lord 1306, for the state of the venerable father Lord Thomas, by divine grace bishop of Exeter, there is accounted for £16 arising from the church of St Eval in Cornwall, from which is accounted in expenses for the annual wages of two chaplains, £6 6s. 8d. Also for the obit of Gilbert Tytyng, 12s. Also to the rector of the chapel of St James, 16d. To the farmer of St Sidwell, 4s. To the collector of the rents of the canons in Exeter for rent, 26s. 8d. Also to the vicars of the church of St Peter for various rents, 5s. 8d. Also to the Friars Minor, 2s. Also to each canon underwritten present in the choir, 2s., to 24 vicars, 24s., to 10 secondaries because 2 are absent, 5s., to 14 boys, 2s. 4d. To each chaplain of the church and of the city and suburb, 1d. each. To the custors for ringing, 12d. To the chapter clerks, 2s.

Penitentiary	Chancellor	R. de Charleton	Archd. of Barn.
W. de S. Elena	J. de Exonia	J. de Bruton	Treasurer
R. de V. Terra	W. de Kilkenny	J. Strange	
Archd. of Totnes	R. de Molton		

Furthermore the vicar of the church of St Winnow, namely Sir Philip, farmer of the aforesaid church of St Eval, accounts that he has spent 7s. 6d. on the prosecution of a certain action about certain tithes of the aforesaid church of St Eval brought before the official of Exeter. Also paid to Sir John, rector of the church of St James, for the diminution of his tithes from the area [belonging to] the Friars Minor, 16d.

At the obit of Master John Nobil, formerly dean of the church of Exeter [3 November], 16s. 9d. To each canon present, 6d., to each vicar present, 3d., to each annuellar and secondary, 1d., to each boy, ½d.

Penitentiary	Chancellor	R. de Charleton	Archd. of Barn.
W. de S. Elena	J. de Exonia	J. de Bruton	Treasurer
R. de V. Terra	W. de Kilkenny	J. Strange	
Archd. of Totnes	R. de Molton		

At the obit of William de Werplisdon, 7s. 5½d.

Penitentiary	Chancellor [*deleted*]	R. de Molton	Archd. of Barn.
R. de V. Terra	J. de Exonia	R. de Charleton	Treasurer
Archd. of Totnes	W. de Kilkenny	J. Strange	

At the obit of Walter de Lechelade [9 November], 7s. 5½d.

Penitentiary	J. de Exonia	R. de Charleton	Treasurer
R. de V. Terra	W. de Kilkenny	J. Strange	
Chancellor	R. de Molton	Archd. of Barnstaple	

At the obit of Robert Gyffard [12 November], 11s. 3d. To each canon, 4d., to vicars, 2d., secondaries, 1d., boys, ½d., annuellars, 1d.

Penitentiary	J. de Exonia	J. Strange
R. de Veteri Terra	W. de Kilkenny	Archd. of Barnstaple
Chancellor	R. de Molton	Treasurer

At the obit of Th[omas] Gapes [18 November], 7s.

Dean	J. de Exonia	Archd. of Barnstaple
Penitentiary	W. de Kilkenny	Treasurer
R. de Veteri Terra	R. de Molton	

[f. 71v]

At the obit of John Rof [14 November], paid by the collector of the rents of the canons 3s. 10d. and the residue cannot be levied. It is ordained by the stewards that it be distributed among the vicars, secondaries, boys, and others who so deserve [*promeruerunt*].

Dean	Chancellor	J. Strange
Penitentiary	J. de Exonia	Treasurer
R. de Veteri Terra	W. de Kilkenny	

At the obit of William de Bruwere, knight [23 November], 7s. 2d.

Dean	Chancellor	J. Strange
Penitentiary	T. de Charleton	Treasurer
R. de Veteri Terra	J. de Exonia	
W. de Kilkenny		

At the obit of William Briwere, bishop, 11s. 8d. To each canon, 4d., each vicar, 2d., each secondary, 1d., each boy, ½d. To each priest present and the other ministers of the church, as it is accustomed.

Dean	R. de V. Terra	W. de Kilkenny	T. de Charleton
Penitentiary	Chancellor	J. Strange	
W. de S. Elena	J. de Exonia	Treasurer	

At the obit of John de Kantia [2 December], 7s. 9d.

Dean	Chancellor	J. de Bruton
Penitentiary	T. de Charleton	J. Strange
W. de Sancta Elena	J. de Exonia	Archd. of Barnstaple
R. de Veteri Terra	W. de Kilkenny	Treasurer

For a certain corpse, deducting deductions, 12¾d., divided between 9 canons, each of whom received, adding ¾d., 1½d.

Dean	R. de Veteri Terra	J. de Bruton
Penitentiary	T. de Charleton	J. Strange
W. de Sancta Elena	W. de Kilkenny	Treasurer

At the obit of Bartholomew, bishop [14 December], 8s. 11d.

Dean	Chancellor	J. Strange
Penitentiary	J. de Exonia	Treasurer
W. de Sancta Elena	W. de Kilkenny	
R. de Veteri Terra		

At the obit of Eustace, by the collector of the rents of the town, 20s. To each canon, 4d., each vicar, 2d., secondary, 1d., boy, ½d., and to the rest of the ministers as is accustomed.

Dean	J. de Exonia	Treasurer
Penitentiary	J. de Bruton	
W. de Sancta Elena	J. Strange	
Chancellor	Archd. of Barnstaple	
R. de Veteri Terra		

To the monks of St Nicholas, 12d., the monks of Cowick, 6d., the monks [*recte* canons] of the Marsh, 3d., the monks of St James, 3d. To the bridge of Exe, 12d. by R., collector of rents. For a certain candle in the church of the Arches, 8d. by William de Okumpton. To the fabric, 2d., to the chapter, 4d. To the collector of rents for his labour, 4d.

[f. 72r]

Here begins the term of the Nativity of the Lord, in the year of the same 1306.

Rents. Robert, collector of the rents of the town, paid from the rent of the town from the term of St John, adding 6s. 8d. which he received from the exchequer, 30s. from the term of St John of the aforesaid year, which payment is called that of St Michael's [term], divided between 12 canons resident in the same term of St John, each of whom received 2s. 6d.

W. de S. Elena	Chancellor	R. de Molton	Treasurer,
R. de V. Terra	J. de Exonia	R. de Charleton	by a canon
Archd. of Totnes	T. de Charleton	J. Strange	
W. de Kilkenny	Archd. of Barnstaple		

At the obit of Richard Blundi, bishop [23 December], 12s. 1d. To each canon, 4d., each vicar, 2d., each secondary, 1d., boy, ½d., and to the rest as is accustomed

Dean	R. de V. Terra	W. de Kilkenny	Archd. of Barn.
Penitentiary	Chancellor	J. de Bruton	Treasurer
W. de S. Elena	J. de Exonia	J. Strange	

At the obit of William de Staneweye, dean [31 December], 13s. 1d. To each canon, 4d., each vicar, 2d., secondary, 1d., boy, ½d., to the rest of the ministers of the church as is accustomed.

Dean	Archd. of Totnes	W. de Kilkenny	J. Strange
Penitentiary	Chancellor	R. de Molton	Archd. of Barn.
R. de V. Terra	T. de Charleton	J. de Bruton	Treasurer
	J. de Exonia		

At the obit of John Wyger [30 December], 8s. 3d.

Dean	Archd. of Totnes	W. de Kilkenny	J. Strange
Penitentiary	Chancellor	R. de Molton	Archd. of Barn.
R. de V. Terra	T. de Charleton	J. de Bruton	Treasurer
	J. de Exonia		

For the corpse of Master Henry de Somersete, dean, deducting deductions, 10s. 4½d., from which each received 9½d. and there remains 1d.

Penitentiary	Chancellor	R. de Molton	Archd. of Barn.
W. de S. Elena	T. de Charleton	J. de Bruton	Treasurer
R. de V. Terra	J. de Exonia	J. Strange	
Archd. of Totnes	W. de Kilkenny		

Memorandum that Master Thomas [de Lechlade], chancellor, executor of the testament of Master Henry de Somersete, deceased, paid 100s. in lieu of the said deceased man's palfrey, divided between 13 canons present at the funeral rites of the said deceased man, each of whom received 7s. 8d. and there remains 4d.

Penitentiary	Chancellor	J. de Bruton Treasurer
W. de Sancta Elena	T. de Charleton	J. Strange
R. de Veteri Terra	W. de Kilkenny	J. de Exonia
Archd. of Totnes	R. de Molton	Archd. of Barnstaple

The new fabric. Memorandum that Sir Robert de Asperton received for the half-share of the canons' prebends from the term of the Nativity of the Lord, in the year of the same 1306, £12.

[f. 72v]

The box. Found in the box on Monday [16 January 1307] next before the feast of St Agnes the virgin, 22s. 6d. From which in expenses: for wine for the whole term, 3s. 4d. For the making of one new cope, 13½d. For buying silk and thread, 2½d. For the repair of thuribles, 10d. For coals bought, 4d. For grease for the bells for four feast days, 4d. For placing candles, 2d. Also to the subtreasurer and clerk, 8d. Also to the seamstress, laundress, and digger, 15d. Also to the custors and the cat, 13d. For buying a book, 12d. Total 10s. 4d. And so remains 12s. 2d. to be divided between the treasurer and the canons, from which 6s. 1d. is delivered to the subtreasurer for the use of the treasurer, and the other half-share is placed in the exchequer in the accustomed place.

At the obit of Master Roger le Rous [17 January], 10s.

H. de Somersete, deceased	Chancellor	J. de Bruton
Penitentiary	T. de Charleton	J. Strange
W. de Sancta Elena	J. de Exonia	Archd. of Barn.
R. de Veteri Terra	W. de Kilkenny	Treasurer
Archd. of Totnes	R. de Molton	R. de Charleton

For the corpse of Sir Roger de Molton [canon], deducting deductions, 5s. 3d., divided between 14 canons, each of whom received 4½d.

H. de Somersete, deceased	Chancellor	R. de Charleton
Penitentiary	T. de Charleton	J. Strange
W. de Sancta Elena	J. de Exonia	Archd. of Barn.
R. de Veteri Terra	W. de Kilkenny	Treasurer
Archd. of Totnes	J. de Bruton	

For the palfrey of Sir Roger de Molton, 66s. 8d., divided among 14 canons present at the obsequies, each of whom received 4s. 9d., and there remains 2d. which the aforesaid canons assigned to the submonitor.

H. de Somersete, deceased	Chancellor	J. de Bruton
Penitentiary	T. de Charleton	J. Strange
W. de Sancta Elena	J. de Exonia	Archd. of Barn.

| R. de Veteri Terra | W. de Kilkenny | Treasurer |
| Archd. of Totnes | R. de Charleton | |

For the corpse of Sir Roger de Stok [vicar choral], deducting deductions, 2s., divided between 14 canons, each of whom, adding ½d., received 1¾d.

H. de Somersete, deceased	Chancellor	J. Strange
Penitentiary	T. de Charleton	Archd. of Barn.
W. de Sancta Elena	W. de Kilkenny	Treasurer
R. de Veteri Terra	R. de Charleton	J. de Exonia
Archd. of Totnes	R. de Molton, deceased	

[f. 73r]

At the solemnity of the Holy Spirit made for the healthful state of Sir William de Puntyngdone on Friday [3 February] on the morrow of the feast of the Purification of Blessed Mary, 18s., distributed among the canons present in the choir each of whom received 4d., each vicar, 2d., each secondary, 1d., each boy, ½d., and there is paid to each of the prescribed people present and also to the clerk of the chapter, 2d. To 15 poor people, 15d., and that the residue should be distributed among the same canons.

H. de Somersete, deceased	Archd. of Totnes	R. de Molton,
Penitentiary	Chancellor	deceased
W. de Sancta Elena	J. de Exonia	R. de Charleton
R. de Veteri Terra	W. de Kilkenny	J. Strange
		Treasurer [*erased*]
		because he was not
		present in choir

And so a distribution being made between the canons, vicars, secondaries, boys present and to the rest as aforesaid and there remains to be divided between the same canons, 8s. 6d., each of whom received 9¼d. and there remains ¼d.

At the obit of Adam de Yuilcestr' [1 February], 7s. 11d.

H. de Somersete,	Archd. of Totnes	W. de Kilkenny	Treasurer
deceased	Chancellor	R. de Molton [deceased]	
Penitentiary	T. de Charleton	J. Strange	
W. de Sancta Elena	J. de Exonia		
R. de Veteri Terra			

For the corpse of Pentecoste, deducting deductions, 11d., divided between 14 canons, each of whom received ¾d. and there remains ½d.

| H. de Somersete, deceased | Chancellor | R. de Charleton |
| Penitentiary | T. de Charleton | J. Strange |

W. de Sancta Elena   W. de Kilkenny   Archd. of Barnstaple
R. de Veteri Terra   J. de Bruton   Treasurer
Archd. of Totnes   R. de Molton, deceased

At the obit of Richard de Brendisworthy [4 February], 8s. in the choir and 25d. to the poor.

H. de Somersete, deceased   Chancellor   R. de Charleton
Penitentiary   J. de Exonia   J. Strange
W. de Sancta Elena   W. de Kilkenny   Archd. of Barnstaple
R. de Veteri Terra   R. de Molton,   Treasurer
                            deceased

At the obit of Ysaac, archdeacon of Totnes [8 February], 7s. 10d.

H. de Somersete,   Archd. of Totnes   R. de Molton,   Treasurer
  deceased   Chancellor   deceased
Penitentiary   J. de Exonia   T. de Charleton
W. de Sancta Elena W. de Kilkenny   J. Strange
R. de Veteri Terra   Archd. of Barnstaple
[*erased*]

At the obit of Thomas Maudut [12 February], 7s. 10d.

H. de Somersete,   Archd. of Totnes   J. Strange
  deceased   Chancellor   Treasurer
Penitentiary   J. de Exonia   Archd. of Barnstaple
W. de Sancta Elena R. de Molton [deceased]   J. de Bruton
R. de Veteri Terra

At the obit of Hugh de Wilton, 7s. 10d.

H. de Somersete,   Archd. of Totnes   J. Strange
  deceased   Chancellor   J. de Bruton
Penitentiary   J. de Exonia   Archd. of Barnstaple
W. de Sancta Elena R. de Molton [deceased]   Chancellor
R. de Veteri Terra

[f. 73v]

At the obit of Ralph Cole [7 March], 7s. 5d.

H. de Somersete,   R. de Veteri Terra   W. de Kilkenny   Treasurer
  deceased   Archd. of Totnes   R. de Molton, deceased
Penitentiary   J. de Exonia   Archd. of Barnstaple
W. de Sancta Elena

For a certain corpse, deducting deductions, 9d., divided between 10 canons, each of whom, adding 1d., received 1d.

H. de Somersete, deceased	R. de Veteri Terra	R. de Molton
Penitentiary	Archd. of Totnes	[deceased]
W. de Sancta Elena	J. de Exonia	Archd. of Barnstaple
W. de Kilkenny		Treasurer

Rents. Memorandum that Robert, collector of the rents of the town, paid 30s., reckoning in them 6s. 8d. arising from the church of St Eval which he then received in the exchequer from the term of St Michael, which payment is called that of the term of the Nativity of the Lord, divided between 14 canons resident in the aforesaid term of St Michael, each of whom, adding 3d., received 2s. 2d.

Penitentiary	Chancellor	R. de Molton,	Archd. of
W. de S. Elena	T. de Charleton	deceased	Barn.
R. de V. Terra	J. de Exonia	R. de Charleton	Treasurer
Archd. of Totnes	W. de Kilkenny	J. de Bruton	
		J. Strange	

At the obit of Robert de Warwast [22 March], 9s. 4d. To each canon, 3d. To the rest of the ministers of the church, as it is accustomed.

Dean	R. de V. Terra	W. de Kilkenny	Archd. of
Penitentiary	Archd. of Totnes	R. de Molton	Barn.
H. de Somersete,	Chancellor	[deceased]	Treasurer
deceased	J. de Exonia	J. Strange	
W. de S. Elena			

The box. Found in the box, Friday in Easter week [31 March], 20s. 7d. From which in expenses: for wine for the whole term, 3s. For mats, 13d. For the repair of one arm [*virge*] of a [or, the] cross, 3d. For rushes, 4d. For coals, 8d. For litter [*litterio*], 1¾d. For belts for the bells, 5d. For lamps, 3d. For placing candles, 1d. Also to the seamstress, the laundress, the digger, 15d. For thread, 1d. For the repair of vestments, 2d. For the repair of one cross, 2d. Also to the subtreasurer and the clerk, 8d. Also to the custors and the cat, 13d. For grease for the bells for four feast days, 4d. Total 10s. And so remains to be divided between the chapter and the treasurer, 10s. 7d.. from which 5s. 3½d. is delivered to the subtreasurer for the use of the treasurer, from which 3s. was paid to Geoffrey de Wydelond for making wax for the feasts of the Purification and Easter in the year, etc., 1306 [1307. modern style], and so is delivered to the sub-treasurer for the use of the treasurer, 3s. 3½d. And the other half-share remains to the chapter.

Memorandum that 4s. 6d. arising from a *wayf* [stolen] horse found in

Stoke Wood [that was] sold, and 18½d. for stone sold in the house in the High Street next to the church of St Laurence, acquired by the law of *onhalde*, [was] distributed among the canons resident in the term of the Nativity of the Lord in the same year 1306, each of whom received 4¾d. and there remains 1¼d.

Dean	Archd. of Totnes,	R. de Molton
H. de Somerset,	by vicar	[deceased]
deceased	Chancellor	R. de Charleton
Penitentiary	T. de Charleton	J. Strange
W. de Sancta Elena	J. de Exonia	Archd. of Barnstaple
R. de Veteri Terra	W. de Kilkenny	Treasurer

[f. 74r]

Here begins the term of Easter in the year of the Lord 1307.

At the obit of Gilbert Tytyng [10 April], 10s. 9½d. To each canon, 4d., and to the other ministers as it is accustomed.

Dean	R. de V. Terra	J. de Exonia	R. de Treasurer
H. de	Archd. of Totnes	W. de Kilkenny	Charleton
Somersete	Chancellor	R. de Molton	J. Strange
[deceased]	T. de Charleton	[deceased]	
Penitentiary		Archd. of Barnstaple	
W. de S. Elena			

For the corpse of the son of Robert de Neweton, deducting deductions, 2s. 0¼d., distributed between 9 canons each of whom, adding ¾d., received 2¾d.

H. de Somersete,	T. de Charleton [*erased*]	R. de Charleton
deceased	J. de Exonia	Treasurer
Penitentiary	W. de Kilkenny	
R. de Veteri Terra	R. de Molton, deceased	
Archd. of Totnes		

For a certain corpse, deductions deducted, 12½d., divided between 10 canons each of whom received 1¼d.

H. de Somersete, deceased	Archd. of Totnes	J. Strange
Penitentiary	W. de Kilkenny	Archd. of Barn.
R. de Veteri Terra	R. de Molton [deceased]	Treasurer
R. de Charleton		

At the obit of W. de Swyndone [16 April], 7s. 3½d.

H. de Somersete,	Archd. of Totnes	R. de Molton	Archd. of
deceased	J. de Exonia	[deceased]	Barn.

Penitentiary	W. de Kilkenny	R. de Charleton Treasurer
R. de Veteri Terra	J. Strange	

At the obit of Master Adam de Sancta Brigida [20 April], 7s. 9½d.

Dean	R. de V. Terra	J. de Exonia	R. de
H. de Somersete	Archd. of Totnes	W. de Kilkenny	Charleton
[deceased]	T. de Charleton	R. de Molton	J. Strange
Penitentiary		[deceased]	Treasurer

At the obit of Robert de Euesham [18 April], 16s. From which to each canon, 4d., vicar, 2d., secondary, 1d., boy, ½d., custors, 8d. Total distributed in the choir, 12s. 4d.

Dean	Archd. of Totnes	R. de Molton	Treasurer
H. de Somersete	Precentor	[deceased]	
[deceased]	T. de Charleton	R. de Charleton	
Penitentiary	J. de Exonia	J. Strange	
R. de Veteri Terra			

At the obit of Henry de Warewyck [28 April], 7s. 10½d.

Dean	Archd. of Totnes	Archd. of Barnstaple
H. de Somersete,	T. de Charleton	Treasurer
deceased	Precentor	Precentor [*sic*]
Archd. of Exeter	J. de Exonia	
Penitentiary	W. de Kilkenny	
R. de Veteri Terra	R. de Molton [deceased]	

The new fabric. Delivered to Sir R. de Asperton from the red chest, 15s. 5d. Memorandum that R. and W., stewards of the exchequer, delivered to Sir Robert de Asperton, warden [*custos*] of the new work, [and] he received for the same work for the half-share of the canons' prebends for the term of Easter in the year of the Lord 1307, £12.

For a certain corpse, deducting deductions, 14d., divided between the canons underwritten, each of whom received ¾d. and there remains 1d.

Dean	R. de Veteri Terra	R. de Molton	Archd. of
H. de Somersete,	Chancellor	[deceased]	Barn.
deceased	Precentor	T. de Charleton	Treasurer
Archd. of Exeter	J. de Exonia	J. de Berkeley	
Penitentiary	W. de Kilkenny	J. Strange	
W. de Sancta Elena			

[f. 74v]

At the obit of Master Thomas de Bodeham [8 May], 20s. arising from the house of the archdeacon of Totnes, from which to each canon present, 8d., to each vicar present, 4d., each annuellar and secondary, 1d., boy, ½d.

H. de Somersete, deceased	R. de Veteri Terra Chancellor	R. de Molton [deceased]	J. Strange Archd. of Barn.
Archd. of Exeter	Precentor	T. de Charleton	Treasurer
Penitentiary	J. de Exonia	J. de Berkeley	
W. de Sancta Elena			

At the obit of Daniel de Longo Campo [11 May], 7s. 10d.

Dean	R. de Veteri Terra	J. Strange
H. de Somersete, deceased	J. de Exonia	Archd. of Barnstaple
Archd. of Exeter	W. de Kilkenny	Treasurer
Penitentiary	R. de Molton, deceased	
W. de Sancta Elena	J. de Berkeley	

Pentecostal offerings, namely on Monday [15 May], 45s. 2d., from which is delivered to the subtreasurer, 6d., the clerk of the chapter, 6d., the subclerk, 3d., the custors, 3d., and of the remainder half, namely 21s. 8d., is distributed to the treasurer and the same is distributed between the 13 underwritten canons, each of whom received 20d.

Also the offerings on the Tuesday following [16 May], 29s., from which is delivered as is given above to the subtreasurer, clerk of the chapter, subclerk, and custors 18d. And so remains 27s. 6d. from which 13s. 9d. is delivered to the treasurer for his half-share and the same is distributed between the underwritten canons, each of whom, adding 3d., received 12d.

Dean	R. de Veteri Terra	J. de Berkeley
H. de Somersete [deceased]	T. de Charleton	J. Strange
Archd. of Exeter	J. de Exonia	Archd. of Barnstaple
Penitentiary	W. de Kilkenny	Treasurer
W. de Sancta Elena	R. de Molton [deceased]	

For a certain corpse, deducting deductions, 7¼d., divided between the canons underwritten each of whom received ½d. and there remains 1¼d.

Dean	R. de Veteri Terra	W. de Kilkenny
H. de Somersete, deceased	Chancellor	R. de Molton [deceased]
	T. de Charleton	

Penitentiary   J. de Exonia   J. Strange
W. de Sancta Elena   Treasurer

At the obit of Master Reginald le Arceuesk [17 May], 7s. 6d.

Dean   Precentor   J. de Berkeley [*erased*]
H. de Somersete, T de Charleton Archd. of Barnstaple
 deceased   J. de Exonia   Treasurer
Penitentiary   W. de Kilkenny
W. de Sancta Elena R. de Molton [deceased]
R. de Veteri Terra

At the obit of Roger de Lemesy [24 May], 7s. 11d.

Dean   Precentor   J. de Berkeley
H. de Somersete [deceased] T. de Charleton J. Strange
Penitentiary   J. de Exonia   Archd. of Barnstaple
W. de Sancta Elena   W. de Kilkenny Treasurer
R. de Veteri Terra   R. de Molton [deceased]

[f. 75r]

For a certain corpse, deducting deductions, 10d., divided between the canons underwritten, each of whom, adding ½d., received ¾d.

Dean   R. de Veteri Terra W. de Kilkenny Archd. of
H. de Somersete Precentor   R. de Molton Barn.
[deceased]   T. de Charleton [deceased]   Treasurer
Penitentiary   J. de Exonia   J. de Berkeley
W. de S. Elena J. Strange

Pentecost. The Pentecostal offerings from Cornwall 20s., divided between the underwritten canons, each of whom, adding ½d., received 18½d.

Dean   W. de Sancta Elena R. de Molton Archd. of
R. de Veteri Terra J. de Exonia   [deceased] Barn.
 deceased   W. de Kilkenny   J. de Berkeley Treasurer
Archd. of Exeter   J. Strange
Penitentiary

For a certain corpse, deducting deductions, 9¾d., divided between the underwritten canons, each of whom received 1d. and there remains ¾d.

H. de Somersete [deceased] Chancellor R. de Molton
Penitentiary   Precentor   [deceased]
R. de Veteri Terra   W. de Kilkenny Archd. of Barnstaple
                  Treasurer

For the corpse of John Fex and other corpses, 2s. 11¾d., divided between 10 canons, each of whom received 3½d. and there remains ¾d.

H. de Somersete, deceased	Precentor	Archd. of Barnstaple
Penitentiary	J. de Exonia	Treasurer
R. de Veteri Terra	W. de Kilkenny	
Chancellor	R. de Molton, deceased [*erased*]	

At the obit of John de Monte Acuto [17 June], 6s. 10d.

H. de Somersete, deceased	Chancellor	J. Strange
Penitentiary	T. de Charleton	Archd. of Barnstaple
R. de Veteri Terra	R. de Molton, deceased	Treasurer

For the corpse of Sir William de Kamuyle, deducting deductions, 5s. 7¼d., divided between the canons underwritten, each of whom received 5½d. and there remains 1¼d.

H. de Somersete, deceased	Chancellor	W. de Kilkenny	Archd. of Barn.
Precentor	R. de Molton [deceased]	J. Strange	Treasurer
Penitentiary	T. de Charleton		
R. de Veteri Terra	J. de Exonia		

Rents. Robert, collector of the rents of the town, adding 6s. 8d. which he received from the exchequer, paid from the rent of the town from the term of the Nativity of the Lord, 30s., which payment is called the payment of Easter [term], divided between 15 canons resident in the aforesaid term of the Nativity of the Lord, each of whom received 2s.

Dean	Archd. of Totnes, by Pug.	R. de Charleton
H. de Somersete, deceased	Chancellor	R. de Molton, deceased
Penitentiary	T. de Charleton	J. Strange
W. de Sancta Elena	J. de Exonia	Archd. of Barn.
R. de Veteri Terra	W. de Kilkenny	Treasurer

30. Foundation of the Chantry and Obit of Dean Andrew Kilkenny, 1305

(Source: D&C 1927. Indenture, with two tags for seals, the left tag bearing part of the seal of Bishop Thomas Bitton. Latin text. The document, issued by Bitton, appropriated the church of West Anstey (Devon) to the use of the dean and chapter of Exeter Cathedral to endow a chantry priest celebrating daily for the soul of Dean Andrew Kilkenny and an annual obit in the cathedral in his memory. Paragraphing has been added.)

To all the sons of holy mother Church who shall see or hear this present writing, Thomas, by divine permission bishop of Exeter, eternal greetings in the Lord. We have attended [to the fact] that Master William de Kilkenny, canon of the church of Exeter, and Sir Walter de Totton', priest, executors of the will of Master Andrew de Kilkenny of good memory, formerly dean in the same church, deceased, have acquired two acres of land with the appurtenances in West Anstey and the right of patronage or advowson of the parish church of the Blessed Petroc of West Anstey in our diocese, at the cost and with the goods of the same deceased, and afterwards out of zealous devotion for the soul of the said deceased have given it under a certain form [*forma*] to the dean and chapter of our aforesaid church of Exeter to be possessed in perpetuity, so that the aforesaid church might be granted and appropriated to the same dean and chapter to their own uses, notwithstanding any contradiction by the king or other intermediate lords, as we have seen to be fully contained in a royal charter and in various other muniments and writings. We have considered, not without bitterness of heart, the paucity of ministers serving God in our aforesaid cathedral church and the poverty of their stipends, and have noticed that the aforesaid parish church of West Anstey, through the carelessness of the rectors living there in former times, is greatly ruined in its resources as is sufficiently vouchsafed to us in all these respects by witnesses and other legal documents.

For which reason we, the abovementioned bishop, who by the duty of our office are not only bound to conserve the resources of our aforesaid church but to increase by lawful means the sustenance and stipends of the aforesaid ministers and to augment the divine cult in our abovementioned cathedral church, and wishing very much to repair the same church of West Anstey which, as has been stated, is culpably ruined in its resources, and so that the prayers of the living may become meritorious for them and turn obstacles to resolutions, having specially called together Thomas de

312

Allemandesworth, now rector of the same church of West Anstey, the dean and chapter of our abovementioned church of Exeter, and all others who had or have an interest in this [subject], and having examined, discussed, and sufficiently appraised all and each of the aforesaid matters, we appropriate and concede the aforesaid church of West Anstey with all its rights and appurtenances to the dean and chapter of the abovementioned church of Exeter, who are the true patrons of the same church of West Anstey, to their own use to be possessed in perpetuity, and by whom the same parish church, we hope and believe, with the help of the Lord, may be reformed into a proper state, with the express accord and consent obtained of the aforesaid rector, dean and chapter, and others who are concerned, by a diligent and sufficient discussion [*tractatu*] for several days, note having been taken in all things in this matter that are to be noted in the form that is required hereunder.

That is to say that on the cession or withdrawing or by the removal otherwise in a lawful way of the said Thomas, now rector of the same church, the aforesaid dean and chapter shall be allowed to enter into and hold possession of the said church with its rights and appurtenances in perpetuity without the consent of us or our successors as bishops of Exeter being required, saving however that a suitable vicar's portion [*vicariam*] in the same shall be ordained and fixed in value by us or one of our successors, to which appropriation, with the consent of the said dean and chapter, we add, and by adding we charge the same dean and chapter with their consent, that after the aforesaid dean and chapter shall have had peaceful possession of the same church in appropriation and have received the fruits of the same for two years, with the deduction of the vicar's portion, the said dean and chapter shall find, furnish, and pay from the money received for the fruits and offerings of the aforesaid church of West Anstey annually in perpetuity a certain priest at the altar of the Blessed Andrew in the abovementioned church of Exeter perpetually celebrating [mass] for the soul of the aforesaid Master Andrew de Kilkenny, at whose expense and with whose goods the said two acres of land with the right of presentation and the advowson of the aforesaid church of West Anstey have been acquired by the aforesaid said dean and chapter, as has been said, and a licence of appropriation procured, as was stated above, and for the souls of Masters William de Kilkenny, formerly bishop of Ely, Henry de Kilkenny, formerly archdeacon of Chichester, Henry de Kilkenny, formerly rector of the church of Bridestowe, the aforesaid William de Kilkenny, canon of Exeter, after his death shall occur, and for the souls of all the faithful departed, 60s. annually at the accustomed terms [of the year] for such payments there, and on the day of the obit of the aforesaid Master Andrew to each canon of the church of Exeter residing in the same city, 12d. To each vicar present in the choir at the exequies for the same Andrew, deceased, 3d., and if present at the celebration of mass for the same, another 3d.. To each [member] of the second form present at the exequies aforesaid, 1d., and if present at mass, another 1d. To each annuellar priest present at the aforesaid mass who does not receive payment with those of the second form or with other members of the church, 1d. To each boy of the choir, 1d. To the bellringers, 4d. To the ministers of the exchequer, 12d. And to each parish priest of the city of Exeter and its suburbs present in choir dress at the aforesaid mass and who has said a collect and held a special memorial for the said Master Andrew, deceased, on the same day or who will say and hold his mass on the next day, promising [to do so] in good faith, 1d.

In addition the aforesaid dean and chapter shall find and furnish from the same money six candles equally divided from a weight of one and a half pounds of wax in all [to stand] before the bodies of poor people brought to the aforesaid church of Exeter without the light of candles, each of which bodies shall have two candles for itself and not more, burning as long as mass is being celebrated in the same church for these deceased people. And if so many bodies are brought to the aforesaid church on one day that six candles are not sufficient for the aforesaid arrangements, the number of their candles ought not to be increased for this reason.

All the residue of the money from the fruits arising from the aforesaid church of West Anstey shall be divided among the canons of the aforesaid church of Exeter present at the abovementioned exequies and mass on the aforesaid obit day annually in perpetuity. Furthermore on the death or removal of the abovementioned priest celebrating for the said Andrew and the other persons aforesaid, another suitable and honest man shall be quickly provided by the dean and chapter of the same church of Exeter, [to do] the same service, who shall be instituted by the same dean and chapter within twenty days of the aforesaid death or removal, according to the custom of the church of Exeter. Otherwise this provision and institution shall then thereby fully devolve to us and our successors. If however it happens that through the poverty of the aforesaid church of West Anstey, when the vicar's portion in the same has been deducted, all and each of the preceding [charges] cannot be fully paid from the fruits of the same church, the aforesaid dean and chapter at the order of the dean, precentor, chancellor, and treasurer, or three of them if the fourth is absent, whose consciences we specially charge in this respect, shall provide, support, and find the aforesaid obit, distribution, chantry, finding of candles, and the other obligations mentioned above in as far as the fruits and offerings of the aforesaid church of West Anstey, after the deduction of the vicar's portion in the same, shall allow them to be paid, so that nothing at all shall be paid from the other goods of the aforesaid dean and chapter for the support of the aforesaid charges. To which, following the form already written to be observed in perpetuity, we wish, charge, and oblige the aforesaid dean and chapter, with their legitimate consent to be charged and obliged, and so declare [them] to be charged and obliged.

In testimony of which both we and the aforesaid dean and chapter have put our seals to be attached to these presents. And we the said dean and chapter, holding all and each of the above to be fixed and firm, unanimously demonstrate our full assent to these matters and have caused our seal to be attached to these presents in witness of the aforesaid matters. Dated at Exeter on Monday [30 August] on the morrow of the feast of the beheading of St John the Baptist in the year of the Lord 1305, always saving the episcopal and archidiaconal right and jurisdiction in the same church. Dated and done in the day and year stated above.

31. Obits from a Psalter of Exeter Cathedral, 13th and 14th Centuries

(Source: British Library, Harley MS 863, ff. 1r–6v. Latin text. The volume contains a calendar of the thirteenth century into which obits have been entered in a variety of hands up to about the mid fourteenth century, often roughly and without clear allignment to the calendar dates. Several names are faint, and others have been mutilated by cropping the edges of the pages. As noted in the introduction, above p. 244, there are many inconsistencies between the dates ascribed here and those in other sources. The latter, when known, are added in square brackets for comparison.)

[f. 1r **January**]

3	Roger de We [?]
4	H. R< >
24	Master Roger <Rows?> [17 January]
28	Adam de <Ylchester?> [31 January or 1 February]

[f. 1v **February**]

4	Richard de Brendesworth [4 February]
5	Isaac [8 February]
12	N.[i.e. Thomas] Maudit [12 February]
15	Leueric, bishop [10 or 11 February]
23	Th[omas Charlton] [21 February]
28	Master Henry de Kylken' [5 March]

[f. 2r **March**]

6	N.[i.e. Ralph] Cole [7 March]
13	Th[omas] de Hamton [4 March]
27	Robert <de Warelwast, bishop?> of Exeter [22 or 28 March]

[f. 2v **April**]

8 or 9	Gilbert de Tyting' [10 April]
11	William de Suendon [16 April]
13	Adam de Sancta Brigid[a] [20 April]
15	Th[omas de] Lech[lade] [15 April]
21	J[ohn] de Vpav[on] [26 April]
27	Richard de Morceter; Master Robert de Heuesham [17 or 18 April]

29 Richard [i.e. Henry] de Warwyk [28 April]
30 Roger de Torych [29 April]

[f. 3r **May**]

5   John de Fareweye [30 April]
8   Master Thomas de Bodh[am] [8 May]
9   William de Kylkenni [9 May]
13 Daniel de Lon[go] Campo [11 May]
18 Reginald le Arc[e]vesk [17 or 19 May]
22 Roger de Lym[e]si [24 May]
27 John, bishop [2 June]

[f. 3v **June**]

3   Thomas and Richard Stapildon [3 October; 11 March]
6   William de G[r]asum [27 June?]
16 Henry de Cice[ster] [16 June]
17 John de Monte Acuto [17 June]
22 James de Berkylae [died 24 June]
26 Master John de Esse [28 June]

[f. 4r **July**]

8   Alice Tiuuertone; Laurence, canon [5 July]
10 Clement, canon [6 July]
12 Master Roger Baret [8 July]
14 Simon, archdeacon [10 or 11 July]
20 Serlo, dean [21 July]
23 W[illiam] Pontynton [24 July]
30 Master John Bradelegh [8 August]

[f. 4v **August**]

4   N. [i.e. Odelina], wife of Herbert the fisher [*Piscator*] [October]
12 Roger [de Winkleigh] [14 August]
15 [No name inserted]
21 John, bishop [25 August]
27 Master John de Sancto Gorano [30 or 31 August]
28 William de Wllaueston [1 September]

[f. 5r **September**]

2   John de Netton [5 September]
7   Bishop Walter [3 September]
11 Bishop Simon [9 September]
12 N.[icholas] Strange [11 September]

18   William de Molend[inis] [10 September]
21   J.[ohn] Welle [28 September]
23   Bartholomew, archdeacon of Exeter [22 or 23 September]
27   Thomas de Bitton, bishop [25 or 26 September]

[f. 5v October]

6   Peter, bishop of Exeter [4 October]
9   Thomas de Derteford, priest and canon
12   Walter, bishop [15 October]
13   J.[ohn] Strang'
14   Henry de Berbilond, vicar [17 October]
18   Martin Durl[ing] [8 October]
20   Master Walter Penbroke [20 October]
22   Athelstan, king [27 October]
24   Henry, bishop [26 October]
27   Thomas la Barbor
29   Henry Bratton [31 October]

[f. 6r November]

5   John No[byl] [3 November]
7   Master W<alter de> Lechelade [9 November]
9   Sir Wil<liam de> Werpelesdon
11   Sir Robert [Gyffard?] [12 or 13 November]
14   Thomas Cape [18 November]
16   John Rof, dean [14 November]
17   N., wife of Herbert [the fisher] [October]
20   William Bruere [23 November]
22   William Br<uere, bishop> [24 November]
24   B[artholomew], dean [27 November]
25   Thomas Herward, archdeacon of Exeter

[f. 6v December]

2   Roger de Otriue
5   John de Kent, formerly archdeacon of Exeter [1 or 2 December]
10   Bishop Bartholomew [14 or 15 December]
12   Bishop Richard [Blund] [23 December]
13   Eustace, priest [17 December]
18   William de Staneweye [31 December]
19   H[enry] de Somersete, dean [22 December]
21   Sir John Wyger [30 December]

32. Obit Calendar of Exeter Cathedral, early 15th Century

(Source: Exeter Cathedral Archives, D&C 3625. Latin text. This is a list of obits celebrated by the cathedral clergy as a whole, including the canons, as opposed to those in the next document who were commemorated by the vicars choral of the cathedral on their own. The list was probably made in about the 1420s. A few editorial identifications have been added in square brackets.)

[f. i recto] **January**

5	William Donebryg and Nicholas Braybrok
17	Roger Rous
21	Robert Bosoun, chancellor
24	Hugh de Wylton
28	Hugh Hykelyng

[f. i verso] **February**

1	Adam de Ilchestr' and William Poundestoke
4	Richard Brendesworth
8	Isaac
12	Thomas Maudit
19	Baldwin Shyllyngford and John his brother
21	Thomas Cherlton
28	Henry Pyk

[f. ii recto] **March**

3	John Wadham
4	Thomas Henton
7	Ralph Cole
11	Richard Stapuldon, knight
14	[William?] Ferby, J[ohn] Michel, Philippa the queen
16	Thomas Barton
22	Robert Warwest, bishop
26	John Lugans
27	Robert Rygge

[f. ii verso] **April**

10	Gilbert Tytyng

14   [John] Dodyngton
15   Thomas Lychelade
16   William Swyndone
18   Robert Euysham
20   Adam de Brigida
26   John Vphauene
28   Henry Warwyk
29   Roger Toryg
30   John Farewey

[f. iii recto] **May**

2   Hugh Courtenay
8   Thomas Bodeham
9   William Kylkenny
11   Daniel de Longo Campo
14   Walter Gybbys
17   Reginald Erceuesque
18   Walter Meryet
21   Robert Stapeldone
23   Richard Hals
24   Roger Limesie

[f. iii verso] **June**

8   Edward, [the Black] prince
10   Roger Chyuelton [Charleton, *added*]
16   Henry de Cicestr'
17   John de Monte Acuto
19   William Nasshyngton
21   Edward [III], king, and Philippa, queen
7   William Granson
28   John de Esse
30   Henry Blacborn

[f. iv recto] **July**

5   Laurence, subdeacon
8   Roger Baret
11   Simon, archdeacon of Cornwall
1   Ralph Ryngstede
16   William Caprun
21   Serlo, first dean
22   Ralph Tregregiow
24   William Puntyngdon

[f. iv verso] **August**

- 8 Richard Coleton
- 11 Simon Grendon
- 13 Richard Braylegh
- 14 R[oger], dean, and John Strecche, knight
- 25 John Graunsson
- 31 John de Gorano

[f. v recto] **September**

- 1 Master William Wollaueston
- 8 John Necton
- 9 Simon [de Apulia], bishop
- 10 William de Molend'
- 11 Nicholas Stranga
- 17 Edmund Stafford and Humphrey, knight
- 22 Bartholomew, archdeacon
- 23 John Shillyngford
- 25 Thomas Bytton
- 28 John Wele

[f. v verso] **October**

- 3 Thomas Stapuldone
- 4 Peter [Quinil], bishop
- 6 Richard Wydeslade
- 8 Martin Derlyng
- 9 John Cheyne
- 11 Thomas Herford
- 12 John More
- 15 Walter Stapuldone, bishop
- 19 Roger Tyfford
- 20 Walter Penbroke
- 21 Sibilla, mother of Graunson, bishop
- 26 Henry de Wodebury [i.e. Henry Marshal, bishop]
- 27 Athelstan, founder

[f. vi recto] **November**

- 3 John Nobyl
- 4 Andrew Kilkenni
- 9 [Walter] Lechelade
- 12 Gyffard
- 14 John Roofe
- 18 Thomas Gape

23 William Bruere
24 William Bruere, bishop
26 Walter Clopton
27 Bartholomew, dean
28 John Prestecote

[f. vi verso] **December**

2 John de Kent
3 William Ekerdon and Ralph Germyn
4 John [XXII], pope
14 Bartholomew, bishop
17 Eustace
22 Henry de Somersete, dean
23 [Richard] Blound, bishop
30 John Wyger
31 William Stanwey, dean

33. Obit Calendar of the Vicars Choral of Exeter Cathedral, early 15th Century

(Source: Exeter Cathedral Archives, D&C 3675, ff. 26r–31v. Latin text. This calendar was drawn up by the vicars choral of the cathedral, and includes both names of people whose obits were kept only by the vicars choral, as well as many of those who were commemorated by the cathedral clergy as a whole and whose names appear in the previous calendar. In this second category there are a few discrepancies of dates between the two calendars, perhaps because the vicars postponed or anticipated a commemoration that clashed with one of their own. Names subsequently added to the list appear in square brackets.)

[f. 26r] **January**

2   Jordan Lydene and John Leaute
5   Nicholas Braybrok, priest and canon
17   Roger Rows, priest and canon
20   Master Michael Lercedekne, treasurer
24   Hugh de Wylton, priest and canon
27   John Alyn and Eve Alyn
28   [Richard Morton, priest and canon]
31   Adam de Hylchester, priest and canon

[f. 26v] **February**

1   William Mey, draper
3   [Master Alan Sarys]
4   [Master Thomas Kyrkby, treasurer; Master W. Elyott, priest; Master Alan Sarys, and Thomasine his wife]
6   William Gerveys and Thomas Gerveys and Alice Gerveys and others, [and Master John Burnebury, formerly treasurer of Exeter]
12   [Edmund Laci, bishop; Henry Webber, dean; Sir John Simon, priest; and John Kelle, Agnes and Juliana, his wives]
19   Thomas Arundel, formerly archbishop of Canterbury
20   Thomas Charleton

[f. 27r] **March**

3   William Brygge, vicar; also Alexander Beare, vicar; Robert, his brother

323

5   Thomas de Hynton, priest, canon
6   [Richard Thryng and Joan his wife and Andrew Thryng and
      Master John Thryng. Master Halneth Arscott]
9   Thomas Cook, vicar, and Thomas and Blithe, his parents, and
      John Ballam, annuellar
11   Richard Stapyldon, knight
12   Peter Carter, secondary. [Sir Martin Dyer, canon, and William
      Burdyam]
16   [Sir John Rowter, annuellar]
17   [William Wilkinson and Joan his wife]
19   [William Upton and Isabel his wife, and Master John Druell,
      archdeacon of Exeter, and Sir John Lovet, vicar, and John
      Coplestone]
22   Robert Warwest, bishop
24   [William Frost and others]

[f. 27v] **April**

10   Gilbert Tytyng, mayor of Exeter
15   Thomas Lechlade, dean
16   William Swyndon, canon
17   Robert Evsham, canon
20   Adam de Sancta Brigida, canon
26   John Uphavene, canon
28   Henry Warwyk, canon
29   Roger Torygg, dean
30   John Fareway

[f. 28r] **May**

2   Hugh de Curtenay and Margaret his wife
5   Thomas Cook, vicar
8   Thomas de Bodeham, canon
9   William Kilkenny
11   Daniel de Longo Campo
18   Walter Myryet
19   Reginald Archeuek, subdeacon
21   Robert Stapyldon
24   Roger Lymsy

[f. 28v] **June**

2   John, bishop of Exeter
6   John Cokworthy, canon
8   Lord Edward the prince
10   Roger Cherleton, canon

16   Henry de Cyrencestria, canon
18   [Henry Helyer and Joan his wife, and Master William Elyott, canon]
23   [Master William Sylke, canon, and W. Godde]
26   Thomas Tankret; Sir John Tankret
27   William, father of John de Grandisson
28   John de Esse, canon
29   Henry Blacborn, canon

[f. 29r] July

5   Laurence, subdeacon
6   Clement, canon
8   Roger Baret, canon
9   Master Maior Parys
10   Simon, archdeacon of Cornwall
14   Ralph Ryngsted and William Pers, canon
16   William Capron, canon
21   Serlo, first dean
24   William Poyngton
31   Alexander the fisher [*piscator*], our brother; Master Robert Dunnyg, priest

[f. 29v] August

6   [Philip Colshill]
7   [Richard Munseaux and Hugh Thryng and John Traci, citizens of Exeter]
8   Richard de Coleton, dean
9   Sir William Wolf, Hugh Balle, Henry Wolf, Robert Wolf and Joan, parents of the same William
13   Richard Brayle, dean
14   Roger, second dean
23   John de Grandisson, bishop, and Peter Penest[r]in, cardinal
30   John de Sancto Gorano, canon

[f. 30r] September

1   William de Wollaveston, canon
3   Walter, bishop
5   John de Necton, subdeacon
9   Simon, bishop
10   William de Molendinis, canon
11   Nicholas Stranga, vicar
16   Edmund Lacy, formerly bishop of Exeter

17 Edmund Stafford, bishop; Humphrey Stafford, knight; Elizabeth his wife
19 Peter Serell, Constance his wife, and John their son. [Sir William Sakerlegh]
20 Master John Polyng, clerk, and Sir John West, priest
23 Bartholomew, archdeacon of Exeter
24 Robert Lywer, canon
25 John Stevenys, canon [and Master John Cobthorne, dean, and Master John Pyttys, and Master Thomas Toker]
26 Thomas Bytton, bishop
28 John Wele, archdeacon of Barnstaple

[f. 30v] October

3 Thomas de Stapyldon, canon
4 Peter, bishop
6 Richard Wydeslade
8 Martin Derlyng
11 Thomas de Herford, canon
12 John More, annuellar
15 Walter Stapyldon, bishop
16 [Alven]
17 Henry Berbelond, vicar
18 Thomas Fylcomb, vicar
19 Robert Tyfford, canon
20 Walter Penbrok, canon
21 Sibilla, mother of John de Grandisson, bishop
23 Master John Sutton, priest
26 Henry Marshall, bishop
27 King Athelstan, founder
31 Henry Bratton, subdeacon and canon; [Sir Richard Helyer, vicar; Laurence Bodyngton, master of the grammar school of the city of Exeter and secondary of the cathedral church; the father and mother of the said Laurence]

[f. 31r] November

3 John Nobyll, dean
4 Andrew Kilkenny, dean
5 [Roger Keys]
8 Christine Fyshher
9 Walter Lychelade
12 Henry Aleyn, our brother
13 Robert Gyffard, canon

14   John Rooff, dean
15   [Master John Rysse]
18   Thomas Gape
23   William Bruer, knight
24   William Bruer, bishop
26   Walter Clopton
27   Bartholomew, dean

[*Undated:* Lord Morton, cardinal; Master John Ryse; Peter Wylyams and his wife]

[f. 31v] **December**

1   John de Kent, subdeacon and canon
2   James Carslegh, John Lydeford, canons, and Master Robert Hereward
3   Ralph German, canon
4   John, pope
5   Roger Bolter, canon
10   Richard Norton, priest; Richard Brounst, vicar; Thomas Pykenet, priest; John Damarell, knight; Isabel, his wife; and John Fortiscu, esquire, and his wife
15   Bartholomew, bishop
16   [Richard Helier, canon]
17   Eustace, canon
22   Richard [*recte* Henry] Somersed, dean
23   Richard Blondy, bishop
24   [William May, Joan his wife, Master John Polyng]
30   John Wyger, brother of the church
31   William Stanwey, dean

34. Obits Celebrated at Exeter Cathedral, 1462

(Source: Exeter Cathedral Archives, D&C 3772. Latin text. These names have been extracted from one of the latest surviving obit accounts that contains a complete and legible list of the obits commemorated by the cathedral community as a whole: canons, vicars, and others. It shows that many of the thirteenth-century obit endowments still generated enough money for commemorations even in the mid fifteenth century, as well as listing obits that had been founded more recently. It is not, however, a totally accurate guide to obit commemorations in the 1460s; comparison with other accounts of the period show that other obits were held in other years, though they were sometimes suspended because their endowments failed to produce enough money, or because the money was directed to repairing the property that formed the endowment. Some editorial identifications have been added in square brackets. The document does not give the dates of the obits.)

[Christmas term, 1461–2]

Richard Blundy, bishop. [John] Wyger. [William] Stanwey, dean. [Nicholas] Braybroke. Michael Lercedekne, treasurer. [Roger] Rows. [Hugh de] Wylton. Richard Marton; Thomas Spafford, bishop; Richard Rotherham; Thomas Fligh; William Rudston. [Adam de] Ilchester. William Mey, draper. [Richard] Brendisworthy. Isaak. [Thomas] Mawdith. Thomas Arundell, archbishop of Canterbury, and John Stevenys. Robert Veysy and Alice his wife. [Henry] Pyke. Thomas Henton. [Ralph] Cole. Richard Stapeldon, knight.

[Easter term, 1462]

William Warewest, bishop. Richard Brounston. Gilbert Tytyng. Thomas Lychelade, dean. [William] Swyndon. Robert Evysham. Adam de Sancta Brigida. [John de] Uphavene. [Henry] Warewyke. Roger Torygge, dean. [John] Fareway. Hugh Courtenay and Margaret, his wife. [Thomas] Bodeham. William Kilkenny. Walter Colles. Daniel de Longo Campo. [Reginald] Archevek. Master Robert Stapeldon. John Shapelegh and Margaret his wife. [Roger] Lymesie. John,] bishop. Edward, prince of Wales. John Druell. Roger Charleton. John Snetisham, chancellor. John de Monte Acuto. Matthew Downe.

[Midsummer term, 1462]

Thomas Brantyngham, bishop; Edward, king, and Philippa his queen. William de Grandisson. John de Esse. Henry Blakborn. Laurence, [subdeacon]. Clement, [chancellor]. Baret, chancellor. Simon, archdeacon of Cornwall. Maior Parys. Ralph Ryngstede. William Capron. Serlo, dean. John Holand, chaplain. [William] Puntyngdon. Roger Coleton, dean. Robert [recte Richard] Brayley, dean. Roger Wynkelegh, dean. John de [Sancto] Gorano. William Wollaveston. Thomas Spafford, bishop, and Richard Roderham. [John de] Necton. Simon de Apulea, bishop. William de Molendinis.

[Michaelmas term, 1462]

Bartholomew, [archdeacon]. John Cobethorn, dean. Thomas Bytton, bishop. [John] Wele. Thomas Stapeldon. Peter, bishop. [Richard de] Wydeslade, treasurer. [Martin] Derlyng. [Thomas de] Hertford. John More. Walter Stapeldon, bishop. [Roger] Tyfford. Sybilla de Grandissono. Peter [recte Henry], bishop. Athelstan, king. John Noble, dean. Andrew Kilkenny, dean. [Walter de] Lychelade. Robert Gyffard. [John] Rooff. William Brounyng. [Thomas] Gape. [William] Brewer, knight. [William] Brewer, bishop. [Walter] Clopton. Bartholomew, dean. James Carslegh; Robert Herward; and John Lydeford. [John de] Kent. Pope John XXII. Bartholomew, bishop. Richard Helyer. Eustace [the] Blynde.

35. Obits Celebrated at Exeter Cathedral, 1548

(Source: Exeter Cathedral Archives, D&C 3686, ff. 39r–43v. Latin and English text. The source of this is a survey of the cathedral obits, drawn up at the time of their confiscation under the Chantry Act of 1547. It lists the obits in five sections, depending on how they were funded and how much was distributed to the clergy taking part. The sections have lengthy titles, and there are analyses of how much each grade of clergy received. Here, only the names of those commemorated by the obits are reproduced, together with the total amount distributed. In the original, forenames and titles are in Latin; these have been translated. A few mistakes have been noted and identifications added.)

[f. 39r]

Annuals and obits in the cathedral church of Exeter granted to the lord king Edward VI in the second year [of his reign] and made on the 15th day of the month of May in the year of the Lord 1548, commissioners: Hugh Pollard, knight, Anthony Hervy, Robert Caree, [blank] Pridysse and [blank] Arescott, esquires or gentlemen.

[f. 40r **First List**]

Bartholomew, archdeacon	5s. 6d.
Martin Derlyng	5s. 6d.
John Tyfford	5s. 6d.
Henry Marshall, bishop	5s. 6d.
John Roff, dean	5s. 6d.
Thomas Gape	5s. 6d.
John [i.e. William] Bruer, knight	5s. 6d.
Walter Clopton	5s. 6d.
John Kentt	5s. 6d.
Bartholomew, bishop	5s. 6d.
Hugh Wylton	5s. 6d.
Adam de Ilchestur	5s. 6d.
John Isaacke	5s. 6d.
William [i.e. Richard] Brendisworthy	5s. 6d.
John Maudytt	5s. 6d.
Ralph Cole	5s. 6d.
Vincent Herte	5s. 6d.

[f. 40v]

William Warwest, bishop	5s. 6d.
Walter Lychelade	5s. 6d.
William Swendon	5s. 6d.
John Kellegh	5s. 6d.
Adam de [Sancta] Brigida	5s. 6d.
John Fareway	5s. 6d.
John de Warwycke	5s. 6d.
Daniel de Longo Campo	5s. 6d.
Reginald Archyvecke	5s. 6d.
John Lymsy	5s. 6d.
John, bishop	5s. 6d.
John de Esse	5s. 6d.
Clement [de Langenford]	5s. 6d.
[Roger] Barett, archdeacon	5s. 6d.
Laurence, dean	5s. 6d.
Simon, archdeacon	5s. 6d.
Serlo, dean	5s. 6d.
Roger Colyton	5s. 6d.
Roger [de Winkleigh], second dean	5s. 6d.
William de Wullaweston	5s. 6d.
John de [Sancto] Gorano	5s. 6d.
Simon de Apulia, bishop	5s. 6d.
John Necton	5s. 6d.
William de Molendinis	5s. 6d.
Nicholas Strange	5s. 6d.

[f. 41r Second List]

John Wele	7s. 10d.
Thomas Stapyldon	12s. 6½d.
Athelstan, king	10s. 9½d.
John Nobyll, dean	8s. 11½d.
Robert Gyffard	9s. 1½d.
Bartholomew, dean	11s. 9½d.
Eustace Blynde	10s. 9½d.
Richard Blundon, bishop	9s. 1½d.
William Stanway, dean	9s. 1½d.
Henry Pyke	13s. 2d.
Thomas Hinton	11s. 9½d.
Richard Stapyldon	12s. 6½d.
Robert Evysham	8s. 5½d.
John Shaplegh	8s. 4d.
Walter Myryett	8s. 5½d.

Robert Stapyldon	8s. 4d.
William Nassyngton	8s. 5½d.
William Capron	13s. 8d.
John Holland	8s. 9½d.
William Puntyngdon	9s. 0d.
Thomas Charlton	9s. 5d.
John Vphaven	8s. 7½d.

[f. 41v **Third List**]

John Coryngdon	23s. 6d.
Edmund Lacy, bishop	27s. 2d.
William Sylke and More	26s. 11d.
Walter Stapyldon, bishop	26s. 10d.
Owen Loyde and others	18s. 2d.
William Fulford	17s. 4d.
Roger Keyse	27s. 2d.
Hugh Thryng	8s. 0d.
Nicholas Gosse	23s. 8d.
John Kyrkeby	20s. 9d.
Richard Helyer	11s. 10d.
Thomas Harrys	24s. 2d.
John Salter	9s. 7d.
John Fulford, archdeacon	28s. 10d.
David Hopton	27s. 2d.
John Stephyns	27s. 6d.
John Veysy	8s. 0d.
Thomas Chyppyngham	22s. 4d.
Richard More	24s. 6d.
John Warde	26s. 4d.
John Colsyll and others	14s. 11d.
Gilbert Tytyng	6s. 2d.
John Yott and others	22s. 6d.
John Bouth, bishop	22s. 4d.
John Eggecomb	23s. 6d.
William Sylke	24s. 6d.
Matthew Downe	12s. 10d.
Ralph Ryngestede	23s. 6d.
John Skynner	5s. 6d.
John Hamlyn	22s. 4d.
Walter [Bronescombe], bishop	£4 4s. 2d.
Peter Willyams	23s. 8d.
Richard Marton and John Ryse	17s. 8d.
John Arundell, bishop	14s. 5d.

[f. 43r **Fourth List**]

John Wynslade	7s. 9d.
Sybil de Grandisson	23s. 6d.
John, bishop	23s. 6d.
William Kilkenny	14s. 10d.
William de Grandisson	23s. 6d.
John de Grandisson, bishop	63s. 11d.

[f. 43v **Fifth List**]

Thomas Bytton, bishop	50s. 2d.
Peter, bishop	11s. 5½d.
Thomas Herttford	5s. 6d.
Walter Penbroke	5s. 6d.
Andrew Kilkenny, dean	23s. 3d.
William Bruer, bishop	8s. 11½d.
John Wyger, knight	5s. 6d.
John Rows	5s. 6d.
Richard Gilbert	24s. 2d.
Hugh Courtenay	27s. 0d.
Roger Toryge, dean	20s. 6½d.
John Speke, knight	44s. 6d.
Thomas Bodeham, archdeacon	14s. 0½d.
Roger Charlton	14s. 1½d.
John de Monte Acuto	5s. 6d.
Thomas Brentyngham, bishop	23s. 4d.
John Mogryge	24s. 2d.
Edmund Stafford, bishop	24s. 6d.

36. Obit Endowments Returned to Exeter Cathedral, 1585

(Source: Public Record Office, C 66/1254, printed in *Draft Calendar of Patent Rolls, 27 Elizabeth I, 1584–5*, List and Index Society, 241 (1990), pp. 5–9. Latin text. On 5 July 1585, Queen Elizabeth I granted back to Exeter Cathedral many (but not all) of the chantry and obit endowments which had been appropriated by the crown in 1548. The names below are extracted from the grant, together with three (printed in italics) that appear in a later copy of it, edited in G. Oliver, *Lives of the Bishops of Exeter and a History of the Cathedral* (Exeter, 1861), pp. 488–93. The grant includes some details absent from the 1548 list. Some names in the grant are coupled together and the couplings are reproduced here, though the persons concerned were not always commemorated on the same day. Mistakes are corrected in brackets.)

Grant to the warden and college of the vicars choral of Exeter Cathedral:
Henry VII; [Lady Margaret], countess of Richmond and Derby; Richard [Fox], bishop of Winchester
Walter Stapledon
John, canon of Exeter [in 1271]
Laurence Dobel
William Good and others
Alan and Thomasina Sares
Peter Carter and William Upton
William Wolfe
William Gervis
Henry Webber
John Symons
John Kelleye
Walter Good
Richard Hellyer
Edmund Lacye

Grant to the dean and chapter of Exeter Cathedral:
John Coringdon and Peter Courteney
Edmund Lacye, bishop
William Sylke and Richard More
William Stapledon
Owen Lloyd and Cardinal John Mourton
William Fulford

Hugh Thringe

Nicholas Gosse

John Kirkbye

Richard Helier

Thomas Harris

John Salter

John Fulforde, archdeacon

David Hopton

John Stephens

John Vesye

Thomas Chepington [i.e. Chippenham]; Bishop [George] Nevill, bishop;
    John Yott; John Hamlin and others

John Warde

Gilbert Tytinge and Thomas Bytton

John Bowthe, bishop of Exeter; Barefoote [i.e. Robert Barforth]; and
    [John?] Bourton

John Edgcombe

Matthew Downe

Ralph Ringstead and John Skynner

Walter [Bronescombe?], bishop of Exeter

Peter Williams; Agnes his wife; and Cardinal John Mourton

Richard Martin and John Ryse

John Arundell, bishop of Exeter

William Kilkenny, Sybil de Grandisson, Bishop John, William
    Grandisson, John Grandisson [bishop] and John Winslade

Peter [Quinil], bishop of Exeter; Thomas Hertford; Walter Pembroke

Walter [i.e. William] Brewer; John Wiger; John Rowse

Andrew Kylkenny

Hugh Courtney

Roger Towridge

John Speke, knight, and his wife

Thomas Bodham

Roger Charlton and Thomas Charlton

John de Mountacute

Thomas Brentingham

Edmund Stafford

Roger Keyes

Bartholomew, dean; [John] Weele; Upham [i.e. John de Uphaven]

Walter Merriott and Nassington

William Capron

John Holland

Walter [Stapledon?], bishop of Exeter

37. Other Miscellaneous Obit Records

Exeter Cathedral Library, MS 3508

(This is a psalter of the first quarter of the thirteenth century (Ker, pp. 814–15). Its calendar contains several obits entered during the thirteenth and fifteenth centuries. Latin text.)

[f. 5v]

13	February	Master Henry Webber, dean of this church

[f. 8v]

10	August	Robert de Westecote
13	August	Roger de Winklegh, dean

[f. 9v]

24	October	Master William Fullyford
27	October	Herbert the fisher [*piscator*]
28	October	Hegge

[f. 10r]

5	November	Master Roger Keys, priest and canon
24	November	Odeline, wife of Herbert the fisher [*piscator*]

Exeter Cathedral Library, MS 3510

(This is a missal of the second quarter of the thirteenth century (Ker, p. 817). Its calendar contains a single obit of that century or the early fourteenth.)

[f. 5v]

11	June	Adam le Yunge

38. Exeter Cathedral Bidding Prayer, *c*.1413–1485

(Source: D&C 2864. English and Latin document. The text was intended for reading aloud to congregations in the cathedral, to ask them to pray for specific people and causes. It was first drawn up during the reign of Henry V (1413–22) and additions were made until at least that of Richard III (1483–5). In the following edition the English has been modernised (except for surnames), and the Latin translated in italics. Additions to the English text are also indicated by italics, modern editorial additions by square brackets, and illegible passages by angle brackets. The paragraphing is modern.)

You shall pray for the state of all Holy Church; for our holy father the pope, with all his college of cardinals; for the Holy Land, that [God] of his high mercy send it soon into Christian men's hand. Also for the archbishop of Canterbury and all other bishops of this land, and in special for our reverend father, the bishop of this see. Also for *our masters* the dean and chapter of this church, and for all the ministers and servants that serveth or have served yet herein *this holy place*.

Also for the good state and tranquillity of this land, for our sovereign lord the king; *the queen*. Also for all the earls [*deleted*] and lords *and nobles* of this land, *for Thomas Selynger, brother of this place*, and for all the commons of this land, in especial for the mayor of this city and the commons hereof, and for all Christian people that we be due and debtors to pray for.

God be merciful to us [Psalm 67], with Glory be to the Father.
Lord have mercy. Christ have mercy. Lord have mercy.
And lead us not into temptation. [But deliver us from evil.]
O Lord, show your mercy towards us. [And grant us your salvation.]
Endue your ministers with righteousness. [And may your holy people rejoice.]
O Lord, save the king. [And hear us in the day when we call upon you.]
O Lord, save your servants and your handmaids. [Whose hope is in you, my God.]
Make safe your people. [And bless your inheritance.]
Give peace in our time, O Lord. [Because there is no other who fights for us, but only you, our God.]
O Lord, hear my prayer. [And let my cry come to you.]
The Lord be with you. [And with your spirit.] Let us pray.

O God, who have poured the gifts of charity by the grace of the Holy Spirit into the hearts of your faithful people, give to your servants and handmaidens for whom we pray your merciful healing of mind and body, so that they may love you with all their might and with all their love perform those things that are pleasing to you. Through Christ our Lord.

Also you shall pray for the soul of King Athelstan, the first founder of this place; for King Edgar, King Edward, King William <the Conqueror?>, King William <the second?>, King Harry, King Stephen, King Harry, King Richard, King John, King Harry, King Edward, King Edward, King Edward, King Richard, King Harry, King Harry, *King Harry, King Edward, King Edward, King Richard.* Also for the souls of Edward <the Black?> prince of Wales, for Thomas <sometime?> duke of Exeter, for John late duke of Exeter, *for Anne's soul, late duchess of Exeter [erased].* For Hugh Courtenay, sometime earl of Devonshire, and Margaret his wife. For William Courtenay, sometime archbishop of Canterbury, and of all the bishops that have been in this place.

For the souls of Leofric, the first bishop of this place; for Bishop Osbern; for Bishop <William Warelwast>; for Bishop Robert; for Bishop Bartholomew; for Bishop John; for Bishop Harry; for Bishop Simon; for Bishop William Brewer; for Bishop Richard; for Bishop Walter <Bronescombe>; for Bishop Peter; for Bishop Thomas <Bitton>; for Bishop Walter Stapeldon; for Bishop James Berkelegh; for Bishop John Graunson; for Bishop Thomas Brantyngham; for Bishop Edmund Stafford; for Bishop John Caterek; for Bishop Edmund Lacy. *Also for the soul of George Nevell, late archbishop of York, sometime bishop of the see. For Bishop John Bowth's soul.* Of Andrew Kylkenny, sometime dean of this church; *for the soul of Master Harry Webber, late dean of this church.* For Master <Roger Bo>lter *and Master Roger Keyes, sometime precentors of* this church. For William W<ynard?>, squire, *Thomas Selynger,* and for all the *brothers and sisters and* good doers of this church, and for all the souls whose mind days be held herein, and for all the souls whose bones resteth in this church or in the churchyard, and for all the souls that abideth the mercy of God in the bitter pains of purgatory, that God of his mercy the sooner deliver them through your devout prayers.

Out of the depths [Psalm 130], without Glory be to the Father.
Lord have mercy. Christ have mercy. Lord have mercy.
And lead us not into temptation. [But deliver us from evil.]
Give them eternal rest, O Lord. [And may perpetual light shine upon them.]
From the gate of Hell. [Draw forth their souls, O Lord.]
I believe that I shall see the goodness of the Lord. [In the land of the living.]

The Lord be with you. [And with your spirit.] Let us pray.

Absolve, we beseech you, O Lord, the souls of your servants our kings, bishops, priests, benefactors, and parishioners, and the souls of all the faithful departed, from the bond of their offences, so that having been raised again in the glory of resurrection they may live among your saints and chosen people. Through Christ our Lord. Amen.

Remember to pray in perpetuity by name and especially for the soul of Master Henry Webber, dean of this cathedral, when he shall die, among the other benefactors of this church, as above, since this was conceded by the chapter on the 21st day of the month of February in the year of the Lord 1466 [1467 modern style].

Glossary

acolyte – one of the minor orders of clergy, ranking beneath a subdeacon

advowson – the right to appoint the rector of a parish church, a right regarded as a piece of property that could be bought and sold

alb – a white garment covering the arms and reaching to the feet, worn by clergy either by itself or beneath some other vestment

amice – a detached linen hood worn with an alb

andiron – a piece of iron-work placed on a hearth to support burning wood

anniversary – a service held on the anniversary of someone's death, usually including the celebration of mass for the dead

annual – a year's worth of masses, said each day for the soul of a dead person

annuellar – a chantry priest of Exeter Cathedral, who celebrated mass with intercessions for the dead

antiphoner – a book containing antiphons: short texts sung before psalms in church

appropriation – a process by which clergy who held the advowson of a church could, with the permission of the king and the bishop, become rectors of the church and appropriate to themselves its revenues (such as tithes), appointing a vicar to serve the parish with a smaller stipend

ash-blower – a small heater, probably for burning incense

Authentica – collections of Roman laws supplementary to the code issued by the Emperor Justinian in the fifth century

Aylsham – a type of cloth from Aylsham, Norfolk

banker – a covering, generally of tapestry, for a bench or chair

barbette – part of a woman's head-dress, covering the neck and the breast

bluet – a woollen cloth, originally of a blue colour

boys of the choir – the usual term in the thirteenth and fourteenth centuries for the choristers of Exeter Cathedral

broach – a pointed rod, e.g. a spit

buckram – a fine linen or cotton fabric

burnet – a good-quality dyed woollen cloth, originally brown in colour

bushel – a container and also a unit of measurement, both solid and liquid, varying locally in amount

byse – a kind of fur, used for lining or trimming clothes

cameline – a fabric made of, or imitating, camel hair

camlet – a fine fabric, originally from the East, of wool, silk, or hair

carde – a fabric used for curtains

carpet – a kind of cloth, often used as a table as well as a floor covering

cellarer – monk in charge of wine and provisions

cauldron – a metal pot, sometimes mentioned alongside sums of money, possibly because pots, being durable and universal in use, were used to make payments or offerings

chancellor – the third of the four chief dignitaries of Exeter Cathedral, who acted as secretary of the chapter and provided lectures on theology or canon law

chandler – a maker or seller of candles

chantry – an endowment to maintain a priest to celebrate mass, usually daily, with prayers for the good estate of living people or the souls of dead ones

chasuble – a sleeveless garment worn over an alb by a priest at mass

chelle – a kind of vessel, very likely an oil lamp

Christ, body of – the reserved sacrament: consecrated bread and wine kept in a church as an object of devotion

clerk of the second form – a secondary

comfrey – an English plant (*Symphitum officinale*) used for medicinal purposes, especially against wounds

cope – an outer garment like a cloak, worn by clergy and often decorated

cordwainer – shoemaker

corporal cloths – linen cloths on which the bread and wine are placed during the mass

Corpus Juris Civilis – the code of Roman law made by the Emperor Justinian in the sixth century, divided into the *Old Digest*, *Inforciatum*, *New Digest*, *Codex*, *Authentica*, and *Institutes*.

court – in this book it is used to mean both the mayor's court of Exeter (called 'the court of the city') and a domestic house, implying a house of some importance

courtepy – a short coat or short cloak

cruets – small containers for wine or water at communion, or for vinegar or oil for meals

curtilage – a piece of ground belonging to a house and forming part of the same enclosure

custors – the four clergy who acted as sacristans or vergers of Exeter Cathedral

dean – the chief of the four dignitaries of Exeter Cathedral, in general charge of the cathedral community

Decretals – a collection of Church laws, supplementing those of the *Decretum*, published by Pope Gregory IX in 1234

Decretum – the basic medieval collection of Church laws, made by Gratian in the twelfth century

demesne – lordship

Digest – see *Corpus Juris Civilis*

dirige – the service of mattins of the dead

divine office or service – the daily services said in church, often with an implication of funeral services or a daily mass of intercession for the soul of a departed person

draught horse – a horse used for haulage

dresser – a sideboard or table

ell – a measure of length, traditionally 45 inches in England

episcopal register – a book containing the official acts of a bishop, such as appointments of clergy to benefices, ordinations, and wills

essoin – a request to be excused from appearance at a court of law

exequies – the service for the dead, said at funerals and on the anniversaries of deaths, consisting of *placebo* and *dirige*

fabric – when used of a building, the structure of walls and roof

farmer – a person in charge of administering something (such as a church and parish or a piece of land) together with the rights and profits that arose from it

fee-tail – a piece of property which had to be inherited by a particular succession of heirs

feoffment – a conveyance of property, usually accompanied by a written deed

fotmal – a unit of weight of lead, about 70 pounds

free bench – the right of a wife to a share of her husband's property after his death

Friars Minor – friars of the Franciscan Order

Friars Preachers – friars of the Dominican Order

frontal – a piece of fabric hanging down the front of an altar

fruits – the profits of a parish, consisting chiefly of tithes

galingale – an aromatic root from the East Indies

gavel-lack and shortford – a legal process by which a lord regained possession of a tenement whose tenant had failed to render the rent or services due

gradual – a text sung between the epistle and gospel during mass; also a book containing such texts

grange – a barn

hauberk – a coat of mail

houve – a kind of hat

indulgence – a letter from a pope or bishop granting remission of punishment for sin in return for some action or devotion, such as saying prayers

Inforciatum – see *Corpus Juris Civilis*

inquisition *ad quod dampnum* – an inquiry, on behalf of the king, as to whether it would damage him to allow property to be granted to clergy

latten – a mixture of metals, similar to brass

lectern – a desk to hold a book used in church for singing or reading from

ledger stone – a flat stone placed above a grave

Legenda Sanctorum – a book containing the lessons to be on saints' days

Liber Sentenciarum – a comprehensive treatise on theology, the most popular being that of Peter Lombard in the twelfth century

livery – a grant of clothes, or cloth to make clothes, to a servant

maniple – a strip of cloth worn by a priest on the left arm during mass

mark – the sum of 13s. 4d. (two-thirds of a pound)

martyrology – a book listing the saints commemorated on each day of the year

mass – the sacrament of the eucharist or holy communion

mastic – resin

mazer – a bowl, originally made of maple wood

ministers – in the Obit Accounts, this refers to the members of the cathedral staff (especially the clerks of the exchequer) who shared in obit distributions

miniver – a kind of fur, often white

missal – a book containing the material needed for celebrating mass

murrain – an infectious disease of animals

obit – an alternative word for **anniversary**

onhalde – apparently the right of a landlord of a property to the profits of the sale of materials belonging to the property

palfrey – a horse for riding, customarily due to Exeter Cathedral from the estate of every deceased canon

park – a piece of enclosed land of any size or use

Parvum Volumen – an anthology of the latter parts of the *Corpus Juris Civilis*

paten – the small dish on which the wafer is placed at the mass

pautener – a large purse or wallet

pelisse – a garment made of fur, or lined with fur

penitentiary – an alternative title for the subdean of Exeter Cathedral, so called because he acted as confessor to the rest of the canons

Pentecostal offerings – a small sum of money required to be paid to Exeter Cathedral each Whitsuntide (or Pentecost) by every household in Devon and Cornwall

perse – the colour blue or purple, or cloth of that colour

Pipe Office – a department of the king's exchequer in London, dealing with royal revenues and debts

pittance – a bequest to a religious house for food

placebo – the service of vespers of the dead

pollard – a base coin

pone – a writ (written order) from the king to the sheriff, removing a case from the county court to the jurisdiction of the king's justices

portiforium – a portable book containing the texts of the daily services said by the clergy (other than the mass), also known as a breviary

posnet – a small pot with a handle and feet, suitable for heating on a hearth

pound Tournois – the standard French currency of the later middle ages; the values in this currency given in the accounts of the executors of Andrew de Kilkenny, however, appear to have been adjusted to their equivalent in English pounds sterling

praiel – the open space in the middle of a quadrangular cloister

prebend – the stipend of a canon of Exeter Cathedral, half of which was donated to the building of the cathedral during the early fourteenth century

precentor – the second of the four dignitaries of Exeter Cathedral, in charge of the music of the choir

psalter – a text containing the words (and often music) of the psalms, sometimes 'glossed' or annotated

pyx – a small box, e.g. a collecting box for money, or a box in which a consecrated wafer was kept and venerated

quire – a pamphlet or loose sheets not bound into a book

rector – clergyman of a parish church who received all the revenues of the parish (compare vicar)

reeve – the official in charge of a manor

relief – a payment made by an heir on succeeding to a property, paid to the superior lord of the property

rent – a rented property, or the rent arising from it

reredos – an ornamental screen covering the wall behind an altar

rochet – a linen vestment worn by clergy, similar to a surplice

russet – coarse cloth, originally of a reddish-brown, grey, or natural colour

samite – a rich silk fabric

sanap – a cloth placed on a tablecloth to protect it

secondary – one of the twelve clerks of Exeter Cathedral, normally aged between about 17 and 24, who occupied the second or middle rank of the choir

selion – a strip of land in a field

selprith – a crop of unknown nature

serge – a durable woollen fabric

sermountain – a medicinal plant (*Laserpitium siler*)

sindon – a fine linen fabric

shortford – see **gavel-lack**

solar – an upper room

solemn service – a thirteenth-century term for a commemorative service on the anniversary of someone's death, later known as an **anniversary** or **obit**

stewards – two canons of Exeter Cathedral who took charge of supervising the cathedral exchequer

stole – a strip of cloth like a scarf, worn round the neck by clergy in church

strandling – a kind of fur, apparently that of the squirrel

submonitor – the junior member of the staff of the cathedral exchequer, perhaps so called because one of his duties was to warn the canons of chapter meetings; also known as the subclerk

succentor – the deputy of the precentor, usually a vicar choral, who supervised the music of the choir

Summa – a work of commentary

sumpter – a pack-horse that carries loads on its back

surcoat – any kind of outer garment worn over other clothes

surplice – a loose white garment with wide sleeves, worn by clergy

tabard – an outer garment covering the body, with or without sleeves

tester – a kind of helmet

thurible – a vessel in which incense is burnt, often hung and swung on a chain

tithes – the dues paid to the rector of a church, based on the produce of land and animals in the countryside and usually consisting of a customary sum of money in towns

Tournois – see **pound**

treasurer – the fourth of the four dignitaries of Exeter Cathedral, in charge of the moveable goods of the cathedral and responsible for the cemetery outside

trental – a set of thirty masses with prayers for the dead, celebrated consecutively during one month

tripe – a cloth similar to velvet

troper – a book containing tropes: musical texts sung during mass

trundle-wheels – small wheels used in tandem with barrows or handcarts

verjuice – an acid juice made of grapes or apples used in cooking or with food

vestments – clothes worn by clergy over surplices, especially the chasuble worn when celebrating mass

vicar – at Exeter Cathedral, one of the twenty-four vicar chorals who deputised for the canons in saying the daily services in church. Elsewhere a clergyman of a parish appropriated to a monastery (see **appropriation**), who received only part of the revenues of the parish

virgate – a measure of land, varying in extent but often of thirty acres

wytweban – an unexplained English word, perhaps 'widow band': an ornamental band forming part of a widow's head-dress

zedoary – an aromatic root somewhat like ginger

Bibliography

Unprinted Sources

Antony House, Cornwall
  Sir William Pole, 'Extracts from Deeds, Charters and Grants'

Exeter Cathedral, Dean and Chapter Archives (D&C)
  394 (Endowment of procession)
  1374 (Grant of cemetery to Polsloe Priory)
  1927 (Foundation of the Kilkenny chantry)
  2074 (Agreement concerning St James Priory)
  2079 (Will of Walter Gervas)
  2121 (Will of Henry de Collecote)
  2122 (Will of Rosamund Kymmyng)
  2232 (Will of William Mounteyn)
  2600–2704/11 (Fabric accounts)
  2781–2 (Stewards' accounts)
  2920 (Controversy concerning the treasurer)
  3550 (Chapter act book)
  3625 (Cathedral statutes and calendar)
  3672 (Cartulary)
  3673 (Obit accounts)
  3675 (Obit book of the vicars choral)
  3764–72 (Obit accounts)
  4037 (*The Ichnography of the Cathedral Church of St Peter of Exeter*, J.
    Jones, 1757)
  4038 (Plan of ledger stones in the choir, *c.*1763
  4708 (Removal of ledger stones from the choir, *c.*1763)
  ED/50 (Will of Henry de Berbilond)
  VC/3018 (Will of Margaret de Collecote)
  VC/3050, 3052 (Will and inventory of Lucy de Collecote, 2 copies)
  VC/3053 (Will of Adam de Collecote)
  VC/3057 (Will of Walter de Collecote)

Exeter Cathedral Library
  MS 3501 (The Exeter Book)

MS 3508 (Psalter)
MS 3510 (Missal)
MS 3518 (Martyrology)
Hope, Vyvyan. Monumentarium [unpublished list of cathedral monuments]

Exeter, Devon Record Office
51/1/series (Deeds)
332A/PF (St Mary Arches Exeter, deeds)
1718A add/PFW (Holy Trinity Exeter, deeds)
Chanter VIII (The Register of Edmund Stafford, vol. i)
Chanter IX (The Register of Edmund Stafford, vol. ii)
Chanter XII (i) (The Register of George Nevill)
Chanter XII (ii) (The Registers of John Bothe, Peter Courtenay, Richard Fox, Oliver King, Richard Redman, and John Arundell)
Chanter XIII (The Register of Hugh Oldham)
Chanter XIV (The Register of John Veysey, vol. i)
Chanter XV (The Register of John Veysey, vol. ii)
ED series (Deeds)
Exeter City Archives:
   Mayor's Court Rolls
   Miscellaneous Roll 67
   Book 53A (Cartulary of St John's Hospital)
Moger Transcripts of Wills

London, British Library
Add. Charter 13913 (Indulgence for Hugh Courtenay)
Add. Charter 27523 (Will of John de Doulys)
Add. MS 17459 (D.T. Powell's topographical collections)
Add. MS 29931 (John Carter's notes and drawings, Exeter Cathedral)
Cotton MS Vitellius D.ix (Cartulary of St Nicholas Priory)
Harley MS 862 (Ecclesiastical formulary)
Harley MS 863 (Psalter and calendar)

London, Islington, Family Research Centre
PROB 11 (Registered copy wills)

London, Lambeth Palace Library
The Register of Thomas Arundel
The Register of Henry Chichele
The Register of William Courtenay
The Register of John Kempe
The Register of John Morton

Printed Sources and General Works

Allan, J., Henderson, C., and Higham, R.A. 'Saxon Exeter', in *Anglo-Saxon Towns in Southern England*, ed. Jeremy Haslam (Chichester, 1984), pp. 385–414.

Aston, Margaret. 'Death', in Rosemary Horrox (ed.) *Fifteenth-Century Attitudes: perception of society in late medieval England* (Cambridge, 1994), pp. 202–28.

Barlow, Frank, and others. *Leofric of Exeter* (Exeter, 1972).

Barlow, Frank. (ed.) *English Episcopal Acta*, vol. 11, *Exeter 1046–1184* (London, British Academy, 1996).

Barlow, Frank. (ed.) *English Episcopal Acta*, vol. 12, *Exeter 1186–1257* (London, British Academy, 1996).

Baschet, Jerôme. *Les Justices de l'au-delà: les representations de l'enfer en France et en Italie: XIIe–Xve siècle* (Paris, 1993).

Bassett, Steven. (ed.) *Death in Towns: urban responses to the dying and death, 1000-1600* (London and New York, 1992).

Bernstein, Alan E. *The Formation of Hell: Death and Retribution in the Ancient and Early Christian Worlds* (Ithaca, NY, 1993).

Bidwell, P.T. *The Legionary Bath-House and Basilica and Forum at Exeter* (Exeter, 1979).

Binski, Paul. *Medieval Death: ritual and representation* (London, 1996).

Bishop, H.E., and Prideaux, Edith K. *The Building of the Cathedral Church of St. Peter in Exeter* (Exeter, 1922).

Boase, T.S.R. *Death in the Middle Ages: mortality, judgment and remembrance* (London, 1972).

Britton, John. *The History and Antiquities of the Cathedral Church of Exeter* (London, 1826).

Brushfield, T.N. 'Raleghana Part IV: Sir Henry de Ralegh, Knight, *Ob.* 1301', *Devonshire Association Transactions*, 34 (1902), pp. 455–81.

Buck, Mark. *Politics, Finance and the Church in the Reign of Edward II: Walter Stapeldon, Treasurer of England* (Cambridge, 1983).

Burgess, C. 'Late Medieval Wills and Pious Convention: testamentary evidence reconsidered', in *Profit, Piety and the Professions in Late Medieval England*, ed. M.A. Hicks (Gloucester, 1990), pp.14–33.

Calendar of Papal Letters, in progress (London, Public Record Office, 1894–1960; Dublin, 1978–).

Calendar of Patent Rolls, in progress (London, Public Record Office, 1901–).

Calendar of Fine Rolls, 22 vols (London, Public Record Office, 1911–1963).

Carew, George. *Sir George Carew's Scroll of Arms, 1588*, ed. J. Brooking Rowe, Exeter, *Devon Notes and Queries*, 1 part 2 (1900–1).

Carter, John. *Some Account of the Cathedral Church of Exeter* (London, Society of Antiquaries, 1797).

Chambers, R.W., Förster, Max, and Flower, Robin (eds.) *The Exeter Book of Old English Poetry* (Exeter and London, 1933).

Cokayne, G.E. *The Complete Peerage*, ed. H.A. Doubleday and V. Gibbs, 14 vols in 15 (London, 1910–59).

Collins, A Jefferies. (ed.) *Manuale ad Vsum Percelebris Ecclesie Sarisburiensis*, Henry Bradshaw Society, 91 (1960).

Conner, Patrick W. *Anglo-Saxon Exeter: a Tenth-century Cultural History* (Woodbridge, 1993).

Cook, G.H. *Medieval Chantries and Chantry Chapels* (London, 1947).

Crawford, Sally. *Childhood in Anglo-Saxon England* (Stroud, 2000).

Cresswell, Beatrix F. *Exeter Churches* (Exeter, *Devon and Cornwall Notes and Queries*, vol 5 part 2, 1908).

Cressy, David. *Birth, Marriage and Death: ritual, religion and the life cycle in Tudor and Stuart England* (Oxford, 1997).

Dalton, J.N., and Doble, G.H. (eds.) *Ordinale Exon*, 4 vols, Henry Bradshaw Society, 37–8, 63, 79 (1909, 1926, 1941).

Daniell, Christopher. *Death and Burial in Medieval England, 1066–1550* (London, 1997).

Duffy, Eamon. *The Stripping of the Altars* (New Haven and London, 1992).

Edwards, Graham R. 'The Idea of "Post Mortem" Purgation in the Western Church to the End of the Middle Ages' (University of Exeter, unpublished PhD thesis, 1983).

Edwards, Kathleen. *The English Secular Cathedrals in the Middle Ages*, 2nd ed. (Manchester and New York, 1967).

Emden, A.B. *A Biographical Register of the University of Oxford to A.D.1500*, 3 vols (Oxford, 1957–9).

Emden, A.B. *A Biographical Register of the University of Oxford A.D.1501 to 1540* (Oxford, 1974).

Erskine, Audrey M. 'The Medieval Financial Records of the Cathedral Church of Exeter', *Journal of the Society of Archivists*, 2 part 6 (1962), pp. 254–266.

Erskine, Audrey M. (ed.) *The Accounts of the Fabric of Exeter Cathedral, 1279–1353*, 2 parts, Devon and Cornwall Record Society, new series, 24, 26 (1981–3).

Erskine, Audrey M., Hope, V., and Lloyd, J. *Exeter Cathedral: a short history and description* (Exeter, 1988).

Feudal Aids, 6 vols (London, Public Record Office, 1899–1921).

Fryde, E.B., Greenway, D.E., Porter, S., and Roy, I. (eds.) *Handbook of British Chronology*, 3rd ed. (London, 1986).

Geary, Patrick J. *Living with the Dead in the Middle Ages* (Ithaca and London, 1994).

Gittings, Clare. *Death, Burial and the Individual in Early Modern England* (London, 1984).

Gordon, Bruce, and Marshall, Peter. (eds.) *The Place of the Dead: Death and Remembrance in Late Medieval and Early Modern Europe* (Cambridge, 2000).

Hadley, Dawn M. *Death in Medieval England: an archaeology* (Stroud, 2001).

Hale, W.H., and Ellacombe, H.T. (eds.) *Accounts of the Executors of Richard Bishop of London 1303, and of the Executors of Thomas Bishop of Exeter 1310*, Camden Society, new series, 10 (1874).

Harding, Vanessa. *The Dead and the Living in Paris and London 1500–1670* (Cambridge, 2002).

Hawkins, Duncan. 'The Black Death and the New London Cemeteries of 1348', *Antiquity*, 64 (1990), pp. 637–42.

Henderson, C., and Bidwell, P.T. 'The Saxon Minster at Exeter', in *The Early Church in Western Britain and Ireland*, ed. S.M. Pearce (Oxford, British Archaeological Reports, British Series, 102 (1982)), pp. 145–175.

Hooker, John. *The Description of the Citie of Excester*, ed. W.J. Harte, J.W. Schopp, and H. Tapley-Soper, 3 parts, Devon and Cornwall Record Society (1919–47).

Hope, Vyvyan. 'Two Incised Slabs with Indents in Exeter Cathedral', *Transactions of the Monumental Brass Society*, 10 part 2 (1964), pp. 102–106.

Horrox, Rosemary. (ed.) *The Black Death* (Manchester, 1994).

Houlbrooke, Ralph A. (ed.) *Death, Ritual and Bereavement* (London, 1989).

Houlbrooke, Ralph A. *Death, Religion and the Family in England, 1480–1750* (Oxford, 1998).

Jones, J. *The Ichnography of the Cathedral Church of Exeter* (no place, 1757).

Jupp, Peter C., and Gittings, Clare. (eds.) *Death in England: an Illustrated History* (Manchester, 1999).

Ker, N.R. *Medieval Manuscripts in British Libraries*, 4 vols (Oxford, 1969–92).

Kurath, Hans, and Kuhn, Sherman M. (eds.) *Middle English Dictionary* (Ann Arbor, Mich., and London, 1956–2002).

Latham, R.E. *Revised Medieval Latin Word-List from British and Irish Sources* (London, 1965).

Latham, R.E., and Howlett, D.R. (eds.) *Dictionary of Medieval Latin from British Sources* (London, 1975–, in progress).

Lega-Weekes, Ethel *Some Studies in the Topography of the Cathedral Close, Exeter* (Exeter, 1915).

Legg, L.G. Wickham (ed.) 'A Relation of a Short Survey of the Western

Counties Made by a Lieutenant of the Military Company in Norwich in 1635', *Camden Miscellany XVI*, Royal Historical Society, Camden third series, 52 (1936).

Le Goff, Jacques. *The Birth of Purgatory*, trans. A. Goldhammer (London, 1984).

Leland, John. *The Itinerary of John Leland in or about the years 1535–1543*, ed. Lucy Toulmin Smith, 5 vols (London, 1907–10).

Le Neve, John. *Fasti Ecclesiae Anglicanae 1300–1541*: vol. 9, *Exeter Diocese*, ed. Joyce M. Horn (London, 1964).

Lepine, David. 'The Courtenays and Exeter Cathedral in the Later Middle Ages', *Devonshire Association Transactions*, 124 (1992), pp. 41–58.

Lepine, David. *A Brotherhood of Canons Serving God* (Woodbridge, 1995).

Litten, Julian. *The English Way of Death: the common funeral since 1450* (London, 1991).

Little, A.G., and Easterling, Ruth C. *The Franciscans and Dominicans of Exeter* (Exeter, 1927).

Lobel, M.D. (ed.) *Historic Towns*, vol. i (London, 1969); *The Atlas of Historic Towns*, vol. ii (London, 1975); *The City of London*, vol. iii (London, 1989).

Lucy, Sam. *The Anglo-Saxon Way of Death: burial rites in early England* (Stroud, 2000).

Marshall, Peter. *Beliefs and the Dead in Reformation England* (Oxford, 2002).

Oliver, George. *Ecclesiastical Antiquities in Devon*, vols i–ii (Exeter, 1840); vol. iii (Exeter and London, 1842).

Oliver, George. *Monasticon Dioecesis Exoniensis* (Exeter and London, 1846).

Oliver, George. *Lives of the Bishops of Exeter and a History of the Cathedral* (Exeter, 1861).

Orchard, Nicholas. (ed.) *The Leofric Missal*, 2 vols, Henry Bradshaw Society, 113–14 (2002).

Orme, Nicholas. 'The Kalendar Brethren of the City of Exeter', *Devonshire Association Transactions*, 109 (1977), pp. 153–169.

Orme, Nicholas. 'The Dissolution of the Chantries in Devon, 1546–8', *Devonshire Association Transactions*, 111 (1979), pp. 75–123.

Orme, Nicholas. *The Minor Clergy of Exeter Cathedral, 1300–1548* (Exeter, 1980).

Orme, Nicholas. 'The Medieval Clergy of Exeter Cathedral: I, the Vicars Choral and Annuellars', *Devonshire Association Transactions*, 113 (1981), pp. 79–102.

Orme, Nicholas. 'The Medieval Chantries of Exeter Cathedral', *Devon and Cornwall Notes and Queries*, 34 (1981), pp. 319–26; 35 (1982), pp. 12–21, 67–71.

Orme, Nicholas. 'The Medieval Clergy of Exeter Cathedral:: II, the Secondaries and Choristers', *Devonshire Association Transactions*, 115 (1983), pp. 79–100.

Orme, Nicholas. *Exeter Cathedral as it Was 1050–1550* (Exeter, 1986a).

Orme, Nicholas. 'Two Saint-Bishops of Exeter', *Analecta Bollandiana*, 104 (1986b), pp. 403–418.

Orme, Nicholas. 'Sir John Speke and his Chantry in Exeter Cathedral', *Devonshire Association Transactions*, 118 (1986c), pp. 25–41.

Orme, Nicholas. 'Mortality in Early Fourteenth-Century Exeter', *Medical History*, 32 (1988a), pp. 195–203.

Orme, Nicholas. 'A Medieval Almshouse for the Clergy: Clyst Gabriel', *The Journal of Ecclesiastical History*, 39 (1988b), pp. 1–15.

Orme, Nicholas. 'The Charnel Chapel of Exeter Cathedral', in *Medieval Art and Architecture at Exeter Cathedral*, ed. F. Kelly, The British Archaeological Association, Conference Transactions, 11 (1991a), pp. 162–171.

Orme, Nicholas. 'Sufferings of the Clergy: Illness and Old Age in Exeter Diocese, 1300–1500', in *Life, Death and the Elderly*, ed. Margaret Pelling & R.M. Smith (London & New York, 1991b), pp. 62–73.

Orme, Nicholas. 'Henry de Berbilond, d. 1296, a Vicar Choral of Exeter Cathedral', *Devon and Cornwall Notes and Queries*, 37 part 1 (Spring, 1992), pp. 1–7.

Orme, Nicholas. 'The Clergy of Clyst Gabriel, 1312–1509', *Devonshire Association Transactions*, 126 (1994), pp. 107–121.

Orme, Nicholas. 'Whose Body?', *Friends of Exeter Cathedral Annual Report*, 66 (1996), pp. 12–17.

Orme, Nicholas. 'Wars and Wonders', *Friends of Exeter Cathedral Annual Report*, 68 (1998), pp. 16–23.

Orme, Nicholas. 'William Elyot, a Fifteenth-Century Registrar and his Books', *Archives*, 26 (2001), pp. 12–17.

Orme, Nicholas. *Medieval Children* (New Haven and London, 2001).

The Oxford English Dictionary, 2nd ed., ed. J.A. Simpson and E.S.C. Weiner, 20 vols (Oxford, 1989).

Platt, Colin. *King Death: the Black Death and its aftermath in late-medieval England* (London, 1996).

Pole, Sir William. *Collections towards a Description of the County of Devon* (London, 1791).

Polwhele, Richard. *The History of Devonshire*, 3 vols (London, 1793–1806, reprinted Dorking, 1977).

Rahtz, Philip. 'Grave Orientation', *Archaeological Journal*, 135 (1978), pp. 1–14.

The Register of Thomas de Brantyngham, Bishop of Exeter, ed. F.C. Hingeston-Randolph, 2 vols (London and Exeter, 1901–6).

The Registers of Walter Bronescombe . . . and Peter Quivil . . ., Bishops of Exeter, ed. F. C. Hingeston-Randolph (London and Exeter, 1889).

The Register of Walter Bronescombe, Bishop of Exeter, ed. O.F. Robinson, vols i–ii, Canterbury and York Society, 82 (1995), 87 (1999).

The Register of Henry Chichele, Archbishop of Canterbury 1414–1443, ed. E.F. Jacob, 4 vols (Oxford, 1938–47).

The Register of John de Grandisson, Bishop of Exeter, ed. F.C. Hingeston-Randolph, 3 vols (London and Exeter, 1894–7).

The Register of Edmund Lacy, Bishop of Exeter, vol. i, ed. F.C. Hingeston-Randolph (London and Exeter, 1909), cited as *Lacy*, i.

The Register of Edmund Lacy, Bishop of Exeter, 1420–1455: Registrum Commune, ed. G.R. Dunstan, 5 vols, Devon and Cornwall Record Society, new series, 7, 10, 13, 16, 18 (1963–1972), cited as *Lacy* I–V.

The Register of John Morton, Archbishop of Canterbury 1486–1500, ed. C. Harper-Bill, 2 vols, Canterbury and York Society, 75 (1987), 78 (1991).

The Register of Edmund Stafford, ed. F.C. Hingeston-Randolph (London and Exeter, 1886).

The Register of Walter de Stapeldon, Bishop of Exeter, ed. F.C. Hingeston-Randolph (London and Exeter, 1892).

Rodwell, Warwick. *The Archaeology of the English Church: a study of historic churches and churchyards* (London, 1981); revised edition, *Church Archaeology* (London, 1989).

Rogers, W. Hamilton. *The Antient Sepulchral Effigies and Monumental and Memorial Sculpture of Devon* (Exeter, 1877).

Rosenthal, Joel T. *The Purchase of Paradise* (London, 1972).

Rose-Troup, Frances. *Lost Chapels of Exeter*, History of Exeter Research Group, Monograph 1 (Exeter, 1923).

Rose-Troup, Frances. 'Exeter Manumissions and Quittances of the Eleventh and Twelfth Centuries', *Devonshire Association Transactions*, 69 (1937), pp. 417–445.

Rose-Troup, Frances. *Exeter Vignettes* (Exeter, 1942).

Rowe, J. Brooking. (ed.) *Sir George Carew's Scroll of Arms 1588, Devon Notes and Queries*, 1 part 2 (1900–1).

Rowe, Margery M., and Draisey, John M. (eds.) *The Receivers' Accounts of the City of Exeter, 1304–1353*, Devon and Cornwall Record Society, new series, 32 (1989).

Rowe, Margery M., and Jackson, Andrew M. (eds.) *Exeter Freemen, 1266–1967*, Devon and Cornwall Record Society, extra series, 1 (1973).

Saul, Nigel. *Death, Art, and Memory in Medieval England: the Cobham Family and their Monuments, 1300–1500* (Oxford, 2001).

Slack, Paul. *The Impact of Plague in Tudor and Stuart England* (London, 1985).

Stephenson, Mill. *A List of Monumental Brasses in the British Isles* (London, 1926).

Stocker, Ben. 'Medieval Grave Markers in Kent', *Church Monuments*, 1 part 2 (1986), pp. 106–14.

Swanton, Michael. 'Some Exeter Cathedral Documents', *Devonshire Association Transactions*, 115 (1983), pp. 123–31.

Swanton, Michael. (ed.) *Exeter Cathedral: a celebration* (Exeter, 1991).

Symonds, Richard. *Diary of the Marches of the Royal Army during the Great Civil War*, ed. C.E. Long, Camden Society, old series, 74 (1859).

Webster, Leslie E., and Cherry, John. 'Medieval Britain in 1973', *Medieval Archaeology*, 18 (1974), pp. 174–223.

Webster, Leslie E., and Cherry, John. 'Medieval Britain in 1978', *Medieval Archaeology*, 23 (1979), pp. 234–278.

Weever, John. *Antient Funeral Monuments*, 2nd ed. (London, 1767).

Index

The names listed below are surnames unless otherwise indicated; the index also includes place-names (with county identities) and major subjects. It does not contain the surnames alphabetically listed in the 'Register of Burials and Funerals' (pp. 44–119) or in the 'Register of Surviving Exeter Wills' (pp. 203–27), which should be consulted separately. Forenames of people without surnames have not been indexed, except for kings, bishops, and a few other important figures. When indexing surnames 'y' is placed with 'i' except when it begins a word.

DEVON & CORNWALL RECORD SOCIETY PUBLICATIONS

Obtainable from the Administrator, Devon and Cornwall Record Society, 7 The Close, Exeter EX1 1EZ

§ No longer available.　* Restricted availability: please enquire

ISSN/ISBN 0 901853

New Series

1§　*Devon Monastic Lands: Calendar of Particulars for Grants, 1536–1558*, ed. Joyce Youings, 1955　**04 6**

2　*Exeter in the Seventeenth Century: Tax and Rate Assessments, 1602–1699*, ed. W. G. Hoskins, 1957　**05 4**

3§　*The Diocese of Exeter in 1821: Bishop Carey's Replies to Queries before Visitation*, vol. I, Cornwall, ed. Michael Cook, 1958　**06 2**

4*　*The Diocese of Exeter in 1821: Bishop Carey's Replies to Queries before Visitation*, vol. II, Devon, ed. Michael Cook, 1960　**07 0**

5§　*The Cartulary of St Michael's Mount*, ed. P. L. Hull, 1962　**08 9**

6　*The Exeter Assembly: The Minutes of the Assemblies of the United Brethren of Devon and Cornwall, 1691–1717*, as Transcribed by the Reverend Isaac Gilling, ed. Allan Brockett, 1963　**09 7**

7*,10*, 13*, 16*, 18*　*The Register of Edmund Lacy, Bishop of Exeter, 1420–1455.* Five volumes, ed. G. R. Dunstan, 1963–1972　**10 0　12 7　15 1　02 X　17 8**

8§　*The Cartulary of Canonsleigh Abbey*, calendared & ed. Vera London, 1965　**16 X**

9§　*Benjamin Donn's Map of Devon, 1765.* Introduction by W. L. D. Ravenhill, 1965　**11 9**

11§　*Devon Inventories of the Sixteenth and Seventeenth Centuries*, ed. Margaret Cash, 1966　**13 5**

12　*Plymouth Building Accounts of the Sixteenth and Seventeenth Centuries*, ed. Edwin Welch, 1967 **14 3**

14　*The Devonshire Lay Subsidy of 1332*, ed. Audrey M. Erskine, 1969　**00 3**

15　*Churchwardens' Accounts of Ashburton, 1479–1580*, ed. Alison Hanham, 1970　**01 1**

17§　*The Caption of Seisin of the Duchy of Cornwall (1377)*, ed. P. L. Hull, 1971　**03 8**

19　*A Calendar of Cornish Glebe Terriers, 1673–1735*, ed. Richard Potts, 1974　**19 4**

20　*John Lydford's Book: the Fourteenth Century Formulary of the Archdeacon of Totnes*, ed. Dorothy M. Owen, 1975 (with Historical Manuscripts Commission) **011 440046 6**

21　*A Calendar of Early Chancery Proceedings relating to West Country Shipping, 1388–1493*, ed. Dorothy A. Gardiner, 1976　**20 8**

22　*Tudor Exeter: Tax Assessments 1489–1595*, ed. Margery M. Rowe, 1977　**21 6**

23　*The Devon Cloth Industry in the Eighteenth Century: Sun Fire Office Inventories, 1726–1770*, ed. Stanley D. Chapman, 1978　**22 4**

24, 26　*The Accounts of the Fabric of Exeter Cathedral, 1279–1353*, Parts I & II, ed. Audrey M. Erskine, 1981 & 1983　**24 0　26 7**

Extra Series